Jonathan Feldman

SAMS
Teach Yourself
Network Troubleshooting
in 24 Hours

SAMS

201 West 103rd St., Indianapolis, Indiana, 46290 USA

Sams Teach Yourself Network Troubleshooting in 24 Hours

International Standard Book Number: 0-672-31488-6

Library of Congress Catalog Card Number: 98-87467

Printed in the United States of America

First Printing: December 1998

01 00 99 98
4   3   2   1

Trademarks

All terms mentioned in this book that are known to be trademarks or service marks have been appropriately capitalized. Sams Publishing cannot attest to the accuracy of this information. Use of a term in this book should not be regarded as affecting the validity of any trademark or service mark.

Warning and Disclaimer

Every effort has been made to make this book as complete and as accurate as possible, but no warranty or fitness is implied. The information provided is on an "as is" basis. The authors and the publisher shall have neither liability nor responsibility to any person or entity with respect to any loss or damages arising from the information contained in this book.

EXECUTIVE EDITOR
Christopher Will

AQUISITIONS EDITOR
Christopher Will

DEVELOPMENT EDITOR
Kate Shoup Welsh

TECHNICAL EDITOR
Scott Humphries

MANAGING EDITOR
Brice Gosnell

PRODUCTION EDITOR
Sara Bosin

COPY EDITOR
Bart Reed

INDEXER
William Meyers

PROOFREADER
Benjamin Berg

LAYOUT TECHNICIAN
Brian Borders

COVER DESIGNER
Aren Howell

BOOK DESIGNER
Gary Adair

The *Sams Teach Yourself in 24 Hours* Series

Sams Teach Yourself in 24 Hours books provide quick-and-easy answers in a proven step-by-step approach that works for you. In just 24 sessions of one hour or less, you will tackle every task you need to get the results you want. Let our experienced authors present the most accurate information to get you reliable answers—fast!

Troubleshooting Cheat Sheet!

TCP/IP Troubleshooting

COMMAND	FLAG(S)	DESCRIPTION
ping *flags host or IP*		"Are you there?"
	-n	Number of times to ping
	-l	Size of data in ping packet
	-f	"Don't fragment" (useful for ruling out fragmentation problems)
arp	-a	Shows ARP entries in station's cache
	-d *IP*	Delete *IP* address from ARP cache
traceroute *host or IP*		(UNIX) Shows each router that a packet passes through to get to a destination
tracert *host or IP*		(Windows) traceroute for Windows
	-d	Don't resolve addresses to host names
netstat	-r	Shows routing table for this station
	-n	Shows output numerically (no host names or DNS)
	-a	Shows socket table for this station
	-e	Shows Ethernet statistics (Windows)
	-i	Shows interface statistics (UNIX)
ethstat		Shows Ethernet statistics (some UNIX)
winipcfg *flag*	/all	Shows Windows 9x TCP/IP configuration
ipconfig *flag*	/all	Shows Windows NT TCP/IP configuration
ifconfig	-a	Shows UNIXnetwork interface configuration
telnet *hostname socketnumber*		Checks a TCP service to see if it's available

Novell TCP/IP Troubleshooting Commands

COMMAND	DESCRIPTION
:load ping *host or IP*	NetWare ping
:load iptrace *host or IP*	(NetWare) traceroute for NetWare
:load tcpcon	The "Swiss Army Knife" of Novell TCP/IP troubleshooting

SAMS

Teach Yourself

Network Troubleshooting

in 24 Hours

Navigating tcpcon

FUNCTION	TCPCON NAVIGATION
Check TCP/IP statistics and error	Statistics menu counts
Check the routing table	IP routing table
Check TCP or UDP socket table	Protocol Information I TCP or UDP I Connections
Check the ARP cache	Protocol information I IP I IP Address Translations

Common TCP/IP Socket Numbers

SERVICE NAME	NUMBER	COMMENT
FTP	21	File Transfer Protocol
Telnet	23	Login service for UNIX, sometimes NT or Novell
SMTP	25	Internet-style server-to-server email
domain	53	DNS services (UDP and TCP)
gopher	70	Internet Gopher
http	80	Hypertext Transfer Protocol—the Web!
pop2	109	Post Office Protocol version 2 (user email)
pop3	110	Post Office Protocol version 3 (user email)
nntp	119	Usenet news
netbios-ns	137	NetBIOS Name Service
netbios-dgm	138	NetBIOS "datagram" service
netbios-ssn	139	NetBIOS "session" service
imap	143	Interactive Mail Access Protocol (user email)
shell	514	"Rlogin" socket — UNIX or NT
printer	515	Line Printer Daemon — Network printing for UNIX
socks	1080	Socks proxy server (Socks 4 and Socks 5)

Novell IPX/SPX Troubleshooting Commands

COMMAND	DESCRIPTION
`:load IPXPING`	IPXPING from the console—tests basic IPX connectivity
`IPXPING.EXE netnum nodenum`	DOS command prompt IPXPING; can be used to ping a server's internal IPX network number (use "1" for the node number) Normally, MAC address is used for nodenum.
`:display networks`	Shows what networks this server knows about
`:display servers`	Shows what servers this server knows about
`:track on`	Displays incoming and outgoing RIP routes

Contents at a Glance

Contents

About the Author

Jonathan Feldman works with UNIX, NetWare, Windows NT, and a whole team of networking propeller-heads for the Chatham County Government in Savannah, Georgia. A multi-disciplinary troubleshooting expert, Jon has also programmed everything from medical office applications to video games. He is a Level II Certified NetAnalyst and writes regularly for *SysAdmin* and *Network Computing* magazines. He has also contributed to *SCO Magazine*, and *The Guru*. Network and system tools that he's written have been downloaded by the likes of SCO, Cisco Systems, BellSouth, and NASA. He has two overly energetic and cheerful kids, Leo and Moshe, and is married to his pal Stacy Feldman. In his spare time he likes to cook, play guitar, and run, but not all at the same time.

Dedication

For Jim Reich: rocket scientist, GM, best man, friend, partner-in-crime, and always!   co-hacker.

Acknowledgments

I could not have finished this book in the time frame that I did without the encouragement, intelligent advice, friendship, and love of my partner and best friend, Stacy Feldman. I am more fortunate than I deserve to be married to such a level-headed and giving person.

My Pop is largely responsible for attempting to beat good, diagnostic techniques into my head at an early age; my hat is off to him. He is one of the best diagnosticians that I have ever met. In particular, I thank him for teaching me how to write SOAP notes, and I thank both of my folks for teaching all seven of us to think and fend for ourselves at an early age, both of which come in handy when troubleshooting anything.

I'm grateful to the entire Reich family, notably Jim and his mom Mary, for allowing me to be a teenage computer (and cookie) parasite decades ago. I probably wouldn't be in this profession today but for the hours I spent in their home hacking away on the Trash-80 and the good old Apple. (Not to mention the fact that I probably owe them thousands of dollars for groceries.)

The long-ago advice of two mentors has helped me immeasurably, both with this book and with my career in general. Harold "Reb" Carter from SUNY Buffalo gave me my first IT job, and showed me the differences between hobbyist computing and professional information technology. John Esak of The Valar Group showed me how much fun technology writing can be, and spent lots of time talking shop with me when I was first getting started.

I'm also indebted to my current employer, the Chatham County Government, particularly my direct supervisor, Renee Bridges, for letting me take vacation time so that I could finish the draft of this book. I feel very lucky to be in a very humane and professional work environment—and to be able to work in a place where I can both learn and teach every day. (Speaking of work environment, Cafe Metropole in Savannah deserves a big thanks for letting me take up their table real estate for the past months!)

Every journey begins with a single step. I'm glad that my agent, Martha Kaufman Amitay, took the first, or you wouldn't be holding this book in your hands. Thanks, Martha!

Finally, I thank Kate Shoup Welsh, Scott Humphries, and Chris Will at Macmillan for their collective professionalism, sense of humor, and hard work on the editing of this book; the end product was much enhanced by the efforts of this team!

Jonathan Feldman

October 1998, Savannah, Georgia

Tell Us What You Think!

As the reader of this book, *you* are our most important critic and commentator. We value your opinion and want to know what we're doing right, what we could do better, what areas you'd like to see us publish in, and any other words of wisdom you're willing to pass our way.

As the Executive Editor for the Operating Systems team at Macmillan Computer Publishing, I welcome your comments. You can fax, email, or write me directly to let me know what you did or didn't like about this book—as well as what we can do to make our books stronger.

Please note that I cannot help you with technical problems related to the topic of this book, and that due to the high volume of mail I receive, I might not be able to reply to every message.

When you write, please be sure to include this book's title and author, as well as your name and phone or fax number. I will carefully review your comments and share them with the author and editors who worked on the book.

Fax: [317-817-7070]

Email: [opsys@mcp.com]

Mail: Chris Will
            Operating Systems
            Macmillan Computer Publishing
            201 West 103rd Street
            Indianapolis, IN 46290 USA

Introduction: Getting Ready to Troubleshoot

Like surgeons about to embark upon a heart transplant, network professionals with years of training and experience gear up to tackle a complex network problem. They might tote complex and costly tools and speak network protocols as a second language. Pretty scary!

Yet, most network problems do not require a degree in rocket science to solve. In fact, just like you are the person who clears the paper jam or changes your toner cartridge on your own photocopier without having to call Mr. Xerox, you can also be the person who unclogs your office's email when it snarls up. Why not? You have a brain, and with a basic understanding of how this stuff works, you can come to logical conclusions just like the next person. You may annoy your dependency-oriented consultant by calling him or her less frequently, but such is the price of success.

Do network professionals really need expensive toys to solve most of your network problems? Not really. The reality is that network folks who rely on network toys rather than their brains, gumption, and common sense do not tend to be very good troubleshooters at all. They tend to concentrate on the accumulation of cool toys rather than solutions that address your business needs.

Most really good networking professionals are able to make these expensive network toys work for them only because of their keen observation abilities and plain old common sense. And much of the time, they don't even need the expensive toy to troubleshoot the problem. Why? Because they understand the fundamentals of "black box" troubleshooting, principles that you can learn in the second section of this book, "Black Box" Troubleshooting Strategies. Of course, they also understand the underlying principles of computer networking, but those principles are actually pretty simple. This is great news, because it means that you do not have to spend $10,000 on a network analyzer to get similar results most of the time.

BLACK BOX TROUBLESHOOTING

"Black box" troubleshooting refers to treating a complex system as a series of simpler systems. Each piece is a "mysterious little black box," a box with hidden stuff in it that makes it do what it does. TThe hidden stuff doesn't matter while you do your "high level" troubleshooting. That is, you don't care *why* one of the pieces of the system is doing what it is doing; the important thing is that it is doing it. Much like object-oriented programming, black-box troubleshooting allows you do more work in less time, since you're not worried about the picky little details!

For example, though you may know nothing about the internals of a fuel pump (and don't really care to know), you still might suspect it as a potential cause of your car's random stalling. Since you treat it as a black box, you rule it out or rule it in as a cause by replacing it with a "known good" fuel pump, and see if the system (your car) starts behaving properly. After a day or so of a trouble-free car, you know that the fuel pump was in fact the cause—all without having to know how a fuel pump works on the inside. Black box troubleshooting is a way for a busy person to troubleshoot just about any problem you can imagine.

Even if you rely on a vendor (and you will; even pros do!), knowing what you are doing can only help speed up the resolution of your problems. Think of it as going into a limited partnership with your professional network installers and troubleshooters—your "vendor." You solve the simple stuff and look like a hero, and you can hand off the really annoying stuff to them.

The ratio of users to network professionals is rather low, and lots of times a person (you, probably) gets roped into being an unofficial, unsung, and (of course!) unpaid network troubleshooter. As long as you are in this capacity, you might as well not be miserable doing it, so it makes sense to get comfortable with the technology and techniques.

Of course, even if you're lucky enough not to have been roped into being an unofficial network troubleshooter, it's likely that your job depends heavily on your network-ability. Whether your job is obviously related to the network, like programming or help desk management, or whether your job simply depends on your access to data, like engineering or medicine, the fact is that you need to be able to share data to get your work done. If you can get past most network bugaboos by yourself, you'll not only be able to pat yourself on the back and allow yourself a congratulatory smile, but you'll also work faster than the guy in the next office who has to wait for the network geek to show up.

Do you have to become a geek yourself to be any good at this? Definitely not. There are topics and levels of detail not covered by this book that are absolutely essential to being a professional network engineer, designer, or manager. But the nit-picky details themselves are not essential to somebody employing black-box troubleshooting, where it is axiomatic that the non-essential details remain hidden. However, you'll learn enough in this book to have a competent conversation with a high-level network support person about your more complex network issues.

You're also about to learn a lot of the simple-but-powerful concepts that professionals rely on. In addition to network fundamentals, even the best troubleshooting professional needs:

- Product documentation
- Site documentation
- Additional books and materials
- Observation and common sense
- Black box troubleshooting
- Other support people

To help you get up to speed on network terms and the framework in which networks live, you'll learn about "The Telephone Analogy" in Hour 1. After you get through that, you'll feel pretty comfortable with this stuff; more importantly, you'll understand a lot of the main terms and principles of networking. This will allow you to understand the way a network conversation flows from start to finish, and you'll start to understand why your network might be broken. You can skip this if you feel comfortable with networking terms and principles and want to dive right into the troubleshooting methods.

Troubleshooting a network, particularly a large network, is very much like figuring out a puzzle. If you've got a basic idea about how the network should work, and if you know which piece depends on which (much like how you always place the edge pieces on a jigsaw puzzle before delving into the middle ones) and the way information should flow, pointing the finger at the general problem area is usually not a problem. Once you figure out the general area of the problem, you can then use basic troubleshooting techniques to figure out which specific piece of the puzzle is causing your grief. After all, you don't need to be a Rembrandt expert to do a jigsaw puzzle of a Rembrandt painting, do you?

Let's take a real-life puzzle that you'd probably be pretty good at troubleshooting. Say that you're a teacher; your problem is that you have three boys who tend to cause trouble in your classroom. You will probably engage in two of the most powerful black-box troubleshooting techniques, "divide and conquer," and "the delta method." You'll realize that one of the boys is new in town, and the only thing that has changed recently in your classroom, which up until now has been serene. You separate him from the group, reasoning that he is almost certainly the cause. By dividing him from the other two boys, and watching the problem move to another section of the classroom, you *rule him in* as a cause, and *rule out* the other two boys. Easy, right? So, right away, before even reading the rest of this book, you've got some ammunition to use against network problems.

Let's consider a similar problem to your classroom problem. Since skilled labor is hard to come by, your retailer has hired some gorillas to come in and install a new PC in your office. They come in, install it, and everything seems fine. The next day, nobody can send email! One of the gorillas decides that it's time to rebuild your email server, but you cleverly realize that the only thing that has changed since yesterday is the new PC. You insist that the gorillas disconnect it from the network, and voila! The problem miraculously goes away. Upon inspection, the new PC's network cable has visible damage to it, which has caused a network problem affecting the email server. One of the gorillas replaces the network cable and walks away muttering something about "still need to rebuild that server." You're a hero, have avoided the risks of having a gorilla rebuild a perfectly fine mail server, and you haven't broken a sweat.

Of course, it's not always that easy. A lot of times, it's tough to know what has changed, or even who's changed it. Or, something may legitimately break without a new element even entering the picture. Unfortunately, since networks are what tie everything together, pretty much anything in the mix, soup-to-nuts, can be a source of trouble. And since everything is tied into the network, it's easy to blame the network. Actually, a lot of times, you simply have to figure out that the trouble is NOT the network!

The bottom line is, you really have to know a little bit about everything in order to start troubleshooting a problem, and then adapt and learn as necessary in order to solve a given problem. And you will!

PART I

Getting Your House In Order

Hour

HOUR 1

The Telephone Analogy: Becoming Familiar with Basic Networking Concepts

Trying to understand the pieces and parts that make up a computer network can be pretty daunting, even to folks who are fairly computer literate in other areas. If you're already familiar with network terms and concepts, you can skip this hour and move on to bigger and better things; if you're not, here's a good way to get comfortable with the basics of network technology.

Getting a handle on something foreign to you by using terms and concepts you already know is a good way to learn it faster. Learning the lingo helps a lot, but even getting good at the jargon does you no good if you don't have something familiar with which to compare the new terms.

The following term comparisons are analogies. They are not identical; be careful not to assume they are.

Therefore, it might help you to consider that computer networks are very much like the public telephone network. Although many differences exist under the hood, there are enough similarities on the surface to allow you to start to get a good concept of how a network really works. In theory, network calls act very much like telephone calls. See Figure 1.1 for a rough comparison of a data network to the telephone system. Also, here's a quick reference list:

Network Buzzword	Telephone Equivalent
NIC (network interface card)	The telephone in your house.
Network media (cabling)	The phone wire.
Address	The telephone number (167.195.162.5 is no more intimidating than 1-212-888-5555).
Router or gateway	The telephone company's central office equipment that connects different "area codes."
Switch or bridge	The local phone box that connects private lines and "party lines" (hubs).
Hub or concentrator	The party line shared by folks in a common area.
Protocol	The language. You can communicate with someone only if you both understand the language being used. Any language can be used for any kind of conversation, but some languages are more suited to certain situations (Italian is best for opera, French for love poems, and so on).
Packet or frame	A sentence of a conversation (not the entire conversation, but one idea from it).

Network Buzzword	Telephone Equivalent
Socket	The extension. Suppose you want to speak to Ms. Jones, who works at Company XYZ. Typically, you'll call Company XYZ's main phone number and ask for Ms. Jones's extension.
Program or service	The entity on the other end of the line that can provide information, or a service that you get during a conversation. Once you get Ms. Jones on the line by asking for her extension, you can then ask her how much a particular gadget costs, or you can ask her to send a technician out to install your gadget. Not all services can handle more than one protocol—just as not all people speak more than one language.
Directory services (WINS, DNS)	The "electronic" phone book. Instead of having to remember that Ms. Jones's number is 1-212-888-5555, you can simply perform an automatic lookup-and-dial on "Ms. Jones."

FIGURE 1.1

A rough comparison of a data network versus the telephone system.

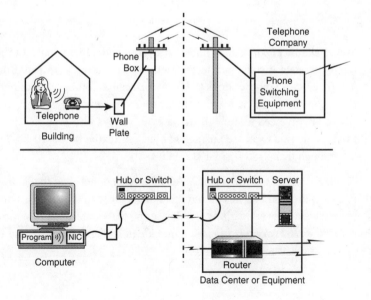

Network Interface Cards

As mentioned earlier, your telephone is very much like the network interface card (NIC) in your computer. Both of them help an individual entity (you, in the case of your telephone, and your computer, in the case of the NIC) talk to others. Also, both the telephone and the network card are oblivious to who is being communicated with and what kind of business is being transacted.

Your telephone is a physical piece of hardware that enables you to connect through telephone company equipment to talk to folks next door or halfway around the world. This is also true of your NIC. It can talk to other NICs on the same line as well as NICs on different lines by using switching equipment that's connected to the line.

MAC Attack

Just as each residence has a unique telephone number, your computer's NIC also has a unique number. However, unlike a telephone, each NIC has a unique number built (or *burned*) into it at the factory; this is referred to as its *burned-in address*, or *BIA*. This address is long enough so that trillions and trillions of addresses are possible. For convenience, the address has a compact form, represented by six hexadecimal bytes.

 Some folks refer to the BIA as the *MAC (media access control) address.*

Yikes! *Hexadecimal* sounds like a witch trial and a math contest rolled up into one. Really, though, it's just a different method of counting—instead of having digits from 0–9 (decimal), you use digits 0–F (hex). Because you have more options for digits (16 rather than 10), you can express numbers more compactly. Don't worry about it, though. All you really need to know is that a byte consists of two of these hex digits and that a MAC address is expressed using six bytes. Actually, 00-00-10-2b-5c-8d isn't too much more tough than 1-800-555-1212, is it?

The IEEE hands out *ranges* of MAC addresses rather than the addresses themselves (for instance, Proteon Inc. has all numbers that start with 00-00-93). This means you can tell who made a network card by looking at the MAC address's first three hex bytes. This is called the *OUI (organizational unique identifier)* and can be useful if you're troubleshooting certain kinds of problems.

The Institute of Electronic and Electrical Engineers (or IEEE; pronounced *eye triple-E*) is the organization that, among other things, acts as a standards body for various electronic standards. One of the IEEE's roles is to act as a clearinghouse for MAC addresses. Because so many network manufacturers exist, it's really important that MAC addresses be tracked. Otherwise, two different manufacturers might accidentally make network cards with the same address, which will cause network problems if two of these network cards end up on the same network. This could happen even though there are many, many possible MAC addresses. A MAC address's six-hex-digit format (or 48-bit address, if you want to sound geeky by talking in binary terms) turns into 281 trillion possible addresses—281,474,976,710,656 to be precise! That's a heck of a lot of combinations. Compare this with the phone system in the United States, where only nine billion phone numbers are available.

OUI ou Non?

Knowing the OUI came in handy for me once when I was experiencing intermittent problems with a new application. The application vendor pointed the finger at one of my network card vendors, who, in turn, told me to get the "latest and greatest" drivers for its network cards to eliminate the problems I was experiencing with the application. Fortunately, I rolled out only a small set of those drivers, which turned out not to be the "greatest." I started to have major network problems and noticed (from the OUIs listed by the network analyzer) that I was only experiencing problems with the cards I had just updated. I undid the update, the network problems went away, and I leaned on the application vendor to solve the original problem. The OUI can really be a useful concept to know.

The OUI only tells you who made the chip, not the manufacturer who put the board together. Creating a microchip is expensive, but putting these chips together on a circuit board that becomes a NIC is less expensive. Because of this cost differential, many vendors purchase other vendors' chips to use on their brand of network cards. For example, although Emulex is on the OUI list as using 00-00-c9, Proteon, Inc. has released network boards with this OUI.

If a network configuration option ever asks you whether you want to override the MAC address of a NIC, say no! This option is intended only for experienced network administrators and can wreak havoc if not used correctly.

Routers

Because each network card on a network has a different MAC address, each network group is assigned a network number. This network number, which defines the "area" of the network, is similar to a telephone area code. Different network area numbers are connected via a router, which, as you might expect from its name, routes packets from one network area (routing domain) to another.

Router is pronounced *row-ter*, not *root-ter*.

You can think of a router as the mystical piece of equipment in the telephone network that connects you from, say, New York to Georgia; routers usually connect geographically separate networks (this isn't always true, but it's a reasonable rule of thumb). More specifically, a router is connected to more than one network number, and it helps network calls get where they need to go (assuming the language in the network call is supported by the router).

This is where the analogy breaks down: Although phone switches care nothing about the conversation on the wire, routers do care. It might help to think of routers as friendly neighbors who can pass your message along (that is, if they speak your language).

Of course, the phone system needs equipment peppered throughout your neighborhood, and it also needs the high-end equipment at the telephone company. The same goes for your network. Two types of network "glue" tie you and your network neighborhood together:

- Hubs (concentrators)
- Switches

1

Think of a hub as a shared neighborhood party line (like the one you used to have at Uncle Harry's cabin in the woods). It used to be cost-prohibitive to give each network card its own channel to talk on, because more silicon "smarts" were required. Just like its name implies, a *hub* is where all of the NICs on the "party line" (or *segment*) come together. Each NIC's wire is connected to the hub in a spoke-like fashion, where they all physically share the same wire.

> A common physical connection like this is generally referred to as a *bus*, and each participant that tries to use this common connection "gets on" or "gets off" the bus.

Because NICs share a common bus, each NIC can "hear" other NICs. NICs have built-in rules for using this common area, which is discussed further in Hour 9, "Ethernet Basics," and Hour 10, "Token-Ring Basics." For the moment, you just need to know that each NIC has been schooled in "netiquette" and has been taught in the factory to play well with others and to share the wire nicely—that is, most of the time. Be aware that if a network card does not obey these rules, this can cause problems on the entire shared segment. (See Figure 1.2 for an illustration of shared versus dedicated telephone lines and network segments.)

FIGURE 1.2

Shared versus dedicated lines.

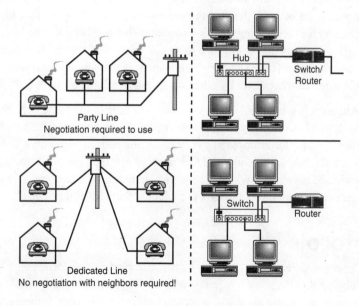

Computers on older networks were actually connected together on the same wire, much like older Christmas lights used to be. Therefore, a physical break in the wire meant that all the computers on one side of the break went down. A hub-based segment fixes this, because each computer has its own physical connection, and the hub ties them all together. The newer method of sharing the wire is called a *star topology*, because it looks like a star. The older method is called *bus topology*—the line from PC to PC is the common bus area.

A new technology called *switching* allows each network card to have its own private line; however, a lot of hub-based shared networks are still in existence (and don't look for them to go away any time soon). You'll find switching to be more and more exciting as you get into network troubleshooting. Similar to the way hubs allow users to get away from the "Christmas light bulb" problem, switches allow users to get away from many of the problems of shared networks. Instead of each computer having to compete for the right to talk when it wants to, each computer can transmit pretty much when it needs to—as long as the computer on the other end is available, of course. Others in the network neighborhood no longer compete for the right to talk on the wire, because each computer has its own connection.

How does this work? In a nutshell, a switch looks at the MAC addresses of two workstations on the network that want to communicate, and it opens up a high-speed private channel for them. A hub has one common channel, but a switch has many, many channels, as well as the intelligence to switch conversations between them. With a fast enough switch (called a *wire speed* switch), workstations conversing on the switch are not affected whatsoever by other workstations talking away at full speed.

Although prices on hubs are very low, switching has become very cheap as well; you can look to this technology as the future of local area networks. Although shared hubs have their virtues (for example, it's easy to see the conversations on a shared line, which is good for troubleshooting), the fact remains that they are more trouble-prone than switched networks (switched networks are much faster and more reliable). As switches get even cheaper, you can expect to deploy them instead of hubs.

Protocols

Your computer "talks" through its network card, but, unfortunately, technology has not advanced to the point where it can speak English quite yet. Instead, your computer uses a more primitive language—a protocol with a much more limited vocabulary. This protocol is most likely either TCP/IP, NetBEUI, or IPX/SPX. You can think of these protocols

1

as languages on a telephone; just as your telephone doesn't care whether you speak German or French, your network card doesn't care whether your computer and the programs that live in it speak TCP/IP or IPX/SPX.

Parlez Vous TCP/IP?

The good news is that you don't have to know much about protocols to troubleshoot—most of the time, your problems won't be protocol related, because protocols are rather simple and well defined. For example, TCP/IP has been around for more than 20 years (a huge life span in computer years), and its feature additions have been rather modest. This means that unlike a typical desktop application, TCP/IP has had an opportunity to stabilize.

This, among other factors, makes TCP/IP (short for *Transmission Control Protocol/Internet Protocol*) pretty much the universal language of network protocols. The Internet has made TCP/IP a household appliance, which means you probably already know something about it. For instance, you probably know that a TCP/IP host name is something like myhost.mycompany.com, and a TCP/IP address looks something like 167.195.160.6.

What's with the three-dotted address? After all, didn't I just say that an address is a six-byte hexadecimal number? Well, it is for network cards, but it isn't for protocols. Just as your telephone number sounds a bit different when you say it in French, your network address is different when you "say" it in TCP/IP. Although they look different, there is a distinct relationship between a TCP/IP address and a MAC address. They are both, for their own purposes, the "telephone number" of your network card; it just depends what language you're speaking at the moment.

TCP/IP addresses are always four numbers between 0 and 254 that are represented in the decimal system you know and love. These addresses are typically assigned by an administrator. An administrator's task is to assign unique addresses to each computer on his or her network.

Why should there be two different addresses? Since the OUI is guaranteed to be unique, why not just represent the TCP/IP address in decimal? Long ago, network cards did not all have unique IEEE-distributed MAC addresses; some were limited to 254 addresses! Because of this, using the MAC address for a TCP/IP address in a large network was not practical, so TCP/IP designers invented a method of translating a MAC address into a larger, more unique value. This obviously isn't necessary with today's MAC addresses, but this translation hangs on to this day.

Duplicate TCP/IP addresses can make your TCP/IP-dependent programs stop functioning. If you assign your own TCP/IP addresses, be sure to keep them unique.

DHCP (Dynamic Host Configuration Protocol) server programs can dynamically hand out IP numbers to computers. This can be a blessing or a curse—would you like it if your phone number changed every few days? On the other hand, DHCP automates the addressing process and tends to eliminate address-duplication errors. You can find practical troubleshooting information on DHCP in Hour 11, "Windows Networking Basics."

Like a phone number, TCP/IP has its network number (or "area code") built right into it. Unlike a phone number, though, the "area code" is the longer part of the number. The shorter part of the number (referred to as the *node* or *host number*) is the local phone number, with the first part of the address referring to the "area code," known as the *network number*. Because TCP/IP network numbers don't have to be a specific length, the length of the network number is calculated with a *network mask*, a number that mathematically specifies how long the network number is.

Fortunately, most small TCP/IP networks have the same network mask, so you can calculate your network numbers just by following an example rather than engaging in horrible binary arithmetic.

The most common use of a network mask in troubleshooting is during configuration verification. Because an incorrect network mask can cause a workstation to malfunction, making sure that a problem PC's network mask is the same as the others is important.

For a network mask whose numbers are all 255, it's pretty easy. Simply write down the IP number with the network mask beneath it; each number that matches up to a 255 is a network number. The remaining number is the node number. (See Figure 1.3 for an example of this.)

Consider a server whose IP number is 192.168.5.10, with a network mask of 255.255.255.0. The network number you get from this is 192.168.5.0, and the node number is 10. Because most simple TCP/IP networks work this way, the binary manipulations for more unusual network masks may be left for those who enjoy pain.

FIGURE 1.3

When figuring out a node number where the mask numbers are all 255, just block (or mask) the network numbers by the corresponding instances of 255 in the mask. The result is your node number.

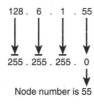

128 . 6 . 1 . 55

255 . 255 . 255 . 0

Node number is 55

Although the concept of network masks and network numbers might seem ugly at first, you really do need to know which portion of your TCP/IP address is your network number. This way you can document it, which, in turn, means that you can troubleshoot it when you need to. These concepts aren't so terrible once you get used to them, so hang in there. (It's the price you pay for being able to "dial out" of your neighborhood.)

Sprechen Sie DLC?

Some protocols can't dial out of the neighborhood. Have they been bad? Are they being punished? No, they're just not very bright and are largely based on the network card's capability to talk to the local network. These protocols can speak only to other MAC addresses and are known as *DLC (data link control)* protocols. They are not routable, which means they can talk only to other stations on the same network. You can think of DLC as the "four-digit dialing" you might find in some hotel telephones (without the ability to press 9 to dial out).

Microsoft's NetBEUI is an example of a DLC protocol. NetBEUI stands for *NetBIOS Extended User Interface*, which tells you nothing unless you know what NetBIOS is— Network Basic Input Output System. In a nutshell, NetBEUI is simply an improvement of NetBIOS. NetBIOS is a simple networking protocol that was used by IBM and Microsoft in early DOS-based file sharing products; NetBEUI is an improvement now used in Windows 95.

Windows 95/98 users always ask me, "Why can't I see other people's work-groups on the network?" Usually, this is because they're asking Windows 9x to use NetBEUI for file sharing, but they're trying to see workgroups on the other side of a router. You can add a routable protocol such as IPX/SPX to solve this problem. (TCP/IP can be used, too, but is more complex to configure.)

Hablas IPX/SPX?

IPX/SPX, in addition to being a routable protocol, is also a very easy protocol to work with from a user's perspective. Instead of having to deal with network masks and figuring out network numbers, you need only look at the server (or router) on a network to get the network number, which is an arbitrary and unique hexadecimal number. The node address is simply the MAC address of the network card. The full address, "area code" and all, looks something like this:

```
0000001D: 000093552899
```

This translates to `network number 1D`, `node number 93552899` and involves no figuring at all. Even better, workstations need no address configuration whatsoever, because the address is simply lifted from the network card's MAC address. Unfortunately, because IPX/SPX (invented by Novell, the makers of NetWare) used to be a somewhat proprietary protocol, it never got the market presence that TCP/IP has. Even though Microsoft has adopted IPX/SPX as a routable protocol for file and print sharing under Windows NT and 95, the juggernaut-like momentum of the Internet (and as a result, TCP/IP) probably means that IPX/SPX will remain the less dominant player. It isn't going away too soon, though. If you have IPX/SPX in your shop, it's definitely worth being familiar with. See Hour 13, "NetWare Networking Basics" for details.

Packets

Another important building block of a network (as important to networking as the red blood cells in your veins are to you) is the *packet* (sometimes called a *frame*). It's the smallest whole unit of communication on the network, much like a sentence is the smallest whole unit of communication in a conversation. (Although words themselves are even smaller units, they're not *complete* units of communication. For example, just saying "dinner" to someone doesn't tell him whether you want to invite him to dinner, eat him for dinner, or skip dinner altogether.)

Only one packet can be on the wire at a time, which makes it tough when multiple users are on the network attempting to complete multiple tasks. For example, suppose the following chunks of conversations traveled the wire in this order:

"Stacy, this is Jonathan. Why don't I pick up some bread for dinner?"

"Jonathan, this is Leo. I'd like you to come home and play."

"Jonathan, this is Stacy. Please do pick up some bread on your way home."

"Leo, this is Jonathan. I'll be home soon and would love to play!"

1

"Stacy, this is Jonathan. Will do."

Tough to follow, huh? Luckily, networks use *packet switching*. The idea of packet switching is simple. Because conversations need to appear to be seamless, each chunk of the conversation contains information to keep track of who is talking and to whom. Suddenly, what once appeared to be one confused conversation becomes two logical ones:

"Stacy, this is Jonathan. Why don't I pick up some bread for dinner?"

"Jonathan, this is Stacy. Please do pick up some bread on your way home."

"Stacy, this is Jonathan. Will do."

"Jonathan, this is Leo. I'd like you to come home and play."

"Leo, this is Jonathan. I'll be home soon and would love to play!"

Because each packet actually has the address (or "phone number") of the person you need to talk to, and because one computer might have more than one program that wants to talk, there's an additional concept called known as a *socket*, which acts very much like a telephone extension. Therefore, just like you might call Frobozz Magic Gadgets and ask to speak to the Wizard at extension 412, when your computer makes a network call, it calls a network address and asks for a socket number.

A socket number is frequently represented by a colon (:) after the address. For example, when you fire up your Web browser to `http://www.co.chatham.ga.us`, you're actually referring to 167.195.160.9:80 (or socket 80 of the TCP/IP address 167.195.160.9). Socket 80 is the standard socket for Web services, called HTTP (Hypertext Transfer Protocol).

HTTP is the name of the service that is usually offered at socket 80 by the program that lives there. However, HTTP also refers to the set of rules that allow for Web transactions that Web servers and browsers attempt to follow. It's important to understand that there are two definitions of HTTP here: the socket name (as in "socket 80 is the socket typically used for HTTP") and the protocol, itself (as in "All Web servers need to follow the HTTP protocol to ensure error-free operation"). Many other protocols and services have this dual reference as well—for example, SMTP, which refers both to socket number 25 (typically used for mail services) as well as the Simple Mail Transfer Protocol's rules of engagement.

Because a socket is the equivalent of a phone extension, the program that picks up the call is the equivalent of the person within the house or company that you want to talk to (see Figure 1.4). The program can do things for you once you "talk"—either give you information or kick off a process that you need accomplished. Some requests can be a combination of both: When you search the Internet, you ask the program on the other end to do a search, and you ask for the answer to your search.

FIGURE 1.4

A socket is the equivalent of a phone extension.

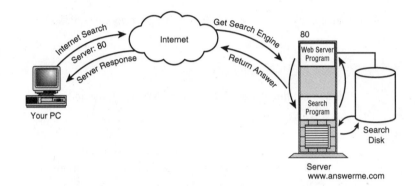

Just like people, some programs (also called *services* because they're server programs) on the other side of the line speak only one language. For example, standard Web servers speak only TCP/IP. However, as previously mentioned, Microsoft file and print sharing services can run on just about anything: TCP/IP, IPX/SPX, and NetBEUI. As with teaching a person a new language, it takes a bunch of effort to program multiple-protocol support into a service, and unless there's payback involved, most programs just pick one protocol and stick with it. The most popular protocol for modern programs? You guessed it: TCP/IP.

What's in a Name?

You've probably asked yourself in one of the preceding paragraphs, "How does www.co.chatham.ga.us get translated into 167.195.160.9?" Furthermore, why use names at all? People can deal with phone numbers, why not just use the IP number? These are good questions. The answer to the latter is that just because people *can* deal with a number doesn't mean that they *prefer* to use a number. Which would you rather remember, 1-800-NETWORK or 1-800-638-9675? Obviously, most people prefer to remember a name. Actually, names are the better thing to use when networking, because numerical addresses can change during a reconfiguration or a move, whereas symbolic names typically stay the same.

Name-to-address translation (also known as *name lookup* or *name resolution*) occurs via name services. Very similar to the speed dial button on your phone, name services are the networking equivalent of an electronic phone book. They're actually a lot cooler than your speed dial: For example, suppose you could say "Mom" to make your phone dial your mother.

DNS

Name services run as a service on any given name server; that is, a specific program runs on a name server that hands out an address when you give it a name. Like your speed dial buttons, you must program in a name entry; entering the correct number for a given name is important.

In particular, TCP/IP name services, although powerful and able to handle millions and millions of names, isn't exactly plug-and-play. The DNS (Domain Name Service) that you use when surfing the Web works pretty automatically for you once it's configured correctly, and it will translate www.co.chatham.ga.us to 167.195.160.9. However, you'll need to know the exact number of your DNS server. Unlike telephone information, DNS servers all have different addresses; verifying that a workstation's DNS server is correct can be an important troubleshooting step (see Figure 1.5).

FIGURE 1.5

Name resolution on DNS.

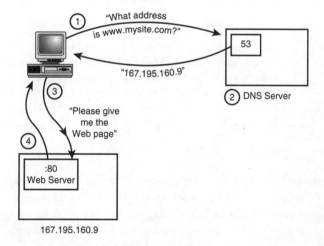

Note that most smaller sites that use TCP/IP usually *don't* have DNS set up. Instead, each workstation has a local (hard drive) "hosts" file that lists the addresses and host names the workstation needs to get to. (Think of this as your personal phone book rather than the corporate directory.) As you can imagine, this gets hard to manage when you have more than a handful of workstations, unless the addresses of the servers never change. As sites grow, or as they get connected to the Internet, DNS servers are added. Can you imagine how big a single file with all the servers on the Internet would be? Fortunately, each DNS server for a given DNS zone is only responsible for its own information.

> A DNS zone (its scope of responsibility for naming) can be huge—for exam-
> ple, .com has millions of subzones (yahoo.com, jotto.com, and so on); on
> the other hand, it can be small—for example, feldman.org lists only one
> host (www.feldman.org) and no subzones.

With DNS servers getting easier to manage and being a mandatory component of Internet access, you can expect to see more of them in smaller shops as time goes on. It's worth mentioning that each DNS server is responsible for only its own zone, so if you can't get to one particular address (say, yahoo.com) but can get to another (say, jotto.com), it may be that the name server responsible for that zone is down. On the Internet at large, this rarely happens, because the DNS organizers require back-up DNS servers for a zone. DNS problems are more likely to happen within a smaller organization's intranet, partic- ularly when all the eggs for that organization are in one basket.

> Remember that you can still dial a number yourself when your speed dial
> buttons are broken. Similarly, if you cannot get to something on your net-
> work, try getting to it by number. For example, rather than going to
> http://www.co.chatham.ga.us, you could try http://167.195.160.6.
> If this works, you know there's something up with name services.

WINS

Not satisfied with DNS, Microsoft invented another naming service for Windows, called *WINS (Windows Internet Name Service)*. WINS is a Windows-specific name service for TCP/IP and is meant for networking geographically distant Windows computers (it typically isn't used on a local area network). WINS not only maps names of servers but also maps names of workgroups and NT domains.

It's unlikely that WINS will be around in the next generation of Windows machines (although it's still around in Windows 98); Microsoft is taking a page from the competi- tion's automatic name services and directory services and will be rolling TCP/IP name services together with their username and password services. This will be called *Active Directory*.

The notion of a directory is similar to the name services concept, but it goes one step further: Instead of simply resolving a name to a number, directory services offer many pieces of vital data on the network. In particular, directory services allow users from all over to log in to the network rather than into a specific server; each server on the network relies on the directory services to assign security rights, and so on.

This is terrific because administrators no longer need to update multiple servers with username and password information; instead, they can administer updates from one point and distribute them throughout the network. Although the long-term goal has been simplification, which makes troubleshooting easier, beware of early implementations. Even Novell's NDS—arguably the "best" directory service around (it's been around a number of years and has a lot of support)—had a lot of problems out of the gate.

Some sort of directory service—whether it's Microsoft's, Novell's, or Acme's—is definitely in your future.

Summary

This hour is a reasonably complete introduction of most of the networking concepts you'll run into. However, as they say, the devil's in the details. This hour will serve as a good foundation on which you can build your troubleshooting knowledge as you read on.

Here are some things to remember:

- A network card acts as your computer's telephone to the outside world. Also, it has its own unique identifier (MAC address) built into it.
- Many LANs are based on a shared bus or "party line." As with real party lines, hurt feelings and even major disasters are caused by those who talk out of turn.
- Segments can be connected with each other via switches. Also, a router may be used to route packets (sentences from a network conversation) to and from differing network numbers.
- Network protocols can be thought of as the different languages humans use. Like humans, programs do not all speak more than one language, so you need to find out what protocol a program uses before you start to troubleshoot it.
- Network naming services, such as DNS and WINS, make it possible for end users to refer to a computer by a symbolic name rather than an address. However, even when the naming service is broken, you should still be able to contact a computer by numerical address.
- Directory services are "naming services on steroids," and they provide more than address-to-name services. They can keep track of any information on a network, including usernames, passwords, and security information.

Workshop

Q&A

Q **Do Apple Macintosh networks work like a telephone network, too? What about AppleTalk?**

A I don't talk about Macs specifically in this book. However, all of the general concepts of networking apply. You still have a network interface, shared media, network numbers, name services, and so on—the specifics are just different. AppleTalk is a protocol and has its own rules and regulations, just like TCP/IP or IPX/SPX.

Q **Shouldn't I learn more about TCP/IP? Don't I need to be a TCP/IP whiz to troubleshoot TCP/IP problems?**

A Learning more is never a waste, but as you'll see in later hours, dealing pragmatically with most TCP/IP problems doesn't really require a deep knowledge of the protocol itself—just a knowledge of workstation configuration and general troubleshooting techniques.

Q **My networking buddy says that switches and routers and bridges are all the same thing. Are they?**

A It depends on who you ask. Certainly, they all take network conversations (traffic) in on one port and spit them out on another. They are also all ways of connecting different segments together. It used to be that switches and bridges were always MAC oriented and only looked at traffic on a DLC level, because handling a routable protocol such as TCP/IP tended to involve calculations, which made things slower. Recent innovations in routing and switching technology have created *Layer 3 switches* (which refers to a protocol rather than DLC) that can act as wire-speed routers. In other words, they take in packets of any kind and spit them out as fast as possible. However, the line does tend to blur with hybrid, high-end equipment. Of course, switch or router behavior depends very much on the manufacturer's specifications; check your manual if you have questions about your switch or router.

Q **How does the concept of intranet versus Internet apply to the telephone analogy?**

A Just think of an intranet as your internal phone system, and the Internet as the world's phone system.

Quiz

1. True or false? Some network cards have name services built into them.

2. What do all network cards have?

   A. Telephone numbers

   B. Burned-out numbers

   C. Burned-in addresses

   D. Telephone addresses

3. Which of the following is a valid MAC address?

   A. 00-55-D5-AA-D5-AA-D5-AA

   B. ad-00-a2-00-ad-30-c0

   C. 00-00-c9-aa-c5-50

   D. c9-aa-50

4. Which definition aptly describes routers?

   A. Routers are combo woodworking and network diagnostic tools.

   B. Routers forward packets from point A to point B.

   C. Routers listen for packets from a troubled network.

   D. Routers can help connect networks with bad MAC addresses.

5. True or false? A hub creates a shared network segment.

6. A _____ TCP/IP address can make TCP/IP-dependent programs stop functioning.

7. If your PC's TCP/IP address is 200.1.5.26 and your network mask is 255.255.255.0, your node address is _____ and your network number is

   _____.

8. True or false? A packet must have a source and a destination address.

9. DNS is a _____.

   A. Socket

   B. Service

   C. Server

   D. Slushee

Answers to Quiz Questions

1. False
2. C
3. C
4. B
5. True
6. Duplicate
7. 26; 200.1.5
8. True
9. B or C

HOUR 2

You Can't Have Too Much Documentation, Money, or Love!

Would you start out on a car trip in a strange country without a map? Of course you wouldn't, but this is what people do every day when they fail to document their ever-expanding networks. When it comes time to troubleshoot, those who don't have a map to go by will just shrug and shake their heads. Undocumented networks are mostly incomprehensible. You need some method of getting your bearings, and network documentation can be an compass in what can be a sea of confusion.

Navigating a Bad Network Neighborhood

There will be those who tell you that complete documentation is too much trouble, or that it takes too much time and doesn't buy you all that much.

This is utter hogwash. (Although many gray areas exist in network troubleshooting, this is one issue that is utterly black and white.) Folks without documented networks are the ones running around with their hair on fire while others with documented networks have fixed the problem, gone to lunch, done something productive, and gone home to spend time with their kids. This may sound rather judgmental, but there's just too much evidence that suggests that you either document once and have a reference during times of trouble or you fail to document at all and end up having to figure out something multiple times during each crisis.

Not only does insufficient documentation waste time when your network is having problems, but it also causes unnecessary fear and confusion during the crisis. You owe it to yourself to have as clear a situation as possible when you start to troubleshoot—believe me, there's enough uncertainty and doubt when you're trying to find your way out of a bad network neighborhood without adding to it due to a lack of a good map.

Documentation Dividends

Enough with the dire warnings and horror stories! Let's set aside all the negatives due to a lack of documentation. On the positive side, you can see tangible benefits to having an acceptable level of documentation. Perhaps the one benefit you'll appreciate most is that a documented network is a network from which you can walk away. You can take a vacation from a documented network without worrying about whether you're going to be called if something goes wrong. Because you're not the only person with access to information about how your network is set up, others can deal with it while you watch the sun rise on your beach vacation without your pager or cellular phone going off. Because the work day is already occupied enough without having to drag somebody around to show him or her all of the nuances of the network, your network documentation does this for you, leaving you time to do other work. Table 2.1 describes the four major types of network documentation.

TABLE 2.1   TYPES OF DOCUMENTATION

Type	Purpose
Logical/functional map	This type of documentation gives an overview of how data flows in general. It leaves out individual workstations and wire runs and simply shows the important parts of the network (such as the servers, routers, and network segments).
Physical/layout map	This type of documentation shows very specific information about the network, including all wires, hubs, local switches, and workstations.

Type	Purpose
Device and cable labeling	This type of documentation consists of physical labels that identify the devices or cables they're attached to in big, bold letters.
Detail/description	This type of documentation can consist of a logical write-up of an application or system, or an everyday log of what's done to a device or system. It includes anything that's not intuitive and not included in manufacturer's documentation.

Logical/Functional Maps

Logical or functional maps are probably the type of documentation that you'll refer to most often. They're used as a sort of "org chart" of your network, and, appropriately, they indicate which device or server is responsible for what function, as well as which devices depend upon other devices in order to work. Details are not as important here; flow is what you're looking for. You'll want to be able to determine, without being confused by unnecessary details, why department A can't talk to the server, but department B can.

Not every PC or printer needs to be on this chart, but every device that somebody else relies on (such as your servers and routers) does. You'll need to make a per-case decision as to whether to include hubs or switches on this type of chart, based on whether these act as a group or stand alone. In other words, on this type of chart, hubs and switches (being a "neighborhood") are usually represented on their own, but there might be cases in which a switch connects two different "neighborhoods" that would be appropriately represented separately. See Figure 2.1 for an example of a simple logical network.

If you have a network that's complex or larger than one site, it's time to grab another piece of paper (it's not worth it to try to cram everything into one map—it just makes your map hard to read). Typically, multiple sites need a separate high-level view, so draw out the site plan for how each site is connected. Each site will be represented by a box that refers to a separate detail map and will indicate how that site links to other maps. See Figure 2.2 for a sample map of a more complex network.

Physical Maps

Physical maps, of course, refer to the physical world—that is, how things really are. Because physical maps are incredibly more detailed than logical maps, you'll want to chew them off in bite-sized chunks. Some sites can get away with just one physical map (usually fewer than 50 PCs in these cases). Most sites usually need a physical map for each floor of the building. This is usually a good breakdown for most sites, because it shows each and every wire running along with each and every PC, printer, switch, and hub, and this can get rather large. Accordingly, for simpler sites, it's really terrific to

FIGURE 2.1

A simple logical map.

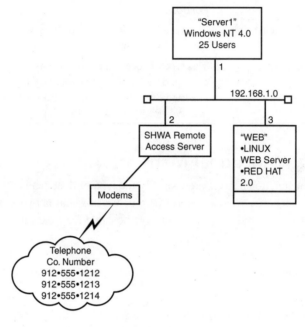

FIGURE 2.2

A more complex logical site map.

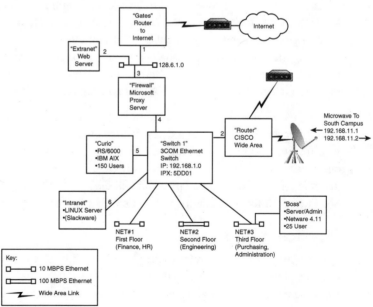

be able to lay your hands on the architectural floor plan of your building and add the network wiring and wire closet layout to it. A more complex site might also need more complex documentation in the form of a physical segment map.

I refer to a *network* as a *physical network* or *physical segment*—a group of hubs that are connected without a router or switch (in other words, the "party line"). Any hubs that are connected via a switch or router are always considered separate physical segments. Large ones can need their own maps.

2

For example, Token-Ring (which I discuss in more detail in Hour 10, "Token-Ring Basics") remains just "one network" even though it can have many hubs attached to it and can span several offices without using routers. Because the physical network is complex in this case, a separate physical segment map would be appropriate (see Figure 2.3). No matter what type of network you have, a physical documentation worksheet can act as a quick reference sheet for all data about that particular physical network (see Figure 2.4).

In general, you'll want to get as detailed as you can. (I've never seen someone crying after a network outage because the maps were too detailed.)

Update your maps as they change. Make this part of your SOP (standard operating procedure) with your consultant, network provider, or PC guy—particularly if you add or change things on your own.

Date your maps! Because things do tend to change, you'll end up with multiple maps of the same general area. If you have a date on each map, it's easy to figure out which map is current.

Using color in your maps can be great, but you might find it harder to share your maps with associates and vendors who are trying to help you (color maps are hard to read via fax, for example). A better idea is to use different symbols for items that need to stand out.

FIGURE 2.3

A sample Token-Ring physical map.

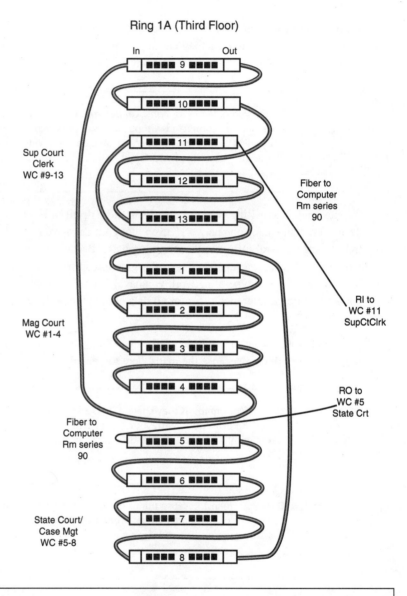

Ring 1A (Third Floor)

In   Out

Sup Court
Clerk
WC #9-13

Fiber to
Computer
Rm series
90

RI to
WC #11
SupCtClrk

Mag Court
WC #1-4

RO to
WC #5
State Crt

Fiber to
Computer
Rm series
90

State Court/
Case Mgt
WC #5-8

Keep it simple! Other people are going to have to read your document, and you want them to actually understand it. Accordingly, try to stay with straight, clean lines and avoid flow chart spaghetti (crossed lines). If you have more detail than you can really fit into one page, add another page.

FIGURE 2.4

A physical documenta-
tion worksheet.

NETWORK DOCUMENTATION WORKSHEET FOR PHYSICAL NET #____ AS OF____
LOCATED IN _____

HUB#	Port#	Wall Box#	Telephone#	IP Adress#	MAC Address#	Location/Description/Person

2

Software for mapping or flowcharting can help you a great deal, but don't
make the mistake of laying out your network map at the same time that
you're learning the new software package. Draw your network map out by
hand if you're unfamiliar with the software—this will make the layout go
faster. Software is great, because minor changes are easy to update.
However, complex software just isn't necessary—any simple drawing program will do. In other words, you don't need to make a career out of network mapping when you've got troubleshooting to do.

Device and Cable Labeling

A map does you no good, of course, if you can't find a device that's shown on the map.
Don't laugh—I've seen plenty of shops where nobody knows where the router is. How
can you reboot the router if you don't know which box the router is? A good troubleshooter will make it a point to label each device clearly and concisely before trouble
strikes; a lack of labeling can really increase your downtime by a remarkable margin.

If you ever visit the U.S.S. North Carolina or a similar World War II battleship,
you'll marvel at all the hoses and pipes that are running throughout the
ship—particularly in the machine rooms. Take a look at the meticulous way

all these pipes are labeled; believe me, they didn't do this for fun. They needed to know which pipe was air, steam, fresh water, brine, gas, or oil—a delay in a repair could literally sink the ship.

If you weren't fortunate enough to have had the Navy meticulously label your network (and your installer hasn't done it either), you'll need to start *today* with "as you go" labeling. Each time you find out what a device is or where a cable is going, slap a label on it. Don't assume that you'll remember—you may have a great memory, but during a crisis, that memory may be on vacation. (Also, remember that you want to go on vacation yourself one day and let someone else troubleshoot all this stuff for you.)

Go out and buy a label maker. They only cost about $50 and are really useful. They pump out quick, clear, and neat-looking labels. Also, you can print a label twice, cut once, and have a two-sided cable label, as shown in Figure 2.5.

FIGURE 2.5

Use a label maker to make two-sided cable labels.

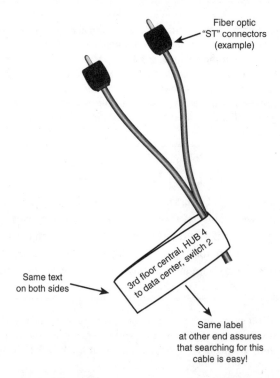

Fiber optic "ST" connectors (example)

3rd floor central, HUB 4 to data center, switch 2

Same text on both sides

Same label at other end assures that searching for this cable is easy!

You should test the labels you buy for adhesion. There's nothing worse than making 250 labels, only to see them all flutter to the ground after a month. As with anything else in networking, a simple pilot test can save you a big headache later. Also, cable labels should be plastic rather than paper; otherwise, as cables get handled, the labels might rip.

Any cable label should be put a good distance from the end (anywhere from 12 to 18 inches, if you have the room). This way, you can read the label once there are 50 or so other cables plugged into the same switch or concentrator.

2

You really need to keep up with your labels when items change or are moved. Troubleshooting can take much, much longer if you think you know which cable is correct but find out later that it's not.

Let's say you have a router that connects your earthbound headquarters with your company's moon base. If the router's name is *LOONIE*, a good device label would be this:

```
LOONIE: Router for moon base, Lockheed Satellite transmitter
```

I've seen folks slap a label with an IP address on such a router; however, this is optional if you have good functional documentation that clearly states that LOONIE has two IP addresses (say, 167.195.160.1 on the earth side and 167.195.161.1 on the moon side). Still, as my grandmother would say, "It couldn't hurt."

LOONIE has two connections in the back (one to your local area network and one to the satellite transmitter); you should label each connection with the device name and its endpoint. For example, the cable going to the satellite transmitter could be labeled this:

```
LOONIE -> Satellite Transmitter
```

Then, the other label might be this:

```
LOONIE -> Data Closet #1, Hub #3
```

Why label the cable that's directly connected to LOONIE as "LOONIE"? Well, suppose you have to disconnect the cable. It would be nice to know where to put it back.

I like to label each end of a cable with both devices that will be connected with the cable. This is so that I don't have to think about which end to put in the cable. I've been at sites where some poor, confused soul has labeled each end with the source rather than the destination, so that all you know is that the LOONIE router has a cable that goes to, uh, LOONIE. Oops! It's best to look at cable labeling from both sides (after all, you bought a $50 label maker, and making labels is easy). It really does save aggravation.

Detail/Description Documentation

The difference between a well-documented site and a professionally documented site is in the details. Detail documentation—although the least practiced documentation type—can augment the other types of documentation very nicely.

Detail documentation in the form of a formal write-up of how a system was configured, along with site-specific standards or frequently used troubleshooting practices, can make it easier for others to retrace your footsteps. This type of documentation, which includes how-to's and cheat sheets, contributes greatly to your ability to actually take a vacation.

You're the captain, so keep a log. It's hard to find a block of time to sit down and write up a formal description of previous troubleshooting techniques, but if you keep a log book near each crucial device, you can document as you go. Make it part of your SOP to write down anything that's done to a server, switch, or router (and at what date and time this operation was performed)—you'll save yourself a bunch of time when it comes to retracing your steps. Log books are also great for providing back-up documentation with a vendor. For example, an entry such as "The new server has crashed each week at 10:00 on Monday night" might lead a vendor to realize that the hard drive cleanup program scheduled to run on the server at 9:50 on Monday nights might be causing a problem.

Is it possible to reverse-engineer an undocumented network? Sure, but this requires a good bit of knowledge. What's more, it's really a waste of time if the network is being installed or changed while the documentation is taking place. See Hour 24, "Reverse-Engineering Somebody Else's Network," if you have a nightmare network that you need to document.

Is this a hint that you should insist on good documentation when you contract out for someone to build a network for you? Yes! Any professional worth his or her salt will probably be labeling like crazy anyway, but just in case you run into someone who thinks that an undocumented network equals job security, you need to get tough. Insist on labels on all cables, and ask for maps. If you have to pay more, either pay up a reasonable amount, which should be nominal (plus you'll save time and money in the long run), or find a different vendor. A lot of vendors are out there, and, ultimately, you're the person who either suffers or benefits from the documentation of the network and cable plan.

Summary

You can be the best network troubleshooter in the world, but without documentation, you're out to sea in a leaking boat. Documentation can mean the difference between ten minutes of downtime compared to two hours or so; therefore, a little work up front can really pay off in the long run.

Each type of documentation is important in its own way—for example, labels on cables, maps of the network cable runs, and functional diagrams of server placement. Also, keeping a logbook can keep history from repeating itself. In other words, it gives you a point of reference when the network goes down.

Workshop

Q&A

Q I label cables by number because each cable function can change and it's time consuming to replace the cable labels. Is this adequate?

A Not in my experience. Folks don't always keep track of what numbers are being used, and a number doesn't describe what's at the other end, thus requiring a separate table to translate the numeric cable number to the physical device (which you'll have to update when you change devices, anyway). Do yourself a favor and just put the description on the cable.

Q What should I document on my maps? What shouldn't I document on my maps?

A Completeness is the key here. Once you get some experience doing this and practice the techniques in future hours, you'll probably look at your initial maps and say, "I didn't need to write that down." However, you'll only know this after you get some experience under your belt. For now, write it all down; you can edit later.

Q This all seems overwhelming. Where do I start?

A Start simple and you'll be fine. You can start by writing down everything that you know about your network—your server name, where it's plugged in, what hub your computer is plugged into, and so on. Then, you can write down the categories of documentation, along with to-do's for each category.

Quiz

1. True or false? Logical documentation shows wire runs and cable boxes.

2. Physical documentation should include which of the following?

    A. Electrical outlets

    B. A small area of very specific equipment and cables

    C. An overall picture of the network

    D. Server-to-server information exchange

3. When labeling the router end of a cable, you should include what?

    A. The router name and the port on the hub

    B. The router name

    C. The port on the hub

    D. Either A or C

4. SOP stands for what?

    A. Some other person

    B. Standard occupational parameters

    C. Standard operating procedure

    D. Some operational processing

Answers to Quiz Questions

1. False

2. B

3. D

4. C

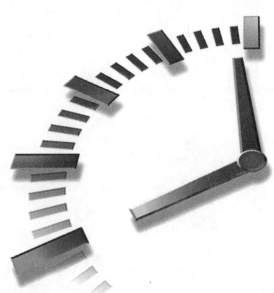

PART II

"Black Box" Trouble-shooting Strategies

Hour

HOUR 3

The Delta Method: Identifying Network Change

It can seem like gremlins are lurking in every server, wire center, and particularly in every Windows 95 PC. Usually, however, what we attribute to gremlins is actually the result of a user who has changed something and subsequently forgotten (or denied) making the change.

We all do this; we're our own worst enemies. For example, say you install a new browser, decide you don't like it, forget to delete it, and then have trouble accessing your company's intranet the next day. If you're lucky, you won't forget you installed the new browser, and you might be fine after uninstalling it. But what happens if you have a really great weekend in between and forget? You might "spin your wheels" for hours while trying to figure out what's wrong.

The Fat Finger Factor

The same principle applies when you're fixing servers and routers. You might make a change to a router or server in order to offer a new service or to fix a problem. If the change seems to work at first, it might be the last thing you think of if a problem surfaces later. For example, if you see that the startup file for your IntranetWare server does not automatically make a certain volume available, you might fix this by editing the file. The next day, you find that Windows NT—but not Windows 95—users are complaining that their time is off by five hours. Related? Couldn't be! Has to be the NT configuration, right? It can't be the server.

However, when this scenario happened to me recently, it was, in fact, the server. This is what I call the *fat finger factor*—while editing any configuration file (no matter how benign your changes are), you might introduce a stray character or two that makes a key command or parameter unintelligible to the server. In my case, the problem was that I had edited the IntranetWare startup file for something quite innocuous and hit a random key by accident at the top of the file. The first line of the file was responsible for setting the time zone. Instead of reading

```
SET TIME ZONE=EST5EDT
```

the line as accidentally edited to read

```
\SET TIME ZONE=EST5EDT
```

When I saved the file with my "benign" changes, all of the sudden the server had no idea what time zone it was in, because it didn't understand the `\SET` command. Because Novell-connected Windows NT synchronizes the time from the server and relies heavily on time zones, my fat finger threw every NT workstation on our network off by five hours (we're in the Eastern time zone, which is five hours off from universal time). Ouch!

The lesson is this: Always point the finger at yourself first. Always be thinking, "What have I done lately"? Then, be prepared to undo your changes. As I discussed last hour, keeping good notes—particularly a formal logbook—is a really good idea. That way, you can compare the date when the problem started to the dates of changes entered in your logbook.

Of course, others in your organization may be equally at fault—particularly if you share responsibility for your network. A logbook helps here, too, but don't solely rely on the logs—it helps to talk to each other and discuss what you've been working on.

When starting to troubleshoot a problem, you should go around and ask everyone if they've changed anything.

It's particularly troublesome when you (or your vendor) do a "fat finger" on a device and don't immediately restart it. When the device does finally get restarted, the change is no longer recent and is therefore hard to point to as the culprit. Of course, when you consider this, it makes sense to think of any device that has been recently restarted as a suspect device.

In general, you should always restart a device after a change has been made to it. A variation on this theme is when another user fat-fingers something and doesn't restart the device. You, then, come along and change something else and are totally innocent of wrongdoing, but when you restart the device, a problem occurs. I combat this problem by restarting a device *before* I start changing things. This way, I know that I am about to change a device that isn't broken.

3

Beware of Vendor

Your vendor probably does have your best interests at heart. However, remember that in addition to wanting to help you out, your vendor also has a schedule, doesn't like to pay people to do more than necessary to get the job done, and has a vested interest in selling you new stuff. Also, because your vendor probably has various projects scheduled, this can mean that someone might show up on your doorstep at a random time (not necessarily when it's convenient for you). You have a right to insist that changes to your network—no matter how necessary—must be scheduled according to your needs. You wouldn't let your plumber walk into your house at any time and fiddle with your water heater, would you?

For larger projects, you should also insist on a rollback plan (also known as *bailout plan*) in case of problems. A rollback plan is executed when things go seriously wrong—that is, when you're worse off when you finish than when you started. You'll have to decide how much this is worth to you: Sometimes, rolling a change back can cost a lot in terms of time and money. For example, if you're converting from a Windows NT server to an IntranetWare or UNIX server, a technician might need to go around to each workstation. Rolling this back can be time intensive and therefore costly. Because a vendor might ask you to eat the cost of rollback, it pays to negotiate this up front for a major project. The cost for "making it work and putting it back if it doesn't" might be a different price than "throwing it in and then dealing with it if it's a problem." It pays to look out for yourself, and if you're dealing with a reputable vendor, he or she won't mind if you bring these types of things up during project negotiation.

 Don't be a pushover, but don't be a pit bull either. Having a good relationship with your vendor is really important; your vendor can either be a cause of trouble or a troubleshooting partner—you want to shoot for the latter.

The Outsiders

Two types of vendors who don't have to get into your building to wreak havoc on your network are ISPs (Internet service providers) , who you rely on to surf the Web and send email, and, of course, telephone companies, who may connect your sites to each other via leased lines. Of these two, the telephone company is the much more mature vendor. Although the various phone companies take a lot of abuse, they've been doing this stuff for decades, and they tend to have good change-management policies in place. Consider that ISPs have only been around in their current form for less than a decade, and it's easy to see why they still have growing pains and therefore a bum rap.

Mondays can be tough. ISPs and phone companies tend to make changes over the weekend when utilization is low. If something that worked on Friday doesn't work on Monday, it's time to pick up the phone and call the appropriate provider and ask what's been changed? The answer will likely be "nothing," but if you can verify that nothing has broken over the weekend at your end and hang in there, the problem may mysteriously vanish around lunch time.

For longer-term problems, you may have to convince them that there's nothing wrong with your computer equipment (or figure out that there is something wrong and apologize for having doubted them). One way of doing this is to set up a test network; if two sites can't talk, you might as well bring the equipment to the same site and connect them directly. Once you do this and see that it works, you have pretty compelling evidence for the outside provider that nothing has changed with your equipment and that something *has* changed between the two sites.

The Risk/Benefit Ratio

New programs are cool. They offer features not offered in older versions, and it's fun to be the first one on your block to have them. Unfortunately, experience shows that for every new feature introduced, there are probably two new bugs in a product. The breakneck speed of Internet time means that software developers have unbearable pressure on them to be first to market. This usually translates into quick product testing, which means that the programs are released with at least a few bugs. Check out any software vendor's Web site—you'll see fixes posted for products that have been out for at least six months.

Because you have better things to do with your day than report these bugs to the software vendor, it's a good idea to *not* be the first one on your block to put a new application or operating system on your network. Unless you desperately need the new features of a new product, you should wait six months after product release to start rolling it out. If you need to do it sooner than that, consider what surgeons call the *risk/benefit ratio*—the amount of risk compared to the potential benefits.

Once you decide you need to start using a new product, you'll still want to make sure you aren't going to have any problems with it right out of the gate. For example, many IT shops were using Windows 95 internally for the better part of a year before they rolled it out to the masses. (Of course, using a new operating system introduces a sea of changes; a year is typically a longer pilot-testing period than you'll want for a new word processor or spreadsheet.) The most important part of pilot-testing is the concept of *limited production*. After you've played with the product in an isolated area, roll out a limited deployment—in other words, install it for a couple of folks who will use it for their daily work and see how it goes. If it goes well, you're usually going to be fine. What's more, if something goes wrong, you only have to roll back a limited number of folks.

Another aspect to keep in mind is the concept of *incremental rollouts*. This means that after a limited deployment, you start giving an application or system to more and more folks rather than doing it "all at once," thus rolling it out in small chunks that get bigger as the rollout becomes more successful. For example, you might give five people a new application. Later, you give the application to 10 more people; then 15, 20, and in your final increment, you might be rolling out 30 people a week (once you're sure that things are working fine). Using an incremental rollout ensures that if you have a problem early on, the least number of folks are affected.

Even if you don't have problems during a rollout, a new application or device can produce secondary effects in another item that doesn't seem to be related to the new item. Accordingly, a good rule of thumb is to shut down new items during network or

3

communications trouble. The trouble might not be related to the new device or program that you've installed, but if you shut it down, you've ruled it out as the source of the trouble.

If the trouble goes away, you can then kick the problem back to the vendor you bought the offending item from (or to the manufacturer). However, make sure the problem is reproducible (that is, make sure it happens repeatedly when you reintroduce the program or device back into the network) before going to your vendor.

You should try to give your vendor as much information as possible, especially when using telephone support, so that the technician can attempt to re-create your situation in his or her shop. Again, backup documentation such as logs and incident reports are key—in fact, technical support tends to pay much more attention to you if you can put your problem in writing.

Summary

Many network problems are the result of human-initiated change. Finding this change involves documenting and communicating your own actions, as well as politely interviewing your coworkers and outside vendors. Even unintended changes due to the "fat finger factor" can seriously damage a network, so it's worth considering where you've been, no matter how unrelated it might seem. You'll also want to figure out where others have been; however, don't rely solely on logbooks. (Although to document is divine, people aren't perfect. They'll sometimes forget to write down what they've done.)

Before deploying a new network toy, it's worth considering whether the risk is worth the potential benefit. Risk is always much higher with new products—you're best off waiting a couple of months before using what might be a pretty green product. Limited rollouts can also limit your potential network risk. You should also always think about a rollback plan, just in case things don't go as expected with a new project.

Workshop

Q&A

Q I've just installed a couple of new Windows 98 workstations. Now, one of my Windows applications isn't working anymore, even though it used to run under Windows 95. What could be wrong?

A There are a couple of things that are somewhat different between Windows 98 and Windows 95—for example, the way the hard drive is formatted. Without seeing your workstations, it's hard to know specifically what is wrong, but you should try to install Windows 95 on one of the workstations to see if 98 as a whole is your problem, or if it's just a hardware problem. (Your manufacturer might have just changed a motherboard on you without your knowledge.)

Q There's someone in my organization who keeps changing things but never admits to it, particularly when things break. What can I do?

A Unless you're this person's boss, you can't do much. However, this person's boss probably sees that this he or she contributes chaos and fear to your organization. Unfortunately, this isn't a technical problem, it's a social one, and is best handled as such.

Quiz

1. An external tape backup unit comes back from repair. You plug it in and boot up your PC. Your PC hangs at the BIOS screen. What do you do?

   A. Call your local repair shop.

   B. Disconnect the tape drive.

   C. Call your brother-in-law who's "into" computers.

   D. Press Ctrl+Alt+Del.

2. You add software to your NT server that requires a reboot. However, you don't remember the last time the server was rebooted. Upon rebooting, you get a message saying that a service failed to start. You uninstall the software and reboot again. You get the same message. What do you do?

   A. Call Microsoft.

   B. Ask around to see if anybody else has changed anything recently.

   C. Reinstall the software.

   D. Ask around to see if anybody else can install this software.

3. True or false? New products are typically "bug free."

4. True or false? Scheduled visits from your vendor (versus drop-in visits) save you time and aggravation.

5. Everybody has been experiencing network disconnects since yesterday. The only changes that have occurred include John installing new virus protection to his PC and Mary receiving a new PC. What's the correct first step in resolving this problem?

   A. Turn off both Mary's PC and John's PC.

   B. Turn off Mary's PC, but leave John's PC on.

C. Turn off John's PC, but leave Mary's on.

D. Fire John and Mary for endangering the common good.

Answers to Quiz Questions

1. B
2. B
3. False
4. True
5. A

HOUR 4

The Napoleon Method: Divide and Conquer

After Napoleon crowned himself Emperor, it's said that Beethoven changed the dedication of his Eroica symphony, originally dedicated to Bonaparte, to read "To the memory of a great hero." I'll try not to swell your head to that extent, but the divide-and-conquer methods in this hour are going to make you into a really great troubleshooter; it worked for Napoleon, and it's going work for you.

Divide and conquer refers to the concept that the location of a given problem can be found more easily by splitting the problem area into smaller, manageable pieces. When you know that a problem is within a given area (say, a certain physical network or within a certain PC or user configuration), you can figure out which portion of that area it's in by splitting the area into pieces.

Nine times out of ten, only *one* network problem is at work at any given time. Unless you've been struck by lightning recently, the odds of you having more than one problem simultaneously are very slim. (That's not to say that domino effects don't exist, though.)

The Numbers Game

Because only one problem usually exists at a time, it should be easy to search for (even in a large network). For example, let's say that I'm thinking of a number from one to one million, and you want to guess what that number is. If you proceed sequentially and guess every number, you could potentially go through 999,999 numbers before getting it right. However, if you divide the maximum number in half, and I tell you "higher" or "lower," and you keep dividing that result in half, you will take *at most* only 23 guesses. That's quite an improvement. Don't believe me? Here's an example:

Me: Okay, I'm thinking of a number from 1 to 1,000,000.

You: 500,000?

Me: No, lower.

You: 250,000?

Me: No, higher.

You: (pausing to calculate 250,000 / 2 + 250,000) 375,000?

Me: No, lower.

You: (getting mad at me for picking a number between 250,000 and 375,000) Let's see, there are 125,000 numbers between 250,000 and 375,000, so the middle of that would be...312,500?

Me: No, lower.

You: (whipping out your calculator) 281,250?

Me: No, lower.

You: (getting good at this now) 265,625?

Me: (astonished) How'd you guess?

In truth, this would probably go on for a couple of more guesses, but you get the idea. The range is initially a 1,000,000—a huge range. Then it goes to 500,000, then 250,000, then 125,000, then 62,500, then 31,250, then 15,625, then 7812, and so on. You can see that you lose zeros pretty fast in only seven guesses; by the time you guess another seven times, you're down to only about 60 possibilities. That should come as no surprise. You can see in Figure 4.1 how fast dividing an area in half cuts down your search.

> If you want to impress your boss or look cool at a geek convention, you can refer to this method of guessing as a *binary search*. As a bonus, you can scrawl its mathematical representation onto the overhead projector:
>
> $n=\log2\ (x)$
>
> Here, x is the maximum number in the sequence, and n is the maximum number of guesses.

FIGURE 4.1

In a binary search, the search area gets smaller and smaller as the number of guesses progress.

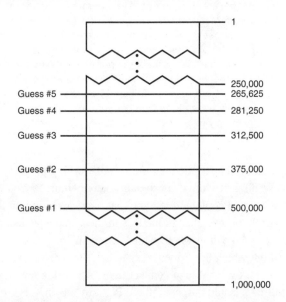

4

Your Waterloo: The Network Is Down!

Now, let's look at what you might do when your network goes down. First of all, how do you know when the network is *down*? Is it a physical network problem or a server or router problem? The answer: divide and conquer. When you're presented with a problem, logically work your way from the entirety of your network (the whole range of numbers from one to a million) to the specific problem (265,625). You'll probably start by trying to figure out if there's only a problem with one person (a *local* problem) or with a large group of people (a *systemic* problem).

If you determine that it's just one person, you're done with your systemic divide-and-conquer technique and can now proceed to workstation troubleshooting (which can require a combination of techniques, including divide and conquer). Otherwise, if it's more than one person, you need to gather more information. Is *everybody* down? Usually not.

I've actually seen a situation in which everybody was down due to an electrician accidentally pushing the emergency off button of an equipment room's UPS. Here's one problem that caused a "domino effect" of a whole bunch of other problems, including no phone service, no network services, and general chaos. This is pretty unusual, and it's the exception rather than the rule.

As network infrastructures are becoming as important as the telephone system, people are starting to get very paranoid about putting all their eggs in one basket. Many servers now have extra (redundant) fault-tolerant power supplies so that if one power supply breaks, the server stays up. Because servers are usually connected to a UPS (uninterruptible power supply or battery backup unit), it's desirable to put each server power supply on a different UPS; otherwise, one broken UPS could take down the server. This might be expensive, but so is downtime. Whether your company has redundant power really depends on whether your management is committed to spending the money to get as much reliability and fault tolerance as possible.

Once you determine which functional group is not working properly, it's time to haul out those maps you so diligently drew after you mastered Hour 2, "You Can't Have Too Much Documentation!" People will tell you that they can't log into the server, that their drive letters are gone, or even that all the PCs in their area have locked up. You'll have to find out from those who call in whether it's "just them" or if it affects everybody. You'll also want to find out which department they're in. Alternatively, you can take a look for yourself: If all the PCs were able to connect to the network a few days ago but now they can't, then for all intents and purposes, these PCs are "down," regardless of whether it's an Ethernet problem or a problem with a switch or server.

Take a look at where these folks are on your functional maps, and see what they have in common or where they connect through. When you do this, it will probably become painfully obvious where the problem is. If two departments are saying that they are down, it might be that the server they use is down—check your detail documentation! On the other hand, if you see from your functional map that all the groups that go through a particular router are down, it's time to check that router. If users from just one segment are calling, it's most likely a problem with the physical network segment.

Physical network segments (or "a bunch of hubs" to use plain language) are exquisitely suited to troubleshooting via the divide-and-conquer method. Why does a physical network segment go down? Usually, because these are shared networks (or "party lines"), the trouble is that somebody is babbling incessantly and not letting anybody else talk (see the Ethernet and Token-Ring hours for specifics). All sorts of fancy new technologies are built into "smart hubs" to detect this and stop it; therefore, this sort of problem isn't as common today.

You'll still see one workstation bring an entire segment down sometimes if you're not totally using switches on your network, because even smart hubs are not as smart as you are (nor are they as smart as manufacturers like to think they are). In other words, there's more than one way a given station can take down the segment.

Segment Searching

Because you're treating a complex system as a series of simpler systems, without needing to know the specifics of each, you don't care *why* the segment is down, you just care that it *is* down. The first thing you can do once you identify that a physical network is down is to refer to your physical documentation to see how many hubs or wire centers are involved with this physical network. These are the basic building blocks of the physical network. Because there are usually not very many of them in comparison to number of PCs on the network, it makes sense to start here. If you have a small number of hubs, it's okay to isolate one at a time to see when the problem goes away. (When it does, you've found the problem hub.)

If you have an untenably large number of hubs connected together, you'll want to use the kind of divide-and-conquer method you used when guessing my number from one to a million—it's a lot faster. Cut off half of them and see if a workstation connected to the remaining hubs can get in. If it can't, you've found the trouble segment. Otherwise, you'll have to try the other half. Continue dividing the troubled segment in half and then in half again. Soon you'll have found the hub that contains the trouble. At this point, you can divide and conquer the hub itself, taking out ports until you find the one that's causing the trouble (see Figure 4.2).

4

FIGURE 4.2

An Ethernet hub with 32 ports requires no more than five guesses.

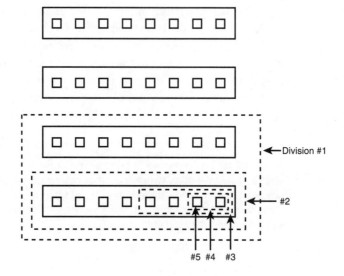

32 Ports – 5 Divisional Guesses

Unlike a shared Token-Ring (where all hubs are connected in a circle, as shown in Figure 4.3), each Ethernet hub is connected to another in a straight line (as shown in Figure 4.4). This means that if you isolate one, you isolate those below it. You can handle this by bypassing the hub you want to isolate and plugging directly into the next hub in the chain. However, be careful that your "cascade" hub is clearly labeled before you start unplugging things.

FIGURE 4.3

A Token-Ring network.

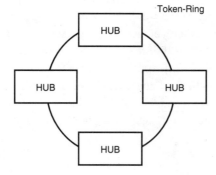

FIGURE 4.4

An Ethernet network.

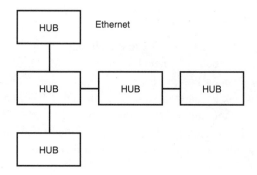

When you find the port that's causing the problem—and even when you first find the hub that has the problem port—make sure you perform a "control" experiment on it (that is, put it back into the main network and make sure it's still causing the problem).

If you isolate the hub that has the "network glue" on it—that is, the server or the router that connects you to the server—the other hubs won't be able to "see" any of the network and will remain "down." If you suspect this hub, it's best to divide and conquer on a port level rather than taking out the entire hub (that is, after verifying that the server or router is okay). If you don't, you'll keep the server or router from talking to the rest of the workstations on the segment, and you'll assume that taking this hub out does not fix the problem (because the stations will still be unable to reach the server or router). In fact, the problem might be with one of the stations on the server hub, which you'll find if you take them out by port rather than by the entire hub.

If you must take out the hub that the server or router is connected to, make sure to test whether it's up or down by checking your documentation and seeing whether a workstation connected to this hub is up.

Once you find the port, it's time to refer to your physical documentation, figure out which node on the network the port belongs to, and then determine the local problem. In most cases, you'll find these types of problems to either be a mangled network cable, a bad network card, or even just a PC that's locked up.

Again, "smart hubs" will automatically figure out certain kinds of problems, and performing this process is somewhat primitive in this era of "automatic transmission" shared networking. However, it's good to know how to drive a standard transmission (just in case you have to); plus, if you know how to troubleshoot a "standard," you're that much better at understanding how an "automatic" works.

Division of Labor

Speaking of primitive, let's hearken back to the old days of the DOS PC. If you've worked with DOS at all, you know that about a zillion little programs, called TSR (Terminate and Stay Resident) programs, would jack themselves up into your PC's memory and sometimes wreak havoc with your other programs. The same was true of the Apple Macintosh computer, only TSRs were called *CDEVs* and *INITs*—and not all of them would work with one another. Therefore, if you didn't have another PC or Mac to compare with, you would have to start getting rid of them one at a time to see if whatever you were trying to do would start working.

Of course, most seasoned tech support operators used to recommend that the first thing you do is to "boot vanilla"—that is, boot without all those startup programs. Guess what they were actually telling you? Divide and conquer! Instead of dealing with each little program, you get rid of them all and then see if you still have problems. This is similar to how you dealt with the previous hub problem—you split them in half and try again until you find the offending program.

Here's how you can "boot vanilla" from Windows 95:

- Start the computer in "safe" mode by pressing F8 right after you turn on your computer (but before you see the blue sky design of the Windows startup screen). You can choose Safe Mode or Safe Mode with Network, depending upon whether you can test whatever it is without the network.
- Press and hold down the Shift key after logging in (this applies to Windows NT as well).

Here's how to "boot vanilla" from DOS:

- Press F8 after you turn on your computer. This will allow you to select which TSRs and/or device drivers to load.
- Back up your startup files by copying AUTOEXEC.BAT to AUTOEXEC.BAK and CONFIG.SYS to CONFIG.BAK; then, get rid of drivers and TSRs manually. You can copy the respective BAK files back to CONFIG.SYS and AUTOEXEC.BAT once you're done.

Every single networked system you have in existence is going to benefit from this same technique. Even though you're no longer in a single-tasking, non-networked environment, this technique still applies.

As I discussed in the last hour, you can find many problems in a networked environment just by thinking about the changes that have been made recently. However, sometimes changes aren't under your control or you're oblivious to them. Good examples of this include browser updates, plug-ins, and virus protection patterns. Therefore, when the change is not obvious, you have to stop banging your head against the wall and get back down to basics.

For example, let's say everybody in your office starts having problems shutting down. They all get stuck at the "Please wait while your computer shuts down" screen. It seems, at first glance, that everybody is going to have to deal with it. Nobody has changed anything recently that they know of, and no one is capable of wading through the guts of what's going on.

Even though this doesn't seem like a network problem, the fact that it just started spontaneously on a bunch of networked computers seems very odd, so it gets dumped in your lap. Fortunately, you realize that even if social engineering does not reveal the source of the change, something *has* changed, and you can at least use the divide-and-conquer method to figure out what it is.

Because your office runs Windows 95, many of the programs that run at startup are in the Startup menu. You get rid of everything in the Startup menu and reboot. All of a sudden, you can shut down again. You return half of the programs to the Startup folder and keep restarting until you find the source of the problem. It turns out to be your email notification program. However, you decide to start up with *just* the email notification problem, and you're able to shut down.

4

In this case, you've got an interaction problem, which is further solvable via the divide-and-conquer method. You put back in half of the programs that were in the startup file, and you manage to track the problem down to a situation where you have both the virus protection program and the email notification program loaded. As you might have guessed, this troubleshooting session actually happened to me—the virus protection program, which is automatically updated from the Internet, had started to interfere with the email notification program. A quick search of the vendor's Web site found a patch for the email client (not the virus protection program) and an annoying problem was fixed.

Obviously, the divide-and-conquer method doesn't always work to ultimately solve your problems. In particular, it's tough to troubleshoot intermittent problems, as well as quantitative (rather than *qualitative*) problems that don't involve a black-and-white (broken or not broken) scenario.

You can remember the difference between qualitative and quantitative by keeping in mind that *qualitative* is the analysis of the *quality* of a situation (as in, "My workstation cannot print at all"). *Quantitative* refers to the analysis of the *quantity* involved with a situation (as in, "My workstation is slower at printing than Sally's").

For example, the divide-and-conquer method might lead you to believe that a new application is causing your network slowdowns (and you might be right). However, it's not always feasible to get rid of a new application, and, furthermore, it might not be clear whether the trouble is *this* particular application or just that the network itself is at a saturation point in general. In this case, you might try a different application, but can you really switch a largely deployed application in a short period of time? You'll probably just end up checking the application to see if it's misconfigured and taking measurements to ensure that the application is behaving properly on your network.

The bottom line is this: Even when the divide-and-conquer method can't directly find your problem, it can at least point you in the right direction.

Summary

A problem that seems insurmountable can become easier to solve if you break it down into smaller parts. Problems tend to be split in two ways: by location or by component (whether it's software or hardware).

Although networks are complex and dependent systems, where one failing component can make it seem like everything has failed simultaneously, typically there's only one problem causing a domino effect. The divide-and-conquer method allows you to find the problem component without knowing why it's causing a failure. When you have large numbers of components or locations involved, divide-and-conquer troubleshooting (also known as a *binary search*) can change your number of guesses from millions to dozens, thus saving you a lot of time.

Although the divide-and-conquer method isn't always the end-all and be-all of the troubleshooting process, it's still a powerful method that can usually pinpoint a culprit in most situations.

Workshop

Q&A

Q Why should I perform divide-and-conquer troubleshooting on my six-node network? It only takes me six guesses to find any problem!

A You're right. Obviously, using the divide-and-conquer method with small numbers might seem more trouble than it's worth. However, you may end up solving the problem in fewer than six guesses.

Q If my router port is having problems, won't it seem like the whole network is down?

A Yes, if you have no local servers. In this case, you can try to contact workstations on your physical segment—this will rule out the physical segment. (For users of Windows 95 file and printer sharing for Microsoft Networks, try to find someone whose CD-ROM or printer is shared. If you have TCP/IP installed, try to ping another workstation on the network—if you can, the network is definitely *not* down.)

Q Although I'm having *some* problems on my workstation, the divide-and-conquer method is problematic for me. I can't get rid of everything in my Startup folder; otherwise, I won't be able to work. Any other suggestions?

A Each situation is obviously different. The divide-and-conquer method might not be your best strategy here. Instead, you may need to ask, "Which of these things is not like the other?" For more information on this troubleshooting strategy, see the next hour.

4

Quiz

1. The divide-and-conquer troubleshooting strategy enables you to do what?

    A. Mathematically calculate a problem resolution

    B. Solve any problem in the world by performing a binary search

    C. Locate a problem by splitting the problem area in half (or removing half of the components involved)

    D. Divide the problem-solving labor among several people

2. You're thinking of a number from 1 to 500. What might my second guess be?

    A. 25

    B. 250

    C. 300

    D. 125

3. What's the first thing you should determine when hearing of a network problem?

    A. Determine whether the problem exists for one user or for multiple users.

    B. Check the router.

    C. Check the documentation.

    D. Determine whether the server has crashed.

4. You track a network problem down to the hub that the segment's router is on. What do you do next?

    A. Start port-level divide-and-conquer proceedings.

    B. Remove the router from the network.

    C. Start to check the router documentation.

    D. Remove the hub from the rest of the network.

5. You've tracked down a problem to a Windows 95 PC, but you have no idea where the problem might be. How do you perform a "vanilla boot"?

    A. By pressing F8 upon bootup and then choosing Safe Mode.

    B. By pressing F5 upon bootup and then choosing Safe Mode

    C. By pressing F8 upon bootup and then choosing Divided Mode

    D. By pressing F5 upon bootup and then choosing Divided Mode

Answers to Quiz Questions

    1. C

    2. D

    3. A

    4. A

    5. A

HOUR 5

The Sesame Street Method: One of These Things Is Not Like the Other

The "Sesame Street" method is more of a game than it is hard work. It's one of the most gratifying and fun ways to troubleshoot (even if you don't hum the song while you work). The principle involved is as follows: Given a group of two or more items on a network, all that's required to troubleshoot the one item that isn't functioning correctly is a comparison to an item that is.

Typically, the way in which items are different is also the reason the non-functioning item is broken. For example, if your children are twins and one of them—the one who eats Super Sugar Bombs instead of Wheaties for breakfast—is hyperactive, it doesn't take a rocket scientist to figure out that you might want to align the twins' diets to try to handle the hyperactive one.

Assuming that the twins have identical activities, are in the same environment for their classes, wear the same types of clothes, and are for all intents and purposes physically identical except for their diets, it makes sense to try to align what they eat in order to *rule out* diet as a possible cause of hyperactivity.

The same principle applies to a misbehaving network appliance: If you find an identical item that happens to be working, changing the problem item's configuration to be just like the one that is working can oftentimes fix the problem.

Servers and Routers

You can apply this principle to just about any object on your network, but it has limited use when troubleshooting devices such as routers and servers. Routers and servers are hardly ever really identical, although they may be similar in function. Sometimes, the similarity of function is enough to compare, but you need deeper knowledge to be able to compare servers that are "mostly the same." It's a lot harder than troubleshooting devices that are "twins."

Servers and routers certainly have "device integrity" similarities—for example, a router that keeps crashing while others are doing just fine might show a different revision of its operating software (or *firmware*). Hardware routers don't run Windows or DOS; instead, they run a "stock car" operating system, which is really pretty simple software (unlike Windows with its zillions of DLLs). The upside of this is that usually you only need to check one revision number; a difference in revision numbers might point out the difference between a working router and a problematic router.

Similarly, you might compare a problematic Windows NT server's patch level and DLL versions to a known "good" server. In particular, NetWare servers have the Config Reader (see Hour 13, "NetWare Networking Basics"), which does a wonderful job of automating the task of comparing the dozens of crucial NLMs (NetWare loadable modules) and patches that live on a given server.

User Objects

Because servers are all configured somewhat differently, it's most useful to apply the Sesame Street principle to user objects that live on your network. By convention, user objects (user logins, associated security rights, and the user's workstation itself) are typically configured at least somewhat the same—if for no other reason than your vendor found it easier to roll them out this way.

In its simplest form, finding out what's "different" is pretty easy: You know that the group of users has been working reasonably well for awhile. Let's say that one user reports that she can't use a particular application; because others are working using *their* workstations and *their* logins, the first step is to figure out whether or not her problem resides in *her* workstation or *her* user login. You can rule out workstation problems by having her log into a different workstation. If the user is unable to run the application at another workstation, you immediately know that the problem is with her login, not her workstation. You can further prove this by having someone else login to the user's workstation, proving that the application on this workstation does indeed work. You next must ask yourself how this user login might be different than the other user logins.

You need to compare apples to apples—in other words, if you try to run an application on a workstation that the application hasn't been installed on, you'll encounter problems. Also, some applications write user-specific files to a workstation, *not* to the network. Beware of these applications. You'll want to perform a control experiment for each type of application—before you have problems—to see whether a user who can work with the application on one PC can also work with it on another PC. If so, you know that the application can "float" from workstation to workstation.

When only a few users in a workgroup report a problem, you should first review what has recently changed. If you come up with nothing (or even worse, if the change was mandatory and not undoable), it's time to start thinking about how those few users are different than the rest of the pack.

5

Ruling out is a really effective troubleshooting technique that's related to, but not identical to, the divide-and-conquer method. If you can start thinking about what a problem *isn't*, you're one step closer to figuring out what the problem *is*.

Ruling out is particularly effective when you find multiple things that are different between objects. For example, if two workstations have different video cards, network cards, and different amounts of RAM, you might give them both the same amount of RAM to rule out the problem as a RAM problem. Then you can move on to giving them the same network card, and so on.

Keep It Simple

You're probably starting to see that a key component of successful troubleshooting is keeping things simple. This is exactly what you do when you start with the "highest" level object when you begin determining which thing is not like the others (see Figure 5.1). In the previous example, why even start investigating the workstation configuration before you can rule it out? Also, why start messing with the PC's video card or network card when you *know* there's nothing wrong with the PC?

FIGURE 5.1

Look at high-level objects first.

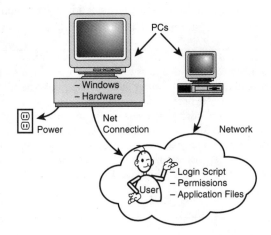

It's useful to think of these items as being in high-level containers that have lower-level containers within them. Until you rule out (or rule in) an upper-level container, it's silly to even look at its subcontainers. You can think of a typical network setup as a "box of workstations" (which contains motherboards, memory, hard drives, and so on), a "box of networks" (which contains wiring, hubs, and so on), and a "box of users" (which contains user IDs, login scripts, and various security attributes).

Thinking of these high-level components in boxes allows you to concentrate on the task at hand without getting distracted, and it will make you a better troubleshooter. If you discover that the network is the problem, you won't get distracted by workstation subcomponents, for example. In other words, once you figure out that the network is the problem, you should only concentrate on the network subcomponents.

To Shotgun or Not to Shotgun?

When you've identified, in general, where the problem lies, the fastest way deal with it is to use the "shotgun" effect—that is, to simply make a problematic object identical to one that's working.

This means that you should point your "troubleshooting shotgun" in the general direction of the target. Have you ever seen a shotgun in use? It's pretty hard to miss your target when shooting with a shotgun, because the shot scatters widely. Anything in front of the muzzle tends to get holes in it. "Shotgunning" a particular object means that you replace everything in that subcontainer in the same indiscriminate way—without spending time analyzing which component is the troublemaker.

Drive duplication can be a big help here, because it's fairly easy to "shotgun" a known "good" hard drive setup to a hard drive setup that's having configuration difficulties (see Hour 16, "Where Do I Start?" for more information). Remaking the user's home directory is another good method of "shotgunning" a problem once you've identify the general target. For example, because UNIX programs are dependent on multiple configuration files in a user's home directory, I sometimes rename a user's home directory, make a new home directory for that user, and then copy a known "good" user's home directory contents into it (see Figure 5.2).

FIGURE 5.2

Shotgunning a user's home directory.

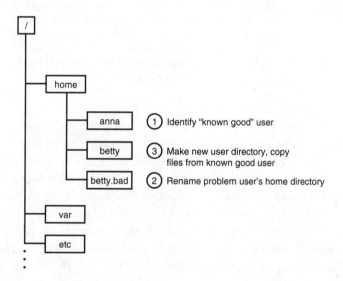

For those times when you can't use this technique (for example, when crucial information would be overwritten), you'll want to consider the following components, listed from the highest level (to the left) to the lowest level (to the right):

```
- Workstation
    - BIOS / Manufacturer
    - Hard drive
        - Operating system configuration (startup files, Registry)
        - Operating system components (DLLs)
```

```
                  - Local applications (versus network)
                  - Virus? Or not!
            - Network card
                  - Cable
            - Video card
            - RAM
            - Power
                  - UPS
                  - Surge suppression
      - User login on server
            - Login script
            - Permissions
            - Application configuration files (user-oriented access list?)
            - User files (home directory)
            - Application itself (versus on hard drive)
      - Port on the switch or hub
```

> Most folks don't realize just how much trouble bad AC power can cause—it's really worth trying to rule out the power of a PC that, for example, is locking up as it gets into the network by plugging the PC into a different wall outlet or adding a power conditioner. A *power conditioner* is a special filtering device that acts to get rid of the jitters and brownouts that can plague AC power (particularly in rural areas).

Again, beware of chasing the low-level components. For example, operating system components can be an adventure in and of themselves; you can literally spend days doing comparisons of these lowest level objects. This might be worth it sometimes, but for most small areas of trouble, keep in mind that information you don't need is information you don't want. This is known as *information hiding*. Keep the fuel pump image from the introduction of this book firmly in mind when you're about to dive into more internals than you really care to deal with. Do you really need to learn all the icky details of what various Windows DLL files do if you can simply copy somebody's known "good" Windows configuration to solve the problem?

On the other hand, if an email program is complaining that it can't load MAPI32.DLL, it's usually worth looking at the MAPI32.DLL file on the hard drive. Sometimes the file is damaged, (it might show a size of 0, for example). Also, you might compare it to a known "good" MAPI32.DLL and realize that it's much shorter than it should be. In this case, copying one file from a known "good" workstation is faster than reloading and reconfiguring the entire workstation. It's a bit of a balancing act—you just need to look at the given situation, see what information you have, figure out how much time it would take to change something out, and take what seems like the quickest and most effective action.

This is actually the hardest part of this method: figuring out what to compare and getting your arms around the items that are proving the problem. For example, if many (but not all) users are reporting a problem, particularly an intermittent problem, it can seem overwhelming at first, because it's hard to say where to start and which pieces of the network might be causing the problem. In cases like this, you'll save your sanity if you start logging the calls and writing down in a tabular format what the problems are, when they happened, under what circumstances, and the configuration of the workstations and users involved. Such a chart might look like the one shown in Table 5.1.

TABLE 5.1 SAMPLE LOG SHEET.

Date	Time	Department	User	Problem	Type of PC
8/11	2:00	Finance	Jack	Illegal operation error—WordPerfect	Clone/486
8/11	2:20	Finance	Leona	Fatal exception 06 (during system boot). Seemed OK afterwards.	Dell/P6
8/11	3:00	Finance	Tracy	Illegal operation error—WordPerfect	Clone/486
8/12	9:00	Finance	Tracy	Illegal operation error—WordPerfect	Clone/486
8/12	10:45	Finance	Jack	Illegal operation error—WordPerfect	Clone/486
8/12	1:00	Finance	Jill	Locked up. Had to reboot when reading email.	Clone/486
8/13	11:00	Finance	Jack	Illegal operation error—WordPerfect	Clone/486
8/13	12:45	Finance	Bill	Illegal operation error—WordPerfect	Clone/486

By looking at this detailed log, it becomes apparent that illegal operation errors are what you're getting the most of. (If you had more incidents listed in the log, it would become even more apparent. The other items are not repetitive and amount to "bumps in the road," not hard errors.) So now you know that "some of these things are not like the others." The ones that are alike are your persistent errors that you're trying to get rid of.

Why isn't Bill calling as much as Tracy or Jack? A quick phone call reveals that he was out of town on the 11th and 12th, so he's not as much of a wildcard as the log implies.

Let's look at a concrete example. I was recently involved in upgrading a department to Windows 95, which included upgrading to a new version of WordPerfect. The word from management was that this was a strategic change, making the possibility of rollback very small; it was up to us to make it work. Although the sample machines I had pilot-tested worked just fine, we started to have problems a day or so after the upgrade. Certain (not all) users began to report illegal operation errors. I was absolutely sure that all users were configured the same—identical login scripts, file permissions, and home directory configuration—but, unfortunately, because we were using clone hardware, I wasn't as sure about the workstations.

I logged the incidents over several days and discovered that some users *never* reported the error. This indicated that the problem was not a moving target and that it was staying in the same places. This is important to establish; some errors do not pop up in the same places all the time—that is, they move from workstation to workstation. This typically indicates a systemic problem rather than a problem with the individual workstations.

Next, I saw that only the PCs that were clones were having a problem with the illegal operation error—none of the name-brand PC users had reported it. Finally, I saw that not all of the users who had clones were reporting errors—only certain of the clones. This led us to believe that there were component problems with certain clones.

Obviously, one group of these things was not like the other! To rule out a user problem, I switched the PC of a user who didn't have the problem with the PC of a user who did have the problem. (This didn't endear me to either user, but it did tell me that the problem was definitely workstation related.)

I took inventory of the workstations that were acting up because I wanted to see what those workstations had in common. I made a new chart of the lower-level components (see Table 5.2). I left out Windows 95 and its components, because I had taken pains during the rollout to make sure that all the workstations were identical in this regard. I also didn't scan for viruses, because I rolled out a scanner along with the Windows installation.

TABLE 5.2 A SAMPLE CHART OF LOWER-LEVEL COMPONENTS

Workstation	Mfr/Bios	Video Card	Hard drive	RAM	Hub/port
Jack	AMI	Brand-X	Quantum	16MB	8/2
Tracy	Phoenix	Brand-X	Connor	16MB	9/3
Bill	AMI	Brand-X	Seagate	24MB	8/1

After looking at the new chart, it became apparent to me that although the PCs all had components-du-jour and had been built with whatever pieces and parts the vendors had lying around, they all, oddly enough, had the same video card.

Just because it was reasonably easy, I swapped out one of the problem workstation's video card with a different video card. As I continued to log problems, it became apparent that the workstation with the new video card was no longer having a problem. I switched another workstation's video card, and the problem went away there as well. Although I tried to update the video drivers on the remaining problem workstations, this did not make the problem go away. The final solution was to replace all the problem workstations' video cards.

Obviously, getting a lot of workstations whose components tend to change on a regular basis isn't a good foundation for being able to easily troubleshoot workstation problems. Because fewer differences equals less time trying to figure out which of these things is not like the others, it makes good sense to practice proactive troubleshooting by attempting to keep all components—software, hardware, and otherwise—to a standard, particularly within the same department or workgroup. See Hour 16 for real-life information from the trenches on how to homogenize your heterogeneous network.

> A *heterogeneous* network is one in which the components are all different; it's more difficult to be a Sesame Street troubleshooter on a network like this. On the other hand, the components used in a *homogenous* network are pretty much all the same. This is a Sesame Street troubleshooter's dream.
>
> Are there really totally homogenous networks in which everything is always identical? Probably not. Like most things in life, the truth lies somewhere in the middle. However, in this case, the key is to keep as many things the same as possible.

5

Summary

If you have something that is broken, comparing it to something that works can be a quick way to establish what *exactly* is broken. Although it's difficult to compare the configuration of seminally different servers and routers, comparing their overall revision levels and file versions can help to rule out a "difference" problem.

This technique works particularly well when you're considering other objects on your network, such as user setups and workstation configurations. Sometimes, if you've troubleshot the problem down to a particular configuration, you can replace it wholesale (or *shotgun* it) with a known "good" configuration. This allows you to avoid dealing with complex issues that you may care nothing about.

For complex problems with multiple complainants, you should keep a troubleshooting log that contains the specifics of how users' workstations and configurations are different. This can help to establish a pattern of how the complainants' configurations are the same.

Workshop

Q&A

Q **How can I tell whether a problem workstation is similar enough to a known "good" workstation to compare apples to apples?**

A You need to have a good sense of when a workstation was installed, who installed it, and so on. Your site's detail documentation will come in handy for determining this. Even documentation in the way of receipts can determine whether a workstation was purchased (and therefore configured) at the same time as another. If you work for a large organization, your purchasing department most likely has asset tags on the PCs. Also, the date of purchase can probably be found somewhere in a database.

Q **How do I shotgun a known "good" user setup?**

A Most network operating systems have some sort of template feature (for example, IntranetWare's NWAdmin), or at worst, they have a feature where you can copy one user to another (NT's User Manager).

Quiz

1. True or false? A hardware router that's having problems should have all its DLL versions compared to a similar router that's not having problems.

2. The Sesame Street method is most applicable to _____.

    A. User hard drive setups

    B. User login scripts

    C. Servers and routers

    D. Both A and B

3. What is *not* part of the high-level workstation "box"?

    A. The hard drive

    B. RAM

    C. The video card

    D. The login script

4. True or false? You need to be a Windows programmer to investigate an error message about a "bad" DLL.

5. When you log problems on a given segment and different people report the same problem each day, the problem is most likely related to what?

    A. The workstation

    B. The user object

    C. Both A and B

    D. The network

Answers to Quiz Questions

1. False. Hardware routers don't have DLLs; they typically just have one version number for their internal software.

2. A

3. D

4. False

5. D

5

HOUR 6

The SOAP Method: Subjective Data, Objective Data, Analysis, and Plan

I hope you've liked all the writing involved in the last hour, because the method of troubleshooting in this hour involves a great deal more of it. Treating a complex problem usually involves a lot of note-taking, because you have to fill in the gaps where your understanding of the problem is incomplete. Up until now, you've treated problems the way you treat a multiple-choice test—with change analysis, divisive reasoning, and matching. Now, we're talking about a fill-in-the-blank test, and it gets a little bit harder; this is the hour where you have to wade through the subjective, match it up with the objective, analyze your data, and plan on what to do next. In other words, this is the hour you want to save for the tough problems.

Doctor Network

First, a little bit about the SOAP method. I first encountered the SOAP method while I was deciding not to be a doctor like my father. Although I had absolutely no interest in sticking needles into people, hanging around my father in his office taught me a lot about troubleshooting. In a sense, medicine is *much* harder than computing—there are hardly any standards, the designer never released the data sheets (much less the full documentation), and the device you're trying to troubleshoot can sue you if you make a mistake. The medical profession has come up with all sorts of diagnostic tricks—we as network troubleshooters have a great deal to learn from the medical profession.

One of those diagnostic techniques is the SOAP method of note-taking. On their patients' charts, some doctors write down on separate lines the letters *S*, *O*, *A*, and *P*, standing for *Subjective*, *Objective*, *Analysis*, and *Plan*, respectively. Therefore, if I went to see the doctor about my stomach, he might write:

S: Patient reports stomach pain; ate hot chicken wings last night; extra work lately.

O: Palpation reveals tenderness in upper right quadrant.

A: Suspect acute gastritis.

P: Treat with antacid x 5 days, bland diet, follow up in 5 days to assess condition.

The subjective is what I say to the doctor, the objective is what the doctor sees, the analysis is what he deduces from his additional questions and reasoning, and the plan is what he will do to try to treat the problem, plus the next step. Doctors are used to not being able to get a black-and-white answer; however, if they have a plan, they are going in the right direction.

Going in the right direction is what the SOAP method is all about. Not every problem you run into as a troubleshooter is going to be solvable within that day or week—particularly problems that are not show-stoppers (emergency room visits). In particular, problems that come and go (intermittent problems) are usually long-term and complex troubleshooting jobs. To be able to wrap your arms around a complex problem, you have to segregate the problem into its component parts—that is, the subjective report and the objective facts. It's particularly important to be able to separate the subjective out—someone may be reporting something that has *some* bearing on the problem but perhaps is not pointing directly at the problem. Consider someone who's reporting chest pains—is this person reporting a heart attack or a muscle problem? The report of pain in the chest is a subjective feeling—the active investigation that reveals a heart attack or muscle pain is the objective finding. The subjective is useful but can only be borne out by investigation.

Just the Facts

When considering the facts in an intermittent or complex network issue (also known in the industry lingo as "troubleshooting a weird problem"), you need to categorize a basic list of objective items that can help point towards a solution:

- Duration of problem (all the time or intermittent?)
- Start of problem (date and time)
- Place (on the network, physical location)
- Number of users involved
- Configuration of workstation (like or unlike others?)
- Number and types of applications involved (running simultaneously with?)
- User name(s) involved, security group(s) belonged to
- Measurements
- Behavior of similar applications

Even though you may have a lot of objective data, you might not have the right objective data to analyze in order to come to the right conclusion. Therefore, your "plan" item on your first couple of tries on a tough problem will probably be to gather more data. Don't give up; the more data you have, the better guess you can make.

SOAP in the Real World

Let's take a case in which a user says she can't run a particular Web applet that she needs for her job. Figure 6.1 shows a logical map of the site; her PC lives at point A on the map.

You visit the user's PC and can run the applet just fine. She frowns at you, and says, "Well, it doesn't work for me." She tries right after you, and it works, but she reports the problem again the next day. You decide to use SOAP on this one:

S: Web applet does not run.

O: Web applet runs *when I try it*.

A: Perhaps the time of day has something to do with it?

P: Come back during the time she usually tries the applet.

6

FIGURE 6.1

*Troubleshooting a
time-related problem.*

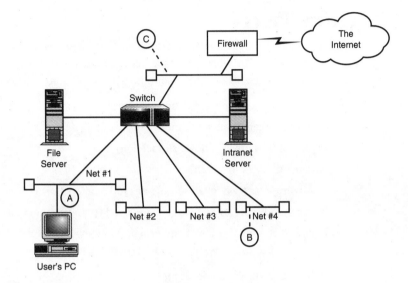

Your analysis of the problem is a good one, and your plan to gather new information
works. You visit her when she usually tries her Web applet, and, sure enough, it won't
work for you. What's going on? This time through, you're the one supplying the subjective data; it's your guess:

   S: I bet that the time of day has something to do with the applet not working.

   O: Web applet does not run at 8:00 a.m.

   A: Could it be related to another network activity on that segment happening at
       the same time?

   P: Try using a different network segment (point B on the map).

An okay plan, but it doesn't work out, as shown from your notes:

   S: Network activity may be different on her segment at 8:00 a.m.

   O: Web applet still fails on a different segment.

   A: My head hurts. What else could be different at this time of day?

   P: Investigate what goes on at 8:00 a.m. on the network as a whole.

She still has problems at 8:00 a.m. on a different network segment. That's fine. You've
now ruled out her network segment, and that's very important to do. You've made a
deduction, and it's wrong. Don't sweat it.

Is It a Virus, Doc?

After getting a cup of coffee, you briefly think about the possibility of one of those viruses that "go off" at 8:00 a.m. on a certain day, but you dismiss it—you have pretty good virus protection. What's more, you used a different workstation that you're sure is virus free when you tested the different segment. Good guess, because things like this have happened—even viruses that don't *do* anything until a certain day at a certain time in the morning can interfere with system operations every day while it checks to see if it's the "right" day to ruin you.

So, it's back to the drawing board.

Getting a Consultation

This is the crucial part, because you're frustrated, and you think you can't possibly solve this problem. It's tempting to give up. Guess what? Pros feel that way, too. The difference, however, is that the successful troubleshooter takes a break and looks at the facts again. Then, much like a doctor, the troubleshooter might "get a consultation" and go right back at it.

Do you have to get a consultation from a pro? Not necessarily. You get a consultation because you're too close to the problem, and you already have preconceptions as to what's going on. Let's say you ask somebody—anybody—what goes on at 8:00 a.m. every day. The answer is going to be "everybody turns their PCs on" or "everybody gets into work" or some variation on this. That turns on a light bulb for you—because everybody is turning their PCs on and logging in at 8:00, might this be the computer equivalent of rush hour on the network?

The answer, of course, is yes, there is a network rush hour. How do you verify this? Well, it's sort of tough. There are two ways:

- Actual measurement (relatively difficult unless you've already read Hour 21, "Tell Me About Your Network")
- Changing the situation (moving the workstation to a place where traffic will be quieter)

Even though you've already moved the workstation to a different segment, you hadn't considered that the segment you were moving to might also be problematic. You can think of this as the equivalent of moving from the Long Island Expressway to the Grand Central Parkway—it doesn't do you a lot of good at rush hour (you've been treating the situation as though there was construction or an accident on one but not the other). Now, your SOAP looks like this:

6

S: The problem might be network congestion.

O: The problem occurs at the same time on different major network segments.

A: Login congestion is likely on major segments, but not as likely on a segment with fewer users.

P: Check maps and try the applet on a "low traffic" network segment (perhaps nearer to the Internet segment and away from segments with server login traffic on them).

You deploy your plan: You temporarily set up a workstation at point C on the map. When you try the applet at 8:00, it works! You have now pointed the finger squarely at network congestion. The next question is, whose problem is this? In other words, is this something that the applet vendor is responsible for, or is this your problem for having a network that's too busy?

Your response to this problem may vary. On one hand, it may be practical to move this person to a less busy segment. However, this might not work, because you can see from your physical maps that the network segments near PCs tend to have a lot of PCs on them and are smack in the middle of the servers. In other words, physical constraints might prevent you from putting this person on a segment without other PCs, because the only hubs near her probably are being used for other users. A hub with less traffic might be in your data center or in another building, outside of her physical reach. (The smart aleck might ask, "Why not ask this person to stop doing her work process at 8:00 in the morning?" Not a great solution—the network is supposed to work, darn it!)

At this point, if you really needed to have this person's workstation live on a busier segment, you have to start application troubleshooting. Why is it that this person doesn't have any other problems, say, with local applications? As you'll see in Hour 19, "Internet/Intranet Troubleshooting," comparing a local application to an Internet application isn't a good idea; using Internet applications is like taking an international flight versus hopping in your car to go to the store. Lots of things can happen between here and Paris. You write down your SOAP again:

S: Applet is not working; other applications are.

O: The applet is the only Internet application in the mix.

A: Internet applications are not local applications.

P: Try a different Internet application during peak hours.

You've now done five SOAP lists. Long and tedious, isn't it? Yet, as you can see, SOAP is a powerful process for refining what you know, as well as a way to take guesses and turn them into fact and a way to keep you moving forward.

You try a different Internet application at 8:00 the next morning, and it works like a champ. Even though it doesn't do exactly the same thing, at least you're now comparing apples to apples—that is, a firewall-dependent wide-area application to another firewall-dependent wide-area application. You try yet another Internet application, just to make sure, and it, too, works just dandy. Here's your latest SOAP:

S: The application itself seems to be at fault.

O: Only have tried two other Internet applications.

A: Measurement of congestion and delay might help but would still lead to vendor.

P: Contact supplier of the applet and relate all notes that led to this conclusion.

Fortunately, this is not a "free" applet, and the supplier is eager to make it work for you. The supplier talks you through taking a network trace, and you email it off to him. He responds that you do have quite a lot of traffic, but not an unreasonable amount. Because you've gathered a lot of notes and have sent them to him, he has a good idea of what's going on and understands that it's probably his problem. Because he wants you as a customer, before too long, you've got a "patched" program emailed to your desk, which you install to your user's PC—problem solved.

In a situation like this, you want to make sure you document the problem—either informally (via email to your colleagues) or formally (say, as an addendum to the product documentation in your library). You might write something like this:

```
10/20/98, JF: Applet has problems running on a busy
network, use Patch 1.2, located on the 'Barbarian'
server's 'FIXES' share.
```

6

Sound crazy? A software supplier fixing something you reported? Not really. Our shop has reported many bugs to suppliers over the years using this procedure, and with great success. When you follow careful SOAP note-taking procedures, you're likely to convince your technical support people that you have a *bona fide* problem that needs to be addressed. However, it's even more likely that you'll come up with the answer yourself—which is really the objective.

Summary

Computer networks have been around less than a century—as network troubleshooters, we should learn troubleshooting techniques from any source we can. The medical profession uses SOAP notes, which can be highly effective in pursuing complex problems. Because you don't necessarily have all the facts when you start chasing a problem, using the SOAP format for note-taking encourages you to analyze your data objectively, collect more facts, and form a plan.

Workshop

Q&A

Q A user says that her workstation hasn't changed, but I've traced the problem down to her workstation. What could it be?

A Remember that what a user *says* is always subjective. You need to take a look for yourself to see what the facts are. Also, talk to other people in her office. Look at her workstation yourself. Odds are that something has changed. This is change analysis, to be sure; however, SOAP reminds you that any user reports are subjective—you need to corroborate the facts yourself.

Q I've reported bugs to manufacturers before, with no success. Granted, there are manufacturers who listen, but how do you tell which ones will?

A Assuming you reported the problem in great detail, my sense is that the smaller software vendors are really the ones who tend to respond to their individual users' problems. The larger software vendors, without naming names, tend to send you a form email that says something like "This will be fixed in the next release" or "Software is operating as designed." Believe it or not, even shareware vendors tend to be really, really responsive to you—particularly after you've registered a large number of licenses with them. They appreciate the business, and it shows.

Quiz

1. *Subjective* means what?

    A. The way someone sees an issue

    B. The cold hard facts

    C. The world according to Garp

    D. The truth of the matter

2. True or false? SOAP notes always lead to a conclusion the first time.

3. A piece of subjective data should be _____.

    A. ignored

    B. collated

    C. divided

    D. investigated

4. Which of the following is not an example of a piece of objective data?

    A. How a user perceives a problem

    B. A measurement

    C. The number of users involved

    D. The timing of a problem

5. Analysis is usually the process of thinking about what?

    A. The cold, hard light of reason

    B. Reasonable subjective data

    C. Objective data only

    D. Subjective data plus objective data

6. True or false? Gathering more data is a common plan.

Answers to Quiz Questions

1. A

2. False

3. D

4. A

5. D

6. True

6

HOUR 7

The Simple Simon Approach

Robert Heinlein's *Have Space Suit, Will Travel* tells a story about two frogs who jump into a milk bucket and can't get out. One frog sees how hopeless the situation is, quits paddling around, and drowns. The other is too stupid to quit and keeps paddling. Pretty soon, he's got an island of butter in the middle of the cream, where he floats until the milkmaid comes and throws him out.

Persistence can be one of the hallmarks of an unstoppable frog or a really good network troubleshooter! Even when you think you're beaten, that "one more try" can beat the thorniest of problems.

As I discussed in the last hour, it's important to "get a consultation" when things seem hopeless. It's easy, fast, and doesn't cost much. What's more, with someone else's perspective in the picture, you can sometimes collect observations or facts that you've missed. Even better, when you explain the problem to someone else, you may be forced into diagramming the flow of the problem, reemphasizing important points, and so on—which usually leads to you getting a better grasp on the problem yourself.

Someone Has Already Solved Your Problem

Wouldn't it be great to quickly and easily get a consultation from an expert? Better yet, wouldn't it be great to get a consultation from an expert for free? You can! Most manufacturers will allow you to search through thousands and thousands of pieces of detailed documentation from technical support personnel. In effect, you end up scanning the knowledge of the smartest technical support gurus in the world. Searching a knowledge base or technical information database can be one of the best ways to avoid reinventing the wheel, particularly with interaction problems (where one piece of software or hardware affects another) or problems caused by poorly worded documentation.

It almost seems too good to be true. Why do the manufacturers do this? Well, to run a good technical support shop, tech managers need good databases that include the problem and resolution of every technical support call, no matter how trivial or tremendous it might be. This allows *them* to avoid reinventing the wheel, as well as saves them tremendous time (and, therefore, tremendous amounts of money). Because support is one of the services that keeps customers coming back, it pays for manufacturers to expend the small amount of effort to make these knowledge bases public. The availability of these knowledge bases also allows software companies to curtail the amount of free phone support they give—they can always point users to the Web database for free yet charge for phone support.

Make sure you don't perform a search from a company's home page. Searches that occur at the main home page typically search the entire company site, including nontechnical information such as press releases. Most companies have a technical support home page that offers a tech-only search.

Just as a company's home page is usually found at www.company.com, most companies' support pages are found at

> support.company.com
>
>   or
>
> www.company.com/support

> Although it seems you would get the best search results by entering as
> many words as possible, sometimes this gives you "search clutter." For exam-
> ple, if you search for `network card error 78E8`, you'll get hits on the word
> *network*, which will match an insane number of documents. Same thing
> with *card* and *error*. You're best off, in this case, to try a search on `78E8`.
>
> If the site offers a more sophisticated search engine, this approach isn't
> necessary. Sophisticated sites should allow searches for the following:
>
> `network card error +78E8`
>
>   or
>
> `"network card error" AND "78E8"`
>
> Both of these mean "don't show me a match unless it definitely has `78E8`
> in it."

Lookin' for Support in All the Right Places

In truth, you can probably do as good a job searching a manufacturer's technical support
database as the first-level support operator who answers when you call for technical support. The key is knowing *what* to search for and *where* to search for it.

For example, suppose you're planning a rollout of Windows NT in your office. Because
you're a careful and responsible person, you're doing a pilot test and going into limited
production. Halfway through the first part of your rollout, a user complains that she's
having problems when using DOS EDIT and other DOS utilities. Apparently, she is
being asked to insert a disk into drive A whenever she runs a DOS program, regardless
of whether a floppy disk is actually involved. This is really odd. You think to yourself,
"Which of these things is not like the other?" and run to another user's machine. You
try the same thing using another user's machine and login, and you get the same results.

You discover that every single machine you've rolled out is having the same problem.
Obviously, you stop the rollout. But now you have an odd problem—why is a fresh new
machine acting this way? As a matter of fact, each machine you've built acts this way. Is
it a hardware error? A software error? If so, which software? Is this a network-related
problem at all?

A lot might possibly go wrong here, so now is a good time to spend a few minutes
searching. Fortunately, you have what to search for right in your face, in the guise of
a very rude error message:

`NTVDM: No disk. Please insert a disk into drive A:`

7

The most obvious place to search, Microsoft's site, reveals nothing of tremendous interest, except that you need to check the NT file path for references to drive A, which aren't there.

In order to figure out where to search for your answers, it's time to *categorize* what you've added to the new machine:

- Windows NT setup
- Intel virus protection
- WordPerfect Suite 8
- GroupWise email and scheduling software

But wait! Hold it right there. You're already missing at least two pieces of the puzzle. You were thinking about application software, but in truth, there are more pieces than you just wrote down. Let's take it from the top and write down what you've *done* to create this new machine. The possible sources of the problem omitted from the previous list appear in bold:

- Unpacked **Dell PC** from box.
- Setup was automatically run. NT and **Microsoft's Service Pack 3** were installed.
- Installed **Novell IntranetWare Client32** (necessary for connection to Novell server).
- Configured **3Com Ethernet** network card.
- Installed Intel Virus Protection, Corel WordPerfect Suite 8, Novell GroupWise.

Enumerating the steps you took to create the workstation lets you come up with a vendor list to search. Your final list contains the following:

- Dell
- Microsoft
- Novell
- 3Com
- Intel
- Corel

Rather than build a new PC from the ground up, which might take anywhere from an hour to two hours (if all goes well!), you go to the following Web sites and key in the error message you received:

- http://support.dell.com

- http://support.microsoft.com

- http://support.novell.com

- http://support.3com.com

- http://support.corel.com

You might begin by entering NTVDM by itself, because this is a unique term (again, you don't want to get hits on common words such as *disk*), and then proceed to search for the entire error message if you get too many hits. (Remember that unless you specify a "weight" to a word—which is not an option on some vendor sites—each word counts the same; therefore, entering **insert disk NTVDM** matches a document with *insert* and *disk* more than it matches a document that has one mention of NTVDM.)

Dell has nothing about NTVDM. Microsoft has zillions of information documents, and NTVDM, by itself, pulls up close to 100 documents. You decide to come back to here if nothing else pans out. On the third try, eureka! As shown in Figure 7.1, a search on NTVDM pulls up only nine documents, a very manageable number. A quick glance reveals a technical document that precisely describes your problem. You click that link to learn more. In this case, you learn that the Novell Client32 in conjunction with a bug in Windows NT Service Pack 3 has caused your problem. The documentation also details a fix (copy NTDOS.SYS from the original Windows NT CD-ROM to your current C:\WINNT\SYSTEM directory).

FIGURE 7.1

Searching several sites rather than spending a lot of time on one can yield pay dirt quickly!

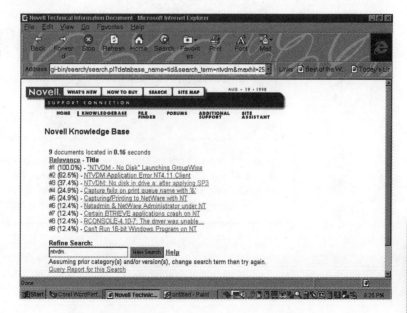

7

> When troubleshooting a potential multivendor problem, don't spend too much time on each site at first—one vendor may have a quick solution, whereas the other vendor may have you sifting through hundreds of documents.

Five minutes after firing up your Web browser, you've solved the problem. Whoa! Talk about standing on the shoulders of giants. You might have spent hours playing divide-and-conquer on this problem if it weren't for the incredible power of the tech support search.

Something Techie Happened on the Way to the Forum

Don't underestimate the power of public forums—Usenet newsgroups and mailing lists can be an invaluable resource. Not all manufacturers promote these groups on their corporate home pages, because Usenet isn't always kind to them (it's not unusual to see postings that read "This product stinks!"). Manufacturers also tend to shy away from Usenet and foreign mailing lists because they have no editorial say on these Wild West public message exchanges. Nonetheless, these forums can be a source of real-world information—stuff you won't get from the manufacturer (although you might have to wade through piles of useless expletives before you hit useful information).

> Don't forget to search manufacturers' support sites before you hit the Web at large. You might save yourself some time this way.

> Most Web search engines (AltaVista, Lycos, and so on) will allow you to specify a search of Usenet instead of Web pages. However, you're better off using a newsgroup-specific search engine such as www.dejanews.com; you can do more specific searches, as well as restrict your search to recent postings.

Fortunately, you can search Usenet as well. If your Internet provider doesn't provide you with Usenet newsgroups, or if your news application doesn't allow searches, you can use Web-based search engines to search for the support topic or error message you're looking for.

In addition to Usenet groups and mailing lists, some manufacturers and resellers also run their own Web-based forums at no charge. These forums are usually pretty good, because in addition to Joe Public, they're monitored by real-life tech support personnel. Even though the manufacturers are not obligated to answer questions posed in public forums, chances are that legitimate questions about legitimate problems are going to be jumped on by the appropriate folks—they do have a vested interest in you being able to use their products without problems. (See Figure 7.2.)

FIGURE 7.2

The Novell Web Forum in action.

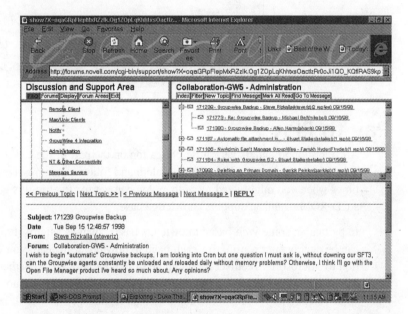

You'll also find forums run by third-party vendors who use them as advertising vehicles. The attraction of these is that the third-party vendors are ostensibly impartial about the product and are mostly concerned with getting it to work for their users. Again, your mileage may vary. (See Figure 7.3 for a sample forum screen for Windows NT.)

7

FIGURE 7.3

A third-party Windows NT support site.

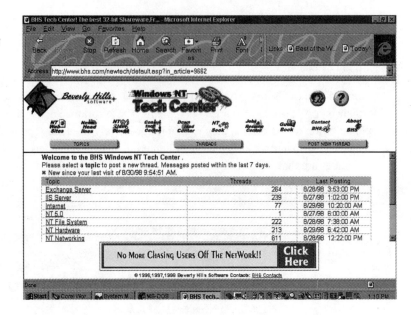

Pay to Play

All free support entails very little obligation on the part of the vendor, but it can be pretty good if you take ownership of the problem and follow up aggressively. Still, there are times when you might need more than you can get for free; in this case, you can invest in a CD-ROM technical support knowledge base.

In particular, some Web-based knowledge bases, such as Microsoft's, are so busy that it can be aggravating waiting for each page to download. Instead, you can buy a subscription to Microsoft's TechNet for a couple of hundred dollars. Whether you love or hate Microsoft, you've got to love TechNet. As with most CD-ROM knowledge bases, you get what you pay for—much more sophisticated features, which result in speedier access. For example, you can refine your search results by product type and you can bookmark. TechNet has every single technical information document available on the Web site, but it runs about ten times faster (see Figure 7.4).

FIGURE 7.4

A Microsoft TechNet session.

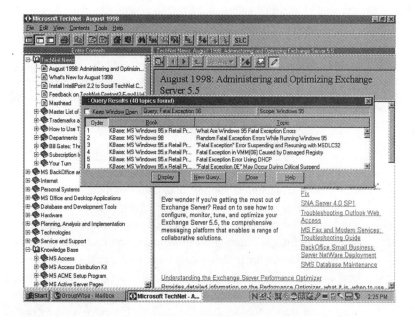

TALKIN' TECHNET

Because I deal quite a bit with problems with Microsoft products, I tend to hit TechNet rather heavily. However, it's sort of embarrassing, because TechNet makes you look like a hero when all the heroism you've shown is a couple of mouse clicks in the right place. For example, a couple of technicians came to ask me for a consultation on a fatal exception error that had been going on for awhile. Instead of running upstairs to look at the workstation in question, I keyed the exact error message into TechNet, which brought up a couple of hits—one of which seemed applicable. We ran upstairs to apply the TechNet suggestion, and the user was fixed in 10 minutes.

TechNet's not only for searches, either. You can also browse by topic, including Microsoft whitepapers and resource kits, making it an excellent source of learning and study.

Tell your boss you can justify buying this stuff with just one or two paid phone calls to technical support or one or two visits from your $150-an-hour consultant.

7

Obviously, if a problem isn't solvable in a reasonable time frame, you'll have to go to the outside for help: Time (particularly downtime) equals money, and a couple of hours of consulting time can be money well spent in comparison to lost man-hours when something critical is down. If you end up having to pay for help from the outside, take heart—your work has not been wasted. Doing your troubleshooting homework can and will save your company hundreds or even thousands of dollars, as you've decreased the up-front work of the consultant.

The "Cadillac" technical support databases out there (for example, MicroHouse's Support Source), cost about $1,000 for a year's subscription. You'll want to think long and hard before plunking down this kind of money. Although these types of resources include carefully researched documentation and multisource technical support sources and are wonderful for professionals who need quick answers, you should think about how often you'll go to them. Although these services usually provide plenty of magazine articles and tutorials and are searchable, you might find your needs adequately filled by Web-based search engines (see Figure 7.5). Unless you do a great deal of troubleshooting (in which case, you also need a raise), these types of services might not be worth getting.

FIGURE 7.5

A MicroHouse Support Source session.

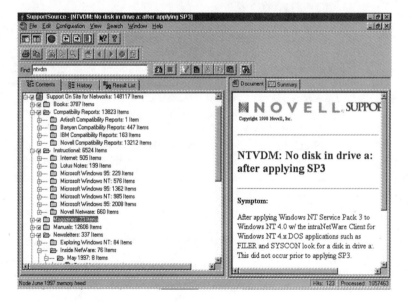

Codependence

If you've read the manual, checked the databases, and you're still stumped, it's time to call the vendor. Whether you pay as you go for what seems to be a hopeless problem or have a support contract, a couple of strategies exist that will help maximize your encounter with a professional technical support person.

Primary in your efforts will be how well you've documented the problem during your troubleshooting efforts. If you've used SOAP notes during the problem, you probably already have exactly what a tech support person is wanting:

- Type of hardware involved
- Type of network involved (maps)
- Application(s) involved
- Time relationship (ongoing, time of day)
- Reproducibility

If you cannot reproduce a problem, neither can the folks at the other end of the phone. However, if you can reproduce the problem on a different workstation or a server, you're that much closer to convincing technical support that your problem is a legitimate problem and not just a product of your network environment.

People who call tech support before they gather this crucial information typically receive the brush-off. (The irony is that once you've done the requisite research and documentation, the culprit is usually apparent, thus canceling your need to call technical support in the first place.) One brush-off technique is the finger-pointing game. Because you, a nonexpert, can't prove that a problem is unrelated to a different vendor, it can be difficult to refute technical support's claim that the problems lies with the other guy.

You can combat this by insisting on documented proof that you can submit to the maligned vendor—the vendor doing the maligning can tell you how to collect this proof—or by administering a test on your own. As you'll see in Hour 21, "Tell Me About Your Network: Network Analyzers & Bits & Bytes," you don't have to be a network expert to be able to submit network traces to technical support. Network traces are basically blow-by-blow accounts of what's happening on the wire, and they can be very useful to the network analyst on the other end of the line.

7

You can also combat finger-pointing by trying the same type of operation "manually," without the influence of the item being pointed at. In other words, if a program complains that it cannot write a file to a server but you think it should be able to, try writing the same kind of file by yourself under the same login and session circumstances (don't reboot or log out). Therefore, if the setup program says this:

```
Can't copy "FOO.EXE" from D:\setup\foo to G:\myapp ñ Retry?
```

You might want to get to a DOS prompt and try typing the following:

```
C:\> COPY D:\setup\foo\FOO.EXE G:\myapp
```

Alternatively, you can use Windows Explorer to copy FOO.EXE from d:\setup\foo to g:\myapp.

FINGER-POINTING FUN

I once had a bizarre problem with a server—certain applications simply would not install. The common thread was that the install program involved complained that it could not write certain files to a certain directory. The application vendors said, "It installs fine on thousands of other servers just like yours!" The server vendor's response was that these programs must be doing something odd while they're installing. "No," I protested, "more than one program is doing this—it must be the server!" The problem was set aside, until one of my technicians had the idea of performing a manual file copy of the files involved. In other words, one of the applications I was trying to install failed while it was copying the file KBSTUFF.SYS, so I simply typed

```
f:\> copy d:\setup\kbstuff.sys f:
```

and sure enough, I got an error—even though I could copy differently named files to that directory (and even though I had file permissions to write to the directory). I called the server vendor's technician back, who said, "I've *gotta* see this!"

The technician requested that I capture the network traffic in between the workstation and the server (the network equivalent of a wiretap). Sure enough, one day after submitting traces to the server vendor, we were told that, yes, the server was replying wrongly to the workstation. The vendor asked, "Do you have virus protection on the server? Software licensing software?" I did, and after removing the virus protection package, I no longer had problems installing any of the applications. Apparently, some sort of interaction problem existed with the various applications I had installed on the server—not the least of which were the vendor's bug-fix patches! The virus protection package was reasonably old, so it hadn't been tested with the latest patches—an upgrade to the virus protection package was in order, but at least I had tracked down the problem.

A given vendor may supply wonderful tech support in addition to a killer Web site. I've been fortunate to deal with some of these vendors—unfortunately, though, they're sort of rare. If you find one, buy its product as much as you can and offer up prayers that it sticks around forever. Seriously, good tech support technicians *can* be major help, so you certainly don't want to rule out calling them.

Summary

Sometimes, the best way to solve a problem is to find out if anybody else has had the problem. Internet search engines, Internet forums, mailing lists, and CD-ROM knowledge bases are excellent ways to extend your troubleshooting efforts. Technical support should be saved as a last resort; if you approach tech support with a documented reproducible problem, you're much more likely to be treated with respect. Brush-offs, such as finger-pointing, can be combated with good notes and a reproduction of the problem without the component that the vendor is pointing its finger at. Working knowledge of diagnostic gear, such as network analyzers, can really help to gather data that ends the finger-pointing game as well.

Workshop

Q&A

Q Why don't you list every technical support site that you know of here?

A This stuff changes every six months; the techniques that you've learned so far will not. (Computer geeks have a saying: "Go to lunch, fall behind.") You'll need to learn how to find particular sites in addition to how to search them once you get there. Just follow the aforementioned guidelines to find a manufacturer's Web site, and you should be okay. There are not many technical support sites outside of the ones provided by manufacturers, but just for fun, you can search for them using standard Internet search engines such as Alta Vista. As an example, try typing "Linux free support", making sure you enter the quotation marks, because each word on its own would result in a huge match.

Q I can't reproduce an intermittent problem. I understand that it's tough to get vendor support until the problem is reproducible, but try explaining that to my boss. Help! What can I do?

A You need to go back to the divide-and-conquer technique, take SOAP notes, and compare the problem area to other working areas. If other workstations or application installations are working fine, it might be time to burn down the barn and

7

build it again. Other than that, disciplined note taking and follow up are your best friends when dealing with an intermittent problem. I feel your pain. Believe me. However, you will prevail if you keep at it. If the problem is important enough, feel free to go ahead and ask your vendor; tech support might be able to give you clues as to what you might have missed in your ruling-out process.

Quiz

1. Which of the following is it best to search a support site with?

   A. As many keywords as possible

   B. One unique keyword

   C. A quoted phrase or error message

   D. Both B and C.

2. A support CD-ROM you want costs $750. Your boss asks you to justify buying it by telling him how many hours of consultant work you can avoid. At $150 per hour (which is the going rate for your consultant), you calculate that you would only have to avoid _____ hours of calling the consultant to justify the cost of the CD-ROM.

   A. 3

   B. 9

   C. 5

   D. 15

3. True or false? Usenet discussion groups are always correct about technical issues.

4. To search the support database of the Frobozz Fabulous FiberSwitch Corporation, where might you start?

   A. http://www.frobozz.com/frotz

   B. http://www.support.frobozz.com

   C. http://support.frobozz.com

   D. http://frobozz.com/www/support

Answers to Quiz Questions

1. D

2. C

3. False

4. C

PART III

The Care and Feeding of Network Appliances

Hour

HOUR **8**

Hard Basics: Guide to Being a Hardware Geek

"We only truly learn by destroying."

—Usenet post, COMP.SYS.UNIX (circa 1980)

Network geeks don't live in a vacuum; we all have to learn how to deal with the things our networks live on. Whether it's a bad circuit board or a corrupt spot on a hard drive, network functions are picky, picky, picky; they stop working when underlying pieces and parts (the *infrastructure*) stop working. Networkers have been fixing (and accidentally breaking) hardware for years. (People may *think* all we do is stare at scores of monitors all over our network command center and stroke our beards thoughtfully, but we've really got our sleeves rolled up. We're the equivalent of a silicon grease monkey.) Once a problem has been troubleshot down to a hardware component, hardware troubleshooting is often necessary. In this hour, I'll cover what to do and what not to do with hardware. I'll also go over the basics of the following topics:

- PCs
- Circuit boards and other pluggable electronics
- Cables
- Monitoring system resources

Because many servers are nothing more than pumped up PCs with faster and better hard drives, CPUs, and so on, many of these hardware techniques apply to servers as well.

The PC Thing to Do

A user's PC is often the culprit of a network problem. Although a PC is essentially just an assemblage of pluggable circuit boards and chips and can be troubleshot from that angle, you should also consider its low-level software configuration when troubleshooting. Your PC's lowest level software is its BIOS (*Basic Input/Output System*), which is responsible for making all the boards and chips talk to each other in a civil manner.

The BIOS

You can get into a PC's BIOS by pressing the Del, F1, or F2 key right after you power on the PC. (Ctrl+Alt+Esc used to be popular, but I haven't seen this one in quite some time.) The BIOS setup screen can range from fairly complex to reasonably simple. Typically, a name-brand PC's BIOS is simpler than a generic clone's, because the name-brand manufacturer exercises greater standardization over which components are connected to its motherboards. A typical BIOS screen is text-based, with no Windows-style controls.

A BIOS setup screen can be compared with other "known good" PCs from the same manufacturer in order to verify that the settings are correct. If you don't have another PC of the same type, you can always reset to the defaults. This can often correct a problem that some nut behind the keyboard might have caused.

For example, certain memory settings are configurable at the BIOS screen, as are certain Plug and Play settings. If one of these is changed to an incorrect value, your system may start malfunctioning in the most interesting of ways. In particular, certain non-Plug and Play network cards, for example, have limited IRQ (Interrupt Request) numbers they can use; if the BIOS reserves these IRQs for Plug and Play devices, your network card will either not work at all or will behave erratically.

8

Be sure to write down your BIOS settings before you reset to the defaults, because you might need some of those settings later. Typically, resetting your BIOS to its defaults won't hurt anything, but you never can tell.

Some PCs have the option to print BIOS settings to a local printer—if yours does, go for it. Printing out your settings beats the heck out of writing everything down.

Name Brand Versus Generic PCs

The components within most PCs are reasonably consistent:

- All PCs have a motherboard.
- All PCs are enclosed in a case, which also houses a power supply to run the entire operation.
- All motherboards house memory, a CPU, a chipset, and expansion slots for daughterboards.
- All motherboards use a BIOS to tie all its components together.

The differentiating factor between PCs tends to relate to the physical layout of components. My experience has shown that cheap clones, as opposed to name-brand machines, can be poorly designed, which can become a factor in situations requiring you to troubleshoot. Suppose, for example, that the PC you're troubleshooting sports a poorly placed motherboard jumper block that comes into contact with an expansion card. (A *jumper* is a movable and removable mechanism that electrically ties two pins together on the motherboard; a *jumper block* is a group of these pins, usually controlling some kind of configuration of the motherboard.) All of a sudden, a jumper set that wasn't connected becomes connected through the metal of the expansion card bracket, and chaos ensues.

Clone PCs are often not compatibility tested with networks the way name-brand machines are, which can add to the fun. The bottom line is this: Spending a few extra dollars for a name brand can help you avoid problems.

Of course, buying a brand name doesn't always mean that things work 100 percent of the time, and you still might run into network issues. However, it's important in a networked environment with large numbers of PCs to be able to have some sort of accountability when things don't work as promised—which you don't often get when buying from the here-today-gone-tomorrow clone market.

Plug and Pray

Of course, each PC also has pluggable components in the form of expansion cards (modems, network cards, video cards, and so on). There are also pluggable microchips that usually have a two rows of 8 to 16 pins that fit into a similarly sized socket. Each of these types of components is susceptible to physical movement or "chip creep" due to the metal expansion and contraction that happens during heating and cooling. What's more, contacts that aren't made of gold are also susceptible to oxidation, much the same way iron rusts.

Any pluggable component (even a cable) is susceptible to these two problems. Fortunately, two simple solutions exist. Many times, pressing down on chips or boards can make an unreliable or intermittent problem go away. If that fails, you can always reseat the component by pulling it out and putting it back in. Chips don't usually need reseating; typically, pushing down on them will do the trick.

If you choose to reseat a chip, be very careful when pulling it out. Otherwise, you can ruin it by bending the small pins. Also, be careful not to allow the pins to fold underneath the chip. You'll want to make certain that each pin aligns correctly with its socket hole.

This problem isn't as bad with modern CPUs because their ZIF (zero insertion force) design does not require you to exert any force on the chip. You'll want to make sure the lever next to the CPU gets raised before you start yanking on the chip—this releases the tension on the CPU.

Therefore, if your PC seems totally dead, you can probably reseat your CPU without worrying too much about hurting anything.

You can cause serious damage to electronic components if you work on them while they're turned on. Make sure any device you're about to work on is powered down.

The interface cards that connect to your motherboard aren't as fragile. You can pull them out and push them back in; this will sometimes fix an intermittent connection or knock dirt away from the pins.

> Electronic components are extremely sensitive to even the smallest amount of static electricity. You must "ground" yourself before touching any components. By touching a metallic ground, you discharge any static electricity that may have built up on your body while walking around. Most computers have a three-prong outlet that includes a ground. If you leave your computer plugged in (but turned *off*) while working on it, you can ground yourself by touching its internal metal chassis.

Dirty Deeds

Cleaning a component or PC can also help clear up odd hardware problems. Dust and dirt can seriously impede the performance and/or reliability of a component. If you're not lucky enough to have a climate-controlled data center, dust will likely be one of your enemies.

> Some people get good results from using a vacuum cleaner to remove excess dust and dirt from the inside of their machines' cases. However, an overly powerful vacuum cleaner can suck up loosely connected jumpers, so be careful. Also a vacuum can create static electricity, which can ruin your whole day.
>
> Although buying canned air is more expensive than using an existing vacuum cleaner, using canned air can give better results because it's portable and you can aim it with pretty good accuracy. However, you don't get rid of the dirt this way; you merely relocate it.

Some people who work with electronics like to use electronic cleaner spray on just about any dusty component. I don't like to use this kind of cleaner on network or computer components—maybe I'm squeamish, but apart from the fact that this stuff tears a hole in the ozone the size of Kentucky, it seems like overkill to me to spray a volatile compound all over your gear. Most times, the aforementioned methods work just fine.

> You can use a soft pencil eraser on the gold contacts of your interface cards to clean oxidation off them.

8

Swap Session

You would be amazed at what can be fixed via a simple hardware swap. As a perfect example of black box troubleshooting, most hardware repair is accomplished by swapping circuit boards and other distinct and separate components. Even pros don't engage in component-level repair anymore; the days of a field technician soldering a new capacitor or microchip onto a broken circuit board have been gone for some time now. To save time, people in the field repair business simply swap out a suspect component for a new, presumably working component.

> It always bothered me that people never repaired these types of things—until I looked at the costs involved. At anywhere from $65–$150 an hour for repairs, it's insanely expensive to repair cheap ($10–$50) electronic gear rather than replace it. Why spend $100 to fix your $40 Ethernet card? You can buy two for the price of fixing it. This probably doesn't make Greenpeace happy, but it sure makes sense economically.

This is even something you can do yourself. Suppose, for example, you've troubleshot a network application's problem to a particular workstation, and you've ruled out the user login and network files.

You've tried to run the Microsoft Exchange client for a user on her workstation, but got a fatal exception error. You logged her into a couple of other workstations, and she worked fine every time.

Therefore, you know that it's a hardware problem, but you don't pass the buck—you're interested in finding out *what* the hardware problem is.

This problem is a good candidate for swapping components. Sometimes it can be obvious what to swap first—for example, if someone's Microsoft Word is repainting the screen badly on one workstation, but not another, you would probably swap the video card first. In this example, it's hard to say what might be causing the fatal exception; fatal exceptions are caused by bad operating system components, local applications, faulty hard drives, bad video cards or drivers, and so on.

While noting whether the problem remains, you swap the following items:

- The hard drive with a "known good" hard drive from a similar PC
- The video card
- RAM DIMMs
- The network card

8

When you swap the memory, the fatal exception error goes away. Furthermore, when you install this memory into a known good PC, that PC starts exhibiting the same lockup problem when you run the network application. It doesn't matter *how* the memory is broken—that is, whether it has bad circuitry on it somewhere or is simply somewhat incompatible with this brand of PC/motherboard. It only matters that it *is* broken.

SIMMs and DIMMs

There are two kinds of common memory nowadays:

- SIMMs (single inline memory modules)
- DIMMs (dual inline memory modules)

A DIMM has contacts on both sides and is therefore more dense pin-wise (168 pins) and data-wise. Although a SIMM has contacts on each side of it, as well, each side leads to the same place on the board. This means that there are actually 60 contacts on a 30-pin SIMM, and 144 contacts on a 72-pin SIMM. SIMMs are also typically slower than DIMMs.

To remove a SIMM from a motherboard, pull outward on the metal clips holding it. This will make it pop from its 90-degree angle from the motherboard to a 45-degree angle. You'll then be able to remove the SIMM. To insert a different SIMM, reverse the process: Put it in at a 45-degree angle, get it nestled in, and push it to a 90-degree angle. You should feel a click when the metal tabs engage the SIMM's holes. (If it's not easy to do, turn it around; you might have it backward.)

A DIMM is even easier: Simultaneously push down (toward the motherboard) the plastic levers on each side of the DIMM. The DIMM will pop up, and you can remove it. To insert a DIMM, simply line it up correctly—it has a different number of pins on each side of its bottom notch—and push it in hard. The plastic levers will engage by themselves.

Depending on which type of memory your machine has, you may have to replace it in pairs or fours—whatever your motherboard documentation refers to as a "bank of memory." The best practice is to swap the entire bank of memory with another known good bank—that way, you don't have to worry about whether you need to keep pairs of memory together, even though some computers consider a *bank* to be one SIMM or DIMM.

Also, you'll frequently find that network application problems are related to component problems; taking half an hour to swap components can save you blank looks from a repair technician. In other words, an intermittent problem on your network might not occur when an outside technician runs diagnostics on what you have determined to be a problem PC. If you can localize the problem, you'll probably save time and aggravation in the long run.

The Cable Is the Network

There are two major types of network cabling widely in use:

- UTP (unshielded twisted pair)
- STP (shielded twisted pair)

Of the two, UTP is the most common. STP, while less sensitive to electromagnetic inter-ference, is also more expensive and harder to work with than UTP. STP is found only in Token-Ring networks. STP is harder to work with because it's very thick and not very flexible. Also, the process for crimping the cable involves stripping the outside, stripping four inside wires, crimping each wire separately, and then assembling a DB-9 housing (much like the housing on a serial mouse). Contrast this to UTP cabling, where you strip the outside wire, place all the wires into a telephone-like jack (RJ-45), and then do one crimp.

 Why is STP only used for Token-Ring? Well, actually, shielded cable was used at one time for Ethernet as well, but it, too, was horrible to work with, and nobody uses it anymore. (See Hour 9, "Ethernet Basics," for more information.)

UTP, which is categorized as CAT-III and CAT-V, is used for 10Mb (megabit) and 100Mb Ethernet, respectively. The categories of wiring are an industry-standard way of referring to the manufacturing specifications for the cable: the thickness (gauge) of the wire, the number of twists per foot, and the electronic resistance of the wire. CAT-III and CAT-V can also be used for Token-Ring. (See Hour 10, "Token-Ring Basics," for more about Token-Ring cables.)

Sometimes, you'll troubleshoot a problem down to a cable. For example, if a user cannot get onto the network, and you run the network card's vendor-supplied diagnostic pro-gram and find that the network card is okay, the next thing to suspect is the cable. It's pretty easy to swap a cable, regardless of whether you're working with shielded or unshielded cable. Therefore, if you swap the cable with a known good cable and this brings the workstation back on the network, you have a broken cable on your hands. In this case, you can simply toss the cable in the trash and buy another.

 Unless you make really, really good cables, you're better off buying your cables ready made. Good cables make a good network.

When troubleshooting UTP wire runs, you'll want to verify that the UTP is nowhere near motors or fluorescent lights, because EMI (electromagnetic interference) can create very odd problems on your network. Because UTP is so easy to work with, lots of people (trying to save a buck) run their own cable. (It's actually easy to slice the housing off of a cable, insert it, and crimp down on it.) However, many times, folks run cable without realizing that EMI even exists. Save yourself trouble by verifying that your UTP runs are nowhere near it.

Using a Multimeter

Because it's expensive to get someone in to pull a cable back into the wall, there may be times when you'll want to verify that a cable is in fact broken (that is, that the problem you're experiencing is due to the cable rather than stemming from some other source, such as EMI or a bad component). In such cases, you can perform a continuity check (that is, you can check whether the current flows through the cable from one end to the other) by using a *multimeter*, a device that measures electrical voltage, amperage, and resistance. You can buy a multimeter for around $10 at Radio Shack or any other electronic supply store.

A multimeter will also tell you whether a cable is open (broken) or closed (okay). After you turn the multimeter's continuity function on, you can see how it works by simply touching the test leads together. You should hear a tone. (This is why testing a cable is sometimes referred to as *toning it out*.) The tone indicates that a continuous electrical path exists between the leads.

If you have both ends of the cable in your hands, you can attach the leads to the same pin of the cable on both sides. (Most Ethernet cables are *straight through*—that is, there's a one-to-one relationship of pins; the same is true of Token-Ring cables.) You should hear a tone when you do this. If you don't, walk one of the leads from pin to pin. If you still don't hear a tone, the cable is broken.

If you hear a tone from more than one pin, this is also a bad thing. This indicates that somewhere along the line, two wires have been shorted together.

Looping Back

If you don't have both ends of the cable in your hands, what can you do? After all, you need to connect both leads to the cable. The answer is to connect two pins together at one end of the cable to create one long wire (see Figure 8.1). Then connect the leads to each end of the long wire (both ends of the long wire will be on the same end of cable, as shown in the figure).

FIGURE 8.1

Continuity check on a cable in the wall.

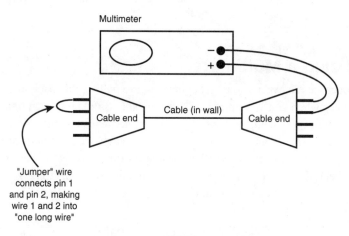

08fig03.eps
Bill K. 10/11/98 ISBN# 72314886

This is called *looping back*, because you create a loop at one end of the cable. Loopback is a powerful diagnostic technique that can also pinpoint which part of your hardware is broken. When you're in a situation where you cannot swap a network card (suppose you only have one high-speed network card in your server), you'll probably want to run the diagnostics program that comes with the network card. This program will likely ask you for a loopback plug—one that makes the network card talk to itself by connecting its send pins directly to its receive pins.

Ethernet uses an RJ-45 plug, where only four pins out of eight really matter. Some Token-Ring cards use a DB-9 plug, where only four pins out of nine really matter. Some can use either a DB-9 or an RJ-45.

If your network card seems okay when you connect the loopback plug to it, you can rule out cable problems by moving the loopback plug farther up the line. For example, you can connect the workstation's cable that normally plugs into the wall in between the network card and the loopback plug. You might need a gender-changer to do this (which looks very much like a telephone coupler for an RJ-45 plug). You plug the loopback into the coupler, the coupler to the network cable, and the network cable into the network card, and then run the diagnostic test again.

If that seems okay, you can connect the loopback plug to the end of the cable that normally plugs into the hub and then test again. This rules out the entire cable run as a source of transmission or reception problems.

Out of Gas on the Information Superhighway

Running out of system resources is enough to make any operating system sing the blues—and stop you from operating properly. Knowing how to rule out (or rule in) a resource problem gets you closer to a solution.

Although it's generally obvious when you run out of disk space, it's a good idea to periodically check how much free space you have left. Remember, Windows allocates "swap" space dynamically; therefore, if you're really low on disk space, swapping may become problematic.

You can think of swap space as an overflow area for your computer's RAM—when you run a lot of programs that don't necessarily fit into the RAM area, an overflow area is used (this is a special file on your hard drive called the *swap area*). When an overflow is about to occur, the operating system copies the least-used RAM to your hard drive. If there's no overflow area...well, you get the point.

Because swapping slows down your machine, you might want to consider simplifying the desktop, which will save a good deal of RAM. Most users can stand to lose a little desktop weight, particularly complex wallpapers, screensavers, and Microsoft's Active Desktop. If you like your desktop the way it is, go for it and buy more physical RAM—you'll be amazed at how fast your machine can go with enough RAM.

Windows

You can check Windows 9x resources by using the System Resource Meter, and you can check hardware limits by using the System Monitor. Both of these programs can be installed from the Control Panel (see Figure 8.2). Here are the steps involved:

1. Choose Start|Settings|Control Panel.

2. Choose Add/Remove Programs from the Control Panel window.

3. Click the Windows Setup tab.

4. Check the Accessories option (if you're using Windows 98, click System Tools).

5. Click Details.

6. Click the System Monitor and System Resource Meter options.

7. Click OK.

8. Insert the Windows CD-ROM when prompted. (Some systems have the Windows setup files installed on the hard drive, so you might not have to perform this step.)

9. Run the tools by using the Accessories|System Tools menu. (No rebooting required.)

FIGURE 8.2

Adding System Resource Meter and System Monitor to Windows 9x.

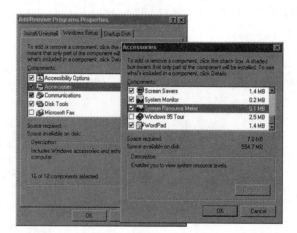

System Resource Meter

You can use System Resource Meter to make sure a given workstation isn't running out of resources. It's particularly effective to run System Resource Meter, try something that you're having trouble with, and watch the bar graph change. You might see it go into the yellow or red, which would indicate resource issues—this might mean you need to add memory, use a less resource-intensive application, or run fewer applications simultaneously.

For example, let's say that you're having trouble printing from WordPerfect—nothing terrible, except that your printed output doesn't look the way it should. You're printing a rather complex newsletter and suspect that you might be running out of gas on your workstation. You run the System Resource Meter and see a new icon appear on your system tray. Because the icon is not green, you suspect that you're running out of Windows system resources. To verify that this is your problem, do the following:

1. Exit all other programs but WordPerfect.

2. Watch the meter go into the green.

3. Try to print again.

System Monitor

System Monitor can monitor just about anything—in Figure 8.3 it's running alongside System Resource Meter to monitor free memory and how hard the CPU is working. System Monitor is configurable for bar graph or line chart operation, and it can display many different resources and statistics. You'll use System Monitor again to check network throughput in Hour 11, "Windows Networking Basics."

Let's say that your computer is running slowly. You wonder whether you're running out of memory, so you do the following:

1. Fire up System Monitor.

2. Select Edit|Add Item and choose Free Memory from the Memory Manager category (to keep track of the free physical memory).

If, in fact, you have approximately 9.1MB of free physical memory, as shown in Figure 8.3, this is *not* why your machine is running slowly. This amount of memory isn't a lot—but it's probably enough that you're not swapping. If the peak value (the dot to the right of the line) is more like .8MB or 1MB, you're probably running out of memory and causing swaps. You could verify this by adding a bar to the graph—Swapfile in Use (again from the Memory Manager category)—and seeing how large this is. If it's more than a couple of megabytes, it's definitely indicating that swapping is occurring. In this case, you should think about getting a memory upgrade or losing a couple of desktop toys.

Windows NT has a very easily accessible CPU and RAM monitor that's built into the Task Manager dialog box (see Figure 8.4). To open this dialog box, press Ctrl+Alt+Delete and choose Task Manager.

FIGURE 8.3

With System Monitor, you can observe how hard your CPU is working and how much memory you have available, among other vital PC statistics.

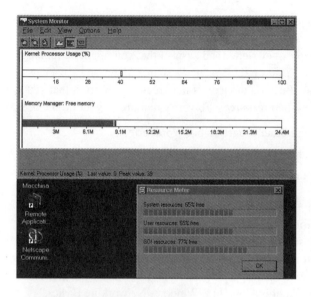

FIGURE 8.4

The NT Task Manager's Performance Monitor is a good way to get a quick and succinct status of an NT workstation.

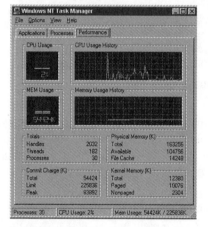

ScanDisk

The hard drive is probably the most fragile resource of your system. It's a good idea once you rule in a workstation to run ScanDisk on the hard drive to rule out hard drive errors. This is particularly true if you're using the first release of Windows 95—it does *not* run ScanDisk after an abnormal shutdown the way later releases of Windows 9*x* do! This can mean that days and weeks of disk problems due to power blips and user resets can go unnoticed. These errors, along with wear and tear on the drive, can accumulate and cause truly strange problems.

It's a really, really good idea to run ScanDisk on a regular basis—say, every week. Most weeks you can probably get away with the Standard check, but every so often (every month or so), you'll probably want to run the Thorough check, just to be safe.

Although you can run ScanDisk from the Programs|Accessories|System Tools menu, you can also run it by right-clicking your hard drive in Explorer and then selecting Properties from the shortcut menu that appears. You'll see a dialog box with a Tools tab, like the one shown in Figure 8.5. On this tab, you can see when you last checked the drive. You can also start a new check from here as well.

FIGURE 8.5

A ScanDisk a day (or week, as the case may be) keeps the trouble away!

Doesn't Do Windows

Not a Windows user? Fret not. UNIX and NetWare were resource checking when Windows was just a glimmer in Bill Gates's eye. Although the methods differ—and aren't as graphical, unless you're using X Window or NetWare 5—the basic idea remains the same: Check your resources when you're having problems and compare these results to what your resources look like when you're *not* having problems.

UNIX

Let's say you're a Linux user, and you want to check your available memory and swap. You can simply type this:

```
INPUT    moria:/$ free
```

OUTPUT

```
                total     used      free      shared    buffers
Mem:            7220      6948      272       2524      3356
Swap:           16416     2396      14020
```

Most UNIX users can check real-time resource use through the VMSTAT command , like so:

INPUT

```
$ vmstat 1
```

OUTPUT

```
procs   memory         page          faults     cpu
___.   _____.  _____  _____  _____  ____
r  b    avm   fre re  pi po fr  sr cy in   sy  cs  us sy id wa
0  0    13376 233 0   0  0  2   6  0  144  807 81  4  5  84 7
0  0    13376 233 0   0  0  0   0  0  129  757 89  2  8  89 2
0  0    13376 233 0   0  0  0   0  0  143  768 85  2  7  91 0
0  0    13376 233 0   0  0  0   0  0  140  567 124 5  1  94 0
0  0    13376 233 0   0  0  0   0  0  147  387 39  1  3  96 0
```

This output looks like Greek, but it's not too terrible once you know the translation. Here are the salient points you should look for:

AVM	Active virtual pages (amount of swap plus physical memory)
PI	Page in activity per second (how much overflow goes to swap)
PO	Page out activity per second (how much overflow drains out)
FRE	The free memory list
US	CPU utilization by users
SY	CPU utilization by system processes
ID	CPU idle time
WA	CPU time spent waiting for disk activity

If you want a report, you should check out the SAR command; using it will show you a report similar to this:

```
smp smp 4.0 2 PENTIUM    09/17/98
00:00:00    %usr    %sys    %wio    %idle
07:00:00    0       0       3       97
08:00:00    0       1       4       95
08:10:00    1       2       9       87
08:20:00    2       4       11      83
08:30:00    3       5       57      35
```

```
08:40:00    2      5      23     69
08:45:00    3      6      61     30
```

Notice how the situation starts to get really ugly at 8:20 (when everyone's had their coffee and is now tearing into things)? At 8:30, the system is only 35 percent idle, as opposed to 97 percent idle at 7:00. As you can see, the SAR command can help you with long-term monitoring. Both SAR and VMSTAT have manual pages that you can access online by typing this:

```
man <sar or vmstat>
```

NetWare

If you're a NetWare user, unfortunately, you have no long-term resource monitoring solution provided by Novell, although third-party solutions are available. You can, however, use the NetWare monitor screen to check out various resources. Simply type

```
load monitor
```

at your console prompt, and you'll see the processor utilization on the front page. Go to the Processor, Memory, or Resource Utilization submenus for more details.

Probably the most important thing to keep track of is the number of cache buffers, which you can track from the Resource menu. If the number of cache buffers falls below 40 percent or so, you'll probably experience problems.

> There's no swap or virtual memory to check in NetWare 3.x or 4.x.

Summary

Knowing how to troubleshoot basic hardware problems can save you loads of time. PCs as a whole are reasonably simple beasts, consisting of pluggable electronic components, some of which can be reseated. Poorly designed cases or motherboards can cause problems, so you can avoid problems by avoiding these.

Keeping clean is just as important as your mother told you; all hardware components react badly to dirt. Use a vacuum or canned air on visibly dusty components; use a pencil eraser on board contacts that seem to have dirt or oxidation on them.

Swapping components is an integral part of hardware troubleshooting. As with the fuel pump on your car, you don't need to know how it works, just that your problem goes away once you swap it.

Unshielded twisted pair cable (UTP) is the most common network cable type. It's fairly sensitive to external electromagnetic interference (EMI). Therefore, you should buy rather than make your own cables.

If your workstation is running out of gas, it can hardly be expected to drive down the street, much less to the onramp of your personal information superhighway. Knowing how to check your system's resources is really useful, no matter which operating system you run.

Workshop

Q&A

Q Shouldn't I leave this hardware stuff to a hardware tech? I might break it!

A If this was stuff that cost thousands to millions per component, I might agree with you. If you're completely out at sea on this issue, grab a hardware troubleshooting book for good details. But really, if you destroy a floppy disk drive or a video card, you're out $50–$100, and believe me, you'll never make that particular mistake again. Just be careful with static electricity, powering off before you work, and putting components back in the same orientation, and you should be just fine.

Quiz

1. How do you get into most PC BIOS setup screens?

   A. Spacebar

   B. Compose-Compose-Execute

   C. F5, Ctrl+Alt+Del, or Enter

   D. F1, F2, or Del

2. True or false? Power should always be on when you're working on a hardware device.

3. You can ground yourself by touching which of the following?

   A. The plastic of the PC case

   B. The screw of your wall outlet

   C. The chassis of your PC (while plugged in)

   D. The dirt in your plants

8

4. True or false? Marginal or incompatible memory can cause network-related problems.

5. To verify a cable's integrity, you can run a _____ test.

A. Compatibility

B. Continuity

C. Craftsmanship

D. Culling

Answers to Quiz Questions

1. D

2. False

3. C. Surprisingly, the screw on your wall outlet is *not* always grounded.

4. True

5. B

HOUR 9

Ethernet Basics

You're probably familiar with the classic battle BetaMax versus VHS, an example of a simple, more accessible technology (VHS) fighting with a complex, more elegant (and more expensive) technology (BetaMax). Some people like one, some people like the other, but no one can argue with the fact that the simpler technology dominates units sold and mind share.

You can chalk up another clash of the titans when you consider Ethernet versus Token-Ring, with Ethernet being by far the simpler and more popular technology. Some folks like Ethernet, some like Token-Ring. If Token-Ring is what *you* have, read on anyway—it's good to know the differences.

Since I've already alluded to the fact that most networks are party lines— that is, lines with more than one network card talking on them—one obvious difference between different network types can be the way in which they share the line. That is, is it a free-for-all or are rules followed?

Not all Ethernet networking is party line based. A fully switched Ethernet network—that is, one with one workstation on each switch port—is actually composed of many two-person networks.

A network with just two participants is called a *point-to-point* network, much like your PC's connection with your Internet service provider.

Although most folks refer to a point-to-point network only when considering outside dial-up and leased lines, the defining quality of a point-to-point network is that there are only *two* stations on the segment. Once you introduce a switch into the picture, you actually only have two stations sharing a common line (the switch port and the PC), so it *is* a point-to-point network—that is, a network with only two end points. The switch then connects folks together much like the phone system does, without others listening or being able to interfere.

Following the Rules: As Long As You Live Under Our Network...

Ethernet is a party line with rules. They're pretty basic and simple rules, but they're rules, nonetheless. The acronym for these rules is *CSMA/CD*, which stands for *Carrier Sense Multiple Access Carrier Detect*. Just as you can listen even as you start talking at the same time another person starts talking, Ethernet network cards listen as they start to transmit to the party line. The carrier in CSMA/CD, like the dueling banshees you hear when your modem connects to another, is a predefined signal that information can ride on top of.

Collisions

If another network card is transmitting while your network card is also transmitting, the signal becomes garbled—the wire can only hold *one* signal at a time. This generates a network error called a *collision*. When a collision occurs, both network cards wait a random infinitesimal amount of time, and try again. Eventually, as shown in Figure 9.1, they do succeed, on a low-population segment. Because each workstation transmits in small, discrete *packets* (discussed in Hour 1, "The Telephone Analogy: Becoming Familiar with Basic Networking Concepts"), it's possible (believe it or not) for a workstation to get a word in edgewise in between another workstation's transmissions. This has always seemed like black magic to me, but it works.

At moment 1 in Figure 9.1, Vizzini and Fezzik simultaneously try to transmit and thus collide. They randomly retry, but it happens to be at the same moment (2). They retry again, and Fezzik gets in at moment 3, followed by Vizzini at moment 4. Poor Vizzini collides with Inigo at moment 4. Vizzini retries at moment 5, nobody does anything at moment 6, and Inigo finally gets the final word in moment 7.

FIGURE 9.1

Collisions!

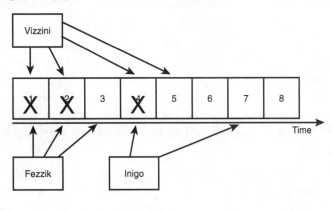

On a small network, collision detection works pretty well. But just as informal meeting rules start to break down when you get more than 10 or 15 people in a conference room, Ethernet, too, turns into a babble fairly quickly when a particular segment is scaled to more than a couple dozen workstations.

Ethernet is really, really easy to *cascade*; that is, you can extend the party line from a hub by simply adding a single cable and an additional hub. Instant upgrade, huh? Buy a hub and hook it up!

Although it's easy to add a hub or two via cascade, you don't want to go crazy on this. Be careful about how large your Ethernet gets—if you add too many hubs, you're going to run into trouble.

Many Ethernet installations in smaller shops have just sort of grown larger rather than having been designed that way from the ground up. This can result in lots of workstations sharing the same segment, which translates into lots of collisions. Take a look at your segment maps and count how many workstations are on each; for optimal performance and reliability, you'll want to subdivide your segments into smaller divisions using a switch.

Framed and Fragmented

It's worth briefly looking at the packet structure of Ethernet. Remember from Hour 1 that a packet is the smallest unit of transmission on a network. There are times when differences in packet sizes can cause problems between two network segments, so you should know the different maximum packet sizes of your networking topologies.

Ethernet's maximum packet, or *frame size*, is 1,514 bytes. This includes six bytes for the MAC address of the source NIC, six bytes for the MAC address of the destination, a two-byte value indicating what kind of packet it is, and a "payload" portion that holds your data (this can be a maximum of 1,500 bytes). Some people (even those who design network analyzers) refer to a maximum value of 1,518 bytes. This number just includes a four-byte error-detection value at the end of each packet. Another 20 bytes of overhead can be found at the beginning of the packet (but this is only of interest to Ethernet switch designers).

Any Ethernet packet less than 60 bytes is considered a *runt*, also called a *short* or *fragment*, and will show up as an error on a software analyzer. A runt can be caused by collisions, so if you see a lot of these, you might want to consider dividing up your users among switches.

Go, Speed Racer, Go

Classic Ethernet runs at 10Mbps (megabits per second). That is, 10,000,000bps (bits per second) can be transmitted on the wire. Divide this by 8 bits per byte, and you get 1,250,000Bps.

> *Bits per second* is indicated with a lowercase *b*, whereas *bytes per second* is indicated with an uppercase *B*. Therefore, 10 megabits per second would be 10Mbps, and 10 megabytes per second would be 10MBps.

That's a lot. It means that about 1MB can be transmitted on the wire every second. Does this really happen? Not unless the Ethernet link is a point-to-point connection without other stations trying to share it. Even though 97 percent of the data is actual "payload," every time you get a collision, it decreases the efficiency of your network and the whole blessed packet has to be retransmitted.

Are collisions a fact of life? You bet. Each time you add more than two Ethernet stations to a segment, you add to the potential for collisions. No big deal; even if you drop 30 percent of your packets due to collisions, you still see about .8MB per second, which is pretty fast.

However, in a highly populated—and thus highly trafficked—Ethernet segment, the collision rate might approach 80 percent. (Makes you wonder why you don't just use a floppy disk.) On a segment such as this, problems might manifest themselves in various ways. Because some applications are timing sensitive, for example, if they don't get their data quickly enough, you might see all kinds of errors. Therefore, it pays to take a gander at your physical documentation and count the hub ports.

> The collision problem leads some Token-Ring proponents to smugly assert that this is why *they* use Token-Ring instead, because it scales much better and can truly provide the bandwidth it advertises. Don't worry. Ethernet is fine. I'll talk about the virtues and the problems of Broken-Ring—I mean *Token-Ring*—in the next hour. Meanwhile, the truth is that all network topologies have their problems—the key is to recognize them and to deal with them in a proactive way that causes you to lose the least amount of hair. (I'll bash Ethernet a little bit during Hour 10, "Token-Ring Basics." It'll be fun, so stay tuned.)

100 Megabit Ethernet

Keeping track of how many workstations are connected to a segment becomes even more important with 100Mb (megabit) Ethernet. (We're not even going to get into 1,000Mb Ethernet, or *gig Ethernet*, because it currently requires fiber-optic connections to achieve these speeds as well as professional installation and maintenance.)

Although 100Mb Ethernet works exactly like Ethernet—even down to the frame size and collisions—it runs 10 times faster. So, instead of about 1Mbps, we're talking about 10Mbps. Presumably, the reason folks install 100Mb Ethernet is to actually get a high-speed network. A large collision domain (fancy talk for "lots of people on a shared segment") can bring your throughput down substantially, so it makes sense to use switching gear to cut down the "party line babble" and run as close to 100Mb as you can.

> For your servers, a *full-duplex* fast Ethernet connection might be the antidote to a slow connection. A full duplex connection to a switch means that you're using both the transmit and the receive wires simultaneously; therefore, you *double* the speed. This means your 100Mb Ethernet pipeline becomes a 200Mb Ethernet pipeline. Wow!

9

Half duplex, the typical Ethernet or Token-Ring connection, is like when you use a radio. One person talks, then the other person talks back.

Full duplex is like using a telephone—both stations can talk at once. Because this is *not* a party line, and because computers (unlike you and I) can do lots of things at once, this does not cause collisions.

Just make sure your Ethernet driver as well as the switch you're going to connect to both support full-duplex operation; the manuals should tell you how to enable this. Most cards and switches will be capable of performing at full duplex if you've purchased them recently, but it couldn't hurt to check.

Cabling Carnival

For a computer-related technology, Ethernet is pretty long in the tooth. This means that there are a bunch of ways of configuring its cabling that are *possible* that aren't necessarily *desirable* as you traverse the next millennium. The good news is that none of the 100Mb stuff is configurable in any of these old, horrible ways, but if you're running 10Mb Ethernet, you might be stuck with older cabling configurations.

It will save you time and money in the long run to replace any of the following network types. They are obsolete and can be replaced fairly cheaply. Here's what needs to get thrown in the trash:

Name	Connector Type	Problems
Thinnet	BNC (Coaxial) 10Base-2	Bus cabling means that one disconnected workstation or cable break takes down the entire segment. It's trouble prone in general and hard to work with versus modern 10Base-T.
Thicknet	BNC (Coaxial) 10Base-5	Bus cabling. It's expensive, trouble prone, and hard to find parts for.
AUI	DB-15	Expensive and hard to find parts for.

All of these bad old network types came before the advent of the UTP technologies (10Base-T, and later, 100Base-T).

The *Base* in Base-T refers to the fact that Ethernet is a baseband—rather than broadband—technology. This is just a geeky term that refers to its method of signal encoding. The *T* simply stands for twisted pair.

People tend to refer to the modern way of connecting Ethernet as either *UTP* or *10Base-T*. The important part, nowadays, is whether you're running CAT-V (100Mb) or CAT-III (10Mb). Again, the CAT designation is simply an industry-standard way of referring to the manufacturing specifications of the cable. CAT-V can hold a lot more signal than CAT-III; therefore, you can run 10Mb Ethernet on CAT-V wiring, but you cannot run 100Mb Ethernet on CAT-III. If you're trying to run 100Mb Ethernet on CAT-III wiring, you're going to run into problems.

 Don't try running 100Mb Ethernet on wiring that's not certified as CAT-V. The world may not come to an end, but it still will be bad.

All sorts of intermittent network errors can occur, which can domino into your applications. What's more, because you're getting a signal and are talking to the network, you might not realize that the problem is due to wiring until you've run around looking at everything else.

Other than that, 100Mb Ethernet is pretty much the same as 10Mb Ethernet, but faster. For example, the maximum cable run for either one is 100 meters (330 feet). Both use RJ-45 connectors, and both require a hub or a switch.

How do you know whether your cable is CAT-V? Well, if it has been installed any time from 1997 on, you can guess that it's probably CAT-V. The only way you *know* is to ask your installer, or to have him or her test it with a cable scanner. I'll talk briefly about cable scanners in Hour 21, "Tell Me About Your Network: Network Analyzers & Bits & Bytes."

A cable plant fails CAT-V certification in at least five ways, so you should ask the installer to "certify" it as part of the installation process. This means that he or she will install using plugs, jacks, cabling, and techniques that are CAT-V compliant and will actually put a meter on the end-to-end product to ensure that theory has become practice.

Also, some folks prefer to use certified cable installers—that is, professional network cable installers with a networking industry affiliation—rather than an electrician, who might be more comfortable with A/C power cabling than network cables.

All UTP Ethernet uses four wires: pins 1, 2, 3, and 6. Do you have to know this to troubleshoot? Only if you want to "tone out" the cable, as illustrated in Hour 8, "Hard Basics: Guide to Being a Hardware Geek." In other words, if pins 4, 5, 7, and 8 have problems, it's not a big deal.

Only NIC-to-hub cables should be straight through—that is, pin to pin. Cables that are used to connect hubs together should be crossover. If you have a multimeter, you might want to experiment to find out which pin on one side of the cable goes to which pin on the other side. Remember, you can do this by putting the meter in continuity mode, placing one test lead on pin 1 on one end of the cable, and then walking your other test lead down each pin of the other end of the cable.

UTP Ethernet cables have four pairs of twisted wires. Pins 1 and 2 need to be from the same pair, and pins 3 and 6 need to be from the same pair (see Figure 9.2). Although the intuitive way to make a cable might be to put pins 1 and 2 together, then 3 and 4, 5 and 6, and 7 and 8, this is *not* correct. 10Mb Ethernet will run on this, but you might encounter strange problems under 100Mb. If you see a cable that looks like it was crimped the wrong way, you might want to exchange the cable with a known good one.

Does it sound like the installation really, really matters with Ethernet? Go to the head of the class! Even jumper cables add to the overall cable plant of a segment (*cable plant* is the term often used to refer to collective cabling). A segment, because it's a party line, is as strong as the weakest link—one bad apple *can* spoil a whole bunch. Again, you'll probably want to use premade cables rather than manufacturing your own.

FIGURE 9.2

Correct Ethernet wire and pin configuration.

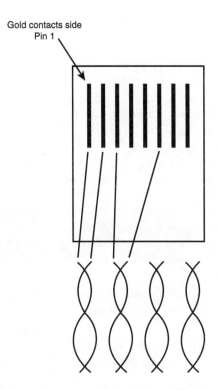

Gold contacts side
Pin 1

9

Down, Down, Down

Chances are that if your Ethernet segments were behaving last week, and the week before, and the week before that, you don't have installation problems, right? After all, nothing has changed. Let's take a look at the way an Ethernet segment might change, and the problems that might ensue.

The "growabililty" of Ethernet has been, in the past, its downfall. Although most folks expanding an Ethernet network nowadays will probably use a switch to add a hub or a couple of hubs, in the past, they would just *cascade* hubs. Adding hubs or extending an Ethernet network can put it outside design specifications. One of those design specifications is called the "3-4-5 rule."

> **THE 3-4-5 RULE**
>
> The Ethernet 3-4-5 rule states the following:
>
> - You may have three populated subsegments (applies to coaxial only, so forget this one).
> - You may have four repeaters or concentrators.
> - You may have five subsegments in a series—that is, one connecting to the next, as with Christmas tree lights.
>
> Because the 3 rule applies only to coaxial networks, let's concentrate on 4 and 5. A *repeater* is a device that regenerates whatever signal is on the wire in order to overcome a wire length limitation (100 meters with UTP). In a nutshell, when you echo a signal down the line, it takes time; too many echoes results in a critical loss of timing.
>
> The 5 rule means that you shouldn't cascade more than five hubs in a row. (A stackable hub with a proprietary link between hubs counts as only one hub.)

Even when you're in spec and nothing has been changed, things still break. For example, network cards can go bad and stop listening while they're transmitting, causing the party line to be tied up. Smart hubs have antijabber circuitry that usually catches this, but even hubs go bad. When smart hubs can't make up for a bad network card, or when they, themselves, are broken, it's time to play divide-and-conquer.

> If you suspect a physical network problem (for example, a particular segment is really slow), you'll need to keep the network up while you're troubleshooting. (People take it badly when you stop them from working just so you can troubleshoot a problem that they do not consider to be a showstopper.) In this case, you should consider putting a two-port switch in place, which will allow you to give a particular hub or group of hubs a separate party line from the rest (see Figure 9.3).
>
> You can get a miniswitch from DataComm Warehouse (www. datacommwarehouse.com), CableExpress (networksnow.com), or any of the mail-order network houses. (As of this writing, NetGear seems to be a reasonably available manufacturer of two-port switches.)
>
> Installation is a snap. Disconnect the cascade cable from the second hub, leaving it plugged into the first hub. Plug that cable into port 1 of the switch. Add an additional cable to the switch in port 2. Connect port 2 of the switch to the second hub. Voila! You're done.

FIGURE 9.3

A small bridge divides the fault domain or collision domain in half, yet users can still operate fairly transparently.

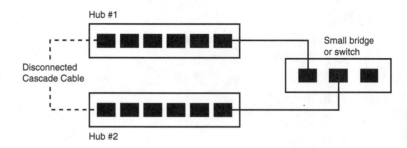

Summary

Ethernet is a really simple physical networking technology. However, like all networks, it has hard-and-fast rules for its design and implementation. Although Ethernet has used many different types of physical cabling in the past, the simplest and most reliable cabling today is UTP.

Ethernet is simple to add to, and that simplicity makes it a target for ad hoc additions that can bring the network outside design specifications. This isn't a big deal with switched networks, because each switch port gives each Ethernet segment (or workstation) its own party line rather than following the rules that apply to larger, cascaded Ethernet networks.

Workshop

Q&A

Q Should I use a switch port for every PC?

A If you're very wealthy, go ahead. Most folks, however, like to put a small hub on each switch port and save dedicated switch ports for servers.

Q Are there errors other than collisions?

A Collisions cause other errors, such as CRC errors and runts. But on the whole, all errors are collision related.

Q Don't people run their own CAT-V cabling?

A Nope. Once something is in the wall, it's really a pain to replace it, so it makes sense to do it only once.

Q The 3-4-5 rule confuses me. Do I really have to learn it?

A Not if you're putting a small hub on each switch port with no additional repeaters.

Quiz

1. During normal error-free transmission, there may only be _____ signal(s) on any given Ethernet segment.

   A. 5

   B. 10

   C. 2

   D. 1

2. What is a collision?

   A. When two network cards try to transmit simultaneously

   B. When two network cards develop bad microchips

   C. When a user accesses the wrong database

   D. When a user transmits incorrect data

3. True or false? Errors are a normal part of Ethernet operation.

4. True or false? Thinnet, Thicknet, and AUI are the most desirable types of Ethernet you can buy.

Answers to Quiz Questions

1. D

2. A

3. True

4. False

HOUR 10

Token-Ring Basics

"Neither bird, nor plane, nor even frog. It's just little
old me...Underdog."

The underdog of LAN topologies, Token-Ring, is jeered at by those who
don't use it and venerated by those who do. What's the straight skinny? For
many folks, Token-Ring has given faithful, speedy, and reliable service for
many years, but predicting its future is hard. Although Token-Ring vendors
have joined the 100Mb ranks by recently announcing HSTR (High-Speed
Token-Ring) gear, as well as gig (1000Mb) Token-Ring products in the near
future, Token-Ring remains more expensive than Ethernet of similar speed,
and it's getting hard to find technicians who are experienced in deploying
and troubleshooting it.

Some folks think that this lack of experienced technicians will be the nail in
the coffin for Token-Ring. The argument is that Token-Ring will go the way
of the superior yet more expensive BetaMax-type technology: Token-Ring
shops will continue to use it for another three to seven years, but new gear,
technicians, and parts will become hard to come by, and therefore will be
expensive. Eventually, cost justification will sway even the most die-hard
Token-Ring devotees to start using other topologies.

One observation is that savvy IT managers are keeping Token-Ring in the mix for now and will distribute it as it breaks—in other words, if it ain't broke, don't fix it! Ripping out an entire networking infrastructure all at once can be expensive and dangerous to one's career if no cost justification exists for it. Nonetheless, IT managers who believe they see the writing on the wall are planning to get rid of Token-Ring as things break or as new networking projects develop.

On the other hand, the availability of High-Speed Token-Ring gear makes it safe and easy to keep doing what they're doing, only faster. Only time will tell if the availability of High-Speed Token-Ring will trigger its rebirth. As I write this, though, it's looking pretty grim for the Token-Ring home team.

Regardless of Token-Ring's future, the fact remains that you're reading this chapter, so either you're interested in what all the hoopla is about regarding Token-Ring versus Ethernet or you've inherited a Token-Ring network. Token-Ring is well-designed stuff, so be of good cheer. Welcome!

Follow the Rules: Share and Enjoy!

Token-Ring, regardless of its dubious market presence, makes one heck of a great shared network. Unlike Ethernet's free-for-all rules, where everybody arbitrarily and randomly talks and then retries if they get an error, Token-Ring's party line has strict rules. Whereas Ethernet is a "be home by 11:00" parent, Token-Ring is the kind of parent who wants to know who you're going with, where you're going, who's driving, and so on. Token-Ring has a lot more rules and therefore has a lot more recovery and manageability.

Just for a moment, think of everybody in a Token-Ring network as being in one big conference room. Suppose there are a lot of people (say, more than 50). How does *anybody* get a word in edgewise? Think about what you might do in such a situation. You'd probably elect a chair, and this chair might give everyone a turn to speak. This is pretty much what Token-Ring is all about. In large groups, Token-Ring is much more efficient than Creepernet, uh, I mean *Ether*net. It's sort of like using parliamentary procedure rather than family discussions: It's a wasted effort for small groups, but a lifesaver for large groups.

First, how does Token-Ring work physically? Each workstation that enters the *ring* can be thought of as filling a seat at the conference table. This is actually how Token-Ring is wired (that is, in a ring rather than in the "star" topology that Ethernet uses). Even though the wiring looks star-like, the *path* of the wiring actually forms a loop from station to hub to station, as in Figure 10.1. You might be wondering why doesn't this act the way Christmas lights do? The answer is because all cables come to a hub; if a break occurs, the hub (called a *MAU* or *multiple access unit*) can route signals around the break (unless something else is wrong).

FIGURE 10.1

Even though a hub is present, Token-Ring's wiring actually forms a ring, which makes it look like a star.

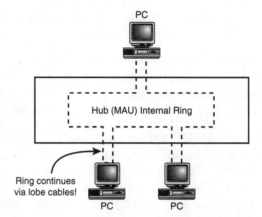

10

Think of each station that connects to the MAU as sitting down at the conference table (the ring). The first station on the network is called the *active monitor* (the elected chair), and it acts as a point of contact for others to report errors, maintains the ring's timing, detects certain kinds of ring errors on its own, and initiates a "do over" if the ring gets certain serious errors. Each station on the network that subsequently joins the ring becomes a *standby monitor* and can take over if the active monitor leaves the ring.

The active monitor is also responsible for issuing a special packet called the *token*. Each packet on the wire is handed from Token-Ring card to Token-Ring card, all the way around the ring. Everyone takes turns speaking, one after the other. When a station has the token, it may transmit its own information.

Error Terror: When a NAUN Is *Not* a Person, Place, or Thing

Token-Ring's pecking order is wonderful when it works. It's also pretty good when it doesn't, because Token-Ring provides a lot of rules for error handling. In the way that a parliamentarian can deal with certain rule infractions without adjourning the meeting, the active monitor of the ring also can deal with certain situations. However, just like any democratic society, each citizen is also left to do his or her part.

For a packet to make it all the way around the ring, each station must transmit the packet to its neighboring station; in the process, each station gleans the location of its neighbors. That is, each station knows the address of its nearest address upstream neighbor (its *NAUN*, pronounced *noun*). Is this important? You bet!

First of all, what's *upstream*? Well, because a Token-Ring passes packets around the ring in sequence, *upstream* refers to the direction in which packets are *not* flowing.

Let's talk briefly about what constitutes *downstream*. Toss out theory, for the moment, and consider this from a purely pragmatic standpoint. You plug a bunch of workstations into a Token-Ring hub, plug in a server, and you're ready to rock and roll, right? *Downstream*, in this case, is the direction from first port to the last port.

Plugging in another hub means that you have some means in which to extend the ring. Each Token-Ring hub (MAU) has a *ring in* and a *ring out*, which are the means for extending the ring. It's simple: Packets flow downstream through the out and then flow into the next hub through the in, which, by definition, is upstream of its ports. This may sound crazy, but when you look at Figure 10.2, it'll make more sense.

FIGURE 10.2

Downstream is always toward the out and upstream is always toward the in of a Token-Ring MAU. The direction of upstream and downstream changes as you move on the ring.

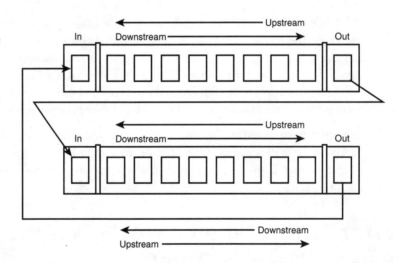

Back to NAUNs. The reason why it's so cool that a station knows its NAUN is because when errors are detected by a particular station, it reports them two seconds later to the active monitor—the Chairman of the Ring. If you're running a network analyzer, you'll see the error report, plus the address of the NAUN. If you see the NAUN reported in the error log, you have a good idea where the error originated.

Think about this for a moment. In a game of telephone, if the guy to my left is responsible for giving me the correct message, and I'm responsible for giving the guy to my right the correct message, when I find out that the message I have is not the correct one, I naturally suspect the guy to my left. If these messages are packets and I'm a Token-Ring card, when I see an error, I naturally suspect the Token-Ring card upstream of me.

Error Types

The types of errors discussed thus far are called *isolating soft errors*. They're *isolating* because they're typically caused by a lone station rather than a generic ring problem, plus they're reasonably easy to track. They're *soft* because getting a few of them is not terribly bad for the ring. Unless you're going to be a Token-Ring geek, it's not worth dealing with the specifics of these errors; however, it's good to know which Token-Ring errors are isolating errors. If you look at an analyzer and it tells you that the NAUN for an error is a certain MAC address, all you need to do is find that MAC address and turn the machine off. No divide-and-conquer techniques required.

Here are the isolating errors:

- Abort delimiter
- A/C error
- Burst error
- Internal error
- Line error

All these errors pretty much mean the machine is ill and needs help. Because you're not interested in being a Token-Ring physician, the best thing to do is to remove the NAUN from the network and see if the problems clear up. After all, you probably haven't put a network analyzer on a segment unless you're experiencing problems—in other words, you probably have to take action after sizing up the situation. Be aware, however, that if you put an analyzer on what is ostensibly a healthy Token-Ring, you'll see a limited number of errors, so don't panic.

Any station that comes into the conversation or leaves the conversation breaks the ring momentarily. This causes a *burst error*. A neighboring station notices this and reports it to the active monitor. *This is as normal to Token-Ring as collisions are to Ethernet.* Having a couple burst errors on a healthy Token-Ring is not a big deal; it's just an indication that someone has turned his or her PC on or off. If you have hundreds of these in a short period, then you have a problem. Don't worry about a couple, though.

Receiver congestion errors are also okay in small amounts—they simply indicate that the workstation is having a hard time keeping up. You'll want to investigate large numbers of these, because they can slow down your entire network. In general, though, a few of these just indicate that some workstation is having trouble keeping pace with the '90s.

Token Analyzers

Finding a NAUN is really easy if you have the right Token-Ring analyzer program. I'll go into this in further detail in Hour 20, "Tell Me About Your Network: Network Analyzers & Bits & Bytes," 135 but for the moment, consider that the right analyzer can give you a NAUN list showing all the MAC addresses on the ring, in the correct order! This is much better than Ethernet because you immediately know which port a given MAC address lives on. As a matter of fact, certain Token-Ring vendors will *give* you a program that collects this information for you—for free. For simplicity's sake, let's say you have two hubs on a given Token-Ring segment (see Figure 10.3).

FIGURE 10.3

A NAUN list depends on which stations are in the ring at the moment.

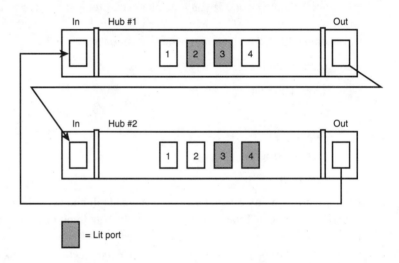

Your PC with the NAUN-listing program (which, fortunately, deals with the workstation name as well as the MAC address) is plugged into hub 2, port number 3. Your NAUN list is shown in Table 10.1.

TABLE 10.1 NAUN LIST

Order	Name	MAC
1	THIS_WORKSTATION	00-00-c9-88-54-22
2	MY-BOSS	00-00-c9-88-54-55

Order	Name	MAC
3	HER-BOSS	00-00-c9-88-54-d5
4	OUR-SERVER	00-00-c9-88-54-f9

Whoa! You have eight possible ports on your two four-port hubs, but only four stations are listed. A quick glance at the hubs reveals that, in fact, only four lights are lit out of a possible eight. First of all, NAUN lists reveal only who is on the network *while* they are on the network. A NAUN lister can't list something that isn't there. Still, you work quickly, hoping that you'll do your figuring before anybody kicks in or out of the ring. By looking at the hubs and correlating the lights that are on to the NAUN list, you deduce that because your workstation with the NAUN lister is #1 on the list and #3 on the hub, then MY-BOSS is #4 on hub #2, HER-BOSS is #2 on hub #1, and OUR-SERVER is #3 on hub #1.

Most of the time, I just do this to quickly figure out the identity of the machine I need to take out of the network. You really, *really* don't want to rely on this as a method for after-the-fact documentation, mostly because people are always clicking in and out of the network at exactly the wrong time. This will start to drive you crazy before too long.

> You'll get large numbers of "frame copied" errors on a switched Token-Ring network if you're using an analyzer that wasn't designed with switching in mind. The analyzer is telling you that somebody claims they got the frame, but it wasn't the intended recipient.
>
> In fact, because the switch has joined two separate Token-Rings, the receiving station could not have received it without the help of the switch. The switch *had* to grab it. The switch grabs the frame on the source network and throws it onto a different destination network, where the destination workstation can get it. The destination network is a separate, physical Token-Ring segment and, as such, has a separate active monitor and so on; it's a separate conference table in a separate room. Therefore, it's okay for the switch to grab the frame meant for the destination—otherwise, it would never get to the destination. In other words, the analyzer is fretting about nothing. Here's the bottom line: Don't worry about "frame copied" errors in this scenario.

Let's Get Physical

Like Ethernet, Token-Ring has overly complex rules about how long the wires can be at what speed using what type of wire, and so on. The most common cable used to be IBM Type 1. Type 1 shielded twisted pair (STP) cable is huge and very resistant to EMI (electromagnetic interference), but hard to work with.

Token-Ring comes in two speeds: 4Mb and 16Mb. If you're using 4Mb, it's time to change. I can't even think of a place where I could get a Token-Ring card that doesn't also do 16Mb, and I buy used equipment shamelessly! As an incentive for you to treat yourself to 16Mb (and to keep the discussion simple) I'm only going to talk about 16Mb rules.

Token-Ring does not have any hard-and-fast cable length limit on any given run. Instead, there's a *total ring length* limitation. If you think about it, this makes sense, because all the cables work together to make one ring, right?

When using STP, the maximum distance around a ring can be 180 meters, or 590 feet. When using CAT-V UTP, your ring distance can be 100 meters, or 330 feet. If you're using CAT-III UTP, you might as well set it all up in your garage—the longest roundtrip can only be 70 meters, or 230 feet. I'm throwing in these numbers for reference only; you're not going to need them unless you start designing Token-Rings.

To actually calculate whether your ring is within cable budget, you must use a complicated formula (which gives me a headache when I look at it) that involves the longest individual cable run, the internal wire distance of each MAU on the network, the inter-MAU cable runs, and the price of tea in China, *ad nauseam*. People who design Token-Ring networks must invoke this mystical little formula. Fortunately for you, though, this formula has little or nothing to do with troubleshooting Token-Ring.

Again, as is the case with Ethernet, if your network was working last week as well as the week before, there's dust all over the cables, and nobody has played with the cable plant, the last thing you would suspect is that the cables have gotten longer all by themselves. If, on the other hand, someone has added a couple of MAUs or a rather long cable to your Token-Ring and it's starting to act flaky, you should disconnect this stuff and see what happens. You don't need to engage in higher mathematics or whip out a tape measure to do this. This is mere change management, and it's a whole lot easier than measuring cables that are already in the wall and in use on a production network.

Packet Jacket

A Token-Ring can have several different packet sizes. They can be anything from 1KB to

If you have a wide-area, routed network or a mixed Token-Ring and Ethernet environment, beware of large packet sizes. Some (actually, more than you would think) TCP/IP applications don't handle fragmentation properly. *Fragmentation* is what happens when you need to put 10 pounds of stuff in 5-pound bags—the packets get split into smaller, more manageable chunks. When a mixed environment is in use, packets will almost definitely get chopped up in order to fit through the smaller interfaces on your router. You can handle this by instructing your applications to use smaller packet sizes, or you can simply dial down the packet size on your Token-Ring. Alternatively, you can ask your vendor to fix things; it depends on how optimistic you feel that day.

10

16KB, with the most popular packet size I've seen being 4KB. The packet size of a given Token-Ring is equal to the smallest packet size specified on the network—that is, you can easily decrease the packet size on a Token-Ring simply by adding a network card that's configured to use a smaller packet size.

Down Town

Most Token-Rings chug away pretty well. The most problematic Token-Rings are usually the largest ones, where error recovery doesn't work as well. (Although you can theoretically put more than 100 workstations on a single Token-Ring, it's suicidal to go above 60, and in this day of cheap switching, you might as well put one or two dozen per segment.) Nonetheless, Token-Rings are known to go down.

A *downed* ring usually results from one of these two causes:

- Beacons
- Excessive errors

A *beacon*, most often, is when a signal loss occurs on the wire. That is, a workstation has not exited the ring gracefully, and the hub thinks the station is still in use. Because the workstation doesn't respond anymore (caused by a broken NIC), its downstream neighbor detects a signal loss and tells everyone. (It can still talk downstream, even though its upstream data has been cut off.)

The active monitor initiates a ring purge (or *do over*). If this doesn't work, the downstream neighbor thinks to itself, "What if it's me?" and hurries to check this out. It removes itself from the ring, performs self-diagnostics, and reinserts itself. This cycle keeps happening until the signal loss is corrected. It's a pretty bad scene until you come along.

Fortunately, you have your trusty Token-Ring monitor program, and the defective workstation has been reported to the active monitor as the reporting station's NAUN. You walk the NAUN list, find the bad workstation, remove it from the hub, and everything is okay. You can then figure out why the signal loss was occurring at your leisure (it's usually a bad card or cable). Most times, this is how a beacon troubleshooting session goes.

Excessive errors are troubleshot in pretty much the same way. You can look at the NAUN of the offending machine and remove it from the network. Even though I've seen all sorts of errors caused by bad drivers, your trouble will most often be with a single card, cable, or hub. If you don't have a Token-Ring monitor (and again, some vendors provide this for free-it's part of what Token-Ring offers over Ethernet) or network analyzer (or if your analyzer provides no clues), the divide-and-conquer method will usually win over any problem.

Summary

If you like Macs and BetaMax, you'll love Token-Ring. Technically superior to Ethernet, Token-Ring nonetheless plays second fiddle to Ethernet on the corporate desktop. It's able to run over STP and UTP, and with a current ring speed of 16Mb, Token-Ring's token-passing scheme for wire-sharing means that more people can share the wire efficiently.

Token-Ring's error-recovery facilities are pretty good, and when these don't work, the NAUN information that the Token-Ring overhead provides can make it easier for a troubleshooter to find a problem workstation.

Workshop

Q&A

Q Seriously, which do you like better? Token-Ring or Ethernet?

A Sorry, I plead the fifth. They both work. Different people like using them for different things.

Q Can I plug a workstation into the ring-in or ring-out port if I don't have to expand a ring?

A No. Sorry, they weren't designed for that.

Q Why do I hear an audible click on my older Token-Ring MAUs?

A A physical solenoid is being triggered to extend the ring. Cool, huh?

Quiz

1. True or false? Errors are a normal part of Token-Ring operation.

2. What is a NAUN?

   A. A person, place, or thing

   B. Near and unusual network

   C. Nearest address upstream neighbor

   D. Nearest application under negotiation

3. *Upstream* refers to which direction?

   A. Toward the "out" of a hub

   B. Toward the "in" of a hub

   C. Toward port 3 of a hub

   D. Toward the out and in of a hub

4. A Token-Ring packet can be as small as ___ KB and as large as ___ KB.

   A. 1, 5

   B. 4, 10

   C. 1, 16

   D. 4, 16

Answers to Quiz Questions

1. True

2. C

3. B

4. C

HOUR **11**

Windows Networking Basics

Microsoft Windows is the Volkswagen Bug of desktop operating systems
and peer-to-peer networks. Truly the "people's network" (although its valves
and carburetor are a heck of a lot smaller than the Bug's), it's pretty simple
to own and drive. For all the slings and arrows that Microsoft suffers at the
hands of the Justice Department and the press, it has taken many of the great
networking concepts (and even some commands) from UNIX, wrapped
them up in a neat and easy-to-use graphical user interface, and gone to town.

In this hour, I discuss Windows 95, Windows 98, and Windows NT 4.0. When
I refer to *Windows*, I mean 9*x* (that is, Windows 95 and Windows 98) and
NT; I'll specify 9*x* or NT when specifics are different.

I'll start off with the theory behind Windows-based networking and talk about the differences between domain and workgroup computing. Because Windows TCP/IP networking has its own nuances, I'll discuss that briefly and then move on to the topics of checking your workstation configurations and using built-in Windows network troubleshooting tools to conquer a host of problems.

DISSED AND DISMISSED

With 31-derful flavors of Windows, why focus on 9x and NT 4.0? Well, NT 5.0 is still pretty late in coming, but even when it arrives, it will be fundamentally similar to NT 4.0. NT 3.51, while functional, doesn't run enough modern applications to make it a real player, and the reliability and speed improvements of NT 4.0 over 3.51 make it a compelling upgrade. If you're still running DOS and Windows 3.x, please don't! Treat yourself by running out to your local electronics house for an upgrade, reformatting your hard drive (back it up first, though), and starting over.

Why so vehement about DOS and Win 3.x? They're a nightmare! Various terminate-and-stay resident DOS drivers have to be manually loaded into the CONFIG.SYS and the AUTOEXEC.BAT; incompatibilities are the order of the day, and memory management is a mess. Everything (networking, in particular) is so much simpler and well integrated with 9x and NT. It's just an exercise in masochism to run the older stuff.

Going Native

Although Windows allows you to connect with everything but the kitchen sink (and I hear that Microsoft is working on this), we'll focus here on only the networking tools Microsoft has invented and provides. If you've got a good handle on the theory behind Windows networking, you'll be better able to troubleshoot it when it's not working. Not surprisingly, there are actually several components to a successful Windows network (I'll define these further as we go along):

- Naming services (WINS, NetBIOS, DNS)
- Authentication services (NT Domain or Workgroup Sharing)
- File and print services (SMB)
- Protocol-specific services (WINS, DHCP)

 Microsoft's whole ball of network wax is sometimes referred to as *Microsoft file and print*.

As you might expect, running a peer-to-peer Windows 95 network is a lot simpler than setting up a Windows NT network over a wide area connection; however, the building blocks are very similar. If you use Microsoft file and print networking, your computer is either part of a workgroup or an NT domain.

NetBEUI

First, we'll look at NetBEUI, which I briefly mentioned in Hour 1, "The Telephone Analogy: Becoming Familiar with Basic Networking Concepts." NetBEUI is a non-routable protocol that runs NetBIOS on top of it; think of NetBEUI as the native tongue of NetBIOS. It's simply the way the NetBIOS message is packaged and delivered to the wire. The downside to NetBEUI is that because it's very simple, it relies on network broadcasts to get a lot of information across.

A *broadcast* is when a network node sends information to *all* other network nodes on a segment, which obviously causes a lot of network traffic. It does this because keeping track of all the nodes on the network is difficult—if a station doesn't differentiate whom to talk to, there doesn't have to be a facility on the network to keep track of who's currently available on the network. Because NetBEUI is a simple protocol, it naturally uses the simplest First, we'll look at NetBEUI, method of talking.

The downside of not using NetBEUI is that TCP/IP is tougher to configure, and IPX/SPX is not well supported by Microsoft. (It's really there only for compatibility with Novell networks.) For small networks, NetBEUI is the way to go—it's actually faster for *small* numbers of PCs because no routing overhead exists. However, anything larger than 30 to 50 stations warrants the extra up-front work involved in TCP/IP configuration.

If you have a larger network, you really shouldn't be using NetBEUI. Broadcasts are the pits; in large enough quantities, they will lead to broadcast storms (that is, one workstation broadcasts, leading other workstations to broadcast). On a large scale, this creates unnecessary network traffic that can wreak havoc on your network. If you're experiencing occasional freezes and hang-ups on your large NetBEUI network, it might be because of broadcast storms.

NetBIOS

NetBIOS (Network Basic Input/Output System) provides name services and session services to the file- and print-sharing programs between two computers. Windows can use the nonroutable NetBEUI protocol to transport NetBIOS to another computer; alternatively, TCP/IP or IPX/SPX can be used in a routed environment.

11

Specifically, NetBIOS handles name services for Microsoft (and older IBM) file and print services. It also serves to carry messages pertaining to the creation of workgroups on the network and makes sure that no duplicate workstation names exist within the workgroup or domain.

One type of NetBIOS error is very common. It occurs when a technician duplicates a "known good" hard drive (see Hour 15, "Beauty Is Consistency Deep") to a "known bad" hard drive and then reboots the problem station. Immediately, he or she sees the following Windows error, which is in fact a NetBIOS error:

```
Microsoft Networking:

The following error occurred while loading protocol number 0.

Error 38: The computer name you specified is already in use on the
network. To specify a different name, double-click the Network icon in
Control Panel.
```

NetBIOS has queried the network to see if the name exists, and, in fact, it does. Of course, the tech simply goes to the Control Panel, clicks the Identification tab, and changes the PC name to fix this problem. This also happens when two people name their workstations the same (like if you had two *2001* fans name their PCs "HAL"). Because it doesn't really matter what a PC is named, if you see this error, you can simply pick a different but similar name, such as "HAL2000."

Browsing

Can the protocol itself deal with the creation of workgroups? No, this task requires a service program on the other side of the wire. You should know that a mechanism, called *browsing*, exists that's part of workgroup or domain network computing.

The browse system consists of a browse master, backup browsers, and client computers. Any client computer can get information about network resources, whether the resources are servers, workgroups, NT domains, and so on. For example, when you click your Network Neighborhood icon, the computer list you see is obtained from the browse master of your workgroup or domain. As you can see, browsing is pretty important— if you can't see the resource, you can't use the resource.

 A Windows 95 computer will only show up on the browse list if it's acting as a server. To make your Windows 95 computer act like a server, do the following:

1. Open the Windows Control Panel by clicking Start|Settings|Control Panel.

2. Click the Network icon.

3.Click Add.

4. Select Service.

5. Click Microsoft and then select File and Printer Sharing for Microsoft Networks.

6. Insert the Windows CD-ROM if prompted and reboot when asked to do so.

I once saw a case in which a user absolutely could not browse others in her workgroup. After checking the network card and cable and finding nothing wrong, we were on the verge of reinstalling Windows—we had tracked the problem down to something about the OS. Before doing this, we checked the Control Panel again; this time, we noticed that the workgroup name had a space in front of it. Argh! We removed the space, and suddenly we could see everybody else.

I've also seen a case in which a workgroup, B&O, was mistyped as B&0 (with a zero rather than the letter O). Be sure to watch out for mistyped workgroup names.

The browse master of an NT domain will always be the NT server that's the primary domain controller (PDC).

Although an NT domain can exist across subnets (that is, via a router), workgroups cannot. Instead, the workgroup exists twice on the two different segments, each one with its own browse master and browse list. That means the browse master on network A has no idea what the browse list is for network B. Computers on segment A will not be able to see those on segment B in their network neighborhood, and vice versa.

11

The *browse master* of a workgroup or domain is the machine that's responsible for keeping a list of participating workstations. If the browse master leaves the workgroup, another browser from the backup browser list must take over. This is only important because mentally ill browse masters have been known to spring up on Windows networks, and this can cause problems. Also, if a workstation claims that it's the browse master when it's not, this can also cause problems.

SMB

Once names are established and workgroups are joined, Windows file- and print-sharing happens through a mechanism called *server message block*, or *SMB*. SMB is featured in NT and Windows 9*x*, but the versions are different. The SMB server program is what makes it possible for other PCs to share a server's files and printers. Contrariwise, the SMB client program on a client PC makes it possible to use SMB-offered files and print-ers on a server. SMB and NetBIOS are somewhat joined at the hip—for example, SMB gets its name resolution from NetBIOS. You cannot run SMB without NetBIOS some-where in the picture.

 In fact, Microsoft networking's multilingual capabilities are predicated on the fact that TCP/IP and IPX/SPX have a facility to carry NetBIOS. If you turn this off in the Control Panel, say goodbye to Microsoft file and print (unless you have NetBEUI installed).

SMB is pretty simple stuff, and it rarely breaks. Problems with SMB usually tend to lie in protocol problems, name service .problems, WINS problems, DHCP problems, and domain and/or security problems.

Eminent Domain

The simplistic SMB protocol was always seen as rather insecure and feature poor. This led Microsoft to adopt a new security model, called the *domain security model*. This model relies on one or more servers that share a common database of usernames and passwords.

I can see you raising your eyebrows. You're thinking, "Shared? Isn't that really inse-cure?" Unless you're a military installation, domain security is probably okay. Microsoft uses reasonable enough encryption technologies that casual folks can't get past it; the upside here is that if one server is down, other folks can still log into the network. What's more, because the domain model shares usernames and passwords among several servers, you avoid administrative hassle when adding users to the network.

Each NT domain must have an NT server that acts as the primary domain controller, and it may have one or several backup domain controllers that act to help out with authenti-cation services while the PDC is up and take over completely if the PDC goes down.

An NT domain is *not* a directory service as I defined it in Hour 1 (we'll talk more about directory services in Hour 13, "NetWare Networking Basics"). It's not really scalable enough to be a directory, and it doesn't carry anything more than usernames, passwords, security groups, and basic information on who a user is. Microsoft has promised a real directory (called *Active Directory*) in NT 5.0. I'm sure it will be wonderful, but you won't catch me installing it on a production network until it's been in the field a good 6 to 12 months.

Workstation Wrestling

If you're using an NT workstation, note that networking to an NT server is slightly different than networking for users of Windows 9*x*. Part of the domain security model is the concept of a *secure workstation*; each NT workstation must be registered with the domain using a valid set of supervisory credentials before it's allowed to participate in file- and print-sharing. Windows 9*x* machines aren't considered to be securable machines, so they don't have to register.

11

SIDs AND YOU

When you install NT, the installation process generates a unique security identification number (SID). It's considered to be a reasonably secure declaration of the identity of the workstation, because it's randomly generated and has billions of possible values.

In NT Workstation, this SID is used as a starting point for generating unique identification numbers for users, groups, and so on that reside on the workstation. In NT Server, this SID is considered to be more than the SID for just that machine; it's the *domain SID* and is used to generate object numbers for the entire domain.

When you create an NT Workstation computer account, the domain controller generates a workstation identification number based on the domain SID. The domain controller establishes a secure encrypted channel with the workstation, based on a shared password.

If you change the computer name, your computer will no longer be considered the same computer that was added to the domain database, and it will not be able to access the domain. You'll have to delete the computer from the domain database using the Server Manager tool and then read it. This doesn't hurt anything, but it does create extra work for you.

SID issues exist when using drive duplication to install Windows NT in a standardized manner—your SID should never be the same on two NT workstations. See Hour 16 for more details.

Part of the concept behind a secure NT workstation is the idea that you cannot access a given workstation until you've identified yourself. On the downside, this can prevent you from accessing even the workstation if the network is down. For example, say you can't get to your NT server because the router that connects you to it is down. If you can't authenticate at all, you're locked out of the workstation and can't do local work. (You cannot simply bypass the login prompt the way you can on a Windows 95 machine; you *must* log in.) Fortunately, because a copy of the last-used domain information is stored (*cached*) on your hard drive, you can authenticate to the workstation anyway.

I've only seen "roaming" users have problems with this—that is, users who use more than one workstation. I've seen a user change her password on the domain one day and then go to another location where there's a network problem and be unable to get into the workstation. The problem? She had changed her password the previous day, and the second workstation hadn't found out about it yet. The solution? She used her old password, and it worked just fine.

> Many manufacturers ship Windows NT with no administrator password. If you can't get into your workstation because you can't communicate with the domain, you can always try logging into the local machine with the username Administrator and no password. This works more often than you'd think. So much for secure workstations!

A Matter of Trust

Because NT domains aren't really a directory service, there must be some way for a user on one NT domain to use the resources of another NT domain. The mechanism that allows users of one domain to use resources of another is called *trust*. Trust relationships can be a one- or two-way relationship.

Say your boss gives you access to the file cabinet with everybody's salaries. He has placed trust in you that you'll not blab everybody's salaries all over town. Similarly, you trust your boss to pay you on Friday. This is a two-way trust relationship. On the other hand, your small children must trust you to put food on the table. You do not trust the older child at the tender age of 6 years old to stay with his 2-year-old brother; his idea of fun would be to feed his dinner to the dog and to feed the dog food to his brother. This, of course, is a one-way trust relationship.

You make NT domain trust decisions in a similar fashion. If you need for folks in domain A to be able to access resources in domain B, but not vice versa, you establish a trust relationship between domains B and A. You would say that A was *trusted* by B, and that B *trusts* A.

If one person in one of your NT domains (domain B) cannot access a resource (a share or a printer) in another one of your NT domains (domain A), you probably want to check the trust relationship. Make sure that the domain providing the resource is *trusting*, and that the domain that needs the resource is *trusted*. Take the following steps:

1. Go to the NT server of the domain with the resources (domain A).

2. From the Start menu, select Programs|Administrative Tools|User Manager for Domains.

3. From the Policies menu in the User Manager, select Trust Relationships.

4. Make sure the other domain (domain B) is listed as *trusted*.

5. Go to the NT server of the trusted domain.

6. Start the User Manager and check the trust relationships again.

7. Make sure the first domain (domain A) is listed as *trusting*.

I've been in a shop where we needed to establish a two-way trust relationship between two domains via a wide-area link. Even though we established the trust relationship properly, it seemed to fail. The system administrator got the following message when he attempted to administer the remote domain:

```
There are no logon servers available to service the logon request
```

The key was in the fact that these were wide-area linked domains, and they relied on TCP/IP as a protocol. They therefore relied on WINS for name services between the domains. WINS was not configured properly; a quick search on TechNet revealed what to do. We ended up reconfiguring WINS between the two domains, ensured that WINS itself worked properly, and the problem went away. (I discuss TCP/IP and WINS in the next section.)

TCP/IP Graffiti

The handwriting on the wall is that more and more Windows functions are going to rely on TCP/IP, particularly over WANs. Accordingly, you'll want to become very familiar with the various TCP/IP concepts and commands that exist, both under Windows and other operating systems. In this section, we'll take a look at the server programs that exist to make your life as a troubleshooter and part-time network administrator as easy as possible by automating network configuration. We'll start out with DHCP, which automatically assigns workstation addresses instead of forcing you to assign them per workstation. Then we'll move on to Windows networking name resolution.

11

DHCP

DHCP (Dynamic Host Configuration Protocol) is probably one of the most important TCP/IP technologies that has arisen in the last couple of years. It allows each TCP/IP workstation to broadcast once during each session and automatically obtain an address and other information from the DHCP server. Actually, the way it works is that a workstation that doesn't know its TCP/IP information must broadcast to the entire segment to obtain a lease on a TCP/IP address from the server. ("Hi everybody! I need an IP address, please.") When the lease runs out, it must rebroadcast to renew the lease. DHCP lease lengths are configurable at the server, as is the DHCP scope—that is, the range of addresses served to client machines. (For example, one server's scope on the 192.168.1 network might be 192.168.1.10 through 192.168.1.50 for a 40-user network.)

DHCP is a much easier way to keep track of IP addresses than assigning them per workstation. I've found that DHCP seriously reduces the number of duplicate IP addresses on a network, which reduces the number of problems you have to deal with.

> Because one of DHCP's good points is that it allows you to quickly change large numbers of workstation IP addresses, you should make your lease length short enough to accommodate weekend reconfigurations—that is, not longer than one or two days.

DHCP is actually integral to using TCP/IP in a happy and healthy way for Microsoft file and print. Finally, you have the option to make workstations that use TCP/IP for NetBIOS name resolution and browsing into nonbroadcast nodes. Yippee!

You can configure workstations within a DHCP scope into point-to-point, nonbroadcast workstations (or *p-nodes*), broadcast nodes (*b-nodes*), or hybrid nodes (*h-nodes*—or node type 0x8—as shown in Figure 11.1) that first try to talk directly and then broadcast if they have no other alternative. The kicker here is that you need to invest in Windows NT to get a DHCP server; Microsoft does not supply a DHCP server for workgroups.

DHCP can potentially distribute many configuration items automatically, one of which is the address of the WINS and/or the DNS server for the network (see the section titled, "TCP/IP Name Resolution," later in this hour). This is awesome, because it seriously cuts down on fat-finger syndrome. You can be pretty sure that if one workstation has the right DNS and WINS information, they all do (rather than wondering if somebody has fat-fingered a given workstation's DNS and WINS info). This saves you a lot of time when troubleshooting.

FIGURE 11.1

The DHCP manager can show you all client leases, thus allowing you to easily figure out which users have which IP addresses.

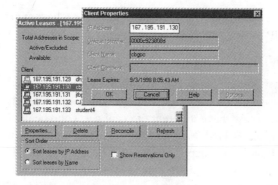

Well, this all sounds wonderful, but what happens if your DHCP server goes down? On a small network where the server *is* the DHCP server, this doesn't matter for small periods of time. The concept of DHCP leases means that unless the lease expired right after the server went down, your folks probably still have IP addresses even without the server. (However, they're probably annoyed nonetheless, because their files are on that server.)

Folks with a 255.255.255 subnet mask typically have two DHCP servers for a reasonably large (less than 300 machines) switched network; this way, they can split the scope into around 127 addresses apiece. Remember, a DHCP *scope* is the range of addresses served by the server. In this case, let's say the subnet address is 167.195.191.0. One server's scope might be 167.195.191.10–167.195.191.127; the other server's scope might be 167.195.191.128–167.195.191.254.

There's a lot to be said for keeping a large amount of eggs in two baskets. (The actual quantity of numbers available for each server's scope will actually be less than 254 divided by 2, because items such as routers and servers have nondynamic IP addresses and use some of the addresses.)

TCP/IP Name Resolution

The thing that always confused me when I started networking with Windows and TCP/IP was this: Why are there two types of name resolution? After the discussion in Hour 1, you're probably comfortable with the fact that any network *name* typically needs to be *resolved* to a network *address*—that is, when you point your browser to www.jotto.com, the browser *resolves* this name-oriented address via DNS (Domain Name Service) to the network address 205.134.224.21.

Therefore, like me, you're probably wondering, why not just use DNS the way other operating systems that use TCP/IP do? It always seemed crazy that Microsoft created a new type of name service just for Windows. Let's take a look at how WINS fits into the Windows TCP/IP picture, and then we'll glance at how Microsoft integrated DNS as well.

Windows WINS!

Windows Internet Naming Service, or *WINS*, was invented to make networking Windows machines easy, even over a wide area. Because you know that NetBEUI is not a routable protocol, it makes sense that a different protocol needed to be used to connect Windows-networked machines. TCP/IP was fine and could carry NetBIOS, but some of the ways that name resolution used to happen in NetBEUI needed to be redone for TCP/IP. In particular, when your domain can be spread over several subnets, using broadcasts for name resolution no longer works—broadcasts typically only affect your local subnet.

WINS is the answer to how machines can resolve names without broadcasting. The WINS server keeps track of Windows workgroups, domains, and machine names on a TCP/IP network. Instead of a machine broadcasting to the network, that machine can instead contact the WINS server and get the necessary information. This is called a *point-to-point* name resolution; machines that resolve names this way are called *p-nodes*. As clients talk to the WINS server, it notes what IP addresses they have and what workgroup they belong to and then updates its database.

The WINS server program, like DHCP, runs only on Windows NT. There's no WINS server for workgroups. Its function is to keep a database of domains, workgroups, and PC names, and to distribute these names and their associated IP numbers to anybody who asks for them.

You have all sorts of options for replicating your database to another WINS server, adding static mappings, and so on, but it's not worth going into in detail here. Check out the NT Resource Kit (available online) if you're interested. The bottom line with WINS is this:

1. You start WINS running.
2. As PCs connect to it, it registers the computer names in its database.
3. WINS distributes this information as required by other workstations and servers.

You can drive yourself nuts with WINS very easily; keep it simple and you'll be okay.

Your NT server that runs the WINS server should use itself as its own WINS server. Sounds crazy, huh?

It's absolutely crucial that you use the latest NT service packs with WINS. Some extremely evil problems have been fixed.

Service packs are accumulated fixes that Microsoft makes available via its Web site or on CD-ROMs. Applying one service pack fixes a whole host of potential problems. A service pack differs from a *hot fix* in that Microsoft has deemed service packs safe for all users, whereas hot fixes are only applicable to users who are having a particular problem.

Using DNS

DNS can be used as a naming service as well, but this will make your initial connections somewhat slower. DNS does *not* have facilities to differentiate between workgroups, domains, and computer names. Each DNS entry specifies a hostname *only*.

Windows 95 automatically uses DNS resolution if other things fail; NT needs this explicitly set up in the network Control Panel under the TCP/IP protocol. Make sure the Use DNS for Name Resolution check box is checked if you wish to use DNS.

Most of the time, you'll *not* want to use DNS; WINS comes with NT and is dynamic and relatively easy to use. DNS is somewhat trickier to set up and doesn't offer as much to the Windows networking world.

The only time you'll want to set up the Microsoft DNS server is if you're acting as a Web server. Because you're then participating in the Internet's network—which is *not* a Microsoft file and print network—DNS is the only option. Using DNS for internal Windows network name resolution doesn't make sense most of the time.

Does all of this seem like a mess? You're not going crazy: It is a mess. There are too many pieces and parts to keep track of with TCP/IP and Windows. Microsoft fans are really, really, hoping that future releases will comb some of the tangles out, and no doubt NT 5.0 probably will, but we'll have to wait awhile to find out. In the meantime, take it slowly; it's not too bad once you get the hang of it. See Figure 11.2 for a sample Windows network that uses TCP/IP. In it, you'll see that PCs are configured upon bootup or lease expiration from the DHCP server on their local segment, which configures them with IP addresses and with the configuration information they need to resolve names from their local WINS server. It's not too awful. You have just a couple of things to set up.

11

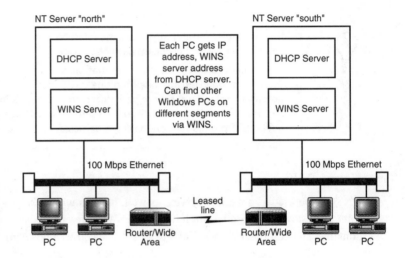

FIGURE 11.2

A sample Windows TCP/IP network.

Static Name Resolution

You should know that in addition to the dynamic name services provided by network name servers, there's a static way for each PC to resolve a network name into a network address. Each PC can have a HOSTS table on its hard drive for resolving hostnames to IP addresses. The HOSTS table is used for normal TCP/IP networking (as in Telnet sessions to a host system as well as pings). Each PC can also have an LMHOSTS file, which is formatted much the same as a HOSTS file but used for NetBIOS name resolution. Both files have a series of lines that look something like this:

```
192.168.10.5 fido
```

```
192.168.10.5 rover
```

This means that 192.168.10.5 is the numeric address for fido, and 192.168.10.6 is the numeric address for rover. (LMHOSTS also has some additional format options to indicate NetBIOS functions such as workgroups.)

Both of these files live in the C:\WINDOWS directory. LMHOSTS.SAM is a sample file you can look at to see the file format and so on. Let me beg of you not to use LMHOSTS files (or HOSTS files) unless you have the smallest network in the world; the tedium of updating many of these files makes you wish you were running after really tough network problems instead. You can consider static host mappings as functionally obsolete, but you should know about it. Just in case there's a naming problem with a workstation, you might want to see if somebody has been monkeying around with LMHOSTS at a given client computer.

Workstation Configuration

Now that I've examined the makeup of the Microsoft file and print superhighway, let's take a look at the roads that connect to it. In particular, let's look at the method of configuring a given Windows workstation, as well as at the given protocols and clients that can be configured on a Windows workstation.

The Network Control Panel

Take a look at the Windows 9x Network Control Panel in Figure 11.3 (see the following section). It shows a high-level picture of the network components configured on that PC. The Windows NT Network Control Panel looks and feels a little bit different, but it ties all your network components together and allows you to manage them and check their configuration from one place. The components include the following:

- *Clients*—These components enable your PC to use a service over a network.
- *Network adapters*—These components and protocols do the setup necessary for you to communicate on the network.
- *Protocols*
- *Services*—As discussed in Hour 1, services are programs that offer information or resources to the network.

I'll treat these components separately in the following sections. We'll start off by discussing clients and then move on to *binding*, the process of letting your workstation know which network components are hooked to one another.

Clients

To talk to any other computer, whether it's another Windows PC or that beefy server in the data center, you always need a *client*. Most times, a client is simply a program that allows Windows to treat server or workgroup resources as though they resided on the local workstation. This is usually accomplished through file and print *redirection*—that is, your G: drive is actually a server drive or your friend Eddie's CD-ROM drive, LPT3 is actually the printer connected to Gloria's printer, and so on. (I get deep into client and generic file and print troubleshooting in Hour 18, "Lots of Different People in Your Neighborhood.")

In order for you to perform drive and printer redirection, you must add driver software to Windows. You add this software by going to your Control Panel and selecting Network, which gives you the dialog box shown in Figure 11.3. Because the Control Panel shows that I have the client for Microsoft Networks and the Novell IntranetWare client loaded, I *should* be able to talk to both Microsoft and Novell networks. Cool.

FIGURE 11.3

The Network Control Panel, where most Windows networking functions are configured, including network cards, protocols, and clients for file and print networking.

Of course, different folks have different strokes, so your different types of servers need different types of clients. Some common ones include the following:

- Banyan DOS/Windows client
- Client for Microsoft Networks
- Novell IntraNetware client
- Various third-party UNIX (NFS, or *Network File System*) clients

Even though Windows ships with many different manufacturers' clients, the versions of these clients on the Windows installation CD-ROM are usually older and possibly buggier than versions you can obtain directly from the manufacturers themselves. You're always best off getting software straight from the horse's mouth.

Binding

So the client is responsible for letting your various programs access file and print network resources. Fair enough. Now, how does the client talk to the network? Well, as we discussed in Hour 1, a client needs to know how to speak the right language, how to use the protocol, and how to ask the network card to initiate a call.

Windows has so many potential protocols, clients, and network cards that Microsoft introduced a concept called *binding*. This helps straighten out what can appear to be an unholy jumble of protocols, services, clients, and network cards. Taking it from the top, each client can be *bound* to one or more protocols. Each protocol, in turn, is also bound to one or more network cards (also called *network adapters*).

> Don't bind more protocols than you're actually using to a network card. Each protocol you bind to an adapter translates into more processing that the CPU must do each time it refers to that adapter. Consider, for example, your dial-up adapter. You probably use it to talk to the Internet via TCP/IP. It would be wasteful to also bind IPX/SPX to this adapter, because the Internet doesn't speak IPX/SPX. In extreme cases, an overly bound network card attached to a very slow CPU can even cause network problems.

> One of the network newsletters I subscribe to points out that one should not use autodetection to detect frame types in an IPX/SPX environment, because this generates unnecessary network traffic and can really slow down the network in large installations.
>
> Frame types are something I haven't talked about so far. In a nutshell, a frame type is the way a packet gets built by a network card. You can think of a frame type as a dialect of the protocol—it's hard for one dialect to talk to another dialect, even though they're the same language. When someone from the Southeast U.S. says, "I'm fixing to wait on you all night," someone who's not from that region might get the wrong idea!
>
> You can find out the frame type in use on your NetWare network simply by typing **config** at your NetWare server's console. You can then enter it manually on your Windows workstations. Because autodetection doesn't always work, this is probably a good idea anyway. I've fixed workstations that were acting odd by getting rid of autodetection.
>
> What if you have lots of workstations? Isn't this a lot of work? Nope. See Hour 16 for tips on how to standardize workstations.

11

Of course, binding is a two-way street; each network card is also bound to one or more protocols. Figure 11.4 shows the Windows 9*x* screen where you can specify which protocols are bound to a given network card (whether that network card is dial-up or not). To see this for your network card, follow these steps:

1. Open the Network Control Panel.
2. Select your network adapter.

3. Click Properties.

4. Click the Bindings tab.

FIGURE 11.4

Showing the bindings on a particular network card.

The Properties dialog box allows you to enable or disable the protocol for a given client or service. (Figure 11.5 shows the Properties dialog box for TCP/IP.) This is the only part of binding that I'm not crazy about; I would rather do it all from one place. In this case, you select the TCP/IP protocol from the Network Control Panel, click Properties, and then click the Bindings tab.

FIGURE 11.5

Showing the bindings for a particular protocol.

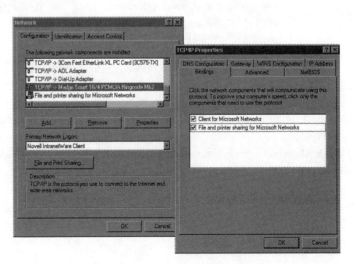

Fortunately, under Windows NT, binding is much more straightforward (see Figure 11.6). Each network card is shown with associated protocols, clients, and services, and everything can be turned on or off from this one place. You reach this dialog box from NT's Control Panel by performing the following steps:

1. Double-click Network.

2. Click the Bindings tab.

3. Select All Adapters on the Show Bindings For list.

4. Show subcomponents by clicking components that have a plus sign next to them. (If you see a component with a minus sign next to it, all subcomponents are shown.)

5. Turn off a bound component by clicking the Disable button; turn it on by clicking on the Enable button.

FIGURE 11.6

Showing bindings for all components on Windows NT.

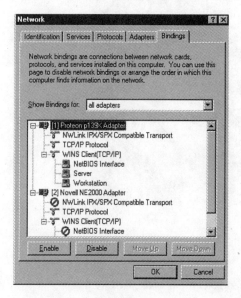

11

Command and Conquer

This is the fun part: You actually get to *do* something. The following sections cover the TCP/IP commands that can give you the information you need to make intelligent diagnostic calls.

winipcfg

Any time you're troubleshooting TCP/IP, you want to know how the workstation is configured. You can go to the Control Panel, but that only tells you a limited amount of information, particularly if the workstation is using DHCP. Instead, get to a DOS prompt in Windows 9*x* and type this:

`winipcfg`

You'll need to click the More Info button or type **winipcfg /all** to get the full output shown in Figure 11.7; otherwise, you'll see a less complete screen. The full screen is a pretty complete and concise summary of just about every TCP/IP option configured on that workstation. Notice that even though my network card is not DHCP assigned, I can still look at its configuration this way.

FIGURE 11.7

WinIPCfg output for a client that doesn't use DHCP or WINS and only uses TCP/IP as a means to access the Internet.

Windows NT users can type

`ipconfig /a`

at a command prompt to get similar text-based output.

A quick comparison of the IP configuration information of two workstations can lead to rapid problem resolution. Of course, any time you compare workstations, make sure you're comparing apples to apples; they should be on the same subnet. Here's what to compare:

- *IP addresses*—The IP addresses of the workstations should be the same, except for the node numbers (192.168.10.5 and 192.168.10.6 are the same ; 192.168.9.5 and 192.168.11.6 are *not*).

- *DNS server(s)*
- WINS server(s)

Chances are, if these settings are different, you've got a configuration problem rather than a hardware or network problem.

Informational Commands

If the problem is more thorny than a configuration issue, it can be useful to know the perspective of the problem workstation; that is, what the workstation can see, what it cannot see, and the state of various informational commands as run from that workstation. You can use various informational commands, as listed in Table 11.1, to see the workstation's perspective on the network (these commands apply for both Windows 9*x* and NT).

TABLE 11.1 INFORMATIONAL COMMANDS

Command	Description
netstat -r	Shows TCP/IP routing table.
netstat -a	Shows all TCP/IP sockets in use (client and server).
arp -a	Displays the MAC-to-IP address translation table.
ping *hostname* or *address*	Checks basic IP connectivity with *hostname* or *address*.
tracert *hostname* or *address*	Traces the route that a packet takes from the current workstation to *hostname* or *address*. Shows each router that the packet goes through on its way to *hostname* or *address*.
nbtstat	Checks the NetBIOS name table.

All these commands (except nbtstat) are more or less lifted from UNIX; see Hour 12, "UNIX Networking Basics," for examples of their use in basic TCP/IP troubleshooting. Hour 18 provides some in-the-trenches techniques.

net

You should also be familiar with the net command. Type

`net ¦ more`

at the command prompt. This will show you the multitudinous net commands you can run. These are mostly file and print related; some relate to networking configuration in general, as well. Some of these functions do not have a graphical equivalent, so set aside about a half an hour when you'll be undisturbed to check 'em out.

11

Friendly, Mon, Real Friendly

Say what you like about any other part of Microsoft networking, but I will defend the built-in statistic-gathering features to the death. Far and away the most wonderful thing about Microsoft networking, the statistic-gathering features in the server and client programs, along with SysMon (the affectionate term for the System Monitor), enable you as Joe User to see how you're doing in terms of performance at any given time. This means you can quickly and easily profile a particular server or network segment. This is something that used to take a network expert and a $10,000 piece of equipment to do, yet Microsoft has now enabled everyone to do it. (Did I mention that I like this feature?)

In all seriousness, this really allows you to do some powerful troubleshooting cheaply. Let's look at a quick example: Suppose we have an application that's for some reason running very slowly for a given person. Other folks are running the application just fine, but our confidence level is pretty low concerning how alike each workstation is. We discover that the user can log into someone else's workstation and work just fine.

Somebody suggests that we nuke the user's hard drive and make it just like a setup that works. This is greeted with stony silence by the user, who happens to be a big shot in the company. Apparently, this is not the path that we will take.

The user says that he runs like molasses, and he seems right from what we can tell of other people's workstations. What's going on? Is it the client or the server? Is this subjective slowness, or is there an objective way of measuring this?

We could break out the $10,000 network analyzer to measure the network throughput by attaching it to the network segment and capturing each packet between the client and server and then doing the math of amount captured divided by number of seconds to get the amount per second. However, because network throughput is easy to measure with the Windows 95 System Monitor, we install this to the user's workstation and add the Microsoft Network client's Bytes Read/Second statistic to our chart. Figure 11.8 shows a monitor session; it reveals that the Microsoft file and print session is running reasonably fast: 625KB–991KB per second. You can't expect much faster than that on a 10Mbps Ethernet network. You can tell that the workstation is working hard keeping up (look at the CPU utilization and free memory). Both drop when this file transfer is happening. In this example, we would see normal output like this when running the application on a different server.

We keep the System Monitor minimized and run the problem application. Yes indeed, it's slow. We're seeing wide-area speeds on a LAN connection. Right away we know that there's truly a speed problem on the network; it has nothing to do with his workstation.

FIGURE 11.8

A monitor session.

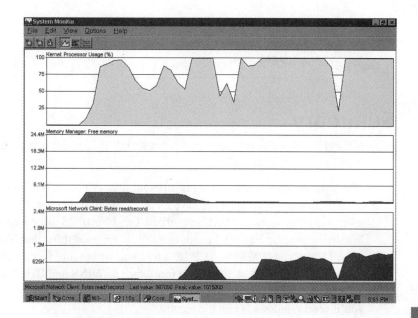

Or does it? We have a different server that runs another department's stuff, so we decide to do the same measurements on that server using the same application. In this case, the measurements are more in line with what we're seeing on other workstations on the LAN. It seems that this particular server and this person's workstation are not happy with each other. The five minutes we spent with the System Monitor accomplished a couple of important things:

- This person is not imagining things; we have objective data to prove it.
- We've discovered that the workstation can connect to a different server without the slowdown problem; we now have a workaround while we further diagnose the problem server or workstation.

In this particular case, the server is definitely a problem. It's *not* a Microsoft server; it's a UNIX server running an older version of an SMB server. However, the server is talking to other PCs just fine. Something about the age of the server and the client software on the user's PC isn't jiving properly.

We (very carefully) reinstall the Microsoft file and print client to the workstation, consistent with other workstations in the department; then we reapply the Windows 95 Service Pack 1. In this case, because we're dealing with a VIP, we make a backup of his hard drive—just in case we cause more problems through this process. After the application of the client and the service pack, we test again with the System Monitor. The problem is gone, and the VIP is happy.

We'll talk more about network throughput in Hour 22, "The Network Is Slow!"

Summary

NT and Windows 9x networking is better than Windows 3.x and DOS's networking. The troubleshooting is also easier.

Windows workgroup networking is different than Windows NT domain networking, but the two methods of networking have many similarities, particularly with regards to the protocols these services travel on. NetBEUI and NetBIOS are the native tongues of Windows; because NetBEUI is not routable, it's a good thing that NetBIOS can also travel on TCP/IP and IPX/SPX. TCP/IP is tricky to set up, and you should really take advantage of the automated TCP/IP setup tools such as WINS and DHCP if you want to use TCP/IP on your network. However, in order to take advantage of these automation tools, you'll need Windows NT in the picture.

Windows has a *lot* of built-in commands and programs for diagnosing and configuring the network; it's worth spending some time investigating them now so that you can use them when problems arise.

Workshop

Q&A

Q I'm using TCP/IP just fine without WINS or DHCP. Come again? Why do I need this stuff?

A You're likely in a nonrouted environment and/or your configuration has been set in stone in the LMHOSTS text files on your hard drive. Hey, if it's working for you, great! When you reconfigure and want to make things a bit more automatic, you might want to change.

Q Why are broadcasts so terrible?

A In a switched environment, all workstations see broadcasts. If you have 300 workstations, each of which broadcasts each time it connects to a drive, uses a printer, and so on, you very quickly have a large amount of broadcast traffic that consumes a lot of network bandwidth, thus making your network slow down. Broadcasting once during DHCP configuration is much preferable.

Quiz

1. True or false? You should probably bind all the protocols you can to a network card, just in case you need them.

2. What does SMB stand for?

   A. Serve My Baguette

   B. Server Mini Broadcast

   C. Service Messaging Broadcast

   D. Server Message Block

3. True or false? WINS is the only naming service available to Windows users.

4. DHCP can distribute _____ to workstations that ask for configuration information.

   A. IP addresses, WINS server addresses, and DNS addresses

   B. IP addresses, Web server locations, and WINS server addresses

   C. IP addresses, DNS addresses, and satellite hookup

   D. IP addresses, WINS addresses, and FTP locations

Answers to Quiz Questions

1. False
2. D
3. False
4. A

11

HOUR 12

UNIX Networking Basics

The most aggravating thing about UNIX is that it has a million flavors. On the other hand, the best thing about UNIX is that it has a million flavors. Lots and lots of network innovations have come out of the UNIX melting pot—the Internet itself probably owes its existence to UNIX-based network inventions. Of course, TCP/IP itself grew up on UNIX computers; therefore, many TCP/IP concepts and commands from UNIX are extremely applicable to other operating systems, notably Windows NT. Even if you have no UNIX in your environment, you still might want to skim this chapter, because you probably have TCP/IP. This hour does not attempt to teach UNIX to the completely uninitiated; however, if you're already familiar with how to log in to the system, you'll learn how to explore the networking components of it.

It's not important to know all the major UNIX vendors; the important thing to know is that a lot of different types of UNIX exist. Although some of the ways they handle hard drives and terminals are very different, many of the TCP/IP commands are very much the same.

Overview

Let's take a 20,000-foot view of how most UNIX servers are configured. Yes, they have the capability to do "file and print" the way Windows networks do, and you can connect your Windows 95 drive letters or LPT ports to a UNIX box (if your Windows 95 PC has an appropriate network client loaded). However, more than this, UNIX servers are typically client/server oriented.

By the way, you'll find very little difference between a UNIX workstation and a UNIX server, other than the speed and redundancy of the hardware.

Client/Server

I'll get into client/server a bit more in Hour 18, "Lots of Different People in Your Neighborhood." For now, it's enough to know that client/server is basically a fancy way of saying, "If I ask somebody for a price of a widget, they give me an answer." (This is unlike file and print, where you would get the entire catalog.) Think of client/server as being question/answer oriented. For example, DNS name services are a great example of client/server. When you pull up www.jotto.com, you don't ask your name server for a list of everyone in the .com zone; instead, you ask it for the IP address of www.jotto.com. It responds with 205.134.224.21. It's a very simple transaction. The client asks the questions, and the server provides the answers. If configured to do so, any machine can act as either the client or the server.

You know the way every salesperson who walks in your door makes sure to mention *e-business*, *VPN*, and *extranet*? That's how it used to be with client/server. It was a hugely overused marketing term a couple of years ago. However, although client/server is now out of favor with marketing types, it describes reasonably well what's happening with UNIX services.

> When I'm teaching a class, I usually refer to any service networking that's not file and print as *service-oriented networking*, but because nobody else in the world uses that term, I'll stick with *client/server* here.

Configuring UNIX

As with any computer, you network a UNIX computer by sticking a network card into its motherboard, plugging it into a hub, turning the computer on, configuring it, and away you go. Not so hard, huh? The trick with UNIX is that the only standards that exist are TCP/IP-based standards. There are no standards for NetBEUI and IPX/SPX; however, these are available through third parties as vendor add-ons (and are beyond the scope of this book).

UNIX servers tend to house mission-critical databases as well as service users via client/server applications. In the past, this has largely been via *Telnet*, a way of running a character-based terminal session on a UNIX computer over the network. Lately, this is being replaced by graphical Windows front ends that do pretty much the same thing (although they might communicate with the UNIX host on a different socket number). Most of this communication is via TCP/IP.

Because TCP/IP seems to win nowadays, it's not much of an obstacle. UNIX's chief problem with most people is that it has many, many cryptic commands that must be typed in to configure the computer. Even though UNIX had a windowing system (called *X Window*) before Windows 3.1 was a gleam in Bill Gates's eye, it has always been a bit "user hostile"—requiring users to edit many configuration files while acting unforgivingly when they made mistakes. In a nutshell, UNIX's windowing system, though finally maturing in the last couple of years, has been a real problem. There aren't any standard ways to configure the network through the window system; therefore, I'm going to talk about command-line network configuration and troubleshooting instead. Don't let that deter you—think of it as an excuse to brush up on your typing. What's more, once you learn this stuff, much of it works under Windows 9*x* and NT—it's just hidden behind the scenes (Microsoft did a great job at making basic network configuration a pretty painless experience).

> I know a lot of people who have been scared by the prospect of playing with their production UNIX systems and have bought a $29 CD-ROM of the Linux operating system, a freely distributed UNIX "workalike." Many people install this to a pretty low-end PC and learn on it. I recommend this highly— you won't be afraid to "learn by destroying," which is one of the best ways

12

to learn. You'll also do an install of what seems to be a complex operating system, and you'll discover that it was actually pretty easy. It's a good way to demystify a seemingly scary endeavor.

Many commercial UNIX vendors have begun to offer free single-user versions of their UNIX flavors, too, for just this purpose. If you happen to have a commercial version of UNIX in production that you want to learn about, you're sitting pretty—it's always best to learn with exactly what you have in production. SCO (www.sco.com) and Sun (www.sun.com), for example, have this policy. (They do charge for shipping and handling, but last time I checked, it was a nominal charge.)

Although Microsoft has tried, NT has not quite eaten UNIX's lunch yet. UNIX's ability to reconfigure without rebooting and the way it keeps going and going and going garners it a good deal of respect from folks who run nonstop data centers. I've seen UNIX servers that have been continuously up for over two years without needing a reboot. (The UNIX administrator in question was a bit of a lunatic, because leaving any server up for that long is just playing with fire, but it's still pretty impressive.)

Friendly Daemons

First a word about a UNIX server's way of keeping track of the various programs running on it. You already know that Windows 95 shows you running programs on the system tray (the gray bar at the bottom of the screen). Well, a UNIX server typically has a couple hundred programs running at once—particularly because each client that connects to the server usually causes a separate program to fire off to serve the client. In Windows 95, that system tray would get pretty crowded! Instead, UNIX uses an internal process table that lists process numbers, the name of the processes, and other information.

A UNIX server, like your Windows 95 PC, can run many programs at once. Not all of them will interact with a user directly. Many of them run in the background. These background processes are called *daemons*. All UNIX services, whether Telnet, HTTP, or FTP, run as daemons.

When looking at a process listing, you can usually figure out which process is a daemon: It has a letter *d* at the end of its name. When talking about a daemon, you usually pronounce the *d* at the end, as in *name-dee* for named.

Suppose that a particular service is not running on a given UNIX server; say, for example, that the Web server doesn't seem to be home. Rather than trying to reboot the server (other services would be interrupted by doing this), you might first investigate whether the Web server process is running and then start it if it's not or stop it and restart it if it is. You usually need to be running as the super user (root) to stop or start processes.

You can cause a great deal of damage when running as the root user; you should use the su (super user) command to temporarily gain root privileges, run your commands, and then exit, rather than logging in as root. Again, you can contribute greatly to your confidence level if you install a play system on a PC—either Linux or another flavor.

Because the root prompt (#) is typically different than the normal prompt ($), I show it in the text to indicate commands that I would run as the root user.

Depending upon the type of UNIX you're running, you would type one of the following commands to look at the process table:

ps -ef

ps -ax

What's up with the -ef and the -ax? Well, these are flags that indicate to the ps (process status) program that you want to view everything in the process table. They're just different on different systems. So, right away, you need a way to figure out which flag you need to use. Buck up! Most, if not all, UNIX systems have all the manual pages right on the system. The man (check manual pages) command can give you details on any command you want. For example, to get specific details on what those -ef and -ax flags with the ps command mean, as well as to find out what other flags are available, you would type this:

    man ps

One of the best ways for you to learn UNIX is to use the man pages; to learn how to use the man command, you can type this:

    man man

12

The ps command stands for *process status*. On a busy system, your screen will zoom by with zillions of processes. Fortunately, you can make the display pause, or, even better, search the table for what you're looking for. Suppose you're looking for the Web server, the http daemon, or httpd. (The http comes from http://, which you type when finding a Web page; it stands for *Hypertext Transfer Protocol*. Therefore, this httpd program is the *Hypertext Transfer Protocol daemon*.) You could type this:

```
ps -ax ¦ grep httpd
```

You might get nothing back—that probably means that httpd has died, and you need to restart it. However, if it's not dead (it's just merely lost its mind), you might get this:

```
52  ?  S     0:01 /usr/sbin/httpd
```

The first number is the *process ID* (or *PID*). This is the number you refer to when you want to do something to this process. For example, the commands for killing and restarting this process might look something like this:

```
$ ps -ax ¦ grep httpd
   52  ?  S     0:01 /usr/sbin/httpd
$ su
Password:
# kill 52
# ps -ax ¦ grep httpd
# /usr/sbin/httpd
# exit
$ ps -ef ¦ grep httpd
  871  ?  S     0:01 /usr/sbin/httpd
```

You'll notice here that I don't need to use su until I actually kill the process and restart it. Then I immediately exit the su session so that I keep my super user risk at a minimum. I also like to recheck the process table before and after I've restarted the daemon just to make sure it's *not* out there after I kill it or to make sure that it *is* there after I restart it.

Should all daemons be there when you check for them? Actually, no. Back in the days when memory was scarce, the concept of a receptionist daemon was invented so that daemons not in use weren't loaded into memory. This receptionist is called inetd (Internet daemon) and is responsible for listening for connections, telling the caller to hold on, and then waking up the right daemon and transferring the call. Daemons that are invoked this way include telnetd (Telnet daemon) and ftpd (FTP daemon), among others. You can see which daemons are invoked by inetd by looking at the contents of inetd.conf, which will look something like this:

```
# If you make changes to this file, either reboot your machine or send
# the inetd a HUP signal:
# Do a "ps x" as root and look up the pid of inetd. Then do a
# "kill -HUP <pid of inetd>".
# The inetd will re-read this file whenever it gets that signal.
# Echo, discard, daytime, and chargen are used primarily for testing.
# Format is:
# <service_name> <sock_type> <proto> <flags> <user> <server_path> <args>
echo    stream tcp   nowait  root    internal
echo    dgram  udp   wait    root    internal
discard stream tcp   nowait  root    internal
```

```
discard dgram   udp   wait    root   internal
daytime stream  tcp   nowait  root   internal
daytime dgram   udp   wait    root   internal
chargen stream  tcp   nowait  root   internal
chargen dgram   udp   wait    root   internal
ftp     stream  tcp   nowait  root   /usr/sbin/tcpd   /usr/sbin/wu.ftpd -a
telnet  stream  tcp   nowait  root   /usr/sbin/tcpd   /usr/sbin/in.telnetd
```

You can start and stop inetd by using the kill commands outlined earlier. This tends
to be a bigger deal than just killing one daemon, because inetd acts as a receptionist for
many services; it's best to use kill -HUP *PID* to make inetd reread its configuration
first.

However, certain really important daemons do run on their own, namely the DNS naming
daemon (named), also sometimes known as in.named. You can stop and restart these in
the same way as with httpd, earlier, without worrying about what other services might
be affected.

In particular to named, if it's running but doesn't give out the right information even after
a restart, you might want to check to make certain the named configuration files are okay
(you can always restore from a "known good" backup). The primary named file lives
under /etc/named.boot, and it refers to several other files that are integral to its operation. See the man page for more information than you ever wanted to know about named.

> It's worth mentioning that the *client* for named on a UNIX server does not
> always perform name lookups from its own name server; not every UNIX
> server runs a name server. Take a look at the /etc/resolv.conf file to see
> how you're configured.

12

Not every service runs on a single daemon. NFS (Network File System, the file and print
service for UNIX), for example, does not. It runs different daemons for different tasks—
biod, nfsd, mountd—and relies on another daemon called portmapper. NFS can be a
beast; if you're lucky enough to use a system that has per-service startup scripts, you
might be able to restart NFS by typing the following:

```
# cd /etc/init.d
# ./S80nfs stop
# ./S80nfs start
```

Usually, systems that use SVR4 (pronounced *Ess Vee Are Four*, short for *System V,
Release 4*) standards, such as UNIXWare or Red Hat Linux, will have these types of
startup and stop scripts. If your system is based more on the University of Berkeley
revision of UNIX (BSD, or *Berkley Standard Distribution*), as is the case with AIX or

Slackware Linux, everything will have a `start` command somewhere in a file called `/etc/rc.something`, but you won't have fine control over starts and stops.

You can check out who's allowed to use a given file system (the equivalent of a share under Windows NT) by looking at the `/etc/exports` file. If you add or change access in this file, you'll need to run the `exportfs -a` command. The host name you add should be listed in the `/etc/hosts` file or in your DNS zone (for example, `company.com`).

Socket to Me

Sometimes, a mere stopping and starting of a daemon won't help. In the case of `inetd`, you may be in a situation where the cure may be worse than the disease. In such cases, you'll need finer diagnostics.

Enter `netstat -a`. This command is to network sockets what `ps` is to processes (remember from Hour 1, "The Telephone Analogy: Becoming Familiar with Basic Networking Concepts," that a socket is like a phone extension that a service listens to for calls). `netstat` lists each socket that's being used for a current connection or being listened to for a connection. It tells you whether things are backlogged, where they are backlogged from, and which socket is in use on both sides of the call. `netstat -an` will allow you to look at the numeric values only, which is valuable when you want to keep name services out of the picture. Let's look at a specific example.

Suppose someone calls and tells you that he can't get into FROTZ. FROTZ is the Financial Remuneration with Overwhelming Trillions of Zeros system. He's very important to your place of employment, Frobozzco, so you're alarmed when someone can't get in. The user at the other end of the line is incoherent with rage and will not answer any of your questions.

You know by this person's name that he's in the Finance department. You can't get an answer to the basic question "Are other people having problems?" Therefore, you decide to find out for yourself. You quickly check the network map and see that Finance lives on the subnet `200.1.1.0`. In order to determine for yourself whether anybody else is having problems, you log in to the FROTZ UNIX host and type the following:

INPUT
```
netstat -a ¦ grep 200.1.1
```

You're rewarded with this:

OUTPUT

```
Proto send-q recv-q Local Address           Foreign Address    (State)
tcp   0      0      frotz.frob.com.telnet   200.1.1.10.1673    ESTABLISHED
tcp   0      0      frotz.frob.com.telnet   200.1.1.25.1975    ESTABLISHED
tcp   0      0      frotz.frob.com.telnet   200.1.1.27.1772    ESTABLISHED
tcp   0      0      frotz.frob.com.telnet   200.1.1.29.1968    ESTABLISHED
tcp   0      0      frotz.frob.com.telnet   200.1.1.33.1492    ESTABLISHED
tcp   0      0      frotz.frob.com.telnet   200.1.1.34.1444    ESTABLISHED
tcp   0      0      frotz.frob.com.telnet   200.1.1.35.2855    ESTABLISHED
```

ANALYSIS I've included the column headings for clarity; you wouldn't actually get them when searching for an address. It becomes apparent very quickly that people from the 200.1.1 network *are* in, and they're working just fine. (Actually, you could have used the who command, which, on most UNIX machines, tells you who is logged in and where they are logged in from. However, netstat will show you *any* service, not just Telnet.) You now know that people from 200.1.1.0 are logged into the system, and you suspect that the user's problem is workstation related.

proto is the protocol. In most cases, it will be tcp or udp, TCP being the equivalent of a phone call (circuit oriented) and UDP being the equivalent of tossing notes back and forth to each other (connectionless). You can find more on UDP in Hour 15, "Firewall and Proxy Server Basics," and Hour 18, "Lots of Different People in Your Neighborhood: In-Depth Application Troubleshooting."

send-q and recv-q are representations of holding places for sending and receiving data in the host's memory. You can think of them just the way you do a print queue; they hold stuff while waiting for processing. Unlike a print queue, they typically will be *empty* during normal operation. That is, these values will typically be 0 for local area networks, because local nets move pretty fast.

What if they're not zero? Well, a changing "send queue" can mean that the other end is processing data but is keeping up somehow. This is usually a normal state for a LAN print server; it really is a print queue, so it processes some data, then catches up, gets some more data, and keeps going. If you see a nonchanging, non-zero send queue for one socket but not others, it usually means that something on the other end has stopped accepting data.

A non-zero receive queue can mean that something on the UNIX host itself is running out of resources, and it's temporarily unable to process the incoming data. In practice, this is relatively rare.

The local address is, of course, the server you're typing netstat on. In this case, because we're discussing the Telnet service, the full address with extension is wefrotz. frobozz.com.telnet. Had we used netstat -an, it would have shown something like 192.168.55.10.23 (Telnet being socket 23). The foreign address is the other address—

12

the client machine. The socket doesn't matter as much here—just about any high-numbered socket that isn't already in use can be used on the client side.

> You can count the number of client/server sockets in use at any given time, say, for an `imap` mail server, by typing this:
>
> ```
> netstat -a ¦ grep imap ¦ wc -1
> ```

> You can find out which services your UNIX machine is offering to the world by typing this:
>
> ```
> netstat -a ¦ grep LISTEN
> ```
>
> This will show you which services are listening for new connections. Because the service names are usually close to or exactly the same as the program names (http service/`httpd` program), you can easily figure out which program is responsible for a given service.

Name Game

Without name services, very little works. Although you can usually rule out a name service problem by trying the same operation by IP address rather than name, name services that fail to work on the server end can be tricky.

> It's important to realize that existing connections will continue to work; it's only new ones that will typically fail.

A UNIX host typically performs a name lookup to whatever its name resolution host is *after* the connection is established in order to get the symbolic identity of the caller. Therefore, if name services have a problem, this can cause a domino effect that causes problems for other services.

I see a lot of problems in the field that are DNS related, even though some of them don't seem to be at first. For example, after a name server dies on a given UNIX host, Telnet sessions to that host can take a *long* time to show a login prompt. That is, even though the connection is accepted, and the `netstat -an` output *shows* there's a connection, *something* prevents the login prompt from being issued.

That something is the DNS server. The Telnet server is configured to look up all connecting Telnet addresses after they connect; although the name server is dead, the Telnet service keeps trying before it issues a login prompt. Depending on the operating system and Telnet implementation, this can result in long delays.

nslookup

The tool for checking name services is called nslookup. As the name implies, it can contact a name server (hence the *ns* in nslookup) and *look up* information from it. If you know your UNIX host is running named and should be answering name queries from itself and others, you can type this:

nslookup *hostname hostname*

You should get a response. If you get an error message, the named that runs on *hostname* is likely down.

> Note that you can use nslookup on any host, not just the one that you're logged into.

There's also an interactive mode that's most helpful for resolving complex DNS issues. I'll go into this feature in Hour 19, "Internet/Intranet Troubleshooting."

Pole Position

Sometimes a UNIX networking problem won't be in the higher-level services and programs—in other words, there will be times when it's not the "people behind the telephone," but rather the telephone or phone system itself. In order to make this determination, you can use a couple techniques and commands.

12

> When *nothing* seems to be working, you might have to find the UNIX console (the terminal that's hard-wired to the server) and log in from there. If the console isn't responsive, the UNIX server has locked up. This doesn't have anything to do with the network—it's a rare occurrence, but it does happen. Your only option here is to wince, turn the server off, and hope that it reboots okay.

Assuming that the console is working, it's time to roll up your sleeves and see why your UNIX server can't be seen from the network. Let's work from the inside out, assuming that, like Dr. Freud, all analysis begins with the self. The basic notion here is that you need a network card to get to anything. Let's check that first:

```
# ifconfig -a
lo      Link encap:Local Loopback
        inet addr:127.0.0.1  Bcast:127.255.255.255  Mask:255.0.0.0
        UP BROADCAST LOOPBACK RUNNING  MTU:2000  Metric:1
        RX packets:0 errors:0 dropped:0 overruns:0
        TX packets:37231 errors:0 dropped:0 overruns:0

eth0    Link encap:10Mbps Ethernet  HWaddr 00:00:C0:82:26:94
        inet addr:167.195.160.6  Bcast:167.195.160.255  Mask:255.255.255.0
        UP BROADCAST RUNNING MULTICAST  MTU:1500  Metric:1
        RX packets:816928 errors:0 dropped:0 overruns:0
        TX packets:654019 errors:0 dropped:0 overruns:0
        Interrupt:10 Base address:0x350 Memory:c8000-cc000
```

The key things to look for are the words up and running. If you don't see them, something has caused your network card to go down. Some network cards will go down due to a bad port on a hub, so try switching the port. A reboot may be in order, or you may indeed have a bad network card. You can also try netstat -i to check the error count and/or run ethstat to see what types of errors you might be getting. This may point to a network problem rather than UNIX problem.

The next thing you need to find out is whether your machine can talk to itself. Try pinging it:

```
$ ping 127.0.0.1
PING 127.0.0.1 (127.0.0.1): 56 data bytes
64 bytes from 127.0.0.1: icmp_seq=0 ttl=255 time=8.5 ms
64 bytes from 127.0.0.1: icmp_seq=1 ttl=255 time=6.8 ms
<CONTROL-C>
-127.0.0.1 ping statistics-
2 packets transmitted, 2 packets received, 0% packet loss
round-trip min/avg/max = 6.8/7.6/8.5 ms
```

Pay careful attention to that address: 127.0.0.1 is a special address, called the *loopback address*. If you can't ping it, you have something really odd going on. Again, a reboot may be in order. This is a *software* loopback, so a problem here does not point to hardware.

> The *loopback address* is a way for you to get your UNIX system to talk to its own TCP/IP programs rather than using the network card to communicate. When you successfully communicate through the loopback, you *rule out* the TCP/IP program (stack) as the cause of your trouble.

Next, try pinging your own network card. If, for example, your server's TCP/IP number is 192.168.99.5, try this:

```
$ ping 192.168.99.5
```

The output from this should look similar to the output for the loopback ping.

If this works out okay, try pinging the router. If this doesn't work, make sure you can see other workstations on the segment. Can they see the router? The router might be down, leading people on all other segments to assume that the UNIX host is down.

I discuss netstat -r (which shows you which route the UNIX host thinks packets should take through the network) as well as traceroute in Hour 14, "Router and Switch Basics." The traceroute command is a great way to find the routers that a packet needs to go through in order to get from point A to point B. The thing to know about it under UNIX is that not all implementations of UNIX have it. Most do, but there are still one or two proprietary implementations of UNIX that do not. However, you can always get it from ftp://ftp.ee.lbl.gov/traceroute.tar.Z. You'll need to be reasonably comfortable with the UNIX command line to use this, because it comes in source code form—it requires you to use the tar command to extract the source code and the make command to compile it.

Summary

UNIX hosts are typically reliable servers used to house databases, client/server applications, and Telnet sessions. They're also awesome for running Web and FTP servers.

Most UNIX services run through background programs called *daemons*. Some service problems can be solved by stopping and starting a daemon process.

Many times, you'll need to run commands as the root user. To get comfortable and become good at this, you'll probably want to set up a play system, where you're able to learn from your mistakes without affecting a crucial system.

You can keep track of the services and clients running on your system through the netstat -a command. A busy UNIX system can have hundreds or thousands of sockets open at any given time; you can track down the socket you're looking for by using netstat in conjunction with the grep command.

Ping is your best friend (as usual with TCP/IP troubleshooting) in determining whether a problem lies with the UNIX server, the network, or the router.

12

Workshop

Q&A

Q **I can't get to a file on my G: drive (it's mapped to my UNIX server's `/home` file system), but the person next to me can. When I log in as her, I can get to the file. What's up with this?**

A UNIX security and file permissions is a reasonably large topic, and I touch on it in Hour 18. To answer your question, though, it's likely that the file or directory belongs to a group that you do not belong to. Look at the group on the file using `ls -la` and add yourself to that group.

Q **We've recently gotten a new Internet Service Provider, and all of our IP numbers have changed. Now, every time I boot my UNIX system, I get "NFS Server Belboz not responding." What's going on?**

A It's likely that the Belboz system is only listed in the `/etc/hosts` file of the UNIX system. View the file, and you'll likely see that the TCP/IP number is wrong; change it to the new number.

Q **I hear that UNIX is less secure than other operating systems. True?**

A No. UNIX's problem is that it is *more configurable* than other operating systems, which means that sometimes it's misconfigured and is therefore less secure. Also, the level of knowledge about the internals of UNIX is pretty high—source code is available for some implementations, which allows hackers to probe for security holes in programs. Actually, even though Windows NT doesn't have source code publicly available, holes have been found in programs there. Just like any operating system, UNIX has several problematic, widespread server programs—such as `sendmail`—that have caused widespread publicity and security panics, but these have always been patched rather quickly.

Quiz

1. True or false? Root access is needed to use all networking commands in UNIX.
2. What does NFS stand for?

   A. Network File Server

   B. Nothing Falls Slowly

   C. Network Failure System

   D. Network File System

3. True or false? named does *not* use inetd as a receptionist server; named runs on its own, all the time, and is not invoked each time a user asks for it.

4. True or false? Linux is the only available free or low-cost UNIX flavor.

5. The difference between a UNIX server and a UNIX workstation is usually what?

   A. Different software

   B. Different bandwidth

   C. Different taste in restaurants

   D. Different hardware

6. It's most desirable to _____ when you encounter a problem with a UNIX service.

   A. Start and stop a process

   B. Reboot

   C. Call the police

   D. Ping

Answers to Quiz Questions

1. False

2. D

3. True

4. False

5. D

6. A

12

HOUR 13

NetWare Networking Basics

I met a traveler from an antique land
Who said: "Two vast and trunkless legs of stone
Stand in the desert. Near them, on the sand,
Half sunk, a shattered visage lies, whose frown,
And wrinkled lip, and sneer of cold command,
Tell that its sculptor well those passions read
Which yet survive, stamped on these lifeless things,
The hand that mocked them and the heart that fed.
And on the pedestal these words appear—
"My name is Ozymandias, king of kings:
Look on my works, ye Mighty, and despair!"
Nothing beside remains. Round the decay
Of that colossal wreck, boundless and bare
The lone and level sands stretch far away.

—Percy Bysshe Shelley

Novell could be compared to the Roman empire; it owned the entire networking map at one time and was considered the only game in town for serious file and print networking. In recent years, however, Novell has lost some significant market and mind share to Microsoft's NT. Has the time come for Rome's fall? Probably not. Novell's products have bounced back considerably from their state of decay five years ago, and they have the only mature directory service shipping today—a really big deal to network geeks. The speed and reliability of Novell servers still make them a compelling choice. Also, because Novell servers run in a nonwindowed environment, they take far fewer resources to run than Windows NT, because they can concentrate on file and print services, not windowing.

Still, a lot of shops out there are ripping out their old Novell 3.*x* servers and putting in NT servers. This is more or less a holy war among geeks: As with the Token-Ring/Ethernet battle, you have your NT zealots and your NetWare zealots. Who's right? Look, they're all crazy.

Nonetheless, I'm going to take a firm stand here: NetWare is good for some things, and NT is good for others. Seriously, there are certain client/server applications that just won't run on a Novell server. However, Novell does offer really fast file and print services, and it has one thing that no other viable commercial network operating system offers: a really good directory service.

NDS Networking

If you have NetWare in your shop and it was a recent purchase, chances are that it was bought because NetWare is where the Novell Directory Service (NDS) lives. Specifically, NDS is a way to have all your server, user, login, security, and configuration information on a distributed, partitioned, hierarchical database, which really makes for one-stop shopping when you're configuring the network.

Whoa! What's this distributed, partitioned, hierarchical stuff? This sounds like a marketing phrase. Well, it is, but it's also pretty cool stuff. In a nutshell, NDS allows you to manage more users and servers with fewer people—which is pretty attractive to management.

NDS is *hierarchical* because it has multiple levels on which information can be stored. This keeps each level uncluttered, and makes things simple for you. Naturally, simplicity makes troubleshooting easier.

Old versions of DOS didn't let you create folders; all your files used to be just sort of plopped in one location on a disk. Can you imagine if you could only save your Office documents to one place? Doesn't that seem crazy? This probably gives you a sense of how important a hierarchy is to a network directory.

The downside to a hierarchical directory is that user names now have multiple parts to them. They still have a name (referred to as the *common name*), but there's also an identifier for where this user fits into the hierarchical *tree*.

For example, `Quizro.finance.ny.frob` refers to the user Quizro, who works in the Finance department of the New York office of Frobozz Magical Gadgets, Inc. You can think of this as an Internet address without the @ sign; it's just taken for granted that the first portion is the user's name.

The NDS is *distributed* because several copies of the database live on multiple servers, making it impossible to lose the entire database if one server goes down. Very neat!

Finally, the NDS is *partitioned* because different levels of the hierarchy can be treated separately. This means the database can have several different segments, not all of which need to be updated all the time. Partitioning your NDS database allows you to cut down on network traffic; if you have 10,000 users, of which only 1,000 at a time are geographically close to each other, why would you want to exchange the entire 10,000-user database when you update it?

Even more importantly, partitioning lets you have a large, connected database without hogging up your wide area traffic. Let's say you run an importing company with offices in New York and Savannah. You have a leased line between these offices that connects the office networks together. Because you pay for the amount of time used or data sent, you're interested in using the line as little as possible. You're also interested in keeping the pipeline clear so that people who are trying to communicate between the offices do so as quickly as possible.

You would want to create a partition between the Savannah site and the New York site, because this tells NDS that the Savannah and New York databases should be treated as separate "distribution" entities. Because they're not joined at the hip, the frequent replication traffic that occurs between the distributed NDS servers will not clog up the pipe between New York and Savannah.

Of course, this makes the NDS attractive, but power comes at a price. Novell servers do not run using the same Windows desktop metaphor that you've come to know and love. Instead, they run using a text-based console, similar to what you used to see under DOS.

13

Don't knock it, though. Again, Novell servers aren't busy fiddling with graphics and windows and the overhead that goes with those things. This lack of complexity and overhead makes for a reasonably easy-to-troubleshoot server that runs faster on less hardware.

Although the server runs in character mode, you'll use the Novell utilities for managing the NDS in the Windows environment; for example, the NWADMN32 tool, which is used by the working network administrator to add, delete, and modify users, groups, security, and so on, runs under Windows NT and Windows 95. This tool is windowed, but because the windowing happens at your workstation, it doesn't bog down the server.

If you have an older NetWare 3.x server, you can get a Windows-based SYSCON system manager program by upgrading to 3.2—apart from its Y2K readiness. Other 3.x versions are no longer supported by Novell. To get NDS, though, you still need to upgrade to 4.x or higher.

If NetWare 3 servers don't support NDS, what *do* they support? Each server must maintain its own list of users and groups, called a *bindery.* The bindery of a server is a standalone entity that does not communicate with other servers at all. If common groups and user names are desired between servers, the network administrators must manually synchronize them.

The bindery has become obsolete with NetWare 4.x and higher, but there's still a *bindery emulation mode*, which makes a NetWare 4.x server respond to NetWare 3.x–style bindery requests.

Das Basics

Any Novell server is fundamentally a 32-bit program called SERVER.EXE that runs from a DOS prompt (yep, just like Windows 3.x used to run from a DOS prompt). This means you still have an AUTOEXEC.BAT file on your C drive—it just typically consists of one line: SERVER.EXE. This server program actually doesn't do much; for example, it can't network on its own or access hard drives. When you load the SERVER.EXE program, the server console screen opens. This screen, shown in Figure 13.1, is a text-based interpreter that can accept various commands.

FIGURE 13.1

RCONSOLE (or Remote Console) allows you to remotely control the server console from your desk.

NLMs

In addition to accepting commands, the server program acts as a traffic cop for all the server resources, and it relies on loadable modules to provide specific services. In general, these modules are referred to as *NLMs*, short for *NetWare loadable modules*. NLMs provide everything from a statistic reporting program (MONITOR.NLM) to configuration programs (INSTALL.NLM); in addition, NLMs enable the server to speak certain protocols (TCPIP.NLM).

Special cases of NLMs include older disk drivers (for example, IDE.DSK), newer disk drivers (for example, IDE.HAM), and network card drivers (for example, NE2000.LAN). All these modules act in concert through SERVER.EXE to make your server talk to the network and respond appropriately to requests. Yikes! There are a lot of pieces and parts. A typical NetWare server has dozens of NLMs loaded at one time. When everything works, it's great.

Trouble Triage

One of the challenges presented to a NetWare troubleshooter is keeping track of all these NLMs and identifying any trouble presented by a malfunctioning NLM. This was really terrible in the past; you had to download many different files to fully "patch" your server. Nowadays, you can simply get the latest service pack from Novell (taking a cue from Microsoft, which has always offered one-stop shopping for fixes). Service packs are really simple to apply.

13

Patch Plethora

Just as Microsoft does for Windows NT, Novell considers certain problems serious enough to issue hot-fix patches (patches that are supplied to the user population before the next service pack is issued). Although not all patches apply for all environments, you might find you need to patch the server in order to fix a certain problem.

> Any time you experience problems with your Novell server, check the Novell Knowledge Base at http://support.novell.com. In addition to using the Novell Knowledge Base to search for your current problem, you can also use it to check out the minimum patch list. This can be a great first step in troubleshooting, because you can easily verify that you have all the patches in the minimum patch list loaded on your server.

As a matter of fact, even if you have Novell's Premium Support, the first thing the support staff will have you do is make sure you've applied the latest and greatest patches. Many, many problems are patch related.

> Patches can fix, but patches can also destroy. You shouldn't get *too* paranoid, though, because the entire industry has come a long, long way toward making the patch process as safe as possible. For example, the patch process now keeps backups of your previous files. Nonetheless, for your own sanity, make sure that you have good, verified backups of your servers before applying any patches. (This applies to *all* patches, not just Novell patches.)

I have to give Novell some credit here: It has been good at 'fessing up to its problems of late. Novell has recognized its problems, taken the blame, and issued fixes for these problems. In some sense, being humbled by Microsoft has been good for Novell, because it's no longer a solitary giant in the networking industry. Now it's a leaner and hungrier network player that, like the car rental company, "tries harder."

NLM Party

What about the NLMs that Novell doesn't provide? In other words, what about third-party NLMs? Examples of these include backup software, network card drivers, software metering programs, and server-level virus protection programs. If you're the type of person who doesn't go for nit-picky record keeping, then keeping track of these revision levels will be a nightmare for you. This is particularly true if you have multiple servers in the mix and have multiple folks working on these servers; you never know if someone has updated one server but not the other.

Accordingly, when you're having problems with one server but not another, you must play the Sesame Street game and compare NLM levels. You can do this manually by typing **modules** at the server console prompt (see Figure 13.2).

FIGURE 13.2

Getting a list of modules from an IntranetWare 4.11 server.

If this seems like a lot of work to do manually, you're right! Go download (for free) the CONFIG.NLM tool (along with the Config Reader) from Novell's site:

http://support.novell.com

CONFIG.NLM reads the configuration of your server and writes a CONFIG.TXT report to your SYS:SYSTEM directory (see Figure 13.3). The Windows-based Config Reader will read the output that CONFIG.NLM drops off in the system directory and process it to make it easy to read.

The Config Reader, shown in Figure 13.4, automatically downloads current information from the Novell Web site and then shows you an overview of your system, points out NLMs that are out of date, and automates the comparison of two given servers. This makes it much easier for you to see how one server differs from another.

13

FIGURE 13.3

CONFIG.NLM *must be loaded on each server before you can use the Config Reader.*

FIGURE 13.4

The Windows-based Config Reader makes it easy to find out "which of these things are not like the other."

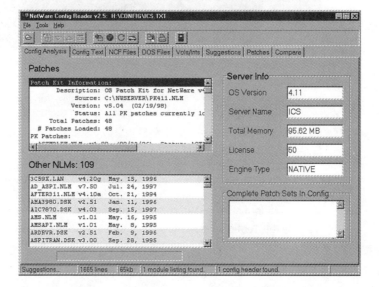

Directory Doldrums

Although NDS is a wonderful thing, sometimes communication problems or hardware problems that have nothing to do with the NDS itself can cause damage to it. This damage can become evident in a number of ways—most notably with problems that have to do with logging in, as well as problems with security levels once you are logged in.

Actually, any program that depends on the NDS can be affected by NDS damage or corruption. This includes—but isn't limited to—print server programs, virus protection programs, automated rollout tools, workstation management tools, and so on.

You can fix many NDS problems simply by typing

LOAD DSREPAIR

at the console prompt and then selecting Unattended Full Repair from the menu (see Figure 13.5).

FIGURE 13.5

Like ScanDisk for your hard drive, DSRepair.NLM *will fix many NDS problems.*

Running DSREPAIR couldn't hurt in many situations, and it allows you to rule out NDS damage when dealing with a complex problem.

Again, make sure you are running the latest Novell patches—many odd NDS problems have been fixed.

13

Your "Friend," the ABEND

If you've run Novell products for any length of time, you know how aggravating it can be to get an ABEND. An ABEND, short for *abnormal end*, is when the server can't handle a situation that has arisen and must terminate its operation because data might get corrupted otherwise. It's a difficult call—would you rather continue working and risk data corruption, or would you rather be down?

What causes an ABEND? In a nutshell, hardware problems and software problems cause ABENDs. It's understandable that a bad CPU or bad memory could take down the entire server—after all, without good memory or a working CPU, it's sort of hard to run programs. But why should one program (such as your Web server program, for example) cause the entire server to go down? Fortunately, the latest Novell server software has started to make distinctions as to what constitutes a major problem versus a minor one.

This is actually one of the really good reasons to upgrade from an earlier version of NetWare to the current versions, IntraNetWare 4.11 or NetWare 5.0.

 Novell called the 4.11 version of its NetWare operating system *IntraNetWare* to emphasize the intranet services included with the product. The 5.0 version has dropped the *Intra* and is, once again, *NetWare*. Don't ask me, man, I didn't do it!

Novell now classifies applications in two different ways:

- Applications that use the same memory and so on that the server program uses (dangerous, but fast).

- Applications that use a special protected mode where the amount of damage they can do to the server itself if they misbehave is minimized (slower, but safer). (Think of this as the rock climber who climbs bare-handed—and quickly—versus the rock climber using pitons, who is slower but safer.)

Novell calls the latter way "running a program in a different domain," but whatever it's called, it's a lot more reliable, and it's automatic in the latest releases. I don't know of anyone who will complain because the server runs two percent slower due to its increased reliability.

If you're still on a lower level of NetWare, or even if you've upgraded to IntraNetWare, you might have hardware-related ABENDs, or ABENDs due to software that isn't running in a protected domain. Refer to Novell TID (Technical Information Document) #2917538 or just do a search on *ABEND Troubleshoot* at the Knowledge Base (http://support.novell.com). It's very well worth your time.

Big Monitor Is Watching

As much as I love the Microsoft System Monitor, I have room in my heart for Novell Monitor as well. Even though it's text based (it's not graphical at all), Novell Monitor is rather complete and can be a troubleshooter's best friend. You simply type

`LOAD MONITOR`

at the console prompt, use the menus, and the world is at your fingertips.

Just about every resource on a Novell server is tracked by the Monitor, and this is a good thing. Here are some really good things the Monitor monitors:

- Server connections and session statistics
- File locks (who's using the file?)
- Hardware resources (CPU, memory)
- Processes (subprograms)

Suppose a user reports that she can't get into the server. Once you've established that others are working with the server, you might try to get in yourself and discover you cannot. A quick check of the monitor screen reveals how many connections are in use—you might see that you're out of server connections.

Each user who is logged into the server uses one server license. If you run out of connections, you'll most likely have to purchase more licenses from Novell.

13

When the server runs out of disk space, you can walk through Monitor's user connection list and see who has been using a lot of disk space lately; the results look something like those shown in Figure 13.6.

In this case, you can see that the evil user JFeldman has written 1,128KB (or 1.12MB) in the one minute he's been logged in. He might not be your culprit, though—1MB usually doesn't overflow a server volume. You should look through the other connections for something more like 5–10MB or more. Also notice the network address: JFeldman's logged in from network 1D, MAC address 00-00-f6-88-d9-4b, and socket 404C.

Once you find the offending user, you get a quick confession. For other ways of finding disk space wasters, see Hour 18, "Lots of Different People in Your Neighborhood: In-Depth Application Troubleshooting."

FIGURE 13.6

You can use Monitor to view connection information.

You might not be able to install software because a shared file is in use. Getting this message is really frustrating, because all Windows will tell you is that you *can't* write to the file, not *who* is preventing you from writing to it.

You can find who's using the file by using the Monitor. Simply go to File Open|Lock Activity menu in the first Monitor menu and then select the file you're interested in. The Monitor will show you the connection numbers of the people who are using the file (see Figure 13.7). You can then navigate the connection list and find out the login names of those people; once you know who the people are, you can kindly ask them to get out of the program for the moment.

FIGURE 13.7

The Monitor can show you who currently has a file "locked."

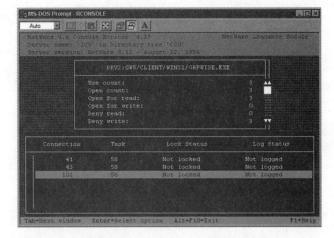

No Need to Fear; Monitor Man Is Here!

Monitor has saved my hide more than once. One time, the network administrator and I were completely stumped by what seemed to be a backup program problem. The backup program, which ran as an NLM, needed to log into the NDS to do its work. Every week or so, the backup program would complain about being unable to log in, and we would reboot the server to enable the backup program to log in again.

The backup software people pointed the finger at Novell: "It's an NDS problem," they said. "There must be something wrong with your NDS; it's nothing to do with our software." Searches on the backup vendor's site as well as Novell's site revealed nothing; fortunately, when we called Novell, they concurred that it certainly sounded like an NDS issue. We pursued this for awhile without getting anywhere.

Then, eureka! During one session of vain attempts to make the backup software behave before we rebooted, a user on the server dropped off due to workstation problems; when he tried to log back in, he couldn't. We checked the Monitor, and sure enough, we were running out of connections. Coincidence? Could be. The next time the backup problem occurred, we checked the number of connections on the server, and sure enough, we were running out each time.

Why hadn't we noticed this earlier? Usually, users were already logged in and working before the backup started acting up. If the backup was acting up, it was usually at 7:00 in the morning, before most folks tried to log in. That meant it was rebooted before others could notice the lack of connections.

We licensed more connections, but even then we kept running out of connections. What was going on?

13

By looking at the Monitor's connection list, we discovered that all the extra connections were coming from the server itself. Remember from Figure 13.6 that a connection display will show the IPX address of the connection station. In this case, the extra connections were coming from the server's unique internal IPX number (see the section later in this chapter titled "IPX/SPX"). This definitely pointed to an NLM.

> This situation would have been awful to troubleshoot without the Monitor. For example, it would have been very difficult to divide and conquer this problem, because it was an intermittent problem and we needed all of our NLMs loaded during the workday. We could not arbitrarily run without given NLMs.

Because of the Monitor's close tracking of such things, we were able to find a resource called *Service Connections* and check each NLM's number of connections (see Figure 13.8). The one with the abnormally large value was our culprit. Once we unloaded this module (which happened to be Novell supplied), all the extra connections went away, and the problem was solved.

FIGURE 13.8

The module that was grabbing all of our licensed connections couldn't hide from the Monitor.

We reported this to Novell. Although Novell already knew about the problem, the patch had not yet made it into the mainstream. Once we did a search on the NLM's name, we found that there was a TID on this problem. Unfortunately, because we weren't really clear on what exactly was going on while we were searching, we didn't get a hit on this. The problem was quickly solved after we applied the patch. Three cheers for the Monitor!

Protocol Problems

If you're the one who installed your server, you're probably already familiar with the INETCFG NLM, which I call the Swiss Army Knife of Novell networking. This NLM, similar to the Windows Network Control Panel, loads network drivers and binds and configures protocols to them. You can use it to quickly glance at the way things are configured.

Alternatively, you can simply type **CONFIG** at the console prompt (*not* LOAD CONFIG; that's the configuration file generator). INETCFG tells you the way things *should* be, whereas CONFIG shows you the way things *are* (see Figure 13.9).

FIGURE 13.9

The CONFIG output of a server that has one network card and one network protocol (IPX/SPX).

If CONFIG doesn't match up with INETCFG, you might have a problem. You can sometimes resolve this by telling the server to enact a networking "do over." Simply type the following:

REINITIALIZE SYSTEM

Scary as this command seems, all it does is reload network card drivers, if necessary, and bind protocols to those cards. It's really fast—so fast that I've run it on a test server, and my session didn't get dumped. However, I sure wouldn't try it on a live production server.

13

IPX/SPX

I've already talked a little bit about how automatic IPX/SPX configuration is. Older versions of NetWare did not have automatic server configuration; they left it up to the administrator. Newer versions will scan the network and attempt to set things up right. Let's take a look at the way things should be on your server's IPX/SPX configuration anyway, because if they're not right, you're in for trouble.

Each IPX/SPX segment needs a network number. This is not a big deal; you can select pretty much any hexadecimal number. The only caveat is that each IPX segment has be unique. The hard-and-fast rule is this: If the segments are connected via a switch, they should have the same network number because the segments are basically the same network. If, on the other hand, network segments are connected via router, they *must* have unique numbers. If the IPX network number for each network segment is not unique, you can run into problems, such as the inability for the servers and workstations on the segments to "see" each other.

NetWare is just full of unique prima donnas; there's another number, particular to each server, called the server's *internal IPX network number*. This number must also be unique, and it can be really useful in tracking down problems (as you saw in "No Need to Fear; Monitor Man Is Here!" when I tracked down the extra connections to the server itself). This number is hexadecimal; if it's the same as another server's number, then it, too, can cause big problems (particularly if a server is acting as a router). In that case, duplicate internal IPX numbers will cause routing to stop working.

If you don't know what a particular server's internal IPX network number is, or what the network number is on the attached networks, just type `CONFIG` (just like with the spaghetti sauce, it's in there).

Server or Router

Each IntraNetWare or NetWare server with more than one network card in it automatically acts as a router. Without giving away too much from Hour 14, "Router and Switch Basics," any router, by definition, needs more than one network card because it connects one network to another network.

The only IPX/SPX routing knowledge that you might need to know from a troubleshooting standpoint is that there are two kinds of IPX/SPX routing: NLSP (NetWare Link Services Protocol) and RIP (Routing Information Protocol). A NetWare server that's configured for RIP can't talk to an NLSP router unless the NLSP router is running in RIP-compatibility mode. (See Hour 14 for a quick comparison of RIP and NLSP.) I haven't seen a lot of problems related to this, but it's worth knowing that there *are* differences between RIP (older) and NLSP (newer).

TCP/IP

You'll configure TCP/IP the way you do any protocol: from `INETCFG.NLM`. The basic configuration is just the way you'd configure a workstation. You do have, however, a couple more things to configure on a server, most notably the *services* that the server offers. To do this, use the UNICON utility. You can use UNICON to check the service configurations, as well as to start and stop the services if you suspect they've gone to la-la land. As you can see from Figure 13.10, UNICON will configure the following items:

- DNS
- NIS (you probably won't need this unless you're a hard-core UNIX shop)
- UNIX print services
- FTP

FIGURE 13.10

UNICON will config-ure UNIX-like services on your NetWare server.

See the UNI in UNICON? Think it might be referring to UNIX? You're right! All these services, though ostensibly generic TCP/IP services, got their start in the UNIX world.

You can also check TCP/IP configuration files (or possibly restore the configu-rations from a backup tape) in the SYS:ETC directory.

13

In particular, the SYS:ETC/RESOLV.CFG is a really important configuration file—symbolic name lookup (DNS) won't work unless this is configured prop-erly.

The TCP Con Game

When you load TCPCON, you can check more TCP/IP-related statistics and functions than you'd ever want to. TCPCON can handle many functions, as shown in Table 13.1.

TABLE 13.1   TCP/IP FUNCTIONS AVAILABLE FROM TCPCON

Function	TCPCON Navigation
Check TCP/IP statistics and error counts	Statistics menu
Check the routing table	IP routing table
Check current TCP or UDP socket table (just like `netstat -a` in UNIX or Windows)	Protocol Information| TCP *or* UDP|Connections
Check the MAC-to-TCP/IP address table (just like `arp -a` in UNIX or Windows)	Protocol Information| IP|IP Address Translations

Other life-saving TCP/IP tools include these:

- **LOAD PING**   Standard ping (but you can ping multiple stations at a time)
- **LOAD IPTRACE**   Novell's answer to traceroute

 Can't load IPTRACE or PING? Believe it or not, these weren't always included in the standard Novell TCP/IP distribution. Load the latest patches, and you'll magically have these tools.

Summary

Novell NDS is one compelling reason shops haven't totally abandoned the Novell network operating system in favor of NT. A Novell server is nothing more than a fancy 32-bit DOS program, but its lean-and-mean paradigm translates into you getting more oomph out of your hardware investment. The server program acts as a broker between the various NLMs that make the system work; therefore, the server itself is basically a conglomerate of NLMs. The modularity of the system also means that one malfunctioning NLM can ruin your whole day, but take heart—tools exist to manage what can seem to be a daunting NLM tracking and upgrading task.

The Monitor can help you with tough troubleshooting jobs, because it keeps track of every resource available to the server. In addition to keeping track of server connections, it keeps track of memory and CPU resources, as well as what each NLM process utilizes.

IPX/SPX is a reasonably easy protocol to configure, but most shops need TCP/IP. Both are configurable through INETCFG.NLM. TCP/IP applications can be configured through UNICON, and many statistics and internal tables can be viewed through the TCPCON. What's more, Novell now includes standard tools such as PING and IPTRACE (traceroute) in its TCP/IP distribution.

Workshop

Q&A

Q Why doesn't Novell just get rid of the concept of ABENDs?

A Every operating system, whether it's UNIX (kernel panics) or NT (the Blue Screen of Death), has unrecoverable errors. It's just the nature of the beast. Nobody wants an operating system to keep running after the foundation has been undermined. The thought is: it's much better to reboot than to have to restore all the lost data due to the server not showing the good judgement to stop playing with the data.

You can type the following command on your Novell server to make it reboot automatically after software ABENDs, which at least automates the recovery process most times (set it to 2 if you want it to reboot after hardware-related ABENDs, as well):

SET AUTO RESTART AFTER ABEND=1

Q My friend who runs a Novell server says that sometimes when he tries to unload an NLM, the console prompt never comes back. Isn't there any way to recover from this?

A Glad you asked. Novell IntraNetWare 4.11 and higher will allow you to type Ctrl+Alt+Esc at the console. This generates the following prompt:

Down server and exit to DOS?

The answer to this question is yes. Although I wish there were a way to run another console prompt, or at least to free up the console prompt when this happens, so far Novell hasn't obliged.

If you still have NetWare 3.x around, you can use the FCONSOLE program to down a server that's not responding; the Ctrl+Alt+Esc key combination won't work.

13

Quiz

1. What does *hierarchical* mean?

    A. Having hieroglyphic translation of ancient computer records

    B. Having multiple levels

    C. Having the ability to recover from errors

    D. Having multiple segments of a database

2. A distributed database can _____.

    A. live on multiple servers

    B. make a set of information more available

    C. Neither A nor B

    D. Both A and B

3. True or false? Partitioning of a large network database makes it more manageable.

4. The main Novell server program is called what?

    A. `SERVER.COM`

    B. `SERVER.EXE`

    C. `SERVER.NLM`

    D. `SERVER.LAN`

5. When you experience trouble with your Novell server, it's a good idea to check what?

    A. The hard disk

    B. The LAN card

    C. Patch levels

    D. Critical NLM BIOS

6. IPX/SPX servers each need a unique _____.

    A. internal network number

    B. Internet network number

    C. Internet nucleus number

    D. internal nucleus number

7. The TCP/IP protocol and basic services may be configured from
   _____.

    A. TCPCON

    B. INETCFG

    C. UNICON and TCPCON

    D. INETCFG and UNICON

Answers to Quiz Questions

1. B
2. D
3. True
4. B
5. C
6. A
7. D

13

HOUR 14

Router and Switch Basics

Although a Beethoven symphony sounds much different than a Bach invention, both follow the same fundamental rules of theory and composition. Although there's an awful lot of room for creativity and inventiveness within the scope of theory and composition rules, if these rules aren't followed, composers may end up with something that sounds like trash cans in the alley.

With the dozens of hardware-based routers and switches on the market, it would be difficult, if not impossible, to address the specific ways that each of them operates. Fortunately, they, too, follow a basic theory and composition germane to routers and switches; I'll discuss the theory behind routing and switching in this hour and throw in a couple of practical suggestions. Combine this with your router or switch documentation, and you'll have a pretty good one-two punch that should take out many of your router- or switch-based problems.

Theory and Practice

Why talk about routing and switching in the same breath? Well, fundamentally, a router and a switch operate in pretty much the same way: Each receives a packet on one of its interfaces and spits the packet out on another interface. It's just that the network layer for a router is different than the layer for a switch; routers work on the *protocol* layer (for example, TCP/IP), whereas switches work on the *data link* layer (that is, they talk directly to network cards).

When network geeks refer to network conversations in layers, they're referring to the OSI (Open Standards Institute) model of networking, which consists of an imaginary cake with the following seven layers:

- Physical
- Data link
- Network
- Transport
- Session
- Presentation
- Application

Note that not all these layers have one-to-one representations in real-life networks. Some of this is really ivory-tower stuff, but some of it is useful when thinking about your real-life network. For example, *physical layer* refers to the electronic rules and signaling that go on in an Ethernet wire, whereas *data link layer* refers to how network cards have card-to-card (MAC) conversations. *Network layer* refers to your network protocol (TCP/IP or IPX/SPX). *Application layer* refers to things such as services (Web and FTP services, for example). All the other stuff is really geeky, and we won't go into it. Whew!

By definition, both routers and switches are referred to as *multihomed hosts*—that is, they have more than one network interface connected to more than one network segment. You can think of this as routers and switches having more than one network they call home. Isn't that sweet?

In reality, although routers and switches are spoken about in different breaths, most large switches have routing capabilities, and most advanced routers have switching (or what used to be called *bridging*) capabilities. Therefore, for practical considerations, it's worth realizing that your switch may be configured to perform routing functions, and that your router may be configured to perform switching functions. See Figure 14.1 for the practical difference between a router and a switch (note the different IP addresses of the networks connected to the router versus the networks connected to the switch).

FIGURE 14.1

The basic difference between a router and a switch: All the networks connected to a switch have the same network numbers.

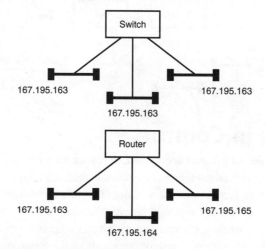

A switch is usually a wire-speed device that's able to spit out packets as fast as it sucks them in. This means that you usually don't switch over a slow link (that is, wide-area link). The reason for this is that data link communication is usually very, very timing dependent—which makes sense, because data link stuff is usually on the same "party line" without a "monkey in the middle." Therefore, you don't want to potentially mess up communications by messing with the timing. This is one instance where a switch and a router don't typically interchange, and where you usually want to use a router somewhere in the mix (see Figure 14.2).

14

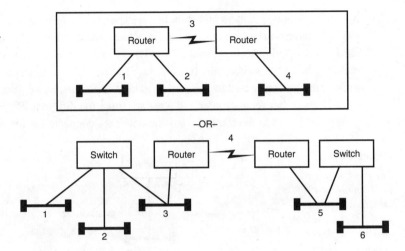

Figure 14.2

Wide-area applications typically have a router in the middle.

Configuring in Comfort

You'll definitely need to get well acquainted with your router or switch documentation. Although the theory behind routers and switches is the same, the way each switch or router is configured differs as much as a Philip Glass libretto differs from *The Magic Flute*. This will be particularly true if you have a limited opportunity to play with your device—for example, when you come into the picture *after* it has been installed and gone into production. (People have no sense of humor about these things. Once any device is in production, for some reason, it's considered rude to start arbitrarily changing things to see what happens.)

In all seriousness, if you can get a hold of the device before it goes into production, so much the better. Being familiar with the commands, error-reporting facilities, and configuration procedure of a device makes you much more able to handle problems as they come up during production.

One thing is reasonably consistent among routers and switches—they are all usually configurable via the following items:

- Telnet
- The Web
- A dumb terminal

The dumb terminal option is the most universal—it allows you to communicate with the device even if the network is down.

If your switch or router has a dumb terminal mode, you can connect your PC's serial port to it using a null modem cable (available at most Radio Shacks or computer supply stores). The connection at the device will either be DB-9 (male) or DB-25 (male); if the connection is something else, it's probably not a dumb terminal port.

After you connect the cable, you can then use just about any modem program (ProComm, HyperTerminal, NetTerm, and so on) to connect to it. The most common settings for dumb terminal mode are as follows: 8 data bits, no parity, one stop bit, 9600bps. This is sometimes written as *9600-8-N-1*.

For some crazy reason, most routers and switches don't allow for backup of their configuration information. So no, you can't hook up a tape drive to a router or switch, and most of them (though not all) won't let you download their configurations to a server that *does* have a tape drive on it. (Were routers and switches invented by Russian Roulette junkies?)

Bottom line: Make sure you have all configuration information well documented. You can usually do a SHOW CONFIGURATION command while logged into the router; if you capture this to a file with your terminal program, you can print it out as a poor man's backup. Regardless, switches and routers are particularly crucial places to keep good change logs.

Router Theory

Each router listens on each one of its multiple interfaces for route requests. Remember from Hour 1, "The Telephone Analogy: Becoming Familiar with Basic Networking Concepts," how we discussed that a packet is the smallest unit of communication between two network cards? Well, when a network card gives the router a packet destined for a different network segment, the router must make a decision as to which of its network interfaces that packet must go out of. If the router is connected directly to the destination segment, it just plops it out of the interface that's connected to that segment; otherwise, it must hand it off to another router that *is* attached to that segment (or is closer to the directly connected router).

Think of the packet as being like you as a teenager, but without a car. You can walk anywhere you like locally, but to go to your friend's house on the other side of town, you need to ride the bus. You can pick up your local bus line, but you might have to transfer to one or more different bus lines to reach your final destination.

14

How does each workstation know the protocol address of its router? Most times, an administrator has entered the address into the workstation's configuration. But you should know that there's also something called *router discovery*, which allows the workstation to search for a router on the subnet.

Routing Tables

Obviously, if the router has a direct connection to a particular segment, it knows how to route the packet there. But what if the router you hand the packet to *isn't* directly connected to the destination segment? How does the router know which "bus line" the packet should take?

Each router maintains an internal table of every network that it knows about. This is called a *routing table*. The routing table consists of a list of network numbers, which interface or router this network number is reachable through, and how costly this route is in terms of time or distance. A routing table for Router 1 in Figure 14.3 is shown in Table 14.1.

FIGURE 14.3

A sample routed network.

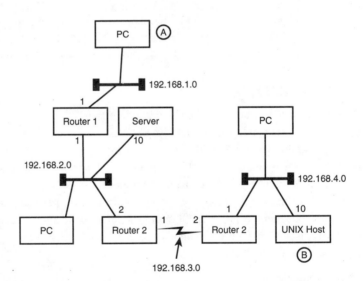

TABLE 14.1   ROUTING TABLE FOR ROUTER 1

Network	Next Hop	Metric
192.168.1.0	192.168.1.1	0 (Direct)
192.168.2.0	192.168.2.1	0 (Direct)
192.168.3.0	192.168.2.2	1
192.168.4.0	192.168.2.2	2

> Depending on your router, the words *next hop* in the router table might be replaced with words such as *destination* or *gateway address*. The word *metric* might be listed as *cost*. In this case, *metric* refers to how many hops away the network is from the router.
>
> For example, look at the map in Figure 14.3 and count how many other routers you must go through to get from Router 1 to 192.168.1.0. Trick question: You don't have to go through any other routers, so the hop count is 0. How many from Router 1 to 192.168.3.0? Right, one hop—through Router 2.

The format of this table will differ depending on what type of router Router 1 is, but the content will be similar. Notice that a routing table can list only "next hop" destinations that are directly reachable by that router. In other words, a router only objectively knows about networks that it's physically connected to, just like a city bus "knows" about only transfer points that exist on streets on its route. All other networks are reachable by routers that are connected to a subnet that this router is connected to.

A Couple of Milliseconds in the Life of Joe Packet

Let's follow a concrete example by tracing a packet through the network shown in Figure 14.3. The PC at point A wants to telnet to the UNIX server at point B. Because we're talking about routing, we don't care about the specifics of the network conversation; we just want to trace how the call gets from point A to point B. Here are the steps:

1. The "middleware" that allows an application program to talk to your network card's driver is called a *stack*. Your PC's TCP/IP protocol middleware (stack) must open up a connection to the UNIX server at 192.168.4.10. The TCP/IP stack knows what its own IP address is (192.168.1.20) and sees that 192.168.4 is not on the same network. Therefore, instead of establishing a conversation with the destination, the IP stack will establish a conversation with the router.

14

2. The IP stack passes the first packet of the Telnet conversation to the router at 192.168.1.1 (Router 1).

3. The router first looks up the destination network in its routing table. In this case, the destination *is* listed in Router 1's routing table as being reachable through the 192.168.2.1 router (Router 2).

> If the destination network is *not* in the routing table, the router drops the packet and sends back a special IP packet saying that this destination is unreachable.

4. Router 1 starts a conversation up with Router 2, whose routing table is shown in Table 14.2.

TABLE 14.2 ROUTING TABLE FOR ROUTER 2

Network	Next Hop	Metric
192.168.2.0	192.168.2.2	0 (Direct)
192.168.3.0	192.168.3.1	0 (Direct)
192.168.1.0	192.168.2.1	1
192.168.4.0	192.168.3.2	1

5. The packet still needs to get to point B from Router 2. Router 2 looks up the destination network (192.168.4) in its routing table and finds out that it does not have a direct connection to that network. Instead, the next hop is at 192.168.3.2 (Router 3), which is on the other side of the wide-area connection. Router 3's routing table is shown in Table 14.3.

TABLE 14.3 ROUTING TABLE FOR ROUTER 3

Network	Next Hop	Metric
192.168.3.0	192.168.3.2	0 (Direct)
192.168.4.0	192.168.4.1	0 (Direct)
192.168.1.0	192.168.3.1	2
192.168.2.0	192.168.3.1	1

6. Finally! The destination, 192.168.4.10, is on a directly connected network! All Router 3 needs to do is to establish an Ethernet-level connection with the UNIX host and hand off all the PC's packets that it receives from Router 2. The packets are flowing and the planets are starting to align—what could be better?

Of course, responses from the UNIX host destined for the PC at point A go from the UNIX host to Router 3, to Router 2, to Router 1, and then to the PC. This might seems confusing when you say it like that, but take a look at the map and refer to each routing table, keeping in mind that the destination is 192.168.1 this time, and you'll see that each lookup will lead to the next correct router.

In real life, this can be somewhat more complicated. Instead of each routing table having four entries, they can have hundreds—or even thousands—of entries. However, the basic principles are unchanged; much of what you need to figure out from a troubleshooting standpoint is how to command your router to show you what its routing table looks like. This way, you can do a sanity check on it. For example, if Router 1's table showed that the next hop to 192.168.4.0 was 192.168.2.10 (the file and print server), you'd raise your eyebrows and start to investigate why Router 1 thought that the best way to 192.168.4 was through a server. (Going through a server isn't in itself terrible—if the server is a multihomed server acting as a router to the proper network. But in this case, it's a dead end.)

Those Dynamic Routers

I heard you ask about four paragraphs ago, "How does the routing table get built?" I wasn't ignoring you; it's a good question. To begin to answer it, let's discuss basic route entry types.

There are two types of routes that can be established in a routing table:

- **Static routes**   A static route is one you type in yourself at the router console. This gets extremely tedious and isn't the greatest way to have a flexible and easily reconfigurable network.

- **Dynamic routes**   Dynamic routing entries are built via routing protocols.

There's one special static route you'll want to know about called the *default* route. This is represented by the destination network 0.0.0.0 and is the route used when a packet has a destination that isn't covered by anything else in the routing table.

Routing protocols are based on the concept that each router "knows" which network it lives on, and that it can communicate which networks it knows about to other routers. Looking at Figure 14.3 again, it makes sense that Router 1 could tell Router 2 about the 192.168.1 network, and that Router 2 could tell Router 1 about the 192.168.3 network—along with the 192.168.4 network, once Router 3 told Router 2 about it. Whoa.

14

It's a good thing this happens more or less automatically, because in a large network, writing this out could get really hairy. Again, here's how dynamic routes would work in this sample network:

Router 1   Tells Router 2 about 192.168.1

Router 2   Tells Router 1 about 192.168.3

                        Tells Router 3 about 192.168.1

                        Tells Router 1 about 192.168.4

Router 3   Tells Router 2 about 192.168.4

Route in Peace: Routing Protocols

There are four common types of routing protocols you should know about—more for configuration checking (making sure that routers are configured for the same routing protocols) than anything else. TCP/IP has two common ones, as does IPX/SPX. The oldest routing protocol, for both TCP/IP and IPX/SPX, is called *Routing Information Protocol (RIP)*.

It's important to realize that different network protocols (TCP/IP versus IPX/SPX) have different routing protocols. Although RIP for TCP/IP works similarly to RIP for IPX/SPX, they are, in fact, different.

RIP

Both the TCP/IP RIP and the IPX/SPX RIP are *broadcast protocols*—that is, each RIP router announces its routing table to everybody on the network every so often. Also, both RIPs calculate route cost based on number of hops rather than how fast a particular route might be (for cases where multiple routers have a path to the same network). RIP can cause lots of network traffic in complex networks because it talks *too much*. (TCP/IP RIP will broadcast to the network every 30 seconds.)

IPX/SPX has a companion protocol to RIP called *SAP*, or *Service Advertisement Protocol*. This protocol is similar to RIP in that it broadcasts information to the network to anybody who might be listening. It's different in that it advertises *servers*, not routers.

The reason for SAP is similar to the reason for RIP—it allows all routers to share information via broadcast. As such, it's pretty chatty.

OSPF and NLSP

If your network is complex and congested, you might want to stop using IPX RIP and go with NLSP. (NLSP replaces IPX's SAP and RIP.) Similarly, if you have a complex and congested TCP/IP network, you'd probably want to replace the RIP with OSPF. OSPF (Open Shortest Path First) for TCP/IP and NLSP (NetWare Link State Protocol) for IPX/SPX are the more advanced routing protocols. They take into account how fast a link might be and assign a cost accordingly. Each NLSP or OSPF router identifies itself to other routers on the same network and learns the routes that those other routers know. If something changes, the routers communicate it directly; because they do a quick check on each other fairly often (usually 10 seconds), a dead router is noticed and the routing tables are updated quickly. Good stuff!

There's not really a lot that goes wrong with routing protocols that aren't domino-effect problems—that is, problems caused ultimately by a bad hub port, cable, or card on the network, or by somebody changing a configuration. Still, it's good to be acquainted with the basics so that you can read the configuration from your router and get the basic gist of what's going on.

All modern servers—whether NT, UNIX, or NetWare—can be configured to be simple and cheap routers. Of course, they need to be multihomed in order to be connected to more than one network.

I use this sometimes to swap out routers. If I suspect that a network problem might be router related, it's a lot cheaper to temporarily put in a PC with UNIX on it acting as a router than it is to purchase a new $10,000 router just to rule out a router problem.

ROUTER RUMBLE!

Be careful if you start to experiment with routers. Unlike servers, which are typically self-contained entities, routers that participate in routing protocols on your network can seriously damage your connectivity if they're misconfigured.

I've seen a situation where somebody plugged a router into network A that was configured to connect network A with network B. This was because the new router was intended to replace the router that currently served network B.

Unfortunately, the new router's second interface was configured as being on network B, and though it wasn't plugged into network B proper, it started to advertise via routing protocols that it knew the best route to network B. This caused confusion in the routing tables; some packets started to go to this router, only to discover that there was an entrance, but no exit! The legitimate router for network B was doing what it was supposed to do, but it was being usurped by the new router.

14

> Here's the lesson: Don't plug a new router into a production network until it's time; instead, test on a disconnected network. Test hubs are cheap enough—putting together a couple of test segments shouldn't cost more than $100.
>
> I've also seen a situation where a RIP router for network C was accidentally plugged into network A. Because RIP routes are broadcast rather than going address to address, the router was able to tell all the routers on that segment that it knew the best way to network C. Again, all of a sudden, folks couldn't get to a network segment that until then had been just fine.
>
> These are, of course, human errors that could have been found by change analysis—if the guilty party had 'fessed up! Both errors were found through examination of the routing table, when someone exclaimed, "Hey! Why in the heck is network B going to *that* IP address?" Fortunately, the networks had been well documented; otherwise, the person looking at the routing table might have assumed that the network B next hop was listed correctly.

Checking Routes

Routing problems can be diagnosed from the router itself, but they can also be diagnosed via a network connected to a router. You can determine whether a router is up just by pinging it (be sure to ping it from a segment that it lives on, because pinging it from a different segment involves different routers). Likewise, you can use the `traceroute`, `tracert`, and `iptrace` commands to see how a packet from the workstation is *actually* flowing through the network. Check the routing table of multihomed servers with `netstat -r` to see what *they* think the routes are. Once you do these things, you can compare the results with how it *should* flow according to your site documentation, and you're one step closer to resolving your problem.

Switch Theory

When I was a boy, we didn't have any of this fancy switching nonsense. We walked uphill in the snow both directions to our networks and used bridges to connect them, and we *liked* it!

Once upon a time, smaller switches were called *bridges* because they bridged two networks together. Today's switches can connect dozens of segments, but they still follow the rules that were invented for their smaller forebears.

Many switches are now used as replacement hubs—shared media becomes very annoying if you have many shared media errors (such as collisions), and you don't get the full capacity of the pipe. As such, they don't speak network protocols the way that routers do.

A switch operates by learning the MAC addresses of each station attached to it. If one MAC address on one segment wants to talk to another MAC address on another segment, the switch connects them together on a private circuit, much like a switchboard operator of old would connect various cables and plugs to appropriate outlets in order to connect various people's conversations together. However, unlike the switchboard operator, the switch could care less about the content of the conversation; it just blithely connects folks who want to talk to each other and separates out the other conversations. This separation of conversations is why folks use switching as a way to speed up their networks.

> Experiencing strange problems on your large switched network? Check out how many simultaneous MAC addresses your switches support—older switches didn't support very many and won't be able to keep large numbers of end stations, which can manifest itself in PC lockups and disconnects.

Does each end station need to know that a switch is in the mix? Nope. This is because the switch will respond when one end station's calls for the other. In other words, Station A in Figure 14.4 wants to talk to Station B, which is on the other side of the switch. Station B never sees the switch; instead, it sees the unmodified frame from Station A, which the switch has lobbed from one segment to another. The frame has a source of A and a destination of B; the switch's MAC addresses never enter the picture. Scary, yet very neat.

FIGURE 14.4

How two stations talk via a switch.

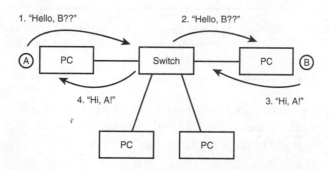

> Always remember that there's a segment on each switch port (whether it's shown or not). In other words, when you see a diagram showing a point-to-point link between a PC and a switch, or a server and a switch, it's unlikely that someone will show the segment in between the node and the switch; instead, just one line between the switch and the node will be shown. However, the segment is there!

14

Wait and Switch

There are two kinds of switching methods:

- **Cut through**   Like it sounds, cut through switching starts transmitting the packet as it comes through, and it's very fast. Of course, if the packet ends up being an error packet, the switch has just introduced an error on the other end.

- **Store and forward**   With store and forward switching, the switch receives the entire packet and then forwards it on to the destination segment. When errors occur here, the switch has the option of dropping the packet rather than propagating the error. Of course, because the switch waits for the entire packet to be received before forwarding it to the destination, there's delay involved.

Store and forward versus cut through involves a tradeoff of reliability versus speed; if you're experiencing problems with your switched network, this is something to keep in mind. The price of speed can sometimes be more than you're willing to pay.

Broadcast News

If you have large numbers of programs, servers, or print servers that rely on data link–level broadcasts (that is, data link traffic destined to *all* stations on a network), remember that each broadcast no longer goes to *one* segment. When switching segments together, a broadcast on one propagates to *all* segments. This can result in large amounts of traffic and can cause unwanted problems.

You'll want to think about when to switch and when to route. Two networks with different protocol addresses do *not* share data link–level broadcasts.

Again, a switch is really dumb. It doesn't know anything about the conversation on the phone—it merely knows who's doing the talking. Can the switch be configured to divide two different segments based on protocols? Sure, but then the switch is basically acting as a router.

Trees Save You

One important aspect of switch operation is what happens when switches are connected together. Because there really isn't any routing protocol when a switch is acting as a switch, what happens if Switch 1 is connected to Switch 2, and Switch 3 is connected to both Switch 1 and 2? Sounds like something evil waiting to happen, doesn't it?

Well, you're right, evil is indeed in the offing. As you can see from Figure 14.5, there are two paths from Station A to Station B. Because Switch 1 forwards the frame from Station A on to the next network, it seems as if Switch 2 *and* Switch 3 would pick up conversation from A and try to forward it to B. If these shenanigans are allowed to go on unchecked, all pandemonium will break loose: The packets will be forwarded forever and ever, your network utilization will go way up, and the bridges will become overworked and go on strike.

FIGURE 14.5

Without the spanning tree protocol, the bridges would cause a loop that would cause the network to malfunction.

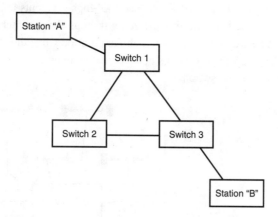

This situation can be avoided by a bridge protocol called *spanning tree*. With this protocol, a special packet is sent out by each bridge or switch on the network; each switch learns about each other switch and stops this kind of nonsense before it even begins by blocking one of the interfaces, such as the one between Switch 1 and Switch 3. If the network changes by a switch being taken out of service, or by a switch losing its mind, the spanning tree will attempt to adjust automatically. All switches that you buy nowadays will give you the option to do this (or will do it automatically), but some (really old) switches won't, and they can cause problems. In this case, you have two options: Don't connect your switches in a loop or stop using the older stuff.

Tree Trunks

As I mentioned in Hour 9, "Ethernet Basics," *full duplex* communication between a switch and a node such as a server is possible. This is true of both Token-Ring and Ethernet switches. This makes the effective bandwidth *double* what it might ordinarily be between the server and the switch: 32Mbps for Token-Ring and 200Mbps for Fast Ethernet.

14

Full duplex is really cool for connecting servers or high-utilization users to switches, but switch-to-switch communications might need even more bandwidth than this provides, because a switch is responsible for many more users than just one. Accordingly, some switches are starting to have the capability to use multiple lines to communicate in between two switches. This is known as *trunking*. This allows you to add as much bandwidth as might be necessary to connect two switches. You can think of this as adding lanes to a highway.

Because the switches in Figure 14.6 have six 100Mbps segments apiece, the *aggregate throughput* (or combined amount of stuff going through these switches) could be 600Mbps. To make sure that there's not a choke point between the two switches, you might connect three full-duplex trunks between the switches, giving you a 600Mbps superhighway between the switches.

FIGURE 14.6

Full duplex and trunking can be a great solution if you need to connect high-capacity switches.

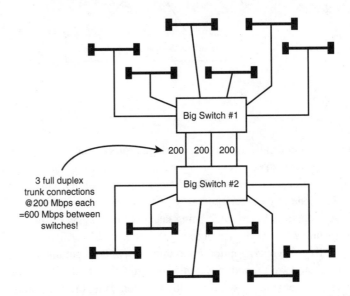

Because trunking is relatively new on the scene—and full duplex is not terribly long in the tooth either—you should definitely suspect compatibility issues if you implement either one or both and your network starts acting screwy.

Summary

You can think of routers and switches as being cousins. Routers switch packets at the network protocol (TCP/IP or IPX/SPX) level, whereas switches route packets at the data link (Ethernet or Token-Ring) level. Switches are usually wire-speed devices, whereas routers can handle delay (as is the case over a wide-area connection). Switches are typically used for one geographically separate area; routers are used to connect geographically disperse areas. A switch can be used as a hub replacement, allowing users to enjoy an unshared line to communicate to other devices on the network.

The documentation that comes with your switch or router should become bathroom reading material if you really want to be able to handle problems. Of course, the theory is really important, but router and switch theory by itself won't do you a lot of good; you'll also need to know specific informational and configuration commands for your devices.

Routers are much more complex than switches, and they communicate back and forth quite a lot via routing protocols. Switches, on the other hand, are pretty dumb, and they only talk to each other to avoid a duplicate path to a workstation. Both switches and routers, however, are more often than not hybrid devices that can route packets at a protocol level or switch packets at a data link level, all depending on how you configure them.

Workshop

Q&A

Q **My boss has been saying that we should chuck all our routing and switching gear and get in some layer-three switches. What the heck is she talking about?**

A Let's first define what a layer-three switch does. To do so, we need to review that icky OSI seven-layer cake I talked about earlier. Here are the OSI layers in order:

- Physical
- Data link
- Network
- Transport
- Session
- Presentation
- Application

14

Without getting heavy into it, *layer-three switching* refers to the network layer, meaning the network protocol (TCP/IP or IPX/SPX, for example). And a device for taking in stuff and deciding what to do with it based on the network protocol is what? Yep, a router. *Layer-three switch* is just a new marketing term for a very fast router. So, the question for you is this: Do you need a new router?

Q I tried to connect to my router/switch with a serial cable. I'm pretty sure that I'm using a null modem cable, but every time I use my communications program, all I see is a bunch of ç characters. Why is my device speaking French to me? Does it think I'm cute or something?

A Don't worry, your device isn't making a pass at you; it's not even speaking French! Any time you see garbage characters like these on a serial connection, it probably means you're running with incorrect communication parameters. If you're using the correct default parameters, as specified by your documentation, somebody has probably improved the connection by ramping up the connection speed and hasn't told you about it. Try 19200bps, 38400bps, or 57600bps. If those don't work, you can always try changing the stop bits or parity—but realize that people usually don't monkey with these on the device end. This problem is typically the result of a speed issue.

Quiz

1. What's the principal difference between a router and a switch?

    A. Data link versus network protocol treatment

    B. Protocol versus network program treatment

    C. Data link versus MAC layer treatment

    D. Protocol versus data network treatment

2. True or false? It's a good idea to connect a switch via a wide-area connection.

3. True or false? You can usually hook a tape drive to a router in order to back it up.

4. A routing table can be built by which of the following?

    A. Static routes

    B. Dynamic routes

    C. Neither A nor B

    D. Both A and B

5. A routing protocol is a way for routers to _____.

    A. assume different bandwidth considerations via networking

    B. exchange known networks and routes

    C. assume routing information internally

    D. exchange network error information

6. Router 88 has a routing table that looks like this:

Network	Net Mask	Gateway Address	Cost
200.1.1.0	255.255.255.0	200.1.1.1	0 (Local)
200.1.2.0	255.255.255.0	200.1.2.1	0 (Local)
200.1.3.0	255.255.255.0	200.1.2.2	1
200.1.4.0	255.255.255.0	200.1.2.2	2

Based on this routing table, how will Router 88 route a packet that's destined for 200.1.3.10?

    A. It will talk directly to the node at 200.1.3.10.

    B. It will talk directly to the router at 200.1.2.2.

    C. It will talk directly to the router at 200.1.2.1.

    D. It will drop the packet and generate an error.

7. How might you make Router 88 send packets that don't correspond to any of its routing entries along to Router 99?

    A. Add Router 99 to Router 88's routing protocol participation

    B. Add Router 99 as a default route for Router 88

    C. Add Router 88 to Router 99's routing protocol participation

    D. Add Router 88 as a default route for Router 99

8. True or false? Each network protocol has its own routing protocols.

9. True or false? Each workstation must have in its network configuration the MAC address of its default switch.

10. Using store and forward switching instead of cut through switching can cut down on which of the following?

    A. The speed required to forward a packet

    B. Errors propagated to other segments

    C. The speed required to format a packet

    D. Errors in the routing information protocol

14

Answers to Quiz Questions

1. A
2. False
3. False
4. D
5. B
6. B
7. B
8. True
9. False
10. B

HOUR **15**

Firewall and Proxy Server Basics

Three can keep a secret if two are dead.

—Benjamin Franklin

This is a *scary* yet kind of fun hour. I hope you've brought your secret
detective code ring and your security blanket. We're going to go seriously
James Bond here; you can expect a couple of nifty devices, explosions, bad
guys, good guys, and gunplay by the end of the hour. (No, not really. This is
a *family* book.)

For some reason, the public perception seems to be that a firewall or proxy
server is the major security concern on any network. In reality, although a
well-configured firewall or proxy server is really, really important, it's only
one piece in a larger security model. Although I won't get into this topic in
tremendous detail here, network security relies on good password policies,
server configuration, diligent application of security-related operating system and application patches, network auditing, and user dial-in policies (just
to name a few things besides firewalls). Just as any responsible corporation

has locks on its doors (the firewalls), it also probably distributes corporate ID tags, has receptionists to greet and keep the public from casually intruding on the work environment, and has an accounting system to keep track of the disbursement of funds. Although not every corporation has security guards—much less security guards with guns—they do have locks on their doors and are basically secure.

> My personal theory about network security is this: The best way to secure a system that's on a network is to unplug it from the hub, disconnect all dial-up ports, burn the Internet router, disconnect the system's hard drive, and start using paper. (For some reason, this is not a popular security policy.)
>
> Failing this, all you can accomplish is best-effort security—and keep good backups. Firewalls are a good beginning to best-effort security. They keep your most obvious entry points locked down and act as a gateway from your inside network to the outside world.

Top Secrets

Let's lay out some definitions here. When most folks talk about firewalls, they usually mean *packet-filtering routers*. As we discussed in the last hour, a *router* is the glue between two or more network segments. Therefore, a packet-filtering router refers to a router that has rules as to who and what is allowed to be routed between its interfaces. Not so bad, huh?

What's a proxy server? First of all, it's *not* any kind of router. So what is it? Like any kind of server, a proxy server offers services. It's basically a multihomed server that accepts requests on a certain socket and *forwards* these requests to a server on the other side.

Think of a proxy server as a big, bad security guard who will go into a bad network neighborhood for you, retrieve what you want, and return it to you—all without exposing your poor carapace to harm. As in voting, the proxy server proxies you—that is, it acts as your agent to go do something and then reports back to you what the results were. Going back to our old friend the telephone analogy, bear in mind that a proxy server is not "telephone equipment"; it's merely an agent that has two different telephones connected to two different telephone systems.

This is hardly the stuff that spy novels are made of. Nonetheless, if you're like most folks, you'll not be configuring your own packet-filtering firewall or proxy server. This is probably a good idea; a misconfigured firewall is almost as bad as no firewall. In some cases, it can actually be worse than no firewall, because it may give you a potentially false sense of security.

15

Granted, we're not doing any soup-to-nuts firewall configuration, but let's take a look at the theory behind it, which will let you start to investigate a given situation and glean what might be wrong.

TCP Versus UDP

Germane to the theory behind firewalling is the idea that connections can be limited based on the service being offered or sought. Because each TCP/IP service has a unique socket number that it listens to (remember from the telephone analogy that a *socket* is the extension number that the service person for the company answers), it's reasonably easy for a router or proxy server to limit connections to these sockets. Because limits are placed on the socket numbers themselves, it follows that the service is also limited. This means you can pick and choose among the services that may travel in or out of the firewall.

Actually, services don't *have* to run on their default socket number; just as your boss can make you sit at a different telephone, a network administrator can change the socket number of a service. This is fairly unusual, but it does happen.

For example, students sometimes run their own Web servers on different sockets because the university has occupied the default Web socket with the official Web server. The firewall upshot here is that if you run a service on a nonstandard socket, people might not be able to traverse the firewall to get to you.

This is reasonably easy with TCP (Transmission Control Protocol) sockets. A TCP connection is a connection-oriented call—like a true phone call, where someone dials someone else and establishes a two-way link.

A UDP (User Datagram Protocol) conversation, on the other hand, is basically like when I throw you a crumpled-up piece of paper containing a message, and you throw one back at me. This is called a *connectionless* session. You can think of the difference between TCP and UDP as the difference between you and me using two tin cans and a string (TCP) to communicate versus you and me passing notes in class (UDP). Keep in mind that a note can be easily misdirected.

It's fairly trivial for TCP connections to be limited, because the reply to the connection is basically within the same connection. It's a lot harder to do this with UDP sockets. A UDP connection throws out a packet and then waits for the reply. Because no connection exists, the firewall must be configured to accept random UDP packets, any of which might be a reply. Typically, a range of UDP ports has to be allowed in through the firewall, which implies a lot of trust.

Some administrators (depending on their site security policies) disallow UDP through the firewall—period. Others rely on SMLI (Stateful Multi-Level Inspection) firewalls, which "remember" the packets that have passed through them and accept responses appropriately.

Packet-Filtering Routers

A packet-filtering router usually depends on access rules—that is, rules you set up within the router software itself. A packet filter usually has a rule set that starts with least common and works its way up to most common. What's a rule set? Typically, a rule set looks something like a routing table but includes sockets as well as addresses. Any packet that comes in is compared against rule 1, then rule 2, all the way to the end. If at any time it matches up against a rule, processing stops. For example, for my 192.168.1.0 network, the rules might be as follows:

- Allow 192.168.1.0:any on if 0 to connect to all:any.

- Deny all:any to connect to all:any.

This means that anybody within my 192.168.1.0 network (provided they come in on router interface 0) can connect to anything they darn well please. If condition 1 was not true, then condition 2 would apply, which denies everything. This is probably the most common firewall configuration: Allow certain sockets (or all sockets) from the inside to go to the outside and disallow all other connections (for example, connections from the outside).

> The most effective packet-filtering routers will have a filter on "which interface" the packet comes in on, in addition to what IP address the packet is from. This helps eliminate *packet spoofing*, where a packet *claims* to be from a certain network, but actually is not.

15

A complex rule set results in confusion and possible misconfiguration. If you're configuring a rule set, you should keep it simple.

You should know that certain applications (such as active FTP) will ask the destination station to initiate a connection back to the requesting workstation, even though it's a TCP application. It's sort of like "Hey Fred, find out when the movie is, then call me back."

Under many firewall configurations, this is prohibited, because it means the firewall has to be configured so that a random workstation from the outside can initiate a connection to a random workstation on the inside. Might as well use a colander rather than a firewall!

You can usually get around this type of application problem by using a different mode of the application—for instance, passive FTP, where only the requesting workstation makes connections. Most browsers default to passive FTP, but not all standalone FTP clients do.

There's usually no logging or accounting on a packet-filtering firewall, although most firewalls will record errors. Here, troubleshooting is very similar to router troubleshooting, with ping, traceroute, and lists of the routing tables and rule sets being your best friends. As with routing problems, symptoms of packet-filtering firewall problems include the inability to reach a host on the other side; unlike a router, though, the symptom of a packet-filtering firewall problem might be the inability to reach a *service* on the other side.

Packet Filter Improvements

Newer firewalls that don't care whether they're good routers—that are more interested in being bang-up firewalls—will do all sorts of new tricks. Some of them will perform network address translations (NATs), which enable you to tell the outside world that you're a different address than you really are. This means that if you change Internet Service Providers, you don't have to change your IP numbers, which is nifty. (It used to be that only proxy servers were good for this, because they use two different routing domains anyway, but the firewall vendors have caught up.)

Stateful Multi-Level Inspection is a really neat technology, too. It allows UDP sockets in on a contextual basis—that is, it reads your note to Jenny and then accepts a note back from Jenny only if it seems as though the contents of that note are relevant to what you sent. This requires a very specialized firewall and is very application specific. If the firewall doesn't "know" Jenny, it can't determine whether the note she sent back to you is real. These firewalls typically come preconfigured with rules for common applications such as Telnet, email, FTP, and so on. If you're having problems using an unusual application through an SMLI firewall, check with the firewall vendor to see how to get support.

Proxy Moxie

Let's dig a little deeper into the theory behind a proxy server. Think of the proxy server as a receptionist for a spy organization that has two sets of phones: the internal organization telephone (the "red phone") and the outside world's phone system. The outside phone system is not directly usable by any of the other agents in the spy agency; they must give a message to the receptionist, who will order out for pizza, arrange for third-party hit men, and so on. The spy organization has it this way so that its circuits are not directly connected to the public telephone network—and a good thing, too! It doesn't mean the receptionist is incorruptible, but at least he's within the organization, fairly trustable, very accountable for his actions, and, of course, easily monitored, because he's the only point of communication between the organization and the outside world.

The important thing to remember is that there are two different types of phone calls, because the receptionist hangs up one line (the red phone) and picks up the outside phone to relay the information on a different call. As such, there are two different routing domains (the two phone systems) involved. Though this sounds mysterious, it really isn't—all it means is that two sets of networks (the red phone and the outside world's phone system) are prevented from talking to each other because the router doesn't share a common network between the two networks (see Figure 15.1).

FIGURE 15.1

A typical proxy server setup.

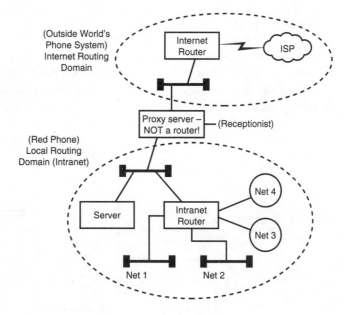

Are there still rules involved as to who may call in or out? Definitely. Similar to a packet-filtering firewall, proxy servers typically have a default policy of "deny every-thing but the following," and you define what *is* allowed. For example, let's say the company executives all reside on network 4 in Figure 15.1. They have ruled that only they may have Internet access, so the only explicit rule that you would set would be this:

Allow all traffic from network 4 from the "inside" interface of the proxy server.

All other traffic, say from network 3, would be denied.

Proxy Type

Here are the two different types of proxy servers:

- **Application proxy**   An application proxy is a very, very specific proxy—it will proxy only one type of application, such as FTP, HTTP, and so on. It will *not* proxy anything else—that is, an FTP proxy will not accept an HTTP connection. If you want to have more applications available through your proxy server, you must make sure that the proxy server is running the proxy services for those applications as well.

- **Circuit-level proxy**   A circuit-level proxy is a proxy that operates on the network
  level only. The most popular circuit-level proxy is called *Socks* (originally developed as a freeware package but now available commercially from several vendors).
  This type of proxy understands protocol and socket number, but that's about it.
  Typically, circuit-level proxies are generic—they can act to handle any sort of
  socket, as shown in Figure 15.2.

FIGURE 15.2

*Application proxy ver-
sus circuit-level proxy.*

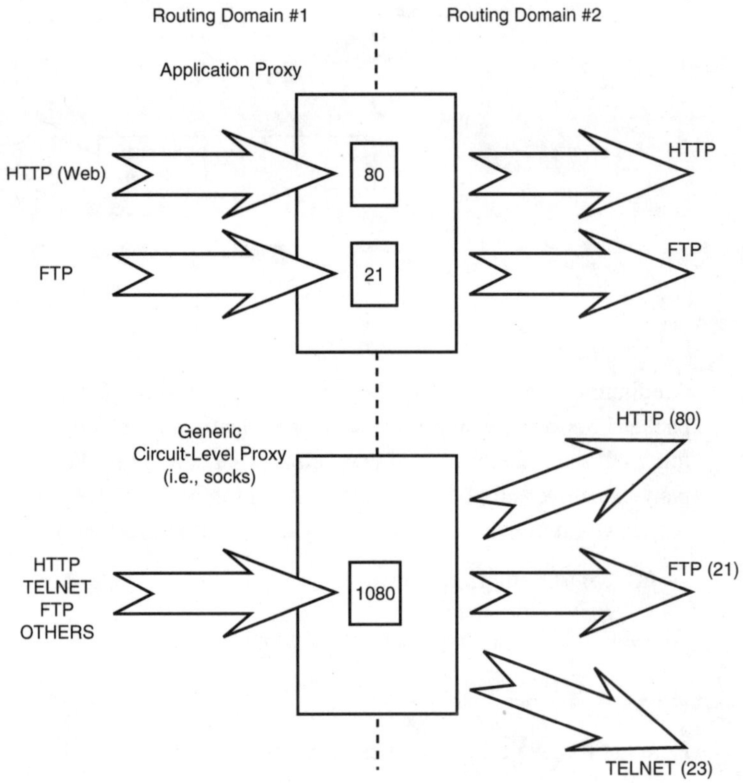

Routing Domain #1   Routing Domain #2

Application Proxy

HTTP (Web) → 80 → HTTP

FTP → 21 → FTP

Generic
Circuit-Level Proxy
(i.e., socks)

HTTP
TELNET
FTP
OTHERS → 1080 → HTTP (80)

FTP (21)

TELNET (23)

What's the difference? Well, for one, a circuit-level proxy is more flexible—it will proxy
any TCP/IP service. However, an application proxy has its merits, too. For example, a
Web proxy (otherwise known as an *HTTP proxy*) will *cache* Web pages and graphics it
has already transferred and, as a result, will serve them up much faster to your users.
This is because an application proxy has inside knowledge about what's going on with
the application, whereas a circuit-level proxy doesn't know anything about the application—just something about the connection. In other words, a Web (HTTP) proxy
"knows" that Web pages are being received from a server and will store them locally, as

15

illustrated in Figure 15.3. The next time any user asks for those Web pages, the proxy will serve them from the cache area, thus saving time. (Don't worry—if new pages are posted, the cache handles this, too.)

FIGURE 15.3

The proxy server stores cache information until it is no longer up-to-date; users can refresh from the proxy server without causing outside network traffic or having to wait.

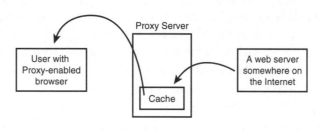

Just Add Software

Every proxy server has client software that needs to be installed on the workstation that will be using the proxy. This can be simple—every copy of Internet Explorer and Netscape Navigator or Communicator has support for the Socks circuit-level proxy, as well as built-in support for the most popular proxy servers. (Figure 15.4 shows the proxy settings for Internet Explorer.)

FIGURE 15.4

The Proxy Settings screen from Internet Explorer.

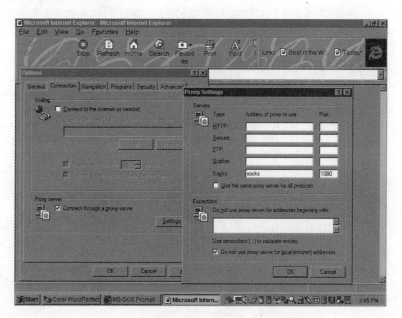

Configuring Your Proxy

The really important thing you should do when configuring the client software is to make sure your proxy server is *not* used for local traffic. Most proxy servers will do fine proxying the amount of traffic that can fit in the pipeline that goes from most sites to the Internet—T1 or 1.5Mbps traffic is a breeze for most servers to handle. However, when a proxy server finds itself forced to also deal with multiple people asking it to handle the local 10Mbps or 100Mbps traffic, things start…to…get…slow. You'll find yourself surrounded by angry villagers waving torches and axes, all of whom want to know why their Internet access is sluggish!

To configure Internet Explorer to avoid the proxy server for local traffic, just make sure the Do Not Use Proxy Server for Local (Intranet) Addresses check box is checked (refer to Figure 15.4). Microsoft assumes that any address in your domain (http://server.mycompany.com) or a server name without a domain (http://server) is a local address. Clever. Netscape is a little more complicated to configure; if you want to do this, you'll need to run a Netscape configuration server.

Of course, even if you configure the software correctly, someone might "unconfigure" it later; it's best to prohibit this type of antisocial behavior at the server. Sure, someone who misconfigures his own workstation will experience malfunctions, but it's better to get one or two trouble calls than lots of pesky "The internet is slow" calls. Trust me on this. People who get slow stock quotes get really, really ugly.

As far as slowness goes, if you see a lot of traffic through your generic proxy server, you might want to investigate specific application proxies. The fact that an application proxy caches frequently used pages can really cut down on your amount of traffic, provide users of those pages a boost in speed, and speed up everybody in general, because those pages are not being loaded over and over again.

Proxy Trouble

You'll need to treat a proxy server as a server that just happens to be connected to two different networks. As such, you'll usually need to be able to log into it in order to troubleshoot it.

Presumably, your firewall will have some sort of secure login. Remember, though, what happens when you assume! Make sure your login session is encrypted; if you don't know, ask your manufacturer. If the login is not encrypted, do not under any circumstances log in from the Internet—it's a trivial exercise for someone to eavesdrop on your login conversation. All of a sudden, your secure firewall is not so secure anymore, because someone from the outside can now log in to it.

When you log in, you can treat the proxy server just as you would a regular workstation. However, remember that it's a regular workstation with a double life: a life on your network and a life on the Internet. You'll do the normal troubleshooting procedures: traceroute, ping, and so on. Furthermore, you can see who's currently using your proxy server by typing **netstat -a** or **netstat -an** (depending upon whether you want numeric output or not).

Pay attention to the LISTENING lines; they're the proxy services themselves. If one of them goes away, it's likely that the proxy program associated with it has died. For example, the Socks proxy service listens on socket 1080. If you don't see something resembling the following, you'll need to investigate whether the Socks program is still running (use netstat -a):

```
Active Connections
Proto  Local Address         Foreign Address  State
TCP    proxy.myhost.com:1080  0.0.0.0:*        LISTENING
```

In this case, the Socks program is definitely running. Whether it's acting nicely is another story. (For example, maybe the access rule for your network has been accidentally deleted: Although you can *connect* to the socket, it's *denying* you the right to use the proxy. You can only verify this by trying to use it from your network.) You can do a similar trick with other proxies if you know their socket numbers. HTTP is socket 80, FTP is socket 21, and Gopher is socket 70, for example.

Same Name Game: DNS and Firewalls

What about name services? Don't you need to be able to speed-dial all those servers on the Internet? Here's the scoop on DNS and firewalls.

Packet-filtering firewalls can be configured to let your DNS servers on the inside perform lookups from the outside. In this case, standard DNS troubleshooting rules apply. The DNS lookup looks something like this:

1. The client workstation asks the local DNS server to resolve www.jotto.com.

2. The DNS on the local server can't find jotto.com; it turns to the outside DNS server.

3. The outside DNS server returns the IP address to the local DNS server.

4. The local DNS server returns the IP address to the client workstation.

5. The client workstation attempts to connect; the packet-filtering firewall grabs the connection and allows it through.

You can determine whether DNS services are working simply by typing **ping *webname***. It's likely that the ping itself will fail—not all Internet servers allow outsiders to ping them, and your packet-filtering firewall may not be configured to let pings through. However, you should be able to resolve the address. For example, if DNS *is* working, a ping to an external host might look like this:

```
C:\WINDOWS>ping www.jotto.com
Pinging www.jotto.com [205.134.224.21] with 32 bytes of data:
Destination host unreachable.
Destination host unreachable.
Destination host unreachable.
Destination host unreachable.
```

The Destination host unreachable message might not be acceptable, but at least you know that name resolution is working, because www.jotto.com is followed by its IP address, 205.134.224.21. If name resolution were not working, the ping session would look like this:

```
C:\WINDOWS>ping www.jotto.com
Bad IP address www.jotto.com.
```

This example doesn't resolve the IP address from the DNS name. The Bad IP address www.jotto.com message from Windows means that the name resolution has failed.

Some proxy servers will allow you to avoid mixing your DNS servers with the outside world's DNS. This is called *proxy DNS*, and it works as follows:

1. The proxy client software tries performing a local lookup on the name (www.jotto.com).

2. The proxy client software fails with the local lookup, assumes that the name is of a remote site, and asks the proxy server to resolve the name and then proxy the request.

3. The proxy server resolves the name from an outside DNS server.

4. The proxy server processes the request and hands the resulting Web page to the client.

15

Notice that at no time is the IP address passed back to the client. This means you *cannot* perform the ping trick outlined earlier if you're using client proxy DNS rather than having your internal DNS servers talk to outside DNS servers. You'll always get the `Bad IP address` *host.outsidecompany.com* message.

 Not every proxy allows for proxy DNS. Socks version 5, for example, *will* proxy the DNS for you if you configure the client to do so, but Socks version 4 will *not*.

Summary

A packet-filtering router is usually what's referred to as a firewall. These routers have rules as to what is and is not allowed into a network on a service-by-service basis. Newer, more specialized firewalls on the market allow for NAT and SMLI, as well as better logging and reporting features than traditional packet-filtering routers.

Proxy servers differ from packet-filtering firewalls in that they're not routers; they act as a workstation on the Internet, and they pass their results back to workstations inside your network. This makes for a bit more setup on the client end and has different trouble-shooting characteristics than a plain router (you need to establish that routing to the device is okay for both networks as well as that the proxy service running on the proxy server is alive and configured properly). Because a proxy server, like a spy ring receptionist, has two separate "phone systems," you sometimes need to log into the proxy server in order to troubleshoot it.

DNS can be a thorny issue; you'll be well served figuring out what type of DNS resolution you have *before* you run into problems (so that you know how to verify DNS connectivity). Certain proxy servers will also proxy DNS resolution, making standard DNS troubleshooting tools unsuitable for troubleshooting Internet name resolution problems.

Workshop

Q&A

Q **Our boss said to get a firewall, so we have one, and it seems reasonably good. Still, I'm concerned about the network internally, because we have lots of PCs with PC Anywhere that have arbitrary dial-in ports. I don't have a lot of money to lock down our network, so I can't invest in expensive network-monitoring programs or audit systems. What can I do?**

A Security people like to refer to most corporate networks as "crunchy on the outside, chewy on the inside," meaning that most folks simply do not invest the time in applying security patches for known security holes. If you're interested in how to improve your security without spending megabucks, check out `http://www.cert.org`. Many vendor-related security alerts (and how to get fixes) are listed there. You should also make a concerted effort to learn as much as you can about network security policies. Good books on this topic include Cheswick & Bellovin's *Firewalls and Internet Security* and Garfinkel and Spafford's *Practical UNIX Security*.

Q My vendor says that its firewall isn't a packet-filtering router or a proxy server. What's up with that?

A I love vendors. They're so funny sometimes. Here's the deal: Packet-filtering routers got a really, really bad rap a couple of years ago when someone figured out how to fake them out. They received a lot of bad press. Therefore, advanced firewalls aren't really considered to be packet-filtering routers anymore—even though they still route packets, they still deal with packets on a network level, and they still filter. Also, they're not particularly the ones with SMLI (which make decisions on the application level). Still, if it walks like a duck...

Q Can't my proxy server be compromised by all the bugs out there?

A Anything's possible. Whether you have a proxy server or a firewall, stay in touch with your vendor and be sure to get security patches as they become available. In general, however, your proxy server should *not* be running other programs besides the proxy programs—unless you're a security expert and can warrant that these other programs won't put the server at risk.

Quiz

1. What's the difference between a proxy server and a packet-filtering router?

    A. Proxy servers filter on the network level, whereas routers filter on the application level.

    B. Proxy servers filter on the application level, whereas routers filter on the network level.

    C. Routers are security risks with improper configurations.

    D. Proxy servers are security risks with improper configurations.

2. True or false? A proxy server is not considered "network glue." Instead, it's considered "just another server" (albeit a multihomed server).

15

3. A packet-filtering router and a proxy server are both _____.

    A. users of Stateful Multi-Level Inspection

    B. multihomed

    C. security loopholes

    D. socket rockets

4. TCP is _____, and UDP is _____.

    A. a pain to configure; wonderful

    B. problematic with government installations; okay with corporations

    C. easy; hard

    D. connection oriented; connectionless

5. A proxy server can be overburdened by which of the following?

    A. Users asking it to proxy local LAN connections

    B. Users asking it to link to infrastructure valence

    C. Too much T1 traffic

    D. Too much searching on a Web site

6. You can use normal DNS troubleshooting tools from within your network if which of the following statements is true?

    A. DNS is being routed through the local DNS servers

    B. DNS is being routed through the proxy server

    C. The router handles internal DNS requests

    D. The proxy server handles all DNS requests

Answers to Quiz Questions

    1. B

    2. True

    3. B

    4. D

    5. A

    6. A

PART IV

In the Trenches

Hour

HOUR 16

Beauty Is Consistency Deep: Saving Yourself Trouble

Network components that are configured consistently—identically, when possible—are a godsend to busy network troubleshooters. In particular, I'll discuss three techniques in this hour that will help you build and maintain as consistent (*homogenous* in geek speak) a network as possible:

- Manual consistency methods (which rely mostly on personal organization skills combined with the exploitation of operating system features)
- Hard drive duplication (cloning)
- The use of newer, automated deployment tools

Apart from the obvious benefits of planning once and deploying many times, these consistency techniques are going to make your troubleshooting life a lot less complex.

In addition, here are four network components that, if kept standardized, can contribute to an easy life as a troubleshooter:

- Hard drive configuration
- Network login scripts
- Network user attributes
- Network application configuration

Having identically configured components means that if one component works in one place, it should work in others as well, unless a hardware problem exists. (Hardware problems also become more obvious if everybody's on the same operating system page.) It also means that you don't have to understand many problems in order to troubleshoot them. Instead of having to understand the nuts and bolts behind a complex network configuration, you can compare simple items to "known good" items (for example, login scripts or user attributes) or quickly redo more complex items.

For example, once you discover that a workstation that's supposed to be identical to other workstations is having an operating system or application problem (you've ruled out the entire user object, user attributes, and network application configuration), you can simply clone its hard drive. This operation takes 15 minutes (versus the hours that you might spend troubleshooting it otherwise). What's more, if the hard drives are indeed all configured the same, cloning the workstation couldn't hurt—that is, at least it won't hurt the configuration that's *supposed* to be on the drive.

To keep from upsetting your users, you need to communicate before you leap. That is, you need to let your users know that keeping data files on their hard drives is a really, really bad idea. Apart from the fact that their data will be lost in the event of a hard drive failure—c'mon, how many people *you* know back up their hard drives every single day?—the cloning of a given hard drive completely overwrites any information stored there.

Here's the bottom line: Troubleshooting starts with identifying whether the problem is local or systemic. If it's a local problem, you can often treat it via homogenization of the workstation or user object. This means that, typically, all you need to spend your brain power on are the systemic problems. If you apply the techniques in this hour, local problems will become no-brainers.

Manual Standardization

You don't really need automated deployment tools in order to get organized (on the other hand, they do make tasks go a lot quicker and easier). Regardless of whether you choose to use power tools or a hand drill to automate your network rollouts, in order to be successful, you definitely need a well-defined work plan. (It's an old saw in the automation game: How can you automate anything that has yet to be done manually?)

Let's look at the parts of your work plan that will need to be addressed whether you automate or deploy manually:

- Divide tasks into workstation-oriented tasks and user setup–oriented tasks
- Make checklists of tasks that must be completed
- Keep good records
- Write down a detailed rollout plan, shoot holes in it, and refine the plan
- Resist the temptation to deviate from the plan

In short, the characteristics of a good network rollout—big or small—are basically your good work habits translated to the computing arena. Try to think of any network rollout as a factory job or as a cookie-cutting session: Anything done to one network object must be done to the next network object.

 Although you can manually configure each object identically, unless you're quite the machine, there's no guarantee that each object will be exactly the same.

Power Tool Time

Your network operating system provides you with the basic tools to help you in your consistency quest:

- **User templates**   These enable you to copy an existing user.
- **User-level login scripts**   Login scripts exist to perform various startup configurations, such as adding a PATH to a user's environment, showing a message of the day, and so on. User-level login scripts are scripts that are run when an individual user logs in.
- **Organizational or group-level login scripts**   Organizational or group scripts run when anybody from that group or organization logs in.

- **User network profiles**   Network profiles are network-stored configuration information, such as your Windows desktop, Start menu, preferences, and so on. (We'll discuss these in more detail later in this hour.)

User Templates

User templates are awesome, but they're really just a takeoff of what network administrators have been doing for years: Creating a "Joe User," testing him out, and then duplicating all his attributes for the other users. As a matter of fact, the only network operating system I know of that actually has a formalized facility for user templates is NetWare (via Novell's NDS). Other systems have various user copy utilities—and frankly, these work just fine, as long as you remember to use them. Figure 16.1 shows the copy user feature for Windows NT.

FIGURE 16.1

You can use NT's User Manager for Domains to copy a domain user.

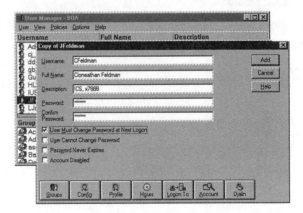

JOE USER

If your operating system doesn't provide user templates, you really should create a Joe User. (In fact, you might have to create several for different departments.) You create his login, his group associations, and his home directory, and you populate his home directory with the various configuration files he might need. For example, different groups of UNIX users might need certain startup files, including but not limited to .xdefaults, .xinitrc, .pinerc, and so on. Similarly, some Windows applications also need user-specific files for terminal emulation settings, Lotus 1-2-3 settings, and so on.

You can copy Joe every time you need to create a new user. Copy his home directory contents to the new user's home directory, and you can rest assured that the new user has everything she needs to get her job done. Think of this as making a boilerplate document in your word processor for a letter you send out every week or so—all you need to do is copy the document, change a few specifics, and you've saved yourself a good deal of time and energy.

User-Level Login Scripts

Every server has the capability to run login scripts for all users. These login scripts perform common tasks for all users. Here are a few examples:

- Show a message of the day
- Set environment variables needed by application programs
- Update workstation software
- Synchronize workstation time to the network
- Set up dumb terminal environments (in the case of UNIX)

You should avoid user-specific login scripts as much as possible, because it's time consuming to configure every workstation one at a time. Instead, do as much as you possibly can in the system login script and the group-oriented login scripts.

Organizational/Group-Level Login Scripts

System-wide login scripts include /etc/profile in UNIX and the system login script in NetWare 3.*x*. These allow administrators to have certain things happen for everyone in the system, which is neat. Of course, you might want certain other things to happen on a departmental level—not on a system-wide basis.

However, until the advent of NDS, administrators haven't had the ability to write a script for users on a departmental basis. This, of course, increases the number of scripts to keep track of, although it also does separate and organize your scripts pretty nicely.

So, are departmental or group-level scripts a blessing or a curse? Well, it depends on whether you need them. If everybody at your company uses the same applications and requires the exact same settings, system-level scripts are your best bet. However, if certain departments in your organization need different settings from others, group-level scripts are almost a necessity.

Tricky Scripts

This is all good and well for NDS users, but what about those without NDS? Fret not—there are tricks that allow you to specify group-level operations from your system login script.

Windows NT's logon scripts are usually .BAT or .CMD files—which, of course, are regular old batch files.

For example, under Windows NT, for each user in your Finance department, a workaround to enable group-level logon scripts would be to specify each user's logon script as FINANCE.BAT, which will run all the commands needed for the Finance department.

But what about users who really do need their own stuff? If certain users really do need their own login scripts (and you should think long and hard about this, because it's much harder to maintain), you can have a line such as the following as the last line of FINANCE.BAT:

```
if exist %USERNAME%.bat %USERNAME%.bat
```

This will run a user-oriented script if such a file exists in the login directory.

In UNIX, if you use the standard ksh or sh shell, you can perform a group test in the /etc/profile script and then execute a particular set of instructions if a person turns out to be in that group:

```
groups ¦ grep -q -w finance && {
  echo "You're in the Finance group, no party for you!"
  cat /finance/message-of-the-day
  PARTY="false"
}

    groups ¦ grep -q -w network && {
        echo "Hello network person, party on!"
        cat /network/message-of-the-day
        PARTY="true"
    }
```

The potential gotcha behind group-level scripts is that some single users may be in multiple groups. For example, let's consider a user in the previous example who's both in the Finance group *and* the Network group. She would end up with a PARTY variable of "TRUE". Is this what you want? If it isn't, you'll need to change this so that the Network group is tested for first.

Oh, all right. If you insist on running NetWare 3.x, you can use SYSCON to edit the system login script to perform group-specific tasks as well. Just go to Supervisor Options|System login script and do something like this:

```
if member of "Finance" then begin
  write "Hi, Finance Person! Parties prohibited!"
  display f:\public\finance\message.txt
  dos set PARTY="false"
end
```

> Don't get *overly* excited about the ability to affect large numbers of users at once. When treating mass quantities, a slip of your electronic knife has the potential of making a lot of people very unhappy all at once.
>
> You should always pilot-test as far away from spectators as possible. If you have a test server, you should use it; in any event, you should use a test group and a test user when testing out a new script or a new way of doing something.

16

Microsoft Profiles

Windows 95 and NT have the capability to store user-specific information on the network, rather than storing it on the local hard drive (although the hard drive has a copy of the information, too). This information consists of the following items:

- The Start menu (shortcuts)
- The desktop (shortcuts)
- Recently used files (shortcuts)
- The User Registry (a roaming version of the Registry with user-specific settings)

Profiles are a wonderful standardization tool, as well as a good network troubleshooting tool. Because the user settings are easily separated from the user's workstation, having the user try something at another workstation is easy and painless—you sometimes don't even have to reinstall applications to have the application settings move with you.

> Because Windows 9*x* ships with profiles turned off by default (so that every user has the same settings), you'll want to make sure you turn them on. You can do this by clicking the Start button, choosing Settings|Control Panel, selecting Passwords, choosing the User Profiles tab in the Passwords Properties dialog box, and then making the appropriate changes (see Figure 16.2).

FIGURE 16.2

The Windows 9x Control Panel allows you to turn profiles on or off for a given machine. Many corporate networks use the settings shown in this figure.

Where do the user profiles live? On a Windows NT network, as well as on Novell 4.*x* and higher, they live in the users' home directories. On Novell 3.*x*, they live in the SYS:MAIL directory, under directories named for the users' unique numeric user IDs. (You can determine what a particular user's unique numeric ID is by choosing SYSCON|User Information|User Name|Other Information.)

If you're going to add or replace something in the user's network profile files, make sure you do it while the user is logged out, because Windows writes a user's profile to the network as he or she logs out of the network. If you don't enact changes while the user is logged out, your changes will be overwritten at the point when he or she logs out.

Send in the Clones

Disk duplication has been one of the innovations that has made using complex desktop operating systems such as Windows a survivable experience for network administrators. It has allowed administrators to treat the whole Windows kettle of DLLs, VXDs, configuration files, and so on as one manageable container. Disk duplication isn't a panacea for all your standardization woes, but it sure helps. The idea behind a disk-duplication rollout is that you get it right once for each functional group and then roll it out many times.

Instead of doing an hour-or-so-long Windows 9*x* or Windows NT install from CD-ROM for each workstation—to the tune of 40 or so hours for 40 workstations—you can perform a 10-minute disk duplication, which translates into a mere six-plus hours for those same workstations.

Yes, Microsoft supports automated setup scripts for Windows NT and Windows 95, which allow you to run unattended setup sessions for large numbers of computers, usually from the network. This also results in identical setups. However, writing unattended setup scripts requires a reasonable amount of "inside knowledge" and will require customization for your site. If you're comfortable with an easy level of programming, you can play with this and get it working—but it takes a long time. Here's the bottom line: It's not as easy and quick as disk duplication.

What's more, in addition to the time consideration, you *know* that each workstation is the same. You don't have to write anything down—even those small tweaks you do to optimize your system—to ensure that all installs have the correct settings.

You'll want to make sure all the workstations' hardware is pretty much the same before you duplicate drives between them; otherwise, you run the risk of intermittent or hard-to-find problems. This typically isn't a big deal—if you're buying 10 to 20 PCs, it's highly unlikely that you're going to purchase them all from different sources. This sanity check comes more into play when you're upgrading folks rather than doing new installs.

Yes, Windows 9*x* is really good at detecting when the hardware changes—but why risk *any* problems? We're looking at using duplication to avoid trouble, not cause it.

Every so often, no matter how sure you are that the duplication is a "known good" one, you should verify that the duplication image is still what you want to be rolling out. For example, file and print software might have changed, and your duplication might need updating.

A duplication session in its simplest form is basically a DOS session with a network boot disk. You boot a DOS disk, load the network client, log in, and then run your duplication software. This allows you to copy the entire contents of the current hard drive to a file on the network or download the contents of the network file to the workstation's hard drive. You have other options, too. You can duplicate disk to disk, to a tape drive, or to a CD-ROM image, all depending on the duplication software you choose.

> Whoa, you say, that's a lot of stuff! Yes, this is true. However, current duplication technology will allow you to compress the disk file on-the-fly, making a 2GB hard drive with 1GB free take up only about 250MB on the network.
>
> Think of this as making a ZIP file of your hard drive—but with all hidden files, system files, and certain drive-specific contents such as the boot sector.
>
> Be aware, however, that not all duplication software will allow you to recover individual files from a duplication file—some will only allow you to restore the entire hard drive.

After you duplicate, you have to change the individual parameters on the new workstation—for example, the machine name and the TCP/IP address (if you're not using DHCP). Advanced duplication software has the capability to do this for you. Cool!

Protection Policy: Automatic Administrative Tools

"Save the users from themselves!" is the cry heard from many a network administrator. I'm sure you've at least thought it. Consider the case of the lady who learned how to change her screen colors—and changed them to yellow, her favorite color. This would have been fine, only she changed *all* the colors to yellow—foreground and background—leaving her with a yellow-on-yellow Windows installation. Kind of hard to read!

Policies

To avoid this type of situation, Microsoft has introduced a special administrative tool called a *policy file*. A policy file, when in the SYS:PUBLIC directory of a Novell server or the NETLOGON directory of an NT server, will enforce certain Registry settings for either default users or specific ones. This makes it sort of tough for users to shoot themselves in the foot, and it keeps you from wanting to shoot them elsewhere.

A policy file can be as restrictive or as permissive as you like. You can lock down the Control Panel in part or in full, restrict application installation, and so on, as shown in Figure 16.3. In short, you can make yourself really, really unpopular with the users. It's a tough call—how much restriction is fair protection versus how much restriction makes a network a fascist police state? This pretty much depends on your corporate culture.

FIGURE 16.3

The Windows NT System Policy Editor can restrict your users from doing just about anything.

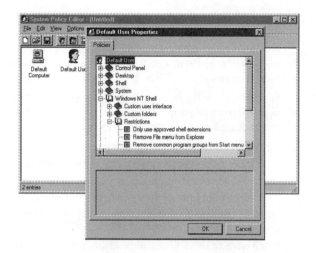

16

Windows policies make it possible for you to ensure that certain Windows attributes stay the same between PCs on your network. Although policies are pretty neat, they've long been considered hard to use. (Try the POLEDIT executable included on your Windows CD-ROM and see if you agree.) However, they are becoming usable—certainly more so since Microsoft introduced its Zero Administration Kit (ZAK).

Check out Microsoft's take on low-cost deployment at
http://www.microsoft.com/NTworkstation/Deployment/deployment/default.asp.

Novell has recently released Z.E.N. (Zero Effort Networking) Works. Among other things, it allows you to administer Windows policies using NDS users, groups, and organizational units. (Z.E.N. also features application deployment tools and remote control.) Take a gander at http://www.novell.com/products/nds/zenworks for more information.

App in a Snap

It used to be that all you needed to do to deploy a network application was give a user a menu option or a shortcut. Windows applications are a lot more complex; some install lots of workstation files, make changes to the user's Registry, and can, frankly, drive network administrators nuts.

Some (but not most) Windows applications are easy to standardize. All you need to do is to install the application into a shared network directory that many people can access. This way, you can configure the application from this central location.

For example, NetTerm, a Telnet application, allows many users to use the same network directory to run the application without running the setup program on each workstation. Here's how to do this:

1. Run NetTerm's setup program.

2. Specify a network location for the program (for example, G:\NetTerm).

3. Create an icon for NetTerm on each user's desktop that points to G:\netterm\netterm.exe, either by visiting the user or by modifying the user's network profile.

You'll have to check your manufacturer's documentation or experiment to determine whether you've got an application that will support this.

For complex applications, application deployment tools are almost as cool as disk duplication. They basically take a snapshot of a PC before a given application is installed and then take one again *after* the application is installed. The differences—whether in the Registry, in the files on the C:\ drive, or wherever—are calculated and stored on the network. These differences can be applied to any PC. You have an instant application with minimum user interaction, and all from the network. This is a great method for standardizing user workstations in conjunction with disk duplication.

The only thing to bear in mind when using one of the application deployment tools—for example, Microsoft's SYSDIFF, Novell's SnAPPshot, or Ghostsoft's Picture Taker—is that you need to make sure you're using a perfectly clean workstation when taking the "before" snapshot. That is, the workstation should *never* have had the application installed on it (ditto for shared components that the application wants). My preference is to keep a freshly installed copy of Windows (along with my file and print client of choice) around as a disk duplication file; I reload a hard drive with this right before taking a snapshot. This ensures that each app has a chance to perform a totally fresh install.

Are there problems with this? There can be—applications are just as capable of conflicting due to automated installation as they are due to regular installation. The key, again, is to test, test, and test some more before you deploy. This up-front work—for any of the standardization techniques we've discussed in this hour—will pay off as you experience easy troubleshooting operations for hours, days, and weeks in the future.

Summary

Using network components that are similar means that you don't have to undertake deep troubleshooting in order to solve many local (not systemic) problems. Besides, heterogeneous components tend to behave the same—which, if they have a "known good" configuration, is a wonderful thing.

Apart from using common-sense work habits while creating users and workstations, you'll also want to check out the built-in cookie-cutter functions of your network operating system, such as user templates and "Joe User" user copies. Although a little bit of scripting knowledge can be a dangerous thing, it can also be a huge help in streamlining user login setups.

16

User profiles and disk duplication are simple and easy ways to ensure uniformity among your users, as well as to guide workstation setups or user setups back in line when they stray. What's more, policy management packages, such as ZAK and Z.E.N. Works, can really help as well. Add application deployment to the recipe, and you've got a mix of strong tools that will help your network stay as consistent as possible.

Workshop

Q&A

Q I've read terrible things about what happens when Windows NT is duplicated. I've heard that Microsoft will no longer support you if you use disk duplication. What gives?

A Welcome, gentle reader, to the "pragma versus dogma" argument. It's true that Microsoft will not support disk duplication done to a workstation after the character mode of Windows NT setup completes. However, this doesn't mean it doesn't work in practice. Microsoft's concerns are mostly due to two things:

- A special, unique security ID (SID) is created for each workstation. Straight duplication will result in each of your workstations having the same SID, which can conceivably cause problems with your network.

- NT doesn't have a chance to query your hardware if you don't run Setup, which can lead to problems.

You should definitely take the SID issue seriously; fortunately, most duplication software vendors provide a SID changer that runs either during the duplication process or following the duplication process, thus getting rid of the first concern. The concern about NT not querying your hardware if you don't run Setup is also valid, but if you follow good duplication practices and duplicate only between sets of identical hardware, you should not have a problem.

Therefore, you've got to make a choice between what works and what's forbidden. It's your call, of course, and you should definitely research and pilot-test further if you're concerned.

The good news is that Microsoft recently announced that future versions of Windows will be designed with increased support for disk-image copying.

Q I've got a special workstation-based Registry setting for a network card that I need to set one time on a bunch of workstations I'm about to roll out. How do I use the policy editor to do this?

A Unless you want to dive into one of the Microsoft Windows Resource Kits and figure out how to add your own policy editor templates and custom Registry settings, I'd apply any workstation-based Registry settings by using the REGEDIT tool right before drive duplication. This will ensure that all your users get the settings. However, there's more than one way to skin a cat, of course.

Q Which duplication software is right for me?

A Duplication software has matured tremendously. There are now a half dozen vendors who offer it. Just surf the Web for the right solution for you. Here are a few options:

- Symantec (Ghost)   www.ghost.com
- Key Labs (ImageBlaster, Lab Expert, and RapiDeploy)   www.keylabs.com
- PowerQuest (DriveImage)   www.powerquest.com
- Microhouse (ImageCast)   www.imagecast.com

Quiz

1. You discover, halfway through a departmental rollout of workstations, that although the file and print client that you've been using is working fine, it's not the latest and greatest. A prudent consistency technique would dictate that you do what?

   A. You start using the latest and greatest client on the rest of the machines.

   B. You start using the latest and greatest client on power users' machines.

   C. You keep rolling out the same client on power users' machines and the latest and greatest on others.

   D. You keep rolling out the same client on the rest of the machines.

2. True or false? It's a good idea, whether or not you opt to use disk duplication, to advise users *not* to rely on their hard drive as a permanent storage medium.

3. Which of the following statements is true concerning user templates?

    A. They're available on all operating systems, making user copies undesirable.

    B. They're not available on any operating systems, making user copies mandatory.

    C. They're not available on some operating systems, but user copies are possible.

    D. None of the above.

4. For consistency's sake, it's best to _____.

    A. use as many individual login scripts as possible

    B. use system- or group-oriented login scripts

    C. Both A and B

    D. Neither A nor B

5. When copying a Joe User, what should you remember to do?

    A. Copy the user object, the system login script, and home directory files

    B. Copy the user object, home directory files, and login script if necessary

    C. Copy the home template

    D. Copy the login template

6. True or false? There are tricks that allow you to perform group-oriented login scripts, even if the operating system does not directly support login scripts for groups.

7. True or false? Disk duplication is appropriate for every workstation installation.

8. A user of yours keeps accidentally changing her display driver settings, leading you to repeatedly troubleshoot a terminal emulation problem. Which action should you take to stop this nonsense?

    A. Edit her Registry

    B. Create a policy file

    C. Neither A nor B

    D. Both A and B

9. When creating any type of application deployment snapshot, you should be certain to do what?

    A. Use a workstation that already has the application installed on it

    B. Use a typical user's workstation

    C. Use a clean workstation, without any installed components already on it

    D. None of the above

16

Answers to Quiz Questions

1. D
2. True
3. C
4. B
5. B
6. True
7. False. It's only appropriate for installation of groups of similar hardware.
8. B
9. C

HOUR 17

Where Do I Start?

You're not obligated to finish the task; neither are you free to neglect it.
—R. Tarfon, *Pirkey Avot* (Chapter 2, Mishna 21)

The answer to "where do I start?" could be this: Every day, try to improve things just a little bit. This is known as *proactive troubleshooting* in geek speak, and you got a good glimpse of what it's about with documentation in Hour 2, "You Can't Have Too Much Documentation, Money, or Love" and homogenization in Hour 16, "Beauty Is Consistency Deep: Saving Yourself Trouble." (We'll look a little more at proactive troubleshooting in Hour 22, "Who Watches The Watchmen?: Network Management Tools.")

The best kind of troubleshooting is the kind where you stop problems before they start. However, *proactive* troubleshooting is a little bit like peace, love, and understanding. (What's so funny?) This is all great and everything, and it's definitely worth shooting for (pardon the phrase); however, no matter how much you make things better, you'll still have to engage in *reactive* troubleshooting when things don't go as planned. Just as you'll continuously work on your proactive troubleshooting by documenting, observing your network, and planning, you'll also continuously be reactively troubleshooting. It's inevitable.

Even though we'd all rather avoid problems before they start by learning what causes problems and enacting policies and procedures to avoid them in the future, even as we do this, new problems have a way of popping up. Proactive and reactive troubleshooting are simply the yin and the yang of the troubleshooting game. You'll never get done with either; all you can do is make each one less painful.

Accordingly, in this hour, we'll reexamine the basics of how to get started with reactive troubleshooting of networking problems, whether those problems are application related, network protocol related, or physical network related. This will allow you to then further hone in on what the problem might be, based on the theory and composition behind the component.

No book can provide you with a cool head during a network combat situation. However, as this stuff is demystified for you, and you start to form your own set of troubleshooting reaction habits, you'll start to see that *whatever* the spooky problem is, the source *will* eventually rear its ugly head if you keep plugging away. At the point at which this all becomes more common to you, your stress level during problem determination will definitely start to decrease.

Identifying the Fault Domain: "In the Beginning…"

Unless you have a crystal ball or some sort of network-management software, your first inkling that something is wrong with your network will have nothing to do with your network and everything to do with your telephone. Particularly if your organization has multiple sites or multiple network segments, you're not always going to personally suffer during a network outage; therefore, you won't know what's happening unless someone (or something) lets you know.

 I'll cover network management software in Hour 22. However, for the moment, let's assume you haven't invested in such software and are relying on your telephone to explode at the speed of light when the network gets into trouble.

First, you should ask the person at the other end of the phone whether other users have this same problem. It may take some doing to tickle this answer out of the caller; he or she is understandably upset, may have lost work, may have a deadline, and so on. You'll need to be polite but firm—you can't provide help if you don't know the scope of the problem.

If other users are experiencing the same problem, then the problem is *systemic*—that is, it's a pretty safe bet that everybody's PC hasn't malfunctioned in exactly the same way at exactly the same time. Therefore, the answer can be found in something that all the PCs have in common—their common network "glue." Here's a list of items PCs are commonly connected to (in the order of "more local" to "less local"):

- Hubs
- Switches
- Routers
- Servers

If you're lucky, the first 90 seconds of the trouble call should tell you where the problem lies, which is pretty cool. Once you know what *type* of problem it is, the troubleshooting takes care of itself. If you know the problem is systemic, you can sometimes practice the techniques we discussed in Hour 4, "The Napoleon Method: Divide and Conquer." If you know the problem is local (PC related), you can relax—at least you don't have a lot of people down. What's more, if you've practiced the network consistency techniques we discussed in Hour 16, your likelihood of getting this person back up quickly is quite high.

Diving into Details

As optimistic as we'd all like to be, you won't always run into clear-cut situations. Sometimes the network isn't down for everybody. When the network infrastructure is not totally misbehaving, some of your calls will come from users who have gotten various illegal operation errors. Perhaps a user will report to you that he printed, but nothing came out.

> Some network problems aren't directly related to the network protocol or physical network attributes. These problems are generally thought of as *application* problems, whether they're client/server programs or file and print–oriented programs. We'll do a lot of in-depth application trouble shooting in Hour 18, "Lots of Different People in Your Neighborhood: In-Depth Application Troubleshooting." Be sure to bring coffee and a hankering to tinker!

Socializing a Solution: Basic Call-Handling Techniques

Let's go over the basic call-handling techniques that are applicable when you're not presented with a clear picture of what's going on. Assuming that that user is having unspecified application problems, how do you probe for more information? Don't forget to apply the SOAP theory—getting as many objective facts as possible about any type of trouble can only help you. Ask the user as many factual questions as you can. Here are some examples:

- What happened?
- When?
- During what? With what applications loaded?
- What were you doing right before the problem?
- Was idle time involved?
- Has this happened before? How was it resolved?

Asking about previous instances of the current problem is really important. Sometimes the history behind the problem will make the problem come into focus for you. For example, someone might tell you that the problem happens repeatedly at the same time every week—a major clue. Sometimes, the user might go so far as to tell you how the problem was fixed last time. A doctor friend of mine says that history is nine-tenths of diagnosis; he's not too far off.

This whole process—particularly if you're not at the workstation involved—can be like groping in the dark. If you don't have a basis for your questioning, it's hard to know which questions to ask. Sometimes, you simply have to go see it for yourself (particularly when the problem being reported is a local problem). Before you do, however, you might want to try to reproduce the problem from *your* desk.

For example, to rule out operator error, you can have the user at the other end of the line reboot the problem workstation—soup to nuts. Have the user power down and ask him or her to describe to you what's happening at each stage of the boot process. When it's time to run the application, bring up the same application on your workstation, and have the user talk you through what he or she is doing to get the error; at the same time, you do the same thing on your end. This process can be tedious, and it takes a bit of practice, particularly if you're familiar with the application but the user is not (or vice versa).

A better option, particularly if it's problematic for you to get across town to a user's workstation, can be to invest in one of the many network remote control packages out there, such as one of the following:

- PCAnywhere
- ReachOut
- RemotelyPossible
- Novell Z.E.N. Works Remote Control
- Microsoft SMS Remote Control

These packages will allow you to watch exactly what the person at the other end is doing, which is really, really helpful. Sometimes you can simply correct what the user is doing. If you can't, though, at least you'll realize whether he or she is reporting the problem correctly.

Of course, a network remote control program does you zero good if a workstation is not talking to the network, so you might want to brush up on your over-the-phone troubleshooting skills anyway.

Protocol Problems

If you think that the application is installed correctly and on a functional workstation but might possibly be the victim of a bad bit of network glue, you should perform some basic protocol troubleshooting steps to gather more data. I basically perform these measures as second nature, just so I don't assume I have the entire picture before I get this objective data.

This discussion is going to be in the context of a Windows PC, but these steps can be taken on any workstation—you'll just use slightly different commands.

TCP/IP

If you're using TCP/IP, you'll follow steps that are similar to the ones in Hour 12, "UNIX Networking Basics."

Step 1: Ping the Loopback Address

First, you'll definitely need to identify your user's PC as well as the resource he or she is trying to get to on your network map. You'll want to get to the user's workstation and see if you can ping the loopback address (127.0.0.1).

As you've probably figured out by now, the loopback address isn't just a UNIX feature. Every station that has TCP/IP on it has a loopback address of 127.0.0.1. It serves the same function as the loopback plug I discussed in Hour 8, "Hard Basics: Guide to Being a Hardware Geek." It allows the IP protocol program to talk to itself without involving any outside influence, such as the network card.

Huh? Without the network card? How can you talk to anything without a network card? Trust me, you can. This is because the TCP/IP protocol (the *stack*) is its own program, and while it can and should talk to the network card, it can also talk to itself, as illustrated in Figure 17.1. This allows you to rule out the stack or the PC environment as the source of the trouble.

FIGURE 17.1

The TCP/IP stack of your computer can talk to itself, allowing you to rule out the PC environment as a source of trouble.

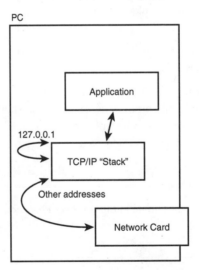

Step 2: Ping the Workstation's IP Address

Next, ping the workstation's IP address. If you don't know what it is, look at the output of the winipcfg command. (This command might tell you something else as well: Are you running out of leases on your DHCP scope? Is the DHCP server down?)

You might get a hardware error during either of these local pings, which means you've got a hardware problem. You'll need to run the network card diagnostics that came with your network card.

> If you can't ping the workstation's own IP address, perhaps the user ignored an error message when Windows started up, stating that a conflict existed with the IP address and Windows was going to disable the protocol—meaning no TCP/IP for you! Try rebooting and seeing if you get such a message. (See Hour 21, "Tell Me About Your Network: Network Analyzers" for tips on hunting down a duplicate IP address with a network analyzer.)

Step 3: Ping the IP Address of Another Workstation on the Same Segment

17

If you *can* ping the workstation, see if you can get to another workstation on the same segment. If you can, it will mean that the workstations involved are functioning correctly on the data link level; that is, they're able to make local calls. If not, you might be dealing with a data link problem.

Don't know the address of a station on the same segment? Try pinging the *broadcast address* (a special address that tells all stations on the segment to respond).

> The broadcast address is typically your IP network number with a 255 tacked on for the node number. Therefore, if your IP address is 192.168.10.5, with a net mask of 255.255.255.0, your node address of 5 would be replaced with 255, giving you 192.168.10.255 as a broadcast address.
>
> Some routers or UNIX workstations will allow you to ping 255.255.255.255 and will figure out the broadcast address for you, but Windows will not.

Once you ping the broadcast address, open the Address Resolution Protocol (ARP) table (this gives you information about IP-to-MAC address resolution) by typing this:

```
arp -a
```

If you see the following message, you've probably got a problem:

```
No ARP Entries Found
```

If other folks on this segment are okay, check the workstation cable and the card. Otherwise, the whole shebang will look something like this:

INPUT

```
C:\>ping 167.195.163.255
```

OUTPUT

```
Pinging 167.195.163.255 with 32 bytes of dat    A
Reply from 167.195.163.255: bytes=32 time<10ms TTL=128
Reply from 167.195.163.255: bytes=32 time<10ms TTL=128
Reply from 167.195.163.255: bytes=32 time<10ms TTL=128
Reply from 167.195.163.255: bytes=32 time<10ms TTL=128
```

INPUT

```
C:\> arp -a
```

OUTPUT

```
Interface: 167.195.163.7 on Interface 1
Internet Address  Physical Address    Type
167.195.163.3     00-00-c9-0b-ec-7f   dynamic
167.195.163.9     00-00-c9-14-93-17   dynamic
167.195.163.15    00-00-c9-1e-30-97   dynamic
167.195.163.17    00-05-24-dd-79-ea   dynamic
```

This technique does two things for you: It gives you a handy list of MAC-to-IP addresses, and it tells you that this network card, in conjunction with the TCP/IP stack, is working fine.

Take notes about what works and what doesn't. You'll begin to see how the picture starts to come together.

Step 4: Ping the Segment's Router

Try pinging the segment's router. Chances are, if you were able to ping other stations on the segment, you'll be able to ping this, too.

Step 5: Ping the Server by Name and IP Address

Ping the server by IP address and then try to ping it by name. The important thing to remember is that you want to troubleshoot by IP number before bringing name services into the picture; otherwise, you might confuse an already complex issue.

If pinging the IP address works but pinging the name doesn't, you should investigate the DNS configuration of the workstation or check the DNS server itself.

You can check the DNS configuration with the nslookup tool in NT or UNIX. (More on DNS in Hour 19, "Internet/Intranet Troubleshooting.")

If pinging the IP address doesn't work, you'll definitely want to "traceroute" the address. Listing 17.1 shows a healthy traceroute from a good workstation to a server (see Figure 17.2).

The traceroute command on most routers and UNIX systems is actually spelled out (*traceroute*), whereas Windows NT/95's traceroute command is typed as *tracert*.

LISTING 17.1 A HEALTHY TRACEROUTE

INPUT

```
C:\>tracert 167.195.165.15
```

OUTPUT

```
Tracing route to mail2.blibdoolpoolp.com [167.195.165.15]
over a maximum of 30 hops:

1  10 ms  10 ms  10 ms  167.195.163.1
2  60 ms  70 ms  61 ms  167.195.174.2
3  60 ms  71 ms  60 ms  mail2.blibdoolpoolp.com [167.195.165.15]

Trace complete.
```

FIGURE 17.2

Using the traceroute command is helpful when you're troubleshooting routing problems.

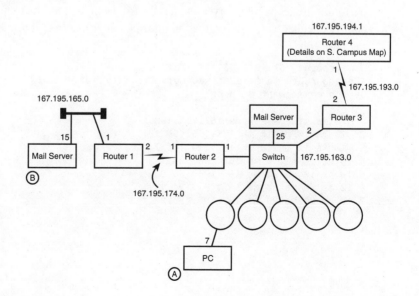

If the only router serving a subnet is down, you might get a `destination unreachable` message, depending on your routing setup. Some implementations of traceroute will show this as `!N`.

This happens because the router isn't alive; therefore, it can't generate the routing protocols that advertise the network to other routers. If no router knows about it and no default route passes it off to another "better informed" router, then the destination probably doesn't exist.

Each and every router involved is shown in the traceroute output. It goes without saying that if you see the traceroute just stop, then you've discovered the most likely point of failure. For example, if the traceroute in Listing 17.1 had stopped at `167.195.163.1` and never made it to the next hop (`167.195.174.2`), it's likely that there's a problem with the wide-area link (maybe the telephone company) or router 1 is down. A *successful* ping of `167.195.174.1` and an *unsuccessful* ping of `167.195.174.2` would verify this. (It would also show that router 2 was doing its job but was unable to contact the other side of the wide-area link.)

 Bear in mind that only *one* interface from each router will be shown on a traceroute. Notice that there's no record of the packet passing through `167.195.165.1` or `167.195.174.1`.

You can also spot misconfigurations with the `traceroute` command. For example, if you try to traceroute the mail server and get the following output, then router 3 is seriously confused, either by bad configuration information or incorrect information from a routing protocol:

```
C:\>tracert 167.195.165.15
Tracing route to mail2.traceroute.com [167.195.165.15]
over a maximum of 30 hops

1 <10 ms <10 ms <10 ms 167.195.163.2
2 <10 ms 10 ms 10 ms 167.195.194.1
3 <10 ms 10 ms 10 ms 167.195.163.2
4 10 ms 10 ms 10 ms 167.195.194.1
5 10 ms 10 ms 20 ms 167.195.163.2
6 10 ms 20 ms 20 ms 167.195.194.1
7 10 ms 20 ms 20 ms 167.195.163.2
^C
```

Here, router 4 says, "Hey, this isn't a packet for *me*, take it back!" Then router 3 says, "Duh, no, George, this is a packet for you!" In this case, you'd have to look at several routers' routing tables to figure out what the deal was. (This is called a *routing loop*, which typically comes about when a router is configured with an incorrect static route.)

IPX/SPX

IPX/SPX is usually a pretty reliable little protocol. Most IPX/SPX troubleshooting comes down to "Can you see it?" and "Am I running out of table space on my hardware routers?"

If you run a Novell shop—or even if you use IPX/SPX to talk to your NT servers—you can use `IPXPING.NLM` to check the response of IPX stations. If you want to run `IPXPING` from a DOS or Windows box, you'll want to go to Novell's site (`http://support. novell.com/cgi-bin/show_file?FileName=ipxpng.exe`) and get the `IPXPING.EXE` file. This allows you to ping servers or workstations.

You ping a workstation based on its IPX network number plus its MAC address, like this:

```
F:\PUBLIC>ipxping 1d 0000c9108c76
0000001D:0000C9108C76 is alive
```

You can also ping a server based on its IPX network number and MAC address, or you can use its unique internal IPX number and use a 1 for the MAC address, like so:

```
F:\PUBLIC>ipxping ddeeff 1
00DDEEFF:000000000001 is alive
```

If you have non-Novell routers in the picture, you should also know that some routers have settable limits. If you start to overrun these limits, you'll experience trouble. If you're having trouble between two sites connected by a hardware router, you should check your router's IPX Service Advertisement Protocol (SAP) as well as its routing table. Most routers will tell you that you're using x entries out of a possible y. If x equals y, you're probably overflowing your tables and should add more entries in the router configuration program.

The biggest cause I've seen of SAP table overflows is the addition of a lot of standalone print servers, such as HP JetDirect cards. These broadcast their presence to the network, and every router will propagate this broadcast to every other router. Most folks I know of have a lot of printers—if each printer has a SAP entry, the table starts to fill up quickly.

In addition to filling up your SAP table, numerous SAP entries can also slow down your WAN. Check your router documentation for ways to filter unwanted SAPs from propagating to your entire network.

17

You can display the names and numbers of IPX/SPX services your Novell network knows about by typing the following command at a NetWare server prompt:

```
display servers
```

Similarly, if you want to see the addresses and quantity of IPX/SPX networks, type the following at the console prompt:

```
display networks
```

These are also good commands to ensure your NetWare server is seeing the network in general.

Summary

It would be nice if you could simply concentrate on improving your network neighborhood each day. Unfortunately, grim reality dictates that in addition to taking proactive measures to avoid or ameliorate trouble, you also need to know how to react. Fine-tuning your reaction habits every day is a good way to lower your stress level and make you a more effective troubleshooter.

Telephone and "trouble call" skills play a large part in determining whether a problem is systemic or local. Sometimes, however, you need to go take a look for yourself, use a remote control program, or let the user guide you to re-create the problem on your workstation.

Once you've ruled out a local problem, you'll want to practice your connectivity-checking habits. Tools such as ping, traceroute, arp, and nslookup, in conjunction with the TCP/IP loopback mechanism, can show you where on the network a problem lies. As you make your way from the local loopback device to the ultimate destination, you'll continue to gather good information about what the problem is—and what it is not. Always troubleshoot numerically before bringing name services into the picture so as not to confuse an issue that may already be quite complex.

IPX/SPX troubleshooting is fairly simplistic, and the few tools you have can point out connectivity problems quite quickly. Some problems can be related to router table overflow, and you can either use router commands or NetWare server-based commands to show you the number of SAP and route entries on your IPX/SPX network.

Workshop

Q&A

Q What happens if I ping the loopback address and it fails?

A You might want to remove and reinstall the TCP/IP protocol from your Network Control Panel. This could fix corrupt TCP/IP stack files. This isn't too common, though, and might be symptomatic of major problems on the workstation.

Q Hey, can you tell me more about this `nslookup` tool, please?

A This is a really great tool, but in my experience, `nslookup` is more useful in a complex DNS environment such as the Internet; therefore, you'll see more about `nslookup` in Hour 19 than you did here. Most networks with fewer than 200 nodes have a very simple DNS environment—checking the configuration at the workstation after doing a ping of a symbolic name tends to show DNS problems just fine. I mention it here because as you get more sophisticated with DNS, it might become part of your initial rote troubleshooting.

Q Are there any more IPX/SPX information-gathering commands?

A Yes. You can type **track on** at your server console and watch your IPX RIP routes go back and forth between your IPX routers. This is more like a sideshow (unless you're really into the IPX routing thing). Most times, other troubleshooting methods are more than adequate to deal with IPX/SPX problems.

Quiz

1. True or false? Proactive troubleshooting is what you do when you get a call saying that the network is down.

2. Reactive troubleshooting habits include which of the following?

   A. User interviews

   B. Rote connectivity checking

   C. Neither A nor B

   D. Both A and B

3. True or false? Finding out whether a problem has occurred in the past can help resolve the problem faster.

17

4. A user has called and said that he can't get into the network at all. You can't get much more out of him. You're able to ping his workstation from your desk just fine, and you see his login on the file server connection list. What do you need to do?

    A. Sever his connection from the file server

    B. Ping him again

    C. Hang up in a fit

    D. Go visit him and see for yourself

5. True or false? You cannot ping a user's workstation, but you can use a remote control program to view his configuration and fix it.

6. What's the TCP/IP loopback address?

    A. `127.0.0.1`

    B. `1.0.0.127`

    C. `128.0.0.1`

    D. None of the above

7. One user can't get into the server SpaceMonkey; a ping to SpaceMonkey from that user's workstation fails. What's your next step?

    A. Ping another server to make sure SpaceMonkey isn't down

    B. Ping SpaceMonkey's loopback address

    C. Look up the numeric IP address for SpaceMonkey and try pinging that

    D. Look up the loopback address for SpaceMonkey and try pinging that

8. My TCP/IP address is `200.1.1.55`, and my net mask is `255.255.255.0`. What's my broadcast address?

    A. `200.1.255.255`

    B. `200.1.1.255`

    C. `200.1.1.0`

    D. `200.1.0.0`

9. After pinging the broadcast address, what do you type to see a table of MAC-to-IP address correlations?

    A. `netstat -a`

    B. `traceroute -a`

    C. `arp -a`

    D. `ping -a`

10. A traceroute reveals that a workstation can't get beyond the third hop. Where might the problem be?

A. The router at the third hop

B. The router at the fourth hop

C. The router at the fifth hop

D. The router at the second hop

Answers to Quiz Questions

1. False
2. D
3. True
4. D
5. False
6. A
7. C
8. B
9. C
10. B

17

HOUR 18

"Lots of Different People in Your Neighborhood": In-Depth Application Troubleshooting

Sadly, most problems won't be reported to you as "I can't update my customer database due to insufficient file permissions" or "A network checksum error due to bad router code is making my print file garbled." (I only wish!) Most times, in addition to the generic troubleshooting mechanisms we discussed in Part II and the initial application investigation techniques we discussed in Hour 17, "Where Do I Start?," you're going to have to do some specific application-level investigation.

This hour, you're going to grab a backhoe and do some major digging in your network neighborhood to aid you in specifically determining where an application's network problem is coming from. We're going to talk about file and print networking, further define its difference from client/server networking, and talk about common problems and diagnostic techniques for both.

Service Definitions

There are two ways to think of the services that a workstation gets from a server:

- File and print
- Client/server

These are the topics of the next sections.

File and Print Services

When most folks think about the common ways that people network and share files, they're thinking of *file and print* services. This is the typical way Windows users share a hard drive with other users and allow remote users to map a drive letter on their PCs to the hard drive on the network.

File and print services allow a user to transfer entire files over the network—and that's it. There are no "smarts" behind the server at the other end; it cannot search a file or files for you the way Yahoo or AltaVista can. File and print networking offers a simple and basic file transfer service.

For example, all application programs that can be run from the network using file and print services require that the application files themselves be transferred to your computer's memory.

Likewise, if you want to search the contents of a file while using file and print networking, you must load the entire file over the network and then use a program at your end to do the actual search. Sort of inefficient, huh?

Just as a point of interest—and as a confession to Geeks Anonymous—I once measured how much network traffic loading the workstation files for a version of WordPerfect caused: about 4MB. Yikes!

In truth, some file and print database programs can identify and ask for slices of files (or *records*), but they still need to comb through these slices—no matter how much of an index the program has—in order to find data for you.

Client/Server Computing

In contrast, client/server computing depends on the server having more intelligence than the simple ability to lump the file onto the network conveyor belt and shove it off to you. As we discussed in Hour 12, "UNIX Networking Basics," client/server systems can answer specific pricing questions about a catalog of items, for example. Rather than shoving the catalog in your face the way a file and print server might do, a client/server system would listen politely to your inquiry about widget pricing, perform a lookup on its local database, and then send the response back to you, as illustrated in Figure 18.1.

FIGURE 18.1

You can think of client/server computing as two intelligent people sitting on two ends of the phone. The client is the one asking the questions, and the server is the one providing the answers.

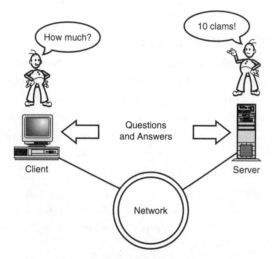

18

What else can a client/server system do? Well, take your Web browser for starters. It's the client of a client/server relationship. Your client says, "Hey, give me your default Web page," and the server spits it out at the client. (We'll look at this more later in the chapter.)

In addition, client/server is what you're using to submit information to a Yahoo search. If you use X Window, thin client, or Java applications, you're using client/server on the bottom line. Of course, the programming on the server end can be rather complex and demanding on the server. (I'm not really going to get deep into this, but it helps to know that—whatever the buzzword involved—any socket-level communication between a client and a server can be fundamentally classified as a client/server relationship.)

With that said, there are higher-level, more complex relationships that depend on client/server underpinnings. For example, you know the file and print clients you load on your workstation? The Client for Microsoft Networks and the Novell IntranetWare Client32? They obviously communicate with the server, ask it questions, and get replies. That means they're client/server, right? Indeed they are, but they're an important enough and complex enough method of networking that they deserve their own treatment. This stuff gets somewhat slippery, doesn't it? Don't worry, that's about as weird as we're going to get.

The File and Print Blues

The underpinning of a file and print client is, of course, the vendor-supplied client you load on the workstation. (Typically, the server vendor supplies you with a setup program, which then automatically loads and configures the client on your workstation. It's really easy.) The first troubleshooting step for file and print is to verify that the client is the correct version. You'll have to check with the vendor for the latest scoop on this, but notice that I say *correct*, not *latest*. It's enough to know that two given workstations (one of which is broken) have identical versions of the client.

How do clients work? Even though the clients may *look* simple, they are, of course, complex internally. Let's look at the NetWare client as an example. In order to make your file sharing and print sharing effortless for *you*, here are some of the things the client must deal with:

- Establishing your login, or *authentication*, to the network
- Locating a server on the network via *Novell Core Protocol (NCP)*
- Connecting to a server volume and then reading and writing files and directories to and from that volume
- Connecting to a server and then transferring files to a printer queue on that server
- Magically making a drive letter or printer appear on your workstation and act as if it were the real thing, even though the files reside on the server (the *redirector*)

Troubleshooting these pieces and parts on an individual basis is more trouble than it's worth—just realize that the client is more complex than it seems.

An interesting note is that the DOS version of the NetWare client used to load all these capabilities *separately*, to allow you to pick and choose which ones you wanted (and thus saving memory). The modules were called *VLMs*, or *Virtual Loadable Modules*.

File and print client software is complex enough that it's pretty vulnerable to domino-effect problems from other workstation software. Verifying good workstation configurations is also really important for file and print troubleshooting.

This section covers the major types of problems you can encounter on file and print systems:

- Problems with printing
- Problems with files
- Problems with applications

I Can't Print!

If you surveyed the entire country and asked administrators which network problem they found most aggravating, my bet is that one of the top answers would be *network print problems*. Therefore, we as troubleshooters want to fix those problems, pronto.

Unfortunately, many delayed resolutions to printer problems are due to insufficient printer documentation. When Cassie and friends refer to the broken printer as "Cassie's printer," that means something to them, but to you as a network troubleshooter, it means zero (unless it's followed by "Oh yeah, that's the finance-10 printer on the PENELOPE server").

Having a table of departments and printers works sometimes, but I find it more convenient when the printer installer slaps a label on it with server/directory/queue name information. That way, you can ask the user, particularly at a remote location, "What's the printer label say?" and be able to immediately start looking in the right place.

18

Let's take a look at what network printing usually entails. You connect to a network printer queue by browsing servers or the directory services tree, and you install drivers appropriate to that printer. So far, this is just like installing a printer that lives on your PC's LPT1 port, right? The only difference is that you're specifying some spooky network location rather than a local port.

What happens when you try to print? To answer that, let's run through these steps:

1. Your application generates a print metafile that it sends to the print driver. *Metafile* is a Microsoft term for a common ground graphics file that both applications and printer drivers know how to read. The print driver can then process the file.

2. The print driver processes the metafile and ends up with a printer-specific spool file. A *spool file* is where a print job is kept until it's printed by the printer. What's a "spool"? Think of a spool of thread, all of which will eventually get used, with the thread nearest to the top getting used first.

3. The *spooler* (the program on your computer that deals with spool files) works with the file and print client to transmit the spool file to the appropriate server's printer queue.

4. The server places the spool file in the appropriate holding directory if the printer is busy. Each spool file is treated on a "first come, first serve" basis.

5. The spool file is transmitted to the physical printer (or a network print server) when the printer is free (after other jobs have printed).

With five potential points of failure (more, in some cases), it's no wonder that print problems can be a big deal. Thankfully, most printer problems can be handled by divide-and-conquer techniques and the Sesame Street method. That is, you'll want to determine whether other users can connect to the printer, as well as whether the user who reported the problem can print to another printer. Lucky for you, I'm going to divide and conquer this entire process for you by breaking it down into five easy troubleshooting steps.

Step 1: Check the Application

Your first step when facing a printing problem will be to check the application. Although this sounds rather silly, I see a lot of printing problems where, say, a database is producing no output for the spooler to process. One would *think* that the database manufacturer might clue the user in that his or her report parameters produced no output, but that's not always the case. (You can always disable the queue and print again to see whether a job is even being generated.)

This might sound crazy, but check to make sure that a Windows 95 user has logged in to the network before you do *any* of these steps.

Windows 95 allows a user to bypass the login window by pressing Esc; therefore, a user might be trying to print to a network printer without being logged in to the network.

More complex problems can occur when an application is either improperly configured or has DLL problems that do not manifest themselves in other ways. For example, I have seen an application that needed special DLLs to print a file; when these DLLs were corrupted, either by another application installing its own versions of these DLLs or by simple hard drive problems, the application stopped printing, even though it otherwise behaved flawlessly.

You can find out whether the printing problem stems from the application by printing from another application—for example, Notepad or the WordPad. In UNIX, type the following to check printing outside of a given application:

```
lp -dprintername /etc/services
```

Step 2: Check the Driver

If two programs on a given workstation are not printing, I like to introduce another printer into the picture. In particular, I like to set up a local printer with a destination of LPT1. If the workstation has no printer attached to LPT1, don't despair—just set it up with a destination of FILE, which will simply direct the output to the hard drive. You can then view that file and make sure it's okay.

To make sure that the print file is actually okay, you can transfer it to another workstation that does have a printer directly attached and then type something such as this:

```
copy /b PRINTFILE LPT1:
```

To rule out driver problems, make sure to use a different driver for your test printer. I like to use "Generic/Text only" for some things, but, of course, this won't work too well if your application is graphical. Because you're ruling out the driver, it doesn't really matter which print driver you use, as long as you're fairly confident that it's a good driver.

> Sometimes, even though you have a good driver, your workstation might be running out of gas while the driver is processing the metafile. Check the resources as we discussed in Hour 8, "Hard Basics: Guide to Being a Hardware Geek."

Step 3: Check the Spooler

Can someone else spool to the server queue? If so, your first guess might be that the problem lies with the workstation. In this case, I want to make darn sure that the printer, as set up on the workstation, is going to a valid queue and has not lost its mind.

To do this, I usually go ahead and set up another printer on this workstation—pointing to the correct server queue—just to make sure. If that doesn't work, I set up another queue to another server, just to prove that queuing is messed up on this workstation. If this works, it means that the problem might not lie with the workstation; you've probably got some sort of communication or security problem between this workstation and the original server queue.

Check whether you can see the server in any other way: Can you log in to it? Ping it? Check your security rights to this queue, or, even better, try to spool to it as someone else.

Step 4: Check the Server

The server might show that it's getting the spool file just fine—whereupon the output just disappears into thin air. A couple things might cause this that aren't limited to communication errors between the workstation and the server. In this case, you might want to rule out a communications problem.

One way you can verify that the server is getting passed a good spool file is by taking a look at it at the moment the server gets it. You can do this by putting the printer in question offline, because the server will delete the spool file after it thinks the printer has processed it. Because you're blocking the printer, spool files will be left alone. You can then take a gander at the spool file that's being passed to the server. Where does the spool file live? Table 18.1 gives you an idea.

TABLE 18.1 Spool File Locations

Operating System	Spool Files Kept In
Windows 9*x*	`%WINSYSDIR%\spool\printers\`*`jobnum`*`.spl`
Windows NT	`%SYSTEMROOT%\system32\spool\printers\`*`jobnum`*`.spl`
(Intra)NetWare	*`QueueVol`*`:SYSTEM\`*`QUEUENUM`*`.QDR`
UNIX	`/usr/spool/lp/temp` (actual queue files)
	`/usr/spool/lp/requests` (control files)

WINDOWS

Usually, the `%WINSYSDIR%` variable (you can show it by typing **set** at a command prompt) is `C:\WINDOWS`, but it could be something else, such as `C:\win95`. Similarly, under NT, `%SYSTEMROOT%` is typically `WINNT`, but it might be something else, such as `WTSRV` for Windows Terminal Server 4.0. `jobnum` is a system-assigned number, and it could be anything—you'll want to troubleshoot on a fairly quiet system so that you don't have to wade through thousands of spool files trying to find *yours*.

NETWARE

Each queue needs a place to store its files; NWAdmin will let you choose a place, such as SPACEMONKEY_SYS. `QueueVol` is usually one of the SYS: volumes on one of your servers, but you should check NWAdmin details of the queue for where it really lives.

Each queue in NetWare also has a unique 8-digit hexadecimal value that's also listed in the properties in NWAdmin. Just fill in the hex number in place of *QUEUENUM*. For example, my queue might live in SPACEMONKEY_SYS:`\system\f00d160d.qdr`.

UNIX

Most SVR4 UNIX flavors keep their spool files here, but some keep them somewhere else. You'll want to check your vendor-supplied documentation.

Once you find the file, what do you do with it? First off, you can always look at it with a regular text file editor. It will probably look like vomit if you're dealing with a laser or inkjet printer. In this case, you might want to temporarily change the driver at the workstation to "Generic/Text Only," unless you speak laser printer fluently. This way, you can read the spool file once you find it.

In addition to reading the spool file on the server end and seeing that it does not contain `Paul is dead` over and over again—or some other such gibberish that might be caused by network communication problems—you'll also want to check the size of the file against the source. Just perform a `DIR` on the filename and compare it to the file on the workstation. (To capture this on the workstation, just set the printer to work offline before printing.)

In some cases, a slight difference in size between the file on the workstation and the file on the server is okay. For example, the Novell UNIX-to-NetWare gateway print filter adds a carriage return to the linefeed at the end of each line (something that DOS-style printers need that UNIX printers don't). This means that the file at the server end will be slightly larger due to the addition of those characters. However, in most cases, a differing spool file size is a *bad* thing.

Step 5: Check the Printer

The last step between your server and your output is the link between the server and the printer. In most cases, if this link is having problems, *everybody* is going to be having problems printing. It's *very rare* that this is a user- or workstation-associated problem. (I've been burned enough that I never say *never*, particularly when strange print problems are involved.)

So, let's assume that Penelope the Bug is sharing her PC's printer with Space Monkey's entire office. Space Monkey can't print, and neither can Quincy. First, you should determine whether Penelope can print. It turns out that she can't.

She's connected to her printer directly via her parallel port and a parallel cable. The cable to her printer is good (you determine this by swapping it out with someone else's printer).

Next, try to print *directly* to the printer, avoiding Windows entirely, by getting to a command prompt and typing this:

```
dir > lpt1:
```

This doesn't work, either, even after you reset her computer. You're pretty sure that her LPT1 port has been fried. Penelope is sad. Fortunately, you brought a spare parallel card. You swap it in, and this solves the problem. Penelope is happy.

There is one special-case server-to-printer link—that of the dedicated network print server. Some of them are configured to be servers (UNIX print servers are usually configured this way) and are therefore contacted directly by client workstations. Others are configured to be subordinate to the server and are therefore contacted by the server after the workstation transfers the queue file (Novell network print servers are generally configured this way). You'll have to check your dedicated print server documentation and configuration to be sure which one you have.

> Even though you cannot perform a `dir > lpt1:` command on a dedicated print server to rule out its link to the printer, some have a button on them (which can be hard to find) that makes them print a test page. Beware of telling a print server over the network to print a test page—you're not testing its local print capability in this case.

File Pile

File problems can be classified into several categories:

- Inability to use a file (read, write, delete)
- Resource problems (out of disk space)
- Application problems (file hierarchy is messed up or files are corrupted)

Several techniques can be used to name your pain for these troubles; because there's more than one problem, there's more than one shooting iron you can use.

Denied!

A file access problem usually manifests itself in a user saying that he can't write or read a file. Alternatively, a user might see the following message:

```
This file is already open, and can only be opened   read-only
```

This can be caused by a few things:

- Someone has set the file to be read-only to protect it from casual overwriting.
- The user lacks the proper security permissions to access the file.
- Someone else has the file open, and because that person is busy with it, the file is locked.
- The user's server connection was dropped by a network error (or whatever) and the automatic reconnect failed because someone else got the connection first. (This is rare.)

Read-Only

A read-only file is easy enough to check. If your workstation is Windows, right-click the file, go to Properties, and see whether the Read-Only check box is checked. If it is, somebody has set it this way. You'll have to go find out why (you can find out who owns the file in the same dialog box).

18

Blanket Security

You'll want to check pertinent files and directories to see that the user can, in fact, access the files in question.

In UNIX, you'll want to look at the full properties of the file and make sure that the file is readable or writable by the user in question. Here's an example of a file's full properties:

```
ls -la mysecretfile
-rwxrwx--- 1 monkey root   140 Nov 14 1997 mysecretfile
```

UNIX file properties are usually the same, even between versions of UNIX. There are three potential clusters of rwx along the left side, each meaning "read, write, or execute permission" for the cluster. The first cluster means "user permission," the second means "group permission", and the third means "world" permission.

In this example, the mysecretfile file is owned by the user monkey, and it belongs to the group root. It's 140 bytes long and was last modified on November 14, 1997. monkey has full read, write, and execute permissions and anybody in the root group can read, write, or execute this file, but the rest of the world cannot do *anything* to this file.

Using a Windows desktop, you can check the file properties. Some network clients, such as Novell's client, will add a tab to the file properties, as in Figure 18.2, where you can check file permissions. Simply right-click any file and select Properties from the menu that appears.

FIGURE **18.2**

File properties, as viewed on a Windows 95 workstation with the Novell IntranetWare client.

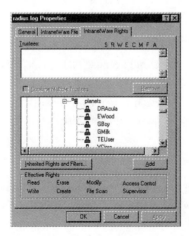

If you know that one user can get to the file but another user can't, you should compare the groups to which the users belong. It's not common practice to assign user-level permissions to files that groups of people need to get to (which works to your advantage).

When all else fails (and you're starting to tear your hair out), you can make the user into a super-user equivalent and try again. (You can do this under Novell by assigning Admin to the user's Security Equivalences tab in the NWAdmin; NT users can be added to the Domain Administrators group as well as the Administrators group.) If the operation succeeds after you've done this, you *know* that you have a security-related issue and can then pursue it further.

> Every security person on the face of the earth is going to have conniptions over me telling you to do this. There *is* danger here, Will Robinson. I'm *not* advocating the practice of normal users running as a supervisor or administrator equivalent—that would be nuts, and it would cause you more problems than you'd know what to do with. (Can you imagine Traci in HR with the power to delete your server's hard drive? I'm shuddering.)
>
> I *am* saying that you can rule out security-related problems this way. If you temporarily allow a user these rights—and then take them away when you're done—this is a powerful method for ruling out (or ruling in) security problems.
>
> Here's the bottom line: As long as you don't forget to take away the security rights when you're done, and you do this for a short, controlled period of time, you should be okay.

18

Flock o' Locks

File locks can cause all sorts of wondrous problems. For example, some backup programs can't deal with a user who has a file open—which causes all sorts of backup problems. Some email programs or database engines keep their files open even while not in use—which causes backup programs to skip them while backing up. Come again? Wouldn't you rather have *any* backup—even risking that the file changed in the middle—than *no* backup of a file? The solution to this is to purchase a backup program with an open file manager, which avoids this sort of thing (a problem found in Novell and Windows, but not UNIX).

Many problems, though, are caused by users being in files. For example, suppose I'm trying to update a terminal emulation program early in the morning, say, at 5:30 or 6:00. I attempt to install the update, only I get a Can't write to file error in the install program. The install program is helpful enough to tell me that it thinks that someone else may be using the file, but that's about it. Alternatively, I might get a call from a user who is trying to update a file, and WordPerfect is telling her that she can only open the file as a read-only file. In both of these cases, if I know the name of the file, I can use server utilities to find out who's using it.

Under NetWare, go to the Monitor's File Open|Lock Activity menu, navigate the volumes and directories, and pick the file, which would show you the server connections that have locks on the files. Then go to Connection Information and scroll down to that connection number, which tells you the user name.

For NT, use the Server Manager to show the files in use, as shown in Figure 18.3, by following these steps:

1. Click the Start menu and then choose Programs|Administrative Tools|Server Manager.

2. Right-click the server you're interested in.

3. Choose Properties.

4. Click the In Use button.

FIGURE **18.3**

The Server Manager can show files (and other resources) that are in use on an NT server.

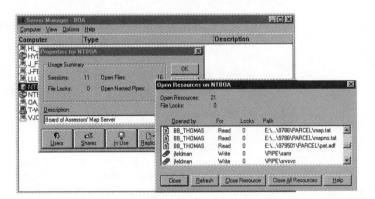

UNIX doesn't have a standard file lock finder. You can find out who's using the file system by using the `fuser` command (see the man page), but this won't work on an individual file level.

My favorite thing to do when I'm updating a program is to not update it. Let's say that I'm updating the NETTERM program, which lives in my G:\NETTERM folder. I need to put the new version out there for users. One of the methods I like to use (which doesn't apply to all cases, but this is a simple application in this case) is to rename the old folder, which means I'm not updating the old program. Rather, I'm installing the new program in the same location. To keep the older version, I drop to a command prompt, and type the following:

```
G:\> move netterm netterm.old
G:\> mkdir netterm
```

If something goes wrong, and I need to quickly put the old stuff back, I can always type this:

```
G:\> deltree netterm
G:\> move netterm.old netterm
```

You could also do this through the Explorer, of course, but you get the picture. The benefit in this case is that the file locks don't apply—I'm not updating the old app; I'm installing a new app into an empty folder.

The only caution here is that you need to go and assign the new folder the same security attributes as the old folder; otherwise, none of your users will be able to see it, much less use it.

18

The Case of the Missing Space

No matter how much disk space you have, it's never enough, is it? Even though hard drive sizes have gone up considerably in recent years, the amount of multimedia being stored online has gone way up, apps have grown in size, and so have their data files. Particularly if you run an enlightened system without file quotas (well, NT doesn't have that ability without third-party software), users can quickly eat up any disk space you throw their way.

In general, when you have acute "diskitis," work tends to grind to a halt. It's important to be able to identify the blockage and excise it quickly. (Novell users: See Hour 13, "NetWare Networking Basics," for a tip on how to use the Monitor to find out quickly who's using the space.)

I know system administrators who always hedge their bets—they either keep a hidden file out there that's a couple hundred megabytes (which they can quickly delete if they get into a full disk situation), or they simply don't dole out all the disk space at once.

Check your operating system manuals; there are ways to add disk space where it doesn't show up immediately. You can also add space on-the-fly. In a nutshell, you can allocate the storage and add bits of it later. Very cool. (Under AIX, see the Logical Volume Manager; under Novell, see INSTALL.NLM.)

On a day that starts out without a disk space problem, it's likely that your remaining disk space has been eaten by any of the following items:

- Large files created that day
- Large numbers of smaller files accumulated over a couple of days
- Large files created in the last couple of days, recently pushed over the edge by normal user activity

How do you find these? If you're like most shops, you have thousands of files and hundreds of directories and subdirectories—wading through these unaided is nuts. Fortunately, you have automation tools to assist you.

Find

The `find` command in UNIX is my best friend. When faced with a space problem, I might type the following:

```
cd /full filesystem
find . -mtime -1 -print ¦ xargs ls -lad ¦ more
```

This means "find everything with a modification date within one day and print out its name with the size, a screen at a time."

Alternatively, I might type this:

```
find . -size +2048 -print ¦ xargs ls -lad ¦ more
```

This finds everything that's over 2048 blocks (1,048,576 bytes, or 1MB).

If nothing turns up, I try the first command with `mtime` set to 3 instead of 1. Something will usually turn up.

The Find tool in Windows is also pretty cool (see Figure 18.4). It allows you to search by date and size. Does this take a long time? Yes. This is why keeping a little bit of hard drive space on the side is probably a good idea.

FIGURE 18.4

The Windows Find tool's advanced settings can help you track down large files (and, thus, disk space hogs).

HEY! STOP THAT RUNAWAY PROGRAM

Sometimes finding the individual files doesn't do you any good. For example, our UNIX system administrator and I came in one Monday morning to find the /usr file system full on the main UNIX system. We saw that most of the files that had been generated over the weekend were print spool files, so we stopped the spooler, deleted the queue jobs, chalked it up to a crazy user, and restarted the spooler. Fifteen minutes later, the file system was full again.

We looked at the spooler control files and saw that they all belonged to one particular user. We did a process list for her:

```
ps -fu mary
```

We killed the lp process that she had been running, stopped the spooler, deleted the queue files, chalked it up to a crazy spool job, and restarted the spooler. Fifteen minutes later...

Apparently, the application she had been using to run a report had lost its mind, and it kept repeatedly printing the report over and over again. Once we killed all her processes, we were okay, but that was a pretty fun half hour.

Here's the lesson: Just finding the files isn't always enough; sometimes you need to find out *why* they're being generated.

18

Application Celebration

Some applications are pretty complicated. For example, email and scheduling applications can be insanely complex with lots of configuration files, incoming, outgoing, administrative, and extra queue directories, and so on. It can be hard to identify a corrupt file—or any other cause—that's the monkey wrench in the works.

Here are some strategies that work with file and print application problems:

- Check server and application logs.
- Change the rules. (Can you simplify them? Can you move the app?)
- Restore from a "known good" point in time.

Happy Fun Logs

A log file typically tells the tale pretty well. You'll want to make sure that your application is configured for verbose- or debug-level logging if you're experiencing problems. You don't necessarily need to be an expert to take action after looking at the logs—you can always search an error message on the Web, or sometimes the log file will suggest an action, like so:

```
file.idx is corrupt—run rebuild process
```

Environment

Changing the environment is pretty case-specific. For example, you might be able to move the application from one server to another to rule out server problems—but I wouldn't do this unless you had reason to believe that the problem was server-related. If you're having problems that seem capacity-related, can you move some users to a different application server?

Restoring from a Known Good Point

If you're not an expert in the application, and neither of the first two strategies work out, the beautiful thing about file-level applications is that they're well-suited to fixing by restoration. You'll still need to know where the application lives in order to restore it, but if you installed it, or if you have the manual, this should be trivial to find out.

> Complex applications sometimes have *more* than one location—an app that exchanges state information with another location *should not* be restored on its own. The app might get really, really, confused if all of a sudden half of its brain gets restored.

EXPERTS INACTION

I've been in a shop where nobody had been trained on the email system; that is, although everybody had been trained on how to *use* the system, nobody had been trained in how to *administer* it. So when the mail system stopped talking one fine morning, nobody really knew how to deal with it.

Log files showed nothing in particular. A search of the Web revealed nothing. Technical support hold times were in excess of an hour, with the promise of a callback later that afternoon—maybe.

All the IT personnel in this shop were highly trained professionals—but not having been trained on the administration of this application, they were just as useless as anybody else in diagnosing this problem. But waiting all day for tech support was not a popular option.

After restoring the system from backup, everything worked—nobody even lost any mail, since the problem had occurred during the night, after the backup ran. To this day, nobody knows what the specific problem was—and nobody cares. Moral of the story: Good backups win.

Client/Server Maitre d'

Client/server troubleshooting basically entails verifying that TCP/IP communications are working okay and then verifying that the server program is answering the phone on the other end—that is, the correct socket is listening at the server end.

Let's quickly review TCP/IP connectivity techniques:

1. Ping by name: Is the name resolvable?
2. Ping by IP address: Is the server reachable at all?
3. Use `traceroute`: Why can't you get there? Where does the packet stop?

State of the Socket Address

Get used to typing the `netstat -a` command—it is *the* tool for troubleshooting client/server application problems. Let's quickly go over what the output of `netstat -a` shows you:

```
Proto Local Address    Foreign Address  State
```

- `Proto`   This refers to the protocol (either TCP or UDP).
- `Local Address`   This refers to the address and socket that the workstation is using to speak.
- `Foreign Address`   This shows the remote address and socket number that you're speaking to.
- `State`   This describes the state of the socket (see the following note).

Does the local socket address matter? No. Just like with a phone call, you can use just about any free extension to dial out—and your computer will do so automatically. The local socket address only matters if the computer that you're sitting on is a server. In that case, it must be listening at the correct socket number; otherwise, nobody will be able to talk to it.

18

Depending on the operating system, you'll see one of the following various states in the State column:

State	Description
LISTENING	"I'm a server, and I'm ready to talk to someone."
ESTABLISHED	"I'm having a conversation."
SYN_SENT	"I'm trying to synchronize the call with someone, but no luck so far."
SYN_RECV	"I'm in the process of synching up with someone."
CLOSE_WAIT	"The other end just hung up; I'm waiting for the dial tone."
TIME_WAIT	"I hung up; I'll get rid of this entry shortly."
LAST_ACK	"The other end said goodbye and will shut down shortly."
FIN_WAIT1	"The socket is closed. I'll get rid of this shortly."
FIN_WAIT2	"The socket was closed by other end. I'll get rid of this shortly."

Services with a Smile

For any client/server service, you'll want to be able to objectively check to see if the server is listening. This usually means trying to connect to it from a client machine. In order to try to connect—or verify a service on the server end—you'll want to know the numeric value of the well-known services, as well as their names.

A list of services is available in C:\Windows\Services under Windows, /etc/services under UNIX, and SYS:ETC\Services under NetWare. You can also check out
http://www.kashpureff.org/nic/rfcs/1300/rfc1340.txt.html for more than you ever wanted to know about standard service numbers, network numbers, and more.

Table 18.2 shows the numeric values of some of the services I work with a lot (and there are many more).

TABLE 18.2 NUMERIC VALUES OF COMMON SERVICES

Service Name	Number	Comment
FTP	21	File Transfer Protocol (Internet)
Telnet	23	Login service for UNIX (sometimes NT or Novell)
SMTP	25	Internet-style server-to-server email
Domain	53	DNS services (UDP and TCP)

Service Name	Number	Comment
Gopher	70	Internet Gopher
HTTP	80	Hypertext Transfer Protocol (the Web)
POP2	109	Post Office Protocol version 2 (user email)
POP3	110	Post Office Protocol version 3 (user email)
NNTP	119	USENET news
netbios-ns	137	NetBIOS Name Service
netbios-dgm	138	NetBIOS datagram service (actual data)
netbios-ssn	139	NetBIOS session service (Hi, how are you?)
shell	514	Rlogin socket (UNIX or NT)
printer	515	Line Printer Daemon (network printing for UNIX)
socks	1080	Socks proxy server (Socks 4 and Socks 5)

What if you don't know the socket number of a client/server program that you're using? Simple—stop the server program and then run netstat -an. Print it out or save it to a file:

```
netstat -an > socklist.txt
```

Then start the server program and run netstat -an again. Compare the two lists. The new socket number that shows up in the second list is the socket number (or numbers) for your client/server program.

18

Connection-Oriented Versus Connectionless Sockets

As we discussed in Hour 15, "Firewall and Proxy Server Basics," for our purposes, there are two types of sockets: UDP and TCP. When a program sends out a UDP packet, it has no way of knowing that the packet got there because it's *connectionless*, rather like a message in a bottle. For our troubleshooting purposes, we hate UDP. It's a very irresponsible child. We like TCP best, because we can quickly tell whether a TCP socket is listening. Because a TCP socket is a connection-oriented socket, we can initiate a call on our own and see whether we get a busy signal or a connection.

One way to check whether the socket is being established is to use the client program itself and then check the workstation's socket list. For example, here's how you can connect with an FTP service in one window and run netstat -an in another window:

```
C:\WINDOWS>netstat -an ¦ find ":21"
TCP 192.168.10.5:1025   192.168.5.1:21   ESTABLISHED
```

Here you have an ESTABLISHED connection, so no matter how much your FTP client is complaining, you do have a *bona fide* socket. In this case, you might want to look at client configuration if you're experiencing problems.

Another way to check whether a remote socket is listening is to telnet to that socket. For example, let's perform a control experiment. You can run an FTP server on a PC and then use Telnet to go to it to see if it's listening. Just so you don't even go to the outside network, use your loopback address (the loopback address in TCP/IP is always 127.0.0.1). You can see the results just by typing this (see Figure 18.5):

telnet 127.0.0.1 21

FIGURE 18.5

You can run a local FTP server on your PC and connect to it with Telnet by specifying the loopback address and socket 21.

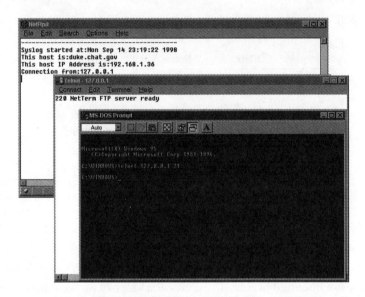

As shown in Figure 18.5, the screen indicates that the FTP server is running. This is a really neat trick, and you can do it with any TCP service. Will you always get a response? No. Sometimes there's no prompt. However, the trick is whether or not you get an immediate CONNECT FAILED from the Telnet program. If you do, odds are that nothing is listening on the other end.

Because the version of Telnet provided with Windows is not very verbose about *why* a connection failed, sometimes I drop to a command prompt and run the character-based `ftp` command. You can specify a socket to it as well, and it returns the proper message when there's no server listening to that socket on the other end. For example, I *know* that I am not running a Telnet server on my PC; to prove it, I'll use `ftp`:

```
C:\WINDOWS> ftp
ftp> open 127.0.0.1 23
-> ftp: connect:Connection refused
```

I can do this to check the listening status of *any* TCP socket.

No matter what operating system you're running, the service number will be the same. For example, any Novell or NT server that gets a print job from a UNIX server is usually listening to the print socket (#515). If you telnet to server 515 and get a `Connection refused` message, it's time to check the server program.

Be aware that not all UNIX printing is socket dependent. There's a method of printing, called *pass-through printing*, that has *nothing* directly to do with the network. It's entirely dependent on your terminal program to react properly to certain invisible codes that are sent with the text. For instance, if your application on a UNIX host sends the `Control-T` code to your Wyse-60 terminal, your terminal—or terminal emulator—will start printing the text that's sent immediately following the code, rather than showing it on your screen. Another code—for example, `Control-R`—will make things go back to normal. Just be aware of this; you might just save yourself some aggravating running around.

I CAN'T SPOOL, TAKE TWO

I was in a shop that bought a new UNIX host, moved some print queues over, and noticed during testing that certain print jobs would just sit there for long periods of time before printing. We noticed that this only happened with wide area–connected printers, as well as printers that were connected to dedicated print servers.

We further noticed that only one printer at a time was printing on any given standalone print server. Our host vendor claimed that it had to be our network, whereas our print server vendor said it had to be the host.

After sending print jobs to multiple queues from the host to one of our standalone print servers, I went to the host and typed the following:

> ```
> netstat -an ¦ grep 515
> ```
> I only saw *one* socket being opened to the print server. That was enough evidence for
> me—apparently, the print services on this (proprietary) version of UNIX didn't support
> more than one printer on a given network host, and it was only sending one job at a
> time. This was why the wide area stuff was acting funny, too—there were more than one
> printer on the other side of the WAN link, and instead of sending multiple print jobs,
> one big print job could block all the other, smaller print jobs. Network traces bore this
> out.
>
> The vendor claimed that this aberrant behavior was "as designed," and declined to fix it.
> So we went and bought something that worked right.

Content Checker

For certain services, such as HTTP, you can actually check content. For instance, Listing
18.1 shows a troubleshooting session with a Web server.

LISTING 18.1   A TROUBLESHOOTING SESSION WITH A WEB SERVER

```
mori    A    ~$ telnet 167.195.160.6 80
Trying 167.195.160.6...
Connected to 167.195.160.6.
Escape character is '^]'.
GET /
<title>Neato Geeky Stuff(tm)</title>
<B>Neato Geeky Stuff(tm)</B><P>
<img src="jonny/smguru.gif">
<B>Leo sez:</B>
<p> Check it out. <I>Lotsa</I> neato geeky stuff.
...
```

Whoa—it's the whole HTML page. This definitely tells you more than a ping—it tells
you that your Web server is up and serving HTML. In other words, who cares if your
Web server is responding to pings? You don't have it there to respond to pings, you have
it there to serve Web pages. If it's responding to pings but not serving Web pages, it is
for all intents and purposes "down." By checking the content like this, you *know* that it's
functioning properly.

> **MAIL FAIL**
>
> If you can telnet to a socket but are still having application problems, it's time to point the finger at the app. I saw a proprietary mail system that was failing at a remote site—the users were connecting but then getting hung up for long periods of time while they were trying to access their mail. We put in a mail server to serve them locally (and get the wide area out of the picture), and the users were then fine. However, when the new mail server tried to talk to the main server, we got lots of disconnected sockets—lots of sockets in the TIME_WAIT state. By *lots*, I mean, 30 to 50. This indicated that there were many successful connections, followed by disconnections.
>
> Odd. Usually, when a connection is established, it will sit there and do its work merrily; disconnects are usually caused by network problems—not the application. However, I could stay connected to a socket using Telnet as long as I liked. This really, really pointed to the app.
>
> A search of the vendor's Web site on the socket state revealed that, with certain router configurations, this problem would occur. The vendor recommended fixing the router but also provided a patch and a workaround applicable to the server and client software, which ending up fixing the problem.

Summary

18

Client/server and file and print networking are the bread and butter of most networked shops. Although file and print networking is, underneath it all, a huge agglomeration of client/server protocols, it's complex enough to warrant being treated differently. File and print services rely on their clients heavily, so you'll want to keep everybody on the same sheet of music.

Printing is one of the most important and aggravating functions on your network. Understanding the print process can help you to quickly pinpoint where a problem is. Printer-oriented documentation helps tremendously, particularly when it's slapped on a label on the physical printer. Knowing how to trace a print problem is really helpful for complex problems.

File errors aren't always necessarily accurate—someone who opens a read-only file might be opening a file that's only read-only to *him* or *her* because of security attributes on that file. Knowing how to navigate your particular server's security is really important here. You can rule out security-related problems by trying the same operation after assigning super-user rights to a user—and then quickly removing them.

Disk space problems can bring your entire operation to a halt. Apart from finding the culprit, you can alleviate the problem by keeping some spare disk space on the side.

Socket-level troubleshooting is the keystone of client/server application troubleshooting after you've ruled out network-level problems. The `netstat -a` command is one of your best friends here. Knowing your service numbers, as well as socket states, can help in diagnosing a problem. In particular, performing the Telnet trick can quickly point out whether a service is running on a given host, and it can sometimes show you whether it's serving up content properly.

Workshop

Q&A

Q What in the blazes is a queue?

A *Queue* is the British-English word for a *line*, such as the line at a bank. It was adopted for use with computing, and it refers to any situation in which something is dealt with on a "first-in, first-out" basis. In a file and print context, a queue is an imaginary line that print jobs wait in to get serviced.

Q I can't print from one particular station, and I've traced it down to something to do with the server, because the queue file is not the same on the server as it is on the workstation. What's the next step in tracking this down?

A If other folks are successfully printing to this server queue, it might be something to do with the workstation. However, this workstation might be on a different network segment than the others that print successfully. Can you move the workstation? That might point to a failing router or switch port.

Q Is there any way to clear somebody's locks on a file without disconnecting them from the server?

A NT can clear someone's lock on a file; Novell cannot. To clear someone's lock on a file residing on a Novell server, you've either got to call the user and ask him or her to stop using the file, or you need to clear the network connection from the server.

Q Is there a Telnet-type tool for UDP to see if a UDP socket is listening?

A To know whether a connectionless socket is listening, you've got to get a response. To get a response, you need to send it the correct kind of "note." So no. The only tool you can use to remotely see if a UDP server is up is the client.

Quiz

1. What's the chief difference between client/server and file and print networking?

    A. You can only get information after a file has been transmitted in client/server print networking.

    B. The client is typically more complex on a file and print client.

    C. Neither A nor B

    D. Both A and B

2. I transmit a query; then the server searches a large database on its local hard drive and sends me back an answer. What's this an example of?

    A. File and print networking

    B. Client/server networking

    C. Neither A nor B

    D. Both A and B

3. During a print troubleshooting session, you've verified that the application is producing output and that the printer driver is working correctly. What would be the next thing to look at in your troubleshooting efforts?

    A. The transfer of the spool file to the server

    B. The transfer of the spool file to the workstation

    C. The transfer of the spool file to the physical printer

    D. The transfer of the spool file to a new department

4. Where does Windows NT store its spool files?

    A. `WINDOWS\Printers`

    B. `%SYSTEMROOT%\System32\Printers`

    C. `%SYSTEMROOT%\Printers`

    D. `WINDOWS\System32`

5. True or false? It's a good idea to allow someone to run with supervisor, root, Admin, or Administrator privileges for a long period of time.

6. In order to find out who has eaten up all of your disk space on a given day, what should you look for?

    A. Files starting with n

    B. Files created that day

    C. Files modified in the last week

    D. Files particular to the most popular application

18

7. True or false: You can use the Windows Find utility to find files that are at least a specific size.

8. True or false? Restoring all application files from a "known good" point in time should be a last-resort method of fixing them.

9. You're trying to get a user's Web browser to work. You pull up a DOS prompt in another window and type `netstat -a` right after you try the browser. You see a connection in TIME_WAIT, but it's to the wrong server and has the wrong socket number. What is most likely happening here?

   A. The browser is suffering from latent network errors.

   B. The browser is misconfigured.

   C. The TCP/IP stack is hosed.

   D. The user needs to update the browser.

Answers to Quiz Questions

1. D

2. B

3. A

4. B

5. False

6. B

7. True

8. True

9. B

HOUR 19

Internet/Intranet Troubleshooting

I remember when a co-worker loudly proclaimed that the Internet was a waste of time and that all of us who were fascinated with it had best find another line of work. Well, although he's a nice enough guy, he's not exactly a terrific fortune teller. The Internet has been more successful than any of us ever dreamed.

The basic idea behind this hour is that the same backhoes and steamrollers used to fix the "information superhighway" at large are also used to troubleshoot your local streets and byways. We'll start off by defining the Internet versus intranets and quickly get into troubleshooting techniques.

Definitions

Nobody needs to define the Internet for you. The source of life, the Mecca of computer civilization, the wellspring from which information flows, the fount of all packets good and ill, is the Internet. In the space of one kid's college career, the Internet has gone from being a pretty nice resource for computer geeks, to being indispensable for geeks, to being indispensable for *everyone*. Many folks used to call the Internet a "noncritical resource," but that's no longer the case, particularly if your business relies on email or a Web page to keep in touch with customers. Nowadays, it's a *vital* resource; if it's down, oftentimes folks can't do their work. For example, this book was edited largely over the Internet. Had it been down—I don't want to think about it!

The millions and millions of TCP/IP-connected computers and networks in the world all network in pretty much the same way that we've been talking about since Hour 1, "The Telephone Analogy: Becoming Familiar with Basic Networking Concepts," but just on a different scale. When your workstation sends a request for a Web page to a server at www.microsoft.com, a name-to-IP-address DNS lookup is done; then a TCP/IP call is sent up to the server, assisted by anywhere from three to a dozen routers in between.

Should troubleshooting your Internet connection differ from the TCP/IP troubleshooting that you've already learned? Not fundamentally. However, with the next level of complexity comes the next level of troubleshooting techniques. In a nutshell, a fault with the Internet connection at your location definitely involves your ISP (Internet service provider) but may not be its fault. We'll talk about the types of firewalls that you might have in your shop and then discuss ways to point the finger at routing problems, name resolution problems, and whether you should call your ISP into the fray for a given problem.

Intranet = Internal

The word *intranet* and its successor *extranet* (a network connecting you and a business partner) are marketing terms that have always confused me. True, *intra* means *within*, and *extra* means *without*, but so what? In our data center, we've usually got an idea of which applications run externally—we call them "public access." In my (admittedly twisted) mind, you might as well call your neighbor's lawn an *interlawn*, your own lawn an *intralawn*, and the border between your lawns an *extralawn*. Give me a break!

Seriously, the term *intranet* does have its uses—but so does the phrase "my network." All it means is that you're using Internet-like applications within the boundaries of your own network—you're using technologies that grew up on the Web. An intranet can be as useful as a Web-enabled telephone directory of all employees, complete with search capabilities, or it can be as useless as a static Web page welcoming you to the Frobozz Magic Intranet. Whatever *your* intranet does, it's likely that you want it to keep on truckin'.

Many of the tools used for diagnosing your Internet connection are applicable to intranet troubleshooting, so read the Internet section carefully. (The techniques covered in Hour 18, "Lots of Different People in Your Neighborhood: In-Depth Application Troubleshooting," are also very applicable to troubleshooting intranets.)

With that said, later on in this hour, we'll cover troubleshooting that's particular to your local network: your internal and external Web services, your email, and the problems that dialup networking users might face.

Cyber Chaos

With all the fancy terms surrounding the Internet, it can be easy to lose sight of the fact that it's just one big TCP/IP network. Let's look at some specific TCP/IP troubleshooting techniques that can pinpoint Internet problems in your shop.

To start with, we'll need to identify what kind of Internet connection your shop has. Once you know what type of Internet connection you have, you'll be better able to identify which of the following techniques are right for you.

Unless you work for a huge multinational company with fault-tolerant Internet connections all over the place, you probably have just one firewall and one domain name (company.com).

Actually, if you happen to work for a huge conglomerate with thousands of dedicated IT (Information Technology) staff members, you'll probably have to read this book in a plain brown wrapper, and you might not have an official chance to practice what you've learned outside of your local area network. The chances of you being allowed to touch network gear or get directly outside the firewall in this type of environment are slim to none. Remember: If any of you are caught or killed, the secretary will deny all knowledge of your actions. This book will self-destruct in five seconds.

19

Internet Identification

More than likely, you have one of the following types of Internet access:

- Method 1: Workstation dialup connections only (see Figure 19.1).
- Method 2: Firewall or proxy direct to ISP (see Figure 19.2).
- Method 3: ISP router only, no firewall (see Figure 19.3).
- Method 4: Firewall or proxy, DMZ (demilitarized zone) network to ISP router (see Figure 19.4).

FIGURE 19.1

A workstation dialing up to a typical Internet service provider.

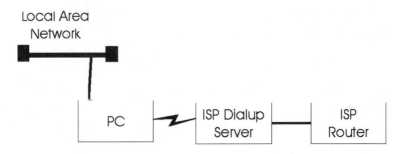

FIGURE 19.2

A firewall or proxy server located on your network that's connected to the ISP.

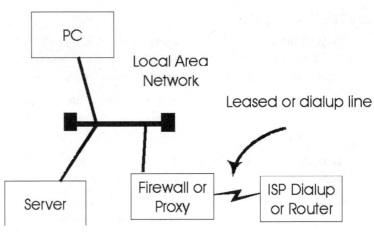

FIGURE 19.3

A router connecting a network directly to an ISP and therefore directly to the Internet (this method is becoming rare due to security concerns).

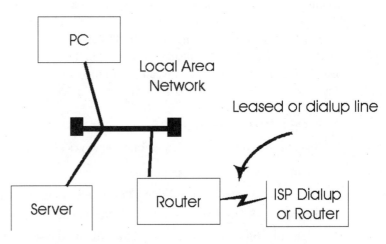

FIGURE 19.4

A typical demilitarized zone setup allows for "permissive" access to public access servers.

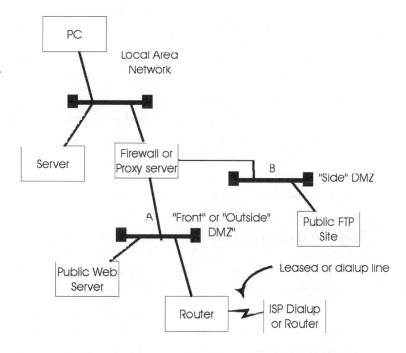

It's important to identify what type of connection you have. How do you find out? Well, method 1 is pretty easy—if you use Windows dialup networking to connect to the Internet, you usually hear a modem dial and you see the dialup networking dialog box before you connect (see Figure 19.5). A dialup connection makes you a "connection unto yourself," and you're actually classified as a method 3 (a direct connection to your ISP with no firewall). In other words, unless your workstation acts as a *router* (Windows 95 cannot, and Windows NT must be configured to do so), nobody else on your network can avail themselves of your Internet connection. (If you do decide to use NT as a cheap router to your ISP, remember that your connection is classified as method 3—you do not have a firewall protecting your network. Beware!)

FIGURE 19.5

The dialup networking dialog box.

19

In general, the first steps for troubleshooting this method of Internet connectivity are pretty easy—you either make the connection or you don't! In most cases, being "down" is due to the ISP's equipment or the telephone company. (Having problems *after* you connect? See "Here I Ping Again," later in this chapter.)

In contrast, if you use methods 2 through 4, you don't usually do anything more than log in to your workstation; the local area network is used as the onramp.

Method 2 is one of the more common configurations, particularly if your ISP *hosts* your Web pages (that is, it runs a server that your Web pages live on, without you needing to run your own Web server). This is a particularly easy way to do things for a small-to-medium sized shop; you only need a wide-area connection (dialup or leased) from the firewall or proxy to your ISP.

Method 3 is sort of unusual. It implies that the user either doesn't care about security—possible, I suppose—or that security is taken care of in the ISP's shop. Although there are still some folks in the United States who don't lock their doors, their numbers are dwindling; so, too, are those who don't have their own firewall.

Method 4 tends to be the norm for most larger shops. What does the presence of an intermediate network, or "demilitarized zone" (DMZ) mean? Machines that don't have to be absolutely and totally secure machines can be placed on the outside network and made available for outside Internet users. The fact that they're "in front" of the firewall or "on the side" of the firewall means that they're treated separately from the production network.

If an outside machine is "on the side" of the firewall, it means that you need outside users to get to the server, but you also want those users to be restricted in some way. Instead of having to configure many servers, you just need to configure the firewall to only allow certain traffic. For example, you might allow FTP sessions from the outside world to get to the FTP server at point B in Figure 19.4 but not allow anything else from the outside.

When a server is "in front" of the firewall, it means that the firewall is *not* protecting the server at all. Sometimes this is done because the firewall would impede the function of the server. For example, because a proxy server requires a proxy client, it would be impractical in this case to use a "side" DMZ for machines meant for public access. In this case, a front DMZ would mean that Internet traffic could reach public access machines without being hindered by the proxy server.

An outside DMZ is cool, because you can walk up to the hub that it's on and monitor your traffic as well as check or use intruder detection software to see if unwanted folks are probing your network. More importantly for our purposes, you can hook a network analyzer or a regular old Windows 95 laptop to it and troubleshoot unhindered by possible firewall restrictions. (Refer to point A in Figure 19.4.)

> Even if you have a proxy server that will not pass ping packets, traceroutes, or DNS lookups, you can plug into your DMZ segment and troubleshoot your little heart out because you're bypassing the firewall.

Seven Years of Plenty...

Once you've identified your firewall type, it's really important—*before* trouble strikes—to try the troubleshooting techniques presented in this hour so that you can know what works and what doesn't work during a "normal" period.

If you don't figure out what's normal for your shop, how will you know when it's broken? In other words, if you have a proxy server that doesn't allow ping—you're not going to *ever* be able to ping, so attempting to ping during an outage will gain you no knowledge. However, if you know that ping typically *does* work through your firewall, then during an outage, if you're not able to ping through your firewall, you might suspect that either the firewall is down or that the link (Ethernet or leased line) to your provider's router is down. You can then investigate appropriately.

Here I Ping Again

You'll start off your Internet connection adventure by doing the same kinds of things you'd normally do internally. The easy part of Internet troubleshooting is that because you more than likely only have one router or firewall, it's pretty easy to point the finger at what's down if you cannot get to the Internet at all.

> This router or firewall is called the *choke point* because it's the point at which all traffic could get choked off if it malfunctions.

If you cannot ping an address right outside your firewall, router, or proxy server, you have a pretty good idea that your choke point is down. Remember to ping by IP address rather than DNS name—you *always* want to make sure that IP connections work before dragging name resolution into the picture. (If IP connections aren't working, you can bet your bottom dollar that DNS resolution isn't working either.)

How do you know what address to ping? Good question! You can ask your provider for the "far side" address of its router. (No, that's not a router with snakes, cows, chickens, and a bizarre sense of humor. It's the router interface farthest from you—the end that isn't connected to your system.) You could also simply keep the IP addresses of several reliable Internet hosts handy. Usually, a ping will resolve a DNS name to an IP address, so just ping a couple of your favorite WWW addresses and write them down.

> You can also use traceroute to trace your path to your favorite WWW address while everything is working and then write down the second hop that traceroute reports. This is probably the "far side" address of your ISP's router.

My preference tends to be to ping my ISP first and then ping an outside address. If your ISP link is up but you can't get to anything else, your link to your ISP could be fine but the ISP's link to the outside world may be having problems. Although your ISP probably already knows that it's having problems with its link to the outside world, it couldn't hurt to call and report this.

DNS Problems

Suppose your IP connectivity is okay. However, although you can ping by IP addresses all day, the second you bring a domain name into the picture, your browser barfs. No problem! Let's take a look at the types of DNS problems you're likely to see:

- Inside-to-outside problems—You can't see others' DNS names.
- Outside-to-inside problems—Others can't see your DNS names.

For either type of problem, the tool of choice is nslookup. The nslookup tool allows you to connect to a given DNS server and find out what that DNS server thinks about things. In other words, when you ping, you're forced to use the DNS server configured into your TCP/IP stack, but nslookup allows you to bypass this and choose which server to talk to. You can specify servers by IP address (when name resolution isn't working at all) or by name (when you're trying to track down a strange problem) and tell nslookup what type of information to give back to you.

Using Windows 95 or 98? Bummer! Although Microsoft has an exact UNIX-like version of nslookup for NT, for some reason, it doesn't supply this program with Windows 95/98. Fret not. You can find reasonable equivalents by searching your local shareware site (www.shareware.com, www.tucows.com, and so on) for "nslookup." I can't find the exact equivalent out there, but several programs offer nslookup-like functionality, including these:

- dns11.zip
- nsb32-5.zip
- lookup.zip
- setuptk.exe

The DNS Hierarchy

To be able to use the nslookup tool effectively, you'll need to know the basics of the DNS hierarchy. Like your hard drive, the DNS has so many individual records that it's separated into many different levels (*folders* on your hard drive; *zones* in the DNS world). Take a look at Figure 19.6. It's drawn as a tree, and you read it from the top down (dots separate the zones). Not too bad, right? That's the way the entire DNS is organized.

FIGURE 19.6

DNS zones, like the folders on your hard drive, are arranged in a tree structure.

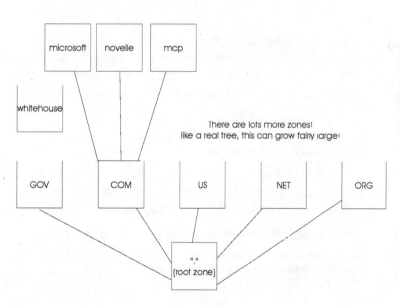

19

Now let's consider how this is implemented in real life. Each zone is usually handled by one *primary* server and several *secondary* servers. How does everybody know which server is responsible for which zone? Each zone also has a special record called the *SOA*, which stands for *start of authority*. Each zone's SOA record details which servers are responsible for that zone, and, among other administrative records, contain contact information for the party responsible for that zone.

Although secondary servers get their information from the primary server for the zone, they otherwise act exactly like a primary server for the zone. Furthermore, the secondary servers may live at any IP address—they do not have to be geographically or physically close to the primary server. The zone is a "logical" concept and has no physical restraints.

Finally, because DNS is hierarchical, if the DNS server that you use does not know the answer for a DNS query, it must kick the query "up the tree" to the zone server above it to see if it can get an answer. If it does get an answer, it stores the answer in its cache. That way, if it gets asked for the same hostname again, it can give an answer back to the DNS client without having to query the zone above it.

With this information in mind, let's look at a real-world inside-to-outside DNS problem.

I Can't See You!

I've been at a site that was having intermittent problems with DNS lookups. Sometimes the DNS lookup was fine; other times, no good—users at Windows workstations would complain that they got an error stating that there's no DNS entry for `www.company.com` (I'll be using fictional addressing in this example). Assuming that the site's DNS server at `200.1.1.6` was responsible for the `ci.monkey.ny.us` zone (standing for Monkey City in the state of New York), our immediate tasks were as follows:

- Make sure that the Internet at large knew that `200.1.1.6` was authoritative for `ci.monkey.ny.us`. I didn't suspect a problem here, but on first blush, this is always a good thing to check.

- Find out "who" the zone server above us was (`ci.ny.us`). I suspected that this was where the problem was (any query that your own DNS server can't handle gets kicked to the next zone above it).

We dug out nslookup and proceeded to check out the first task:

```
> server a.root-servers.net
Default Server: a.root-servers.net
Address: 198.41.0.4
```

```
> set type=soa
> ci.monkey.ny.us
Server: a.root-servers.net
Address: 198.41.0.4

Authoritative answers can be found from:
     US  nameserver = NS.ISI.EDU
     US  nameserver = RS0.INTERNIC.NET
     US  nameserver = NS.UU.NET
     US  nameserver = ADMII.ARL.MIL
     US  nameserver = VENERA.ISI.EDU
     US  nameserver = EXCALIBUR.USC.EDU
     NS.ISI.EDU  internet address = 128.9.128.127
     RS0.INTERNIC.NET  internet address = 198.41.0.5
     NS.UU.NET  internet address = 137.39.1.3
     VENERA.ISI.EDU  internet address = 128.9.176.32
     VENERA.ISI.EDU  internet address = 128.9.0.32
       EXCALIBUR.USC.EDU  internet address = 128.125.51.11
> server ns.isi.edu
Default Server: ns.isi.edu
Address: 128.9.128.127

> ci.monkey.ny.us
Server: ns.isi.edu
Address: 128.9.128.127

ci.monkey.ny.us
origin = ns.ci.monkey.ny.us
mail addr = hostmaster.ci.monkey.ny.us
     serial = 29981
   refresh = 3600 (1 hour)
   retry = 600 (10 mins)
   expire = 86400 (1 day)
   minimum ttl = 3600 (1 hour)
```

Okay, cool. We went directly to a "root" server—that is, a server that has the authority for all the root zones (.com, .us, .gov, and so on)—and asked it what it knew about our little Monkey City. It responded that we needed to go to another server, one that knew all about the .us domain. We then asked that server about the same thing, and it responded appropriately, so we were in good shape.

All root servers, in addition to being in the "dot" or "root" zone, are also in the root-servers.net zone. Each server is designated with a letter, so you can go to b.root-servers.net, c.root-server.net, and so on.

19

Our next task was to find out what the zone above us was:

```
> monkey.ny.us
Server: ns.isi.edu
Address: 128.9.128.127

Non-authoritative answer:
monkey.ny.us
    origin = Buggy.net
    mail addr = postmaster@Buggy.net.savannah.ga.us
    serial = 1998080901
    refresh = 3600 (1 hour)
    retry = 1200 (20 mins)
    expire = 12096000 (140 days)
    minimum ttl = 14400 (4 hours)

Authoritative answers can be found from:
monkey.ny.us nameserver = dns2.Buggy.net
monkey.ny.us nameserver = dns1.Buggy.net
    dns2.Buggy.net  internet address = 128.6.1.9
    dns1.Buggy.net  internet address = 128.6.1.10
```

Okay, apparently the servers that are authoritative for monkey.ny.us are called dns.buggy.net and have IP addresses of 128.6.1.9 and 128.6.1.10, respectively. Because these servers are on the same subnet, we took a look at how far away they were and how long it took to get a packet from here to there.

A ping session revealed that, in fact, certain packets were taking anywhere from 800ms (an eighth of a second) to 1,500ms (a second and a half). Whoa! A second and a half is an *eternity* in networking. Could, perhaps, the slow connection to the zone server next up in the tree pose a problem? It sure could! DNS only waits for so long before it decides that no answer is in the offing and returns an error to the client. So how did we resolve this?

There were two answers here. The folks in question needed to upgrade their line to the Internet because their own traffic was killing them (one person's download was cramming the line so full that DNS traffic wasn't responding fast enough). What's more, a traceroute revealed that the ns.ultra-monkey.net server was 16 hops away. Sixteen hops is, well, a lot. Asking their ISP to take responsibility for the monkey.ny.us zone also helped with this problem, because this meant that there was only one hop between the users and their parent zone.

Sometimes, someone else's DNS servers are down. This will generally mean that you can't look up DNS names for one domain *only*. Most sites have multiple DNS servers, so this shouldn't happen, but it does. This probably means that you'll just have to sit tight and wait for the zone in question to have its problem resolved.

In a nutshell, here are the things that typically cause you to be unable to look up outside addresses (an inside-to-outside lookup problem):

- Too much lag between you and your upstream zone
- Upstream DNS servers are unreachable
- The DNS server is down or unreachable for a particular zone

You Can't See Me!

Let's say that you stop getting email—even "junk" email. You pick up the phone and call your friend Space Monkey, who tells you that his email is getting bounced back to him. He's terribly busy being a successful businessman so he hangs up before you can get details. However, he does mention that he can't get to your Web pages either. You suspect that there's probably an "outside-to-inside" DNS problem, because you can ping everybody in the world and can resolve their DNS addresses inside to outside.

So, how do you check the how the outside world looks you up? The first thing you do is (you guessed it) fire up nslookup. Let's start off by checking your DNS server, the most likely culprit:

```
$ nslookup - dns.frob.com
Default Server: dns.frob.com
Address: 167.195.160.6

> www
Server: dns.frob.com
Address: 127.0.0.1

Name: wizard.frob.com
Address: 167.195.160.10
Aliases: www.frob.com

> mail
Server: dns.frob.com
Address: 127.0.0.1

Name: dragon.frob.com
Address: 167.195.160.8
Aliases: mail.frob.com
```

Hmm. Everything looks OK from a local standpoint.

Many (but not all) DNS servers on the Internet are called "dns" or "ns" to designate whether they're domain name servers or just name servers in general.

19

Well, your DNS server is, in fact, dealing with the world—when it gets queries about your domain, it answers just fine. If this wasn't the case, you would troubleshoot it further: Is it down? Have its data files been corrupted? (If so, you should restore from a backup.)

The DNS server is okay, so we'll move on to other possible problems. Using nslookup again, let's find out how the root servers are telling others to look up your server. In other words, we need to look at the SOA record for your domain, starting from the beginning:

```
$ nslookup - moria.co.chatham.ga.us
Default Server: moria.co.chatham.ga.us
Address: 167.195.160.6

> set type=soa
> server a.root-servers.net
Default Server: a.root-servers.net
Address: 198.41.0.4

> frob.com.
Server: a.root-servers.net
Address: 198.41.0.4

Authoritative answers can be found from:
frob.com nameserver = NS4.frob.com
frob.com nameserver = NS2.frob.com
NS4.frob.com internet address = 167.195.160.15
NS2.frob.com internet address = 167.195.160.6
```

Whoa! What's going on? There's an IP address listed here for a server you don't know about. Actually, you do know about it, but it's a server that's due to be rolled out next month, not *this* month. Apparently, one of your co-workers has jumped the gun and told the powers-that-be on the Internet that your name server has moved to this new address. Unfortunately, your current name server isn't listed due to a paperwork foul-up. A quick visit to the www.internic.net page (the clearinghouse for most domain names) and a discussion with your co-worker fixes this.

This scenario is unlikely (although I've seen it happen). However, it gives you an idea of the type of havoc that can go on in the world of DNS. I've even seen companies where a disgruntled system administrator has *stolen* the domain name after having left the company, leaving the company unable to get email or Web visits from the outside.

Eek! Can this happen? Unfortunately, yes. Two contacts are listed on a DNS entry: the administrative contact and the technical contact. If a system administrator lists himself as both, he can do an address change to his home address and then, after leaving the company, change the SOA record to something else. There's not a lot you can do about this (from a technical standpoint). Your best bet is to pursue this from a business standpoint:

Let the InterNIC (`www.internic.net`) know what's happened and enter into a "domain name dispute." More than likely, you'll be able to get your domain name back without having to get legal-eagle about it.

Routing Problems

Let's say that you can get to certain Web sites but not others—or your email is having trouble getting to some sites but not others. The best thing to do in this case, after making sure you can resolve the name, is to traceroute to the site's IP address.

For example, our library system was having trouble reaching a certain Web address. I used traceroute on the IP address and found that my traceroute packet was being chucked back and forth between two routers repeatedly. This routing loop definitely indicated a routing problem, but it was hard to know who was responsible for it.

I reported the problem to the library's ISP, but also wanted to let the folks who were responsible for the routers know about it. How do you know who's responsible for a router? Here's comes nslookup again!

Each IP address on the Internet *should* (but does not always) have a corresponding DNS name in a special zone called `in-addr.arpa`. This is so you can quickly resolve an IP address to a DNS name using a special kind of record called a *pointer*, or *PTR*. If you check the SOA for the DNS name—or for the network number—you can frequently find out the responsible party for the address. The only catch is, you need to enter the address in *reverse*. This is to make it convenient for the DNS zones. However, don't worry too much about it—the important part is that you need to enter the addresses backward. For example, let's say that the two routers that were looping were `192.168.1.10` and `192.168.2.5`. During my troubleshooting session, I fired up nslookup, as follows:

```
$ nslookup
> set type=PTR
> 10.1.168.192.in-addr.arpa
Server: dns.frob.com
Address: 209.52.182.122

10.1.168.192.in-addr.arpa    name = router10.foo.net

> 5.2.168.192.in-addr.arpa
Server: dns.frob.com
Address: 209.52.182.122

5.2.168.192.in-addr.arpa    name = router5.foo.net

> (Ctrl-D)
$ whois foo.net
[rs.internic.net]
```

19

```
    Registrant:
John E. Monster (FOONET-DOM)
P.O. Box 4242
Indianapolis, IN 46219

Domain Name: FOO.NET

Administrative Contact:
Monster, John E. (JEM12) monster@FOO.NET
317-555-1400 ext. 5066 (FAX) 317-555-1800
Technical Contact, Zone Contact:
Monster, Joey (JM48) joey@FOO.NET
317-555-1400 ext. 5067
Billing Contact:
Monster, John E. (JEM12) monster@FOO.NET
317-555-1400 ext. 5066 (FAX) 317-555-1800

Record last updated on 07-Aug-98.
Record created on 25-Sep-97.
Database last updated on 29-Sep-98 08:19:55 EDT.
```

> You can find out responsibility information for *any* zone using the whois utility. If you don't have UNIX, there are Windows utilities that offer the same functionality—for example, Internet Anywhere Toolkit (www.tnsoft.com).

Okay! I've got all the information I need to report these shenanigans! Foo.net owns both of these routers, and the whois for foo.net provides an email address for the technical person responsible for this zone. I emailed both my ISP and joey@foo.net, gave them the traceroute output, told them what IP address I had done the traceroute from, and the problem cleared up in a matter of hours. Sometimes, you'll get a friendly letter back telling you what the problem was—other times, you'll be greeted with stony silence. I've had it go both ways, but at least I could tell the folks at the library what the problem was and that I had reported it.

Intranet Troubleshooting

If you have a complicated intranet with many DNS zones, you can troubleshoot it much the same way that you troubleshoot an Internet problem—with nslookup, traceroute, and ping. Similarly, the applications that make an intranet run are similar in nature to the applications that you'll run on the Internet, so you can apply the techniques discussed in the following sections to your Internet servers as well.

Your Web Server

My favorite Web server troubleshooting technique (which I mentioned briefly in Hour 18) is to telnet to socket 80 of a Web server and see whether I can use the GET HTTP command. (Most times, this will make the server shoot the main index page my way.) If I can, that means the server is responding to HTTP requests, and users should have no trouble accessing the server to get HTML pages. This is a good indication that the network between you and the Web server is okay.

Most Web server problems fall into three categories:

- Reliability problems
- Third-server problems
- Network problems

We won't discuss network problems here—they're addressable using the techniques we discussed in the "Cyber Chaos" section, earlier, as well as in Hour 17, "Where Do I Start?" and Hour 18.

Reliability Problems

Reliability problems fall into two subcategories:

- Capacity problems (server overload)
- Crash problems (server dies with a blue screen, kernel panic, and so on)

If your server is truly so popular as to be overloaded (really unlikely unless you provide an incredibly popular service on the Internet), you'll first want to check your server log files. Are the hits that you're getting "official" hits? Or has one of your users posted a non–work-related (but very popular) Web page? Overload is really unlikely on an non–Internet-connected server. Most Web servers can handle hundreds, if not thousands, of users without a problem. It's when you start to get hundreds of hits *per second* that you really have a problem.

If you really want to be that popular, you'll have to collect your log files and involve your server vendor and ISP, and you'll probably have to upgrade two things: your Web server and your Internet connection. Based on the amount of Web data shown to be transferred in your logs, these two vendors will make recommendations about how you can upgrade.

It's more likely, particularly for a non–Internet-connected intranet server, that your problems will be crash related. Take heart—most reliability problems are revision related or related to other software on the server. Make sure to get the latest version and/or patches for whatever Web server you use, as well as to use divide-and-conquer and rule-out methods on other services that run on the server.

19

For example, I ran an NFS server on one NT server in conjunction with a Web server. The server kept dying with the blue screen of death on a regular basis—that is, until I removed the NFS server from it and replaced it with an NFS server from a different vendor.

You'll also want to keep current on service packs for your operating system. For example, as of this writing, NT Server 4.0 should have Service Pack 3 installed, and Service Pack 4 is just around the corner.

In a nutshell, you can overcome Web server reliability problems by exercising the divide-and-conquer practices from Hour 4, "The Napoleon Method: Divide and Conquer," and look up specific error messages by using the techniques from Hour 7, "The Simple Simon Approach: The Benefits of Being Too Stupid to Quit, But Too Smart to Keep Tackling a Complex Problem Head On."

Third-Server Problems

Even though your Web server is running smoothly and dishing out HTML to beat the band, you still might experience problems with your intranet applications. Intranet applications tend to rely on more than one server, so it's a good idea to have a diagram of how these applications interact with each other. For an example, see Figure 19.7, a diagram of an intranet application called Knowledgenet. See how the Web server itself is just one piece. For the application to work, the remote control "thin client" server must be functioning, and the CD-ROM server must also be functioning. Notice how the CD-ROM server only speaks IPX/SPX and is a Novell server—it's *not* a TCP/IP server.

FIGURE 19.7

A sample "thin client" multiprotocol, multi-server intranet.

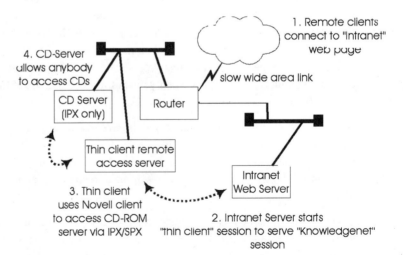

The bottom line is this: Even though your Web server is functioning, any one of the other two components malfunctioning makes the entire intranet application stop working. Again, documentation is key here; if someone tells you that the Knowledgenet application is not working and you pull up this diagram, you naturally know which servers to check.

Email Fail?

Proprietary email is basically a client/server application or, in some cases, a specialized file-sharing application. When trouble arises with your proprietary email system (such as GroupWise, Lotus Notes, or Exchange), you're best off checking your product documentation and using the file-and-print or client/server troubleshooting techniques we discussed in Hour 18.

However, each one of these proprietary email systems also supports Internet/intranet standards and provides gateways to hook up to the Internet at large. Internet (and therefore intranet) email has three components:

- SMTP—Simple Mail Transfer Protocol (server-to-server communication)
- POP—Post Office Protocol (client-to-server communication)
- IMAP—Internet Mail Application Protocol (client-to-server communication)

You can telnet to socket 25 to check whether SMTP gateways are up and accepting connections. Here's an example:

```
$ telnet wpo 25

Trying 167.195.160.7...
Connected to wpo.co.chatham.ga.us.
Escape character is '^]'.
220 wpo.co.chatham.ga.us GroupWise SMTP/MIME Daemon 4.11 Ready
1993, 1996 Novell, Inc.
```

You can also telnet to the POP socket (socket 109 and socket 110, depending on the version of POP that you're using) and the IMAP socket (socket 143) to make sure that the servers that are supposed to be accepting these types of connections are up. Here's an example:

```
$ telnet moria 143
Trying 167.195.160.6...
Connected to moria.co.chatham.ga.us.
Escape character is '^]'.
* OK moria.co.chatham.ga.us IMAP4rev1 v10.170 server ready
```

19

If you're having trouble getting outside mail from the Internet to your intranet, you'll want to use nslookup to check your MX record for your zone. An *MX record* is a special record denoting the "mail exchanger" for your zone. Here's an example:

```
$ nslookup
> set type=mx
> co.chatham.ga.us
co.chatham.ga.us    preference = 10, mail exchanger =
➡moria.co.chatham.ga.us
moria.co.chatham.ga.us internet address = 167.195.160.
```

If it's not the right server or if you don't even have one, you'll need to change this on your DNS server or ask your ISP to do it for you.

Dialing Difficulties

Do you run into problems with the following types of dialing?

- Dialing out of your intranet and into the Internet
- Dialing out of your intranet and into somebody else's intranet

Huh? Dialing *out* of your intranet and into the Internet? Even when you have an Internet connection? Don't laugh—it happens more often than you'd think. Either there's a Neanderthal policy handed down from above that the Internet will *not* be used for personal use or folks just don't feel comfortable using the Internet for non–work-related business.

Dialing out of your IP network and into someone else's intranet is also reasonably common. Therefore, let's take a look at the technical implications of dialing out of your IP network and into another IP network (whether the Internet or another intranet), along with some common problems that folks encounter.

Dialout DNS

When you dial someone else's IP network, you are using that person's IP numbers on one of your interfaces as well as relying on that person's DNS servers to look up names. Because these DNS servers (more than likely) do *not* hold the symbolic names of your servers, it's likely that name resolution will fail for local hosts. Because a DNS server will return a "no such host" message rather than failing with no response, your computer will *not* go to the next DNS server in the list to try again—your request will simply fail.

You'll want to let users know that they might not be able to get to "local" TCP/IP applications while they're dialed in to another network.

Microsoft dialup networking will offer to "clear the existing DNS servers." Let your users know that they should *not* do this; otherwise, they'll be unable to access your local area network services.

There's one more thing that you should know about DNS and dialout. You can specify up to three DNS entries in the Windows Control Panel. If you have a user who will be dialing out of your intranet, you should not specify more than *two* in the normal Windows Control Panel. The reason for this is that if three already exist, when the dialup adapter tries to add one more (for the remote network), it will fail and the user won't be able to resolve remote names.

Summary

Your intranet operates pretty much the same as the Internet at large—just on a smaller scale. Accordingly, troubleshooting strategies that work on one will also work on the other.

Part of getting ready to troubleshoot your Internet connection is identifying what type of connection you have. After you've done so, you'll want to practice troubleshooting measures using nslookup, ping, and traceroute to see if these tools will work through your firewall. To be able to rule out IP connectivity issues versus DNS problems, you'll want to keep a few IP numbers of reliable hosts on the Net handy.

If you have a DMZ (demilitarized zone) segment "in front" of your firewall, you can plug a laptop or other workstation into it for the purposes of troubleshooting, even if the firewall will not allow diagnostic tools to work through it.

A little DNS knowledge goes a long way when troubleshooting Internet problems—whether you're having trouble resolving a hostname or others are having trouble seeing your hosts. The nslookup tool will give you a lot of help when troubleshooting DNS issues.

Routing problems may be addressed similarly to routing problems on your own network; the key lies in finding out who is responsible for those routers and alerting them. Once again, nslookup to the rescue!

Problems with your Web server and intranet applications are typically either capacity related, reliability related, or related to an entirely different server (as with the CD-ROM server in a previous example). Although it's possible for a Web server to run out of gas, this is not true for the majority of intranet servers. Good documentation and staying current on operating system and Web server patch levels can help you avoid or resolve many problems in this arena.

19

Workshop

Q&A

Q **I've read that the Internet at large uses different routing protocols than a typical local area network, so how can troubleshooting techniques on my intranet apply to Internet troubleshooting?**

A True, the routers on the Internet are major beefcakes, and I hear that some of them use steroids. Although they're drugged drones, they still must obey basic rules of routing: A packet that comes in on one interface must be routed to another interface and passed off to the "next hop" or dropped if the destination is unreachable. Seriously, the routing protocols are merely methods of routing table updates—as such, they don't matter to us, because we're not ISPs. We just care about pointing to the trouble and reporting it. If a packet isn't doing what it's supposed to be doing according to a traceroute, we have a reportable problem, and that's where our responsibility ends. Here's the bottom line: Let the ISPs worry about the routing protocols, just so long as they route our packets properly.

Q **My proxy server connects straight to my ISP via a leased line, and I cannot use ping, traceroute, and nslookup through it. I'd like to be able to troubleshoot my own problems, but I have no DMZ and my firewall's getting in the way! Any suggestions?**

A Get a dialup account from your ISP (you might even be able to get a freebie if you have a big and expensive leased line for the main part of your business) and troubleshoot using that. The dialup account will allow you to be on the ISP's DMZ, and you should be able to use standard troubleshooting procedures from there.

Quiz

1. What does ISP stand for?

   A. Internet supplier partner

   B. Internet service provider

   C. Internal stud professional

   D. Interior service provider

2. Which of the following is a legitimate way of connecting to an ISP?

   A. Workstation dialup connections

   B. Firewall or proxy direct to ISP

   C. Neither A nor B

   D. Both A and B

3. What does DMZ stand for?

    A. DNS main zone

    B. Demilitarized zone

    C. Demilitarized zebras

    D. DNS mystical zodiac

4. What's the main tool for resolving DNS problems?

    A. dnslookup

    B. nslookup

    C. ping

    D. traceroute

5. If the DNS server you've queried doesn't know the answer to your question, what must it do?

    A. Scream and cry

    B. Ask one of your internal file servers

    C. Ask its "parent" zone server

    D. Ask the ISP

6. True or false? An SOA contains information about a zone's name servers and point of contact.

7. To look up the hostname for the host 167.195.160.6, you would fire up nslookup and type

    ```
    set type=ptr
    ```

    and then type what?

    A. 167.195.160.6.in-addr.arpa

    B. 6.160.195.167.in-addr.arpa

    C. 6.160.195.167.in-reverse.arpa

    D. 167.195.160.6.in-address.arpa

19

Answers to Quiz Questions

1. B
2. D
3. B
4. B
5. C
6. True
7. B

HOUR 20

Network Troubleshooters Just Wanna Have Fun

Curse you! You know our goal is to give you the opposite of what you want!
Since you want nothing we must give you everything!

—Mordac, "The Preventer of Information Services"
Scott Adams' *Dilbert*, September 17, 1998

Let's say you've been tasked by your boss to get good at network troubleshooting. So far, she's been wonderful and has bought you this book, sent you to a class or two, and things are just great. Only problem is that nothing's broken in almost forever. It's as if the network gremlins *know* that you're prepared for them and are waiting until your guard is down—they're waiting until you forget the stuff you've learned before they pounce.

Well, you can foil their crafty little plans by plying your troubleshooting trade to help the masses have a little bit of fun. This hour deals with stuff you'll need to know in order to play various games and use non—work-related toys through your firewall or proxy server. And why not? You've worked hard, you deserve it.

For those of you who've paged directly to this hour—don't! This hour assumes that you've already engaged in the sweat involved in the past 19 hours and that you have a basic grasp of TCP/IP troubleshooting, particularly the concepts involved in Hour 18, "In-depth Application Troubleshooting," and Hour 19, "'Lots of Different People in Your Neighborhood': Internet/Intranet Troubleshooting."

Seriously, learning how to use games (during your *own* time, of course) and toys on the Internet is a great incentive to practice your Internet and client/server troubleshooting. It teaches you how to perform these types of troubleshooting techniques on a noncritical basis—in other words, you're unlikely to get stressed out helping somebody do something that's strictly optional. What's more, you're then more of an expert at this type of troubleshooting technique when *real* trouble arises. Let's face it, network troubleshooters and IT (Information Technology) people, in general, have a bum rap for being sociopaths. Helping people do fun things has the following benefits:

- It's enjoyable.
- It's a good learning experience.
- It's helpful in establishing a rapport with users.
- It's a way to avoid a Dilbert-like work environment.

As you'll see, configuring toys for use on your network combines a knowledge of your network, the ability to dig into the network sockets in use on your PC, and the ability to use dialog boxes. With that said, let's dive straight into some common applications that people tend to need help setting up on your network. Again, if you're caught, or killed, the secretary will deny all knowledge of your actions.

Finding Your Firewall

First, you have to figure out whether you're using a proxy server or a packet-filtering firewall. Assuming that you have a working browser, it's no problem. Fire up your browser and load a fairly complex page off of the Internet (one that takes more than a second or two to load). Then get into a DOS prompt and type the following:

```
netstat -a > before.txt
```

Then type this:

```
netstat -a > after.txt
```

However, do *not* hit Enter yet. Switch to the browser and refresh the page. Then *quickly* switch back to the DOS prompt and hit Enter. After you do this, you'll have two files: `before.txt` and `after.txt`. The difference between these files will show what additional sockets have been opened when you refresh the browser screen—this will show you whether you're using a proxy server or a packet-filtering firewall. Let's say that you do this for a Web page at `www.quizro.com`:

```
C:\windows> fc before.txt after.txt
Comparing files before.txt and after.txt
****** before.txt
 TCP   duke:1071        frotz.frob.com:23    ESTABLISHED
****** after.txt
 TCP   duke:1572        socks.frob.com:1080  ESTABLISHED
 TCP   duke:1071        frotz.frob.com:23    ESTABLISHED
```

Here's the rule of thumb: If you see a hostname that's *different* than the hostname you were going to on the Net, you're using a proxy server. (In the preceding example, you don't see a socket established to socket 80 of `www.quizro.com`. Instead, you see a socket to `socks.frob.com`; therefore, you're using a proxy server.) The hostname you see is the name of the proxy server; the socket number is the proxy socket number. You can use this knowledge to configure your toys later.

If you see a connection directly to the outside Web site, you likely have a packet-filtering firewall. A packet-filtering firewall acts similarly to a router; it will automatically route your request for a connection to the outside, so you don't need to know the name or location. Easy!

However, you do need to know the name of a proxy server in order to configure your browser or any toys. Common names for proxy servers are "proxy," "socks," "http," and "firewall," among others. You can, of course, perform an `nslookup` to scan through your DNS names to see probable names for proxy servers:

```
$ nslookup
Default server: 192.168.1.6
> ls -d mycompany.com
[ns.mycompany.com]
 mycompany.com.          SOA     ns.mycompany.com postmaster.mycompany.com.
 (1017 10800 3600 604800 86400)
 mycompany.com.          NS      ns.mycompany.com
 ns                      A       192.168.1.6
 ns                      A       192.168.3.6
 ntserver                A       192.168.1.10
 mailserver              CNAME   ntserver.mycompany.com
 cotton                  A       192.168.3.7
 socks                   CNAME   cotton.mycompany.com
```

20

In this output, you can see that "cotton" is the real name of the "socks" server, which is at 192.168.3.7. However, it's probably less effort to pick up the telephone, call corporate IT, and *ask*.

If *you're* responsible for all the networking at your shop, and you've been handed an undocumented network, see Hour 24, "Reverse-Engineering Somebody Else's Network," for more tips on how to explore services on your network.

Socks Stuff

Socks is a really common generic proxy server. The bummer about any generic circuit proxy server is that unless a given application has built-in support for it, you need to use a separate socks client. Two companies distribute free client software that will "socksify" your games or other fun toys:

- NEC (http://www.socks.nec.com)   This is the least intrusive client; that is, it runs as a "launcher," without the need to modify system files. You use dialog boxes to configure it with the name of your socks server, the socks port (by default, port 1080), and the names and locations of the program files that you want to use the socks server. See Figure 20.1 for a sample configuration. As you can see, this is really simple.
- Hummingbird Communications (http://www.hummingbird.com)   This client gets underneath your network DLL files and intercepts all TCP/IP connections. The Hummingbird client is a lot more intrusive to your PC because it replaces Windows system files with its own files. Another bad thing about the Hummingbird client is that it's not obvious when a workstation is using it; that is, there's no icon that appears on your desktop. Therefore, troubleshooting in general gets tougher, because you might not realize that the client is running on the workstation.

Do these clients work *all* the time for all programs? No, but at least one of these clients will work for the majority of software out there. If you have success with either of them, it's a lot simpler (and safer) than monkeying around with firewall configuration.

To find out whether someone has installed the Hummingbird socks client on a PC, check the C:\Windows\System directory for a file named WSOCK320.DLL—if you see this file, it's likely that the Hummingbird client has been installed on the PC.

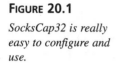

FIGURE 20.1

SocksCap32 is really easy to configure and use.

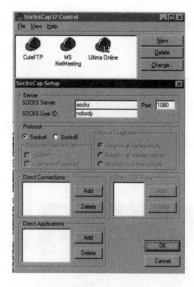

There's also no graphical setup. You must configure the client by editing the SOCKS.CNF file in your Windows system. Here's an example of how I might set up a Hummingbird configuration file for a simple two-segment network:

```
Direct 192.168.1.0 255.255.255.0
Direct 192.168.2.0 255.255.255.0
@SockD4 = 192.168.2.10 0.0.0.0 0.0.0.0
```

In a nutshell, this file means that you're directly connected to 192.168.1.0 and 192.168.2.0. Traffic to those segments will not use the socks server. All other traffic will be passed to the socks 4 server at 192.168.2.10.

In a nutshell, Hummingbird's client is extremely configurable yet hard to configure, and it adopts a "grab everything that goes on in the network and deal with it according to my configuration file" policy. Although this client works with more applications than does the NEC client, it affects *all* rather than *some* applications you run. The NEC client, on the other hand, is less intrusive, more friendly to configure, requires a separate configuration for each application, and sometimes doesn't work for certain applications because it *is* less intrusive.

Let's take a look at some common toys; you can apply the techniques used for these to other fun apps. We'll start with simple examples and get more complex as we go.

20

AOL Instant Messenger

Okay, what's the deal here? What is AIM? AIM is a fun way for folks to talk back and forth across the Internet in real time. However, it wants you to establish a TCP connection to one of AOL's servers in the field, and your firewall may be preventing this.

Make sure that your firewall allows TCP socket 5190 on an outgoing basis (it does if your firewall policy is to allow everything from the inside to go out). If you have a socks or HTTPS (HTTP Secure) proxy server, no problem. As you can see in Figure 20.2, the setup screen for AIM gives you the option to configure it for these types of proxy servers. It's very friendly.

FIGURE 20.2

The AOL Instant Messenger can use socks 4, socks 5, or an HTTPS proxy.

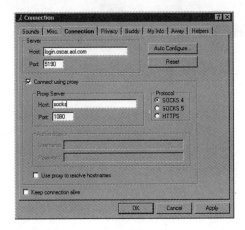

AOL NetMail

America Online allows its users to check their email outside of their regular software by using a Web-based interface. A special plug-in is downloaded for your browser, and you can read your email in a jiffy. The Web component doesn't pick up on your browser's proxy settings; you simply need to configure it similarly to your browser, as shown in Figure 20.3. (You can also use the earlier tips to find out where your proxy server is.)

NetMail is similar to AOL's Instant Messenger; it uses one outgoing-only TCP connection to port 5190 on the server side.

FIGURE 20.3

AOL NetMail supports socks 4 and socks 5; if you only have application-specific proxies such as FTP and HTTP, you may be out of luck.

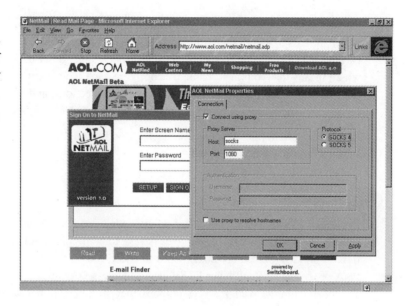

ICQ

Mirabilis's ICQ is arguably the most popular real-time chat program out there. It has great support for socks servers, as you can see from Figure 20.4. However, this is one program that is hard to use with a filtering firewall; although it only needs one TCP port (4000) to contact the ICQ server on the Internet, the workstation must then be able to get connections initiated from the *outside* on many TCP ports—that is, *incoming* connections on your network. (Configured for socks, ICQ needs *no* incoming connections; it simply uses the established connection you create through the proxy.)

FIGURE 20.4

Socks 4 and socks 5 are the preferred proxy servers for ICQ; a filtering firewall is much harder to configure.

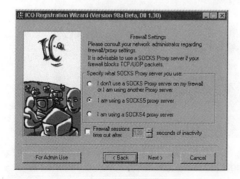

20

Without using socks, the ICQ client software prefers at least *12* incoming ports; even worse, it likes to assign them randomly. To make life easy on you or your firewall administrator, ICQ allows you to specify a "static" port range rather than a random port range, which means that you must manually configure each ICQ client. Still, many organizations have an outgoing-only policy on firewall connections, and it's hard to justify opening up so many incoming ports just to let people run a Net toy. Sheesh!

Here's the bottom line: You *can* use ICQ with a filtering firewall, but it's a lot easier and safer to simply use it with a proxy server.

RealPlayer

RealPlayer allows you to view "streaming" video and audio from the Internet—without waiting for it to download. RealPlayer is easy to configure if you use one of its preconfigured proxies (see Figure 20.5). Unfortunately, most networks don't have a "RealPlayer PNA proxy" or a "RealPlayer RTSP proxy." Unless your business relies heavily on audio and video from the Web, it's very unlikely that management has decided to install such proxy servers.

FIGURE 20.5

RealPlayer works best with its own proxies, but it does support an HTTP application proxy as well.

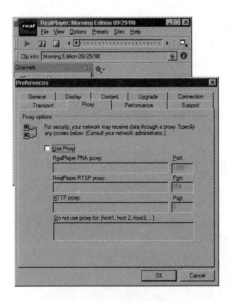

An HTTP proxy is supported, and this is how you'll want to go if you have an HTTP proxy. However, I'm frequently asked how to configure RealPlayer for use over an "outgoing-only" socks 4 or 5 proxy server.

Here's the scoop: For some reason, RealPlayer will *not* work with NEC's SocksCap32; either RealPlayer is using 16-bit network functionality or it works some nonstandard black magic with TCP/IP.

How do I know that it doesn't work with the NEC client? I ran RealPlayer through the NEC socks client, and while it tried to connect, I ran `netstat -a` in a DOS window. I saw that RealPlayer was trying to directly contact the host on the Internet, because I saw a foreign IP address and a `SYN_SENT` socket state. (See Hour 18 for socket state details.) Had it talked properly to the NEC client, I would have seen a socket to my socks server in the `ESTABLISHED` state, or at worst, `CLOSE_WAIT` or `TIME_WAIT`. This would have told me that my problem was *not* with the client software.

In any event, RealPlayer *will* work using the Hummingbird socks client. You'll still have to do some RealPlayer configuration, however. Socks 4 does not support UDP, and some socks 5 servers are not configured for any incoming connections at all. To get RealPlayer to work without touching your proxy server, you'll want to configure RealPlayer to use TCP connections only. You sacrifice some speed by doing this—TCP connections are slower than UDP connections—but who cares? See Figure 20.6 for the proper setup to make RealPlayer only use TCP connections.

FIGURE 20.6

Sometimes you'll need to specify TCP-only connections for RealPlayer to work through a firewall.

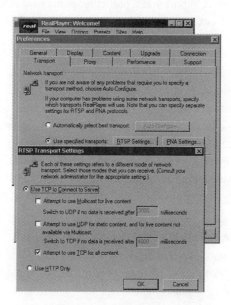

20

Game Strategy

Some games are very well behaved. For example, Origin's Ultima Online is extremely proxy friendly. It uses TCP connections only, and it initiates the connection from the workstation—that is, from inside your network. As such, it will run from the NEC or Hummingbird socks launcher or through a packet-filtering firewall without a problem. I really like network toys that work like this—no muss, no fuss, no problem!

Other games, such as Blizzard's StarCraft and Diablo, want you to open up incoming UDP and TCP sockets on your firewall. (All of Blizzard's Battle.Net games use TCP and UDP port 6112.) Again, they will not work on an "outgoing-only" firewall or a proxy server; they require incoming access to your network. Although I'm a huge StarCraft fan, I'm not a huge fan of opening up incoming ports on a firewall to allow game play. You've got to draw the line somewhere, I suppose.

Of course, there are other things that will keep your network toys from working; don't forget basic black box troubleshooting strategies. In particular, you'll want to monitor system resources (some of these toys are resource hogs) and check, as we did in Hour 18, whether the server on the other side of the Internet is "listening" for connections. If you're able to telnet to the TCP port that a particular game uses (and TCP is the only thing it's trying to use), it's extremely unlikely that your firewall is interfering with the operation.

Summary

You can practice your network troubleshooting skills and create goodwill with your network users all at the same time. Network toys such as chat programs, streaming video and audio, and games are loads of fun to use on your network, but they are usually designed for home use or for a specific corporate customer. To successfully use these, you'll either need to enable their built-in proxy support, add an external client for proxy support, or fix your firewall to allow their socket numbers to pass through unmolested.

If your company policy allows incoming connections, it's a simple matter to add additional ports to your firewall configuration. Nonetheless, I personally hate adding incoming ports merely for network play, because it's "unnecessary" diddling with a very important piece of network security equipment. You should think twice about doing this!

Workshop

Q&A

Q How do I figure out which port a specific game or toy uses?

A I'd be very surprised if the vendor didn't tell you. Still, some don't. You'll want to do the "difference" trick again to find out which port your Net toy uses. Dial into your personal Internet account, and type the following:

```
netstat -a > before.txt
```

Then run the game, stay connected, get back to a DOS prompt, and type this:

```
netstat -a > after.txt
fc before.txt after.txt
```

You'll be rewarded with the socket number(s) that your game uses. This method has two drawbacks: UDP ports won't show up this way, because there is no "connection." Also, you have no idea whether there's a different TCP connection used at login versus during gameplay.

If you *must* know exactly which ports your game uses—check out Hour 21, "Tell Me About Your Network: Network Analyzers," and use a network analyzer to capture the packets of a game session. You'll have to do this from your DMZ, unless you have a serial (dial-up) analyzer. At this point, you should ask yourself whether you really want to play *that* badly?

Quiz

1. You can find the address of your proxy server by checking the _____ while using a functional browser.

    A. socket pocket

    B. socket list

    C. route list

    D. route rocket

2. True or false? The Hummingbird socks client (versus the NEC socks client) applies to *all* applications that are run on the workstation on which it is installed.

3. We used an `nslookup` command to list all entries in a company's DNS zone. What was that command?

    A. `netstat -rn company.com`

    B. `ls -la company.com`

20

    C. `ls -d company.com`

    D. `netstat -d company.com`

4. An application can be configured to use UDP or TCP connections. In order to use this application with an outgoing-only firewall, you would have to configure the application to do what?

    A. Use TCP connections only

    B. Use UDP connections only

    C. Use both UDP and TCP connections

    D. Use neither UDP nor TCP connections

Answers to Quiz Questions

1. B
2. True
3. C
4. A

Hour 21

Tell Me About Your Network: Network Analyzers

Sure, most network troubleshooting cases that you'll encounter will be "elementary, my dear Watson" (solvable by deductive reasoning alone). However, to solve your most hard-boiled network crimes, you'll need to get a wire tap to give you the evidence you need. Network analyzers provide a type of "wire tap" that allows you to gather objective data about a networking problem.

Like a wire tap, network analyzers shouldn't be used indiscriminately; you definitely want to use your noodle before you use your analyzer. You should always formulate a theory before breaking out the analyzer—otherwise, *what* are you looking for? (After all, it's a big network out there.)

Still, when you run into a problem that needs an analyzer, it can be the difference between a stone wall and a breakthrough. After you've formulated a theory, analyzers can *prove* your theory by providing you tangible evidence to either sift through yourself or to give to a vendor for analysis.

What the Heck Is a Network Analyzer?

I have to smile every time I talk about network analyzers: I always think about a piece of network gear reclined on a couch, with some Freudian white-bearded psychoanalyst asking it about its origins. As silly as that seems, this picture isn't far off—a network analyzer's primary job is to listen while other network gear talks.

Here are the two basic kinds of network analysis tools:

- Cable scanners (hardware analyzers)
- Packet sniffers (software analyzers)

A cable scanner's primary job is to test the electrical characteristics of your network wire. As we discussed in Hour 9, "Ethernet Basics," CAT-V cable needs to have certain electrical characteristics, without which you'll get data link errors. A cable scanner will test any particular cable run "end to end" and let you know if something is out of whack.

Some of the more sophisticated scanners will also listen to the signal on the wire to see whether there are physical or data link problems on your network. For example, the only way to truly detect collisions on an Ethernet network is to use a cable scanner. A cable scanner is fairly simple to use (turn it on, plug it into the hub, and watch for errors). However, it operates differently than other scanners and is expensive! (Typically $3,000 and up for a modern scanner.)

In contrast, software network analyzers will *only* listen to data link traffic, and they do not test the physical cable that the traffic is running on. A software analyzer is typically a PC with a special type of network card in it. Software analyzers rely on network cards that are able to run in "promiscuous" mode—that is, they're physically able to listen for packets that are *not* destined for themselves. Nosy, nosy, nosy!

Software network analyzers are typically not very expensive. Some of them do run $10,000, but many of them are less than $1,000. See http://feldman.org/analyzers.html for a list of some of the less expensive software analyzers.

Also, check out the Network Monitor that comes with Windows NT Server 4.0. It lives in C:\WINNT\SYSTEM32\NetMon and works either with NT Server or NT Workstation. It only captures packets to or from the station that you use it on, and it has other limitations. A full-featured version of Microsoft's Network Monitor is only available if you purchase Microsoft's SMS (Systems Management Server). Still, the "vanilla" free version is a good way for you to get familiar with how this stuff works.

Finally, because software analyzers capture entire data link packets from the wire, they are able to use sophisticated software to *decode* these packets and allow you to examine them for protocol and application problems. (See Figure 21.1 for a sample decode window.) The fact that software analyzers are not hard-coded into chips makes them extremely flexible; you can evaluate and purchase different ones as you need them, install them on a laptop, and use the one that seems to best suit the problem at hand! There are a lot more options and applications for a software analyzer than for a cable scanner; we'll examine software analyzer theory and practice in the remainder of this hour.

FIGURE 21.1

Decoding the reply packet for an ARP (Address Resolution Protocol) exchange.

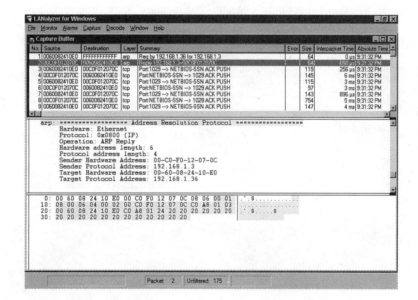

Typical Operation

Most network analyzers have two modes of operation:

- Capture
- Decode

During the capture phase, the analyzer can perform statistic gathering, including number of errors per station, number of packets transmitted/received by each station, network utilization (how congested the network is), and so on. The really cool analyzers will show you graphs, let you sort by "most talkative station," and so on during the capture phase. The decode phase allows you to sift through the specific data that the analyzer captured (the equivalent of reading the transcript of a party-line wire tap).

21

Captive Packet

Capturing *everything* on a shared network is possible—although it's resource intensive on your analyzer! Consider a busy 100Mbps network: At a conservative estimate of 6MBps, that would mean you would need 360MB of physical memory (virtual memory simply isn't fast enough to keep up) to capture a minute's worth of data.

Token-Ring and 10Mbps Ethernet aren't this bad, roughly only requiring 90MB and 36MB respectively of physical memory to keep up with a minute's worth of data. Still, that's a lot of stuff to sift through and store. How do analyzers deal with this?

Most analyzers have a certain "buffer space" they allocate to capture data. When the buffer is full, you have an option to stop capturing or you can simply discard data at the "end" of the buffer to make room for new data (see Figure 21.2).

FIGURE 21.2

An analyzer can either discard the oldest data once the buffer is full or stop capturing altogether.

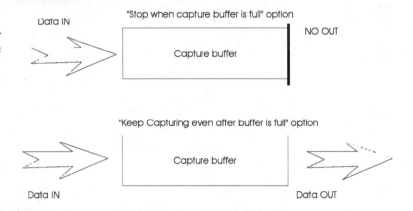

Check with the maker of your software analyzer to see what kind of PC hardware you need to keep up with the network that you're analyzing. For example, some hardware isn't able to run fast enough to capture 100Mbps Ethernet and will end up missing some traffic.

How do *you* deal with this? In other words, are network troubleshooters expected to pore over hundreds of megabytes worth of data to find the damning conversation? No! Just as police aren't expected to listen to 50 random wiretaps at once, an effective network troubleshooter should only be expected to scan through a limited number of network conversations at a time.

As we'll discuss later, you usually won't be capturing all the data on the wire—when you are, you're primarily concerned with statistic gathering, and you're not really interested in looking at the specifics of what each packet contains. Therefore, the fact that the analyzer can't keep up is okay. Many times, depending on the scenario, you'll tell your analyzer that you're only interested in the following items:

- Certain protocols
- Certain workstations
- Certain services

This way, you seriously cut down the amount of data you need to sift through. As we'll discuss later, this is a very important function of any analyzer.

Secret Decoder Ring

After a capture, the analyzer will allow you to look at the data you've captured. The analyzer will "decode" the bits and bytes from within the packet into human-readable form. Will *all* the bits and bytes be translated? No, probably not. Why not? Well, there are three types of translations that your analyzer has to accomplish before you can view data:

- MAC
- Protocol
- Service

The MAC layer is sort of simple: There aren't that many ways that you can put data on the wire, and the specifications for this are fairly well laid out. It gets a little more complicated with the protocol layer, because the analyzer needs to "understand" the language's bits and bytes in order to display what's going on. It gets very complicated when you get into services. There are hundreds and hundreds of services, and it's just not possible for every analyzer to be good at decoding each one. (Think of it as expecting your translator in another country to also be a good golfer, electrician, doctor, technician, dancer, and architect. Sure, you *might* find such a translator—but you'd probably have better luck finding several translators with those skills.)

Here's the bottom line: Not every analyzer can handle every service. Although the common ones, such as Telnet, DNS, and Microsoft and Novell file and print, are pretty well covered, others are covered scantily, and still others are not available at all! (For example, I don't know of *anybody* who makes a decoder for the popular Internet chat package ICQ. ICQ is a fairly proprietary service.)

Is this a disaster? Not really. Even though the analyzer can't *decode* the service so that you can read it, it's still *capturing* what's going on. If you're working with tech support for a proprietary service, you can bet that they'll be able to read your trace using in-house decoders. After all, for our purposes, one of the primary reasons to use a network analyzer is to capture evidence to submit to a vendor, and if the vendor can't decode its own service, we're all in trouble.

21

Dave, I'm Afraid I Can't Analyze That

Some network analyzers have an "expert" mode, which, during packet capture, makes a guess at what could be wrong with your network. In theory, this is wonderful. You and I can't sort through hundreds of conversations at once; this is the sort of job that's well suited to a computer.

In practice? Well, my experience with "expert" analyzers has convinced me that they're somewhat less than *expert*. Sure, they pick up on workstations that are running slowly—they're very good at seeing that a workstation has a significant delay in responding to a request. They're also good at seeing duplicate IP addresses and other simple problems. But *expert*? Not really. Idiot savant would be more like it. In my opinion, a complex network problem *must* be dealt with by a human; there are just too many unknowns, too many guesses, and too much intuition involved to have a computer do it. Teaching a computer how to solve complex network issues would probably be just as hard as teaching a computer how to think.

I definitely don't want to run down analyzers with an "expert" feature—they can be really useful for common simple problems. Just don't think of an expert analyzer as a panacea for all your hard network problems. However, in combination with your own situation analysis, expert analyzers can be very powerful allies in your troubleshooting wars; they tend to point you to *bona fide* problems that need further investigation.

Net Therapy 101: Techniques for Using Your Analyzer

Each analyzer is different; choosing your weapon appropriately is one of the first steps toward success with a network analyzer. For example, when having general trouble with a Token-Ring segment (the segment is beckoning and therefore "down"), I would *never* use Network Associate's Sniffer Token-Ring Analyzer, because it doesn't keep up with the Token-Ring NAUN list during capture (an important part of troubleshooting Token-Ring segment errors). They make another tool, the Sniffer Token-Ring Monitor, that would be more appropriate, because it does keep up with the NAUN list. When troubleshooting a NetWare Token-Ring network, I like to use Novell's LANalyzer. It, too, supports a NAUN list (which Novell calls the *ring monitor*) and is good with NetWare-specific protocols and services.

For instance, for a problem that involved NT workstations, Token-Ring, and Novell, I planned on using Novell's LANalyzer, because my problems seemed to be Novell related. I was not having problems talking to UNIX hosts or Microsoft hosts. I also knew that the problem was *only* Token-Ring related (Ethernet stations were not having the problem), so I planned on using Triticom's LANDecoder if I didn't see anything obvious with LANalyzer. I've found LANDecoder's Token-Ring decodes to be very complete. (We'll talk more about this problem later on in this hour—it's a goodie!)

Here's the bottom line: Your scenario always dictates which tool you need. There's more than one tool out there because there's more than one problem out there! Because you can't buy *all* the tools available, it pays to know your network environment thoroughly before you invest. This way, you can buy the most appropriate tools for you.

Cold-Filtered Ice-Brewed Packets

As I mentioned earlier, knowing how and when to filter your capture data is one of the most important skills you can have when using a network analyzer to capture network traffic. Otherwise, you'll likely be searching for a very small needle in a very large haystack! Even veteran computer geeks get discouraged if they do not filter their data.

Several types of filters are available:

- Station filters—Which workstation and/or server data to capture
- Protocol filters—TCP/IP, IPX/SPX, and NetBEUI
- Service filters—Which services to show
- Generic filters—Hexadecimal values within a packet

Not every kind of filter is available on all analyzers; for instance, some analyzers won't filter every kind of service, but you can get around this by using a generic filter.

Let's look at how to make one analyzer filter by service. For example, Novell's LANalyzer won't allow you to specify "display" Telnet sessions, but it *will* tell you when a packet is a Telnet session (or another kind of session). All you need to do is to click the section of the decode display that you're interested in. In our case, we're interested in a NetBIOS session, TCP socket 139, which translates to hexadecimal 8B (see Figure 21.3).

Notice how several bytes are highlighted; these are the bytes in the packet that are the *hex codes* that identify this packet as a NetBIOS session. You can then double-click these bytes, and LANalyzer will bring up a generic filter window already filled with these values. You can apply this to other services as well. Very cool!

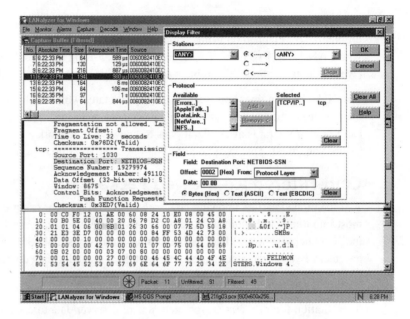

FIGURE 21.3

*Novell's LANalyzer
allows you to filter on
any field in the decode
area just by double-
clicking it.*

Here are the two ways an analyzer can filter:

- Precapture—This is useful when you don't want your buffer to overflow with
  needless data.

- Postcapture—This is good for when you've already captured the general data in
  question and want to refine your search.

Killer Packets

Here's a case in point for how filtering applies to troubleshooting a busy server. I saw a
problem in which a UNIX server started to have trouble sending print jobs to a Novell
server. The Novell server would all of the sudden, and at seemingly random times, generate errors on its UNIX services screen (PLPD) and stop processing. Only a reload of the
PLPD.NLM file would make the server start processing UNIX print again. Our first question was, "Who changed something on the Novell server?" The answer was...nobody.
Nothing had changed on the Novell server. No interrogation or torture was spared to verify this; we were absolutely certain that nobody had changed anything in the time frame
that we were talking about.

This was a really tough problem to troubleshoot: A search on the Novell support site for
the particular PLPD error message revealed nothing, and the problem was still popping
up intermittently. We needed an answer relatively quickly, because this print gateway was
responsible for processing print for a time-sensitive function. Because we were relatively

certain that nothing had changed on either the Novell server or the UNIX server (in fact, the UNIX server was printing fine to other Novell servers), we decided to see what was happening on the network. Maybe some errant evil packet was causing the PLPD server some mental illness.

We connected a sniffer to the server's segment (because we suspected something bad was happening to the server) and considered what we wanted to filter on:

- Because we knew something was happening to the Novell server, we would only capture packets destined for the Novell server's MAC address.

- Because we knew that this was a very busy file and print server, it wasn't feasible to capture *all* packets destined for this server.

- Because we knew that the problem was with PLPD (and knew that PLPD accepted UNIX print services via TCP/IP), we would only accept TCP/IP packets. This eliminated most of the packets destined for this server, which were Novell file and print IPX/SPX packets. This left us with a test setup that looked something like what's shown in Figure 21.4.

FIGURE 21.4

The test setup for a tough NetWare-to-UNIX printing problem.

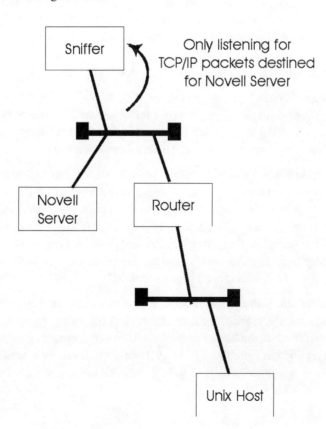

21

As soon as the problem occurred again, we looked at the packet capture. There are two important concepts here: First, we ran and stopped the analyzer right after the trouble report. Second, we synchronized the clock on the network analyzer to the network time before we started capturing, and we asked the user who reported the problem to also report the time of the problem. Because this was a pretty busy print service, we were sure that the problem report was within plus or minus two or three minutes, so we now only had to consider packets around the time of the report, thus limiting how much junk we had to wade through.

Skipping to the end of the trace, we first filtered on the LPD TCP socket, number 515. We did see a problem: The server stopped responding to the LPD requests from the UNIX host at the end. Well, we knew *that* without taking a trace. Still, this was useful: It let us know *where* in the packet list the problem occurred. Therefore, we got rid of the LPD filter, jumped to the packet where the problem occurred, and looked at the packets right *before* the problem.

Apparently, right before the problem occurred, there was an ARP request (TCP/IP's Address Resolution Protocol). Remember, each TCP/IP address must have a corresponding MAC address in order for two network cards to talk. The ARP request I saw was responding with the *wrong* MAC address. An ARP packet with the wrong MAC address typically means that someone else has used a TCP/IP address that's the same as yours, thus interrupting communications—but that was *not* the case here.

We tried to find the MAC address reported by the ARP request, but there was no such network card on our network. Not only that, but I couldn't find the OUI of the MAC address in my OUI table, which was also suspicious. Furthermore, this was a network where only one or two well-known vendors' cards were in use.

Because there was no such device on the network, we next looked at the switch configuration (remember from Hour 14, "Router and Switch Basics," that devices on different sides of a switch do not actually talk directly to each other). Because there was a MAC-level problem, we naturally suspected the switch. We asked the person responsible for switch configuration if anything had changed in the last couple of days—and, in fact, something had. He therefore changed the configuration back to the way it used to be, and the problem went away. Tough problem solved!

Two things still bothered me, though. Why could I ping the Novell server at all if the ARP was incorrect? Well, because ARP is "redone" every couple of minutes, by the time I was on the scene troubleshooting, the ARP was correct again; therefore, I could ping the server without a problem. The switch was only *sometimes* messing up the ARP; usually, it was just fine. Second, why did a bad ARP mess up the LPD service? That's a tougher question, and one I wasn't going to find the answer to, mostly because it didn't matter. The PLPD.NLM file (and for that matter, the TCPIP.NLM file) on the Novell server in question was somewhat old, and an interruption in the data stream was apparently driving it berserk. After the switch configuration was fixed and the ARP problem went away, everything was okay once more (and that, after all, is what's really important).

View Zoo

Finally, when viewing specific packet traces, you'll want to explore your view options. Most analyzers have a menagerie of options that allow you to be flexible about which attributes of the trace you're viewing at one time. Some of these attributes include the following:

- Hexadecimal representation of packet
- Capture time
- MAC and/or protocol and/or service decodes
- Protocol or MAC address
- Network name (DNS and NetBIOS)

> Many network analyzers have a name-gathering feature; that is, they "read" the packets as they go by and see whether there's a name identifier in any of them. If there is, the analyzer will make an entry in its name table, which will allow you to *later* specify a capture filter or view based on a network name. This, of course, is a much more "user friendly" way to specify a filter or view data.
>
> Be aware that some analyzers do *not* capture names automatically; they offer it as a manual operation on data that you've already captured, during the viewing portion of your analysis.

Even with a Windows-based analysis tool, your brain can only process so much input at one time; being able to specify view options lets you "keep it simple" so as not to overwhelm yourself with too much information. Accordingly, you can view strip charts that summarize certain aspects of your data, as shown in Figure 21.5, which divides network traffic by application.

21

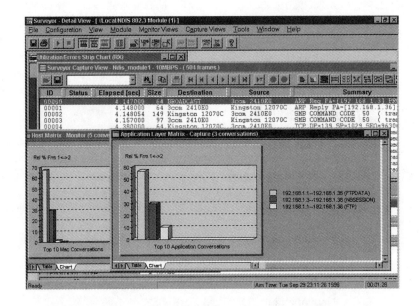

FIGURE 21.5

Shomiti Surveyor and other analyzers can graph "top talkers" and other statistics, thus helping you to interpret raw data.

You can also change your packet decode display options—in particular, how time and network names are displayed. Because a network is a timing-sensitive animal, the time-related options are particularly important. Your *relative* or *interpacket* time is important because it's the delay in between two packets. A value that looks way out of line with other packets indicates a delay caused by network glue such as routers or switches—or, more likely, a delay caused by processing at the other end of the conversation (by a busy server, for example).

General Capture

As helpful as capturing specific packets can be toward finding a solution to a specific problem, there are times when you'll want to run your analyzer "wide open" in order to get a general overview of your network segment.

For example, when everybody on a given segment is complaining that they're running slowly, you would probably want to break out an analyzer that will statistically analyze the segment while it's capturing. The analyzer will likely keep a running total on several things:

- Errors per station
- Frames received per station
- Frames transmitted per station
- Total utilization of the network
- Total errors on the network

On the slow segment, you might see that the total utilization of the network was running high, say, 65 percent (Ethernet tends to degrade after 35 percent, so this is really high). You would probably want to know why the utilization was high: Is it due to many users, all of whom are using a fair portion of the pipe, or a couple of users hogging up the pipe? A good way to find this out would be to sort your statistic list. For example, if you used Novell's LANalyzer to sort your statistics by "packets out," by clicking the column head, you'd immediately find out that there's one station that seems to be hogging up the pipe (see Figure 21.6).

FIGURE 21.6

Analyzers can sort active stations by just about any statistic.

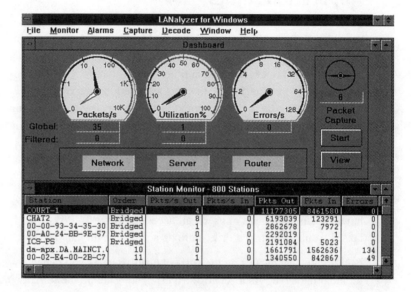

You might want to capture specific data from this station to find out just what type of traffic was being generated—even quicker, check your MAC documentation and make a phone call to determine what the user in question is doing. In this case, let's say your phone call reveals that the user was doing a backup of his hard drive to the network. You'd probably want to politely ask him to stop doing this during peak hours and suggest other methods for hard drive backup, such as a tape drive.

Just to make sure the network is otherwise healthy, you would also sort your station list by errors. A couple of errors here or there is fine—you just want to make sure there isn't one station that's jamming up the freeway by behaving badly.

21

Appropriate Analysis

Let's take a look at a couple of scenarios in which analyzer use is appropriate. Notice that in all of them, we arrive at a theory, which we then prove through the use of the analyzer. We'll take a look at a vendor-related application and service problem first, examine what to do with a MAC address whose location you're not sure of, and finish up with a problem that requires the use of two network analyzers at one time.

Application Antics

Let's travel back to Hour 18, "Lots of Different People in Your Neighborhood: In-depth Application Troubleshooting," to the problem in the "I Can't Spool, Take Two" section. Remember that we had a UNIX host that would not spool more than one print job to a given network print server at one time, even if that print server had multiple printers attached to it. In other words, the host assumed that each print server only had one printer—a seriously wrong assumption! In this scenario, even though I had proved to myself that the host was at fault by using black box troubleshooting, I wanted evidence to submit to the vendor to prove that its stuff worked differently (wrongly) from other vendors' implementations of UNIX printing in order to try to force the vendor to fix it.

It was fairly easy to take a trace of this by specifying a capture filter of the print server's MAC address or TCP/IP address. Why not the UNIX host? Because the UNIX host had hundreds and hundreds of users, all accessing it via TCP/IP—had I specified the UNIX host, I would have had a little more data than I could handle.

I set up two test queues on the suspect host—queue1 and queue2—one for each printer on the print server. As a "control experiment," I set up the same two queues on another host. I started the analyzer capture, went back to my desk, and quickly printed two jobs to the two test queues. I went back to the analyzer, stopped the capture, and saved it to disk, giving it the filename problem.

Then I did the exact same procedure, but used another host to print to the queues. I called this trace file good, because this capture illustrated what happens with a UNIX host that's not brain dead. (Although the vendor didn't immediately act, our salesperson saw that we acted on this objective data and bought something else, which had good long-term effects on our leverage with this vendor—so it was worth doing. In fact, when we started having more problems with the machine and implementation of UNIX, we were given a new machine in reparation.)

Here are the important points to remember when submitting analyzer traces to a vendor:

- Traces should be small. Filter as much as you can.
- Traces should be discrete. As shown earlier, you should take several traces showing a "good" event versus a "bad" event.

- Traces should be backed up with an objective and succinct description of the problem, describing what troubleshooting measures were taken.

Identifying a Station

I've been at sites where the MAC addresses weren't terribly well documented, so any MAC-related error was difficult to run down. For example, suppose Windows exclaims that there's a duplicate TCP/IP address on MAC address `00:00:C9:05:89:62`. It doesn't do a troubleshooter a lot of good if the MAC addresses aren't documented, and if your analyzer doesn't automatically identify network names for you, you might think you're out of luck. Same goes for when your expert analyzer tells you that `00:08:02:55:29:2A` is probably a bad network card and is causing many network errors.

Hey, no problem—you've got a wiretap! You can listen in to all the MAC traffic generated by this workstation, and it's likely that you'll get *something* that will identify the user. By taking a look at the data in the hexadecimal or character-oriented decode window, you can see various data that might lead you to identify the workstation's user (or department).

This is something that takes a little practice, but use your head and you'll get good at it in no time. For example, filtering on Telnet sessions will give you the entirety of a user's Telnet. Go to the beginning, and you'll get the login name. Check the middle data out, and you might see a report or a menu screen that only a particular user or department uses. This is a good opportunity to get good at reading your protocol decodes. If you have the time on a noncritical problem, you should go for it!

 If you're filtering on TCP sessions, look for a SYN packet. This is the beginning of a TCP session—the equivalent of saying "hello?" when you first pick up the telephone—and it likely has the username in a nearby packet.

Broken Ring

Consider the case we talked about earlier this hour: The Windows NT rollout onto a Token-Ring network using Novell servers. Although there were hundreds of Windows 95 PCs that were working just fine, the first pilot test of a Windows NT workstation revealed connectivity problems with the servers—that is, none of the new workstations could see *any* of the new Novell servers, but they could see *some* of the older servers. However, all of them could connect to all UNIX and NT servers using TCP/IP. Take a look at Figure 21.7 for a diagram of the scenario: All workstations were on Token-Ring, new servers were on Fast Ethernet, and older servers were connected to Token-Ring. The newer servers were NetWare 4.11; the older ones, 3.x.

21

FIGURE 21.7

*A problem requiring a
capture on two seg-
ments simultaneously.*

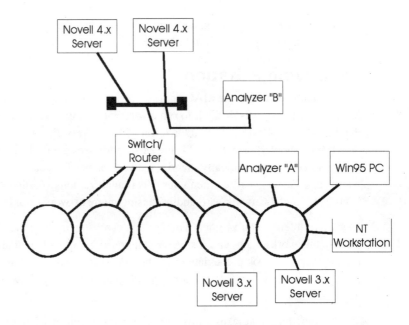

Because the pilot test was on one segment, we tried moving one of the workstations to a different segment. Oddly enough, we could now communicate with *different* Novell 3.*x* servers. Apparently, we could only see Novell servers attached directly to the ring that we were on. This led us to believe that there was a switch problem.

In order to see whether the switch was passing data properly, we connected two analyzers to the network: one to a segment that the workstation was on (point A) and another to a segment that a "problem server" was on (point B). Each packet that passed through the switch should have had a corresponding packet coming out on the other side.

In the spirit of keeping the trace files small, we set point A up to capture packets *from* the test workstation. Because the packets at point B would *not* appear to be coming from the MAC address of the test workstation (instead, they'd appear to be coming from the switch), we purposely had the workstation connect to a low-use test server and captured all data going *to* that server. We booted up the NT workstation and attempted to log in to the test server. As soon as the login failed, we stopped both analyzers.

The analyzers revealed that the switch was, in fact, dropping packets (it was not that "bad" packets were getting to the server and being misunderstood). Great. So what was happening?

We did the same test with a Windows 95 machine and compared the results. Ah ha! The Windows NT machines were using "source routing," a Token-Ring link layer protocol, whereas the Windows 95 machines were not. (We don't need to know what source routing is to troubleshoot this problem; it's enough to know that this was the *difference* between the two traces.) Because the switch was not configured to allow Token-Ring source routing, it was dropping the packets. We had two possible solutions: configure the switch to allow source routing or configure the NT workstations without source routing. Either option was fairly easy and quick. Case closed!

Limitations and Solutions

As you can see, using an analyzer can be as much of a time sink as you're willing to let it be. If you were the kid in elementary school who had a good time reading the dictionary, you'll have a great time poring over protocol decodes. If, however, you need to get a lot of work done, you might have to sigh and save the protocol decodes for a less busy time—and employ your black box troubleshooting skills to isolate if and where you need to use your analyzer.

As far as physical limitations go, remember that an analyzer can only listen in on a party line. You cannot listen to a station that has a point-to-point connection to a switch, because there's no hub to connect to and listen in on. What to do?

Look in your switch documentation for a feature called *port mirroring*. This allows you to specify which port of the switch you want to listen in to. Just plug your analyzer in on another switch port, and the switch will do its own wiretap on the port and tell your analyzer all about it. Cool!

If your switch doesn't support port mirroring, you can always "roll your own" wire tap, as illustrated in Figure 21.8. Simply do the following:

1. Obtain a mini-hub (Ethernet) or a "node doubler" (Token-Ring).

2. Unplug the network cable from the station you wish to "wire tap."

3. Plug that station's cable into the mini-hub's cascade port or node doubler's "lobe."

4. Connect a network cable from the mini-hub or node doubler to your analyzer.

5. Connect a network cable from the mini-hub or node doubler to the target station.

This has the effect of creating a shared segment on the switch port, and you can now listen in.

21

FIGURE 21.8

You can roll your own wire tap for a switch port simply by getting a "mini-hub" and creating a segment between the switch and the end station.

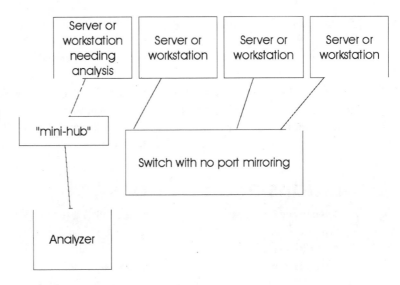

Many analyzers are starting to offer *remote monitoring agents* (or *probes*) that allow you to monitor several different segments using one analyzer. These "agents" are merely small programs that run on a workstation or a server and have the collection function of an analyzer without the decodes or the statistical analysis functions. The agents then pass on the collection data to the master analyzer, which is located anywhere on the network you want it. Of course, this only works if the network and the workstations with the probes are up, but it's a great solution for multiple segment problems and ongoing monitoring, because you can do this from your desk.

Summary

A network analyzer is a tool that listens to network packets on a shared segment and decodes them into human-readable format. Some are horrendously expensive, some are not. The neat thing about them is that they run on most PCs if you have the right type of network card—that is, a "promiscuous" network card, which is able to listen to all network packets.

Depending on the analyzer, you can expect to see many functions that will help you analyze the raw data that the analyzer captures. Some of these functions include capture filtering, sortable statistical displays, "expert" analysis of data, and customizable views.

There's more than one analyzer available on the market, because there's more than one problem out there. Different analyzers are good for different things. In particular, Token-Ring needs certain features not present on generic analyzers.

Knowing what and when to filter is a really important part of learning how to use an analyzer. Once you learn how to take small manageable trace files, you'll be able to quickly go through them and find what you need in order to vanquish your problems—or to entice your vendor to help out.

Analyzers, like any tool, have limitations, but if you have your wits about you, they're a powerful addition to your troubleshooting arsenal.

Workshop

Q&A

Q C'mon, Jonathan! Network analysts spend years learning how to sift through protocol data. How do you expect me to learn this in an hour?

A The key here is to limit the scope of what you're expecting to accomplish. True, although you're probably able to learn the various protocols and service nuances that underlie the everyday programs and services that you know and love, why would you want to? Analyzers are simply an effective way for you to apply your black box troubleshooting skills. Don't get discouraged if you don't understand everything you see on the decode screen—just remember to keep asking yourself questions such as "which of these things is not like the other?" and you'll do very well. If you feel you need or want to dig deeper, grab a protocol book and have fun. However, in many cases, that won't be necessary.

Q Where can I get an Ethernet mini-hub or Token-Ring node doubler?

A The same place you can get a mini-switch: Just visit one of the various network supply houses that have homes on the Net. I've had good luck with www.networksnow.com and www.datawarehouse.com, but any of them can supply these items to you.

Quiz

1. True or false? The difference between a cable scanner and a network analyzer is that a cable scanner can solve all network-level problems.

2. Most analyzers have which two modes of operation?

    A. Capture the flag and a secret decoder ring

    B. Packet capture and packet decode

    C. Capture of data and decode of Ethernet

    D. View and sort

21

3. A network analyzer requires a computer and a _____ network card.

   A. promiscuous

   B. promethean

   C. amorous

   D. packetized

4. True or false? Identifying how and when to filter is a highly important part of learning how to use an analyzer.

5. A filter can be _____.

   A. workstation related

   B. protocol related

   C. Both A and B

   D. Neither A nor B

6. True or false? If your analyzer does not gather network names (such as DNS or NetBIOS), it's impossible for you to identify whose computer corresponds to a particular MAC address.

7. You're about to connect an analyzer to a network segment. For best results, what should you have done first?

   A. Sniffed packets

   B. Formed an option

   C. Come up with a theory

   D. Decided not to use a filter

Answers to Quiz Questions

1. False

2. B

3. A

4. True

5. B

6. False

7. C

Hour **22**

Who Watches The Watchmen? Network Management Tools

Nothing strengthens the judgement and quickens the conscience like individual responsibility.

—Elizabeth Cady Stanton

"Network management" is possibly one of the most overused phrases in networking. Used to mean everything from change management to network monitoring to remote reconfiguration, network management started out as an amorphous marketing blob of a phrase used to soothe you into parting with your money. It used to be that you could buy tens of thousands of dollars worth of hardware and software, end up with a proprietary solution that didn't do you much good, and be left with the net result of being tens of thousands of dollars poorer.

Not anymore! Today's network management packages can provide powerful tools to help you coordinate the task of keeping track of hundreds of network devices and thousands of network stations. Although the high-end management stations and associated network probes can be costly, you now have a choice between comprehensive and complex or simple and slick tools to help you monitor your network's general health or to simply report proactively when things stop working.

Certain management packages include everything but the kitchen sink. In particular, they include tools that we've briefly discussed:

- Automated network application deployment tools (Hour 16, "Beauty Is Consistency Deep: Saving Yourself Trouble")
- Remote control and support (Hour 17, "Where Do I Start?")

For this hour, we'll define a network management tool as any tool that helps you monitor your network infrastructure gear, applications, and servers remotely. You'll see how network management can help you take the bull by the horns and build a more reliable network.

Big Monitor Is Watching

The germane function of network management is, in fact, the monitoring of key services and infrastructures. As network troubleshooters, we are interested in seeing when things are about to fail, as well as when they fail. When we monitor, we're interested in the following items:

- Performance—Is the resource running out of steam? What's it running out of?
- Uptime—How long has it been up? Should we restart it as a preventative measure?
- Availability—Is the resource available, or is it down?

Because you could monitor literally hundreds of individual resources via the network—for example, the power supplies in your server, each hard drive, the internal temperature of the CPU, its network card buffers, and so on—network management packages have introduced the concepts of *thresholds* and *alerts*.

When a resource goes outside the thresholds you or the manufacturer set up, an alert to the network is generated, and you get notified about it. This is the basic concept behind network monitoring.

Depending upon which network management package you choose, this can be more or less automatic. Some management packages use proprietary methods of monitoring (which is not a terrible thing if it works and is easy to use) and some use standards-based monitoring. Which one is right for you? It really depends on how large your shop is, what tools your vendor provides when you buy your network gear, and how well they fit

22

into a management solution. We'll explore this further, but first, let's look at what monitoring standards exist.

MIB: Men In Black? My Information Buddy? Mental Illness Bonanza?

Network management, like all networking, is full of crazy acronyms. Three of the most important acronyms (which also double as important TCP/IP standards) are SNMP, MIB, and RMON.

See `ftp://rtfm.mit.edu/pub/usenet/news.answers/snmp-faq/part1` and Part II, "Black Box Troublshooting Strategies," for answers to common questions about SNMP, RMON, and MIBs.

SNMP stands for *Simple Network Management Protocol* and is a standard way of providing certain network information to nodes that request it, while allowing privileged nodes to change that information. How is this accomplished?

SNMP is just another TCP/IP service, a service that lives on UDP socket 161. A workstation, server, router, switch, or other network device that has the SNMP service running on it is called an *SNMP agent*. Any SNMP agent provides certain variables to requesting management stations. A common set of well-understood variables is known as an MIB; MIBs compose information available through SNMP. Figure 22.1 shows an MIB browser from MG-Soft (`www.mg-soft.com`).

FIGURE 22.1

The MG-Soft MIB browser is a good way to start getting familiar with SNMP and MIBs.

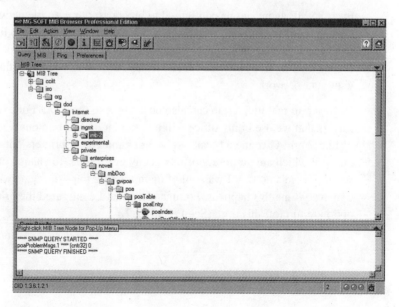

Whoa! What's an MIB? MIB stands for *managed information base* and is a shorthand way of referring to all the resource variables that exist in one group. For instance, just about all SNMP agents will respond to MIB-I and MIB-II variables, such as SysContact, SysName, SysLocation for record keeping, and ifOutOctets and ifInOctets, referring to the number of bytes received or transmitted by an interface (if). Of course, you need a network management station to be able to read variables from an agent.

Many manufacturers provide their own MIBs, because they have specific information that isn't contained in the general MIBs. For example, my GroupWise system has a couple of specific variables in its MIBs that wouldn't be useful for any other system (for example, poaUndeliverableMsgs, which stands for *Post Office Agent's Undeliverable Messages*). Presumably, the agent that lives on the device or software already knows about its MIB; however, an MIB file exists that allows you to "export" the MIB to a network manager that doesn't know about it.

The MIB browser from Figure 22.1 provides a good way for you to tool around the MIB and SNMP world. It includes an MIB compiler so that you can insert vendor-supplied MIBs and check out the information that the agent supplies. Cool!

Okay, so having an SNMP agent on a device allows you to keep track of millions of resources at once. This is neat, but what about alerts? That is, when something goes out of its threshold, how does SNMP tell you about it?

Each SNMP agent can be configured to broadcast a trap to the network (*trap* is just another word for an alert). If your network management station is listening for traps, it will raise a red flag to let you know about it. For example, it can page you or do whatever you wish. Traps provide excellent ways of letting you know that something is wrong with your network.

However, in real life, a trap can also be a silly extravaganza. For example, the print servers that we use in my office will all send an SNMP trap out when their printers are offline. Argh! Give me a break. We've got hundreds of printers out there on the network, many of which are purposely offline at any given time (to change paper, add forms, and so on). There's no way I want all of them sending traps to my network management station every time this happens. Fortunately, when I configured the print server, I had the option to turn off this trap. (See Figure 22.2.)

FIGURE 22.2

A dedicated print server with an SNMP configuration via a Telnet session.

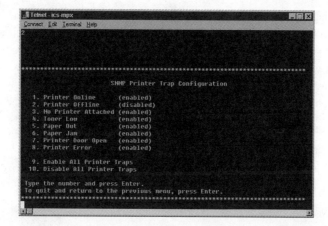

Some SNMP agents can be configured to send several different "levels" of traps to your network manager. This way, you don't get paged for silly stuff. For example, my GroupWise MIB defines certain traps as "informational" (for instance, when the post office first starts up) and others as "critical" (for instance, when the post office must go down). Obviously, I'd like to be paged for critical issues but not for informational ones.

RMON

The Internet MIBs (MIB-I and MIB-II) are a set of variables that allow individual devices to keep track of their internal status. But what about the status of the segment that the devices are on? That's where RMON comes in. RMON (Remote Monitoring) is an MIB defined specifically for a probe device—that is, a device whose sole purpose is to keep track of network traffic statistics. Is this much like a network analyzer? Well, yes and no. Each RMON probe does keep track of network statistics much like your analyzer does when it's capturing packets. However, RMON probes aren't expected to sit there and continually capture packets; instead, they're meant to sit there and continually gather statistical data about the network and other network stations. (Yes, some RMON probes will also act to capture specific packets from the network in conjunction with a network analyzer.)

Because RMON probes are always active, when you have a problem, there's a pretty good chance that the probe has picked up what's going on. For example, rather than connect your sniffer or other network analyzer to the segment and chance missing the problem event on the network, you can simply ask the RMON agent what's been going on. Because RMON keeps track of utilization of each station, if the network is slow, you can check the statistical data and see your top talkers. Very neat.

A package that supports RMON in combination with RMON probes also allows you to perform long-term statistical analysis on multiple segments, as well as create a baseline of how your network runs when it is healthy. This is really important when trying to figure out why the network is slow *today* when it wasn't *yesterday*; we'll discuss baselining more in Hour 23, "The Network Is Slow! Getting a Definitive Answer to a Subjective Question." Here are some examples of SNMP-compliant management packages:

- Kaspia Network Audit Technology (www.kaspia.com)
- Technically Elite MeterWare (www.tecelite.com)
- HP OpenView (www.hp.com)
- IBM NetView (www.ibm.com)
- NetScout (www.netscout.com)

Network Management Nonstandards

I love standards because they ensure that everyone is reading from the same sheet of music. However, SNMP management stations and RMON tend to be large, expensive solutions, and sometimes they're overkill for what you want to do. Accordingly, many vendors provide their own proprietary monitoring tools or will even give you a combination of SNMP and proprietary monitoring software. There's nothing wrong with this. If it works for you, great!

For example, Dell provides a modified version of HP OpenView's Server Manager—all it can do is monitor Dell servers, but if Dell servers are all that you have, no problem! ALR, Compaq, and HP all do this type of thing as well.

Sometimes switch vendors and hub vendors will also provide their own monitoring package. Olicom, for example, provides a neat little Windows-based switch manager application that collects switch statistics, reports trouble, and so on. Such packages are handy when all you have are one vendor's switches, but this approach starts to break down if you've got to run 12 different programs to monitor 18 different pieces of equipment.

In addition to vendor-supplied monitoring tools for particular pieces of gear, you can also use third-party monitoring tools that generically monitor any service or server that you choose. These tools work as follows:

1. Get a list of IP numbers and services (socket numbers) that the user wants to monitor.
2. Every so often, try to *poll* the service (check it using the appropriate protocol).
3. If something doesn't respond correctly, sound the alarm (via pager, email, and so on).

22

This is actually a pretty cool way of monitoring your services; after all, SNMP might be working, but in the final analysis, you want to know that your *service* is working. Who cares if SNMP thinks that your Web server is up? If it's not actually responding to the service when a network station tries it, it might as well be a boat anchor! Many third-party packages are available; some monitor whether generic TCP sockets are "alive and listening," whereas others are complex utilities that are designed to monitor specific applications such as email or network databases.

Here are some examples of service monitoring packages, listed from the primitive to the sublime:

- Sitter (`ftp://feldman.org/pub/sitter`)   A primitive Linux `bash` script that checks ports using the Telnet trick and complains to the console when problems are found. This definitely must be manually reconfigured for your site.

- Netoscope (`http://www.basta.com`)   A Windows utility for checking socket availability of certain servers. Issues audible alerts or runs a program (such as email) when problems occur.

- IPSentry (`http://www.ipsentry.com`)   A socket-monitoring package that runs under Windows. It tries whichever IP addresses and sockets you want, as often as you like. It can also page you when a problem occurs.

- WhatsUp and WhatsUp Gold (`http://www.ipswitch.com`)   This is a graphical network polling package with paging features. WhatsUp Gold has Web access, SNMP features, and IPX monitoring, as well. WhatsUp Gold also has the dubious distinction of being quite expensive for a polling package (close to $1,000 at this writing).

So when do you use "pollsters" rather than SNMP managers? It depends on what you need. In my experience, only larger shops tend to use the SNMP managers; they tend to be expensive, resource intensive, and complex to install and maintain.

Of course, SNMP managers also provide you with lots of information. In particular, the SNMP managers will provide you *service-level* information—that is, not only will they tell you whether the resource is "up" but also how fast it responds, how many bytes of resources are left, and so on. This makes SNMP managers very valuable if you're looking to optimize your network. SNMP managers are excellent for keeping long-term track (baselining) of how your network and resources look on a normal day. As you'll see in Hour 23, baselining is a very important part of problem determination when, as they say, "The network is slow!" After all, if you don't have a sense of how things typically are, how can you tell when something is out of range? Long-term service-level record keeping is also a way to know—and a way to show your boss—that everything is operating efficiently and is working properly.

Still, simple network polling packages can be extraordinarily effective, even for large shops, but particularly for smaller shops. They're typically inexpensive compared to the costs of deploying even a modest SNMP installation, and they're very easy to configure and use. Although most network polling packages don't address service-level issues, look for more of them to do so in the future. Of course, you'll never have the rich level of information that SNMP provides, but you might not need it. In short, a polling package is a one-stop application where you can monitor many services easily. Figure 22.3 shows one of them.

FIGURE 22.3

Basta's Netoscope just keeps polling away!

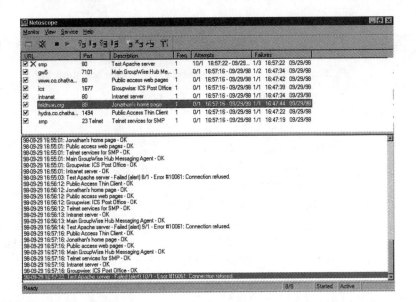

Real-Life References

Network management can be as expensive as you let it be. Of course, ostensibly, when you install a network management station and configure your network for management, you're trying to save time and avoid downtime—both of which contribute to your bottom line.

Still, before you go out and plunk down your hard-earned dollar, be sure to go and check references on any expensive network management package. More than that, try to find businesses that operate the way yours does. You can learn from their experience with network management, and you can possibly avoid some expensive mistakes—or be told, "C'mon in, the water's fine!" Either way, you'll know what to expect from your network management experience.

Summary

"Network management" can be a slippery phrase; it's used to refer to everything but the kitchen sink. In its most helpful form, network management involves network monitoring, which allows you to assess the health of your network.

SNMP (Simple Network Management Protocol) is at the heart of complex solutions; many vendors supply reasonably complete MIBs and agents for their equipment and software, which can then be read by SNMP management stations. SNMP management stations are really good at long-term resource trend monitoring and can help you "baseline" your network.

SNMP agents can broadcast traps to the network, which are then picked up and acted on by management stations. Typically, notification (such as activating a pager) is the best that most management stations can "manage." SNMP traps can be annoying or they can be a blessing, depending on whether they're waking you up in the middle of the night for a printer jam or to alert you that a public safety system is down.

Generic socket-polling packages for TCP services are also available, and so are service-specific polling packages. The generic packages are limited in that they typically only tell you whether a service is "down" or "up" (that is, they're pass/fail graders). They generally don't report how well the service is doing on resources and response times.

Some of the service-specific and vendor-supplied monitoring utilities, such as the monitoring applications that come with certain servers, switches, and routers, will give you an SNMP-like wealth of information without the overhead that SNMP implies.

Depending on the amount of money you're going to spend on a network monitoring solution, you'll want to do some legwork and check references thoroughly before you invest. Although any polling software solution is typically cheap enough to be throwaway if it doesn't meet your needs, a complete SNMP solution is expensive enough in time and money invested that investigating how well it does in a similar shop is a good idea.

Workshop

Q&A

Q How do I configure my SNMP agents to send traps to my SNMP management station?

A You don't. SNMP broadcasts its traps, which will get to your management station.

Q I've got three file and print servers, one intranet server, forty workstations, an Internet firewall, a DMZ, and a Web server on the outside. What type of network monitoring is right for me?

A You said "monitoring," without saying "predict" or "resource," so my bet is that you're probably just interested in whether things are up or down, not in baselining or resource management. In particular, Web monitoring is accomplished just fine by polling. I'd invest a small amount of money in a polling solution and then plan to investigate an SNMP solution if polling isn't enough for your needs. From the size of your network, however, I'd guess that the polling will suit you just fine.

Quiz

1. When you monitor a network, you're typically interested in what?

   A. Resource utilization

   B. Availability

   C. Neither A nor B

   D. Both A and B

2. True or false? Network polling packages, unlike SNMP solutions, typically provide you with a detailed picture of resource utilization and device statistics.

3. What is an SNMP trap?

   A. When a vendor entices you to spend too much money on an SNMP solution

   B. A network broadcast to a certain socket, caused by a problem on an SNMP agent

   C. A point-to-point communication between two management stations

   D. An event that occurs after a server's power goes off

4. What is RMON?

   A. An SNMP MIB

   B. A standard for the types of information a probe can supply to a management station

   C. Both A and B

   D. Neither A nor B

22

5. Good SNMP management stations, unlike service polling software, will allow you to what?

    A. Broadcast

    B. Baseline

    C. Brag

    D. None of the above

6. What are the advantages to using polling software?

    A. Cheap, quick setup, lets you know when things are down

    B. Cheap, quick setup, allows you to configure end stations

    C. SNMP compliant, quick setup, lets you know when things are down

    D. SNMP compliant, allows for baselining, allows you to configure end stations

7. True or false? Polling software, unlike an SNMP solution, probably doesn't require extensive research and reference checking before purchase and deployment.

Answers to Quiz Questions

1. D

2. False (it's the other way around)

3. B (it's UDP socket 162, by the way)

4. C

5. B

6. A

7. True

HOUR 23

The Network Is Slow! Getting a Definitive Answer to a Subjective Question

One of the most frustrating trouble reports you can get is that the "network is slow." Particularly when you're sitting at your desk and using the network just fine, it's hard to believe reports like this and even harder to do something about it—you can't fix what doesn't seem broken! Still, you've got a user reporting with a *bona fide* complaint, so your job is to track down this seemingly invisible problem.

Tracking down and vanquishing network slowdowns can be tough—but rewarding. The key to finding network slowdowns is to divide the problem into smaller, manageable pieces; that is, once you identify *everything* that's involved in a user's connection, it becomes much more possible to test each piece individually and pinpoint which piece is causing the slowdown. The reason one user can sit on the same "network" as other users and run fine while they run slow as molasses is because network sessions can be complex beasts. Simplifying things enables you to troubleshoot quickly and effectively.

Here are the two kinds of slowness reports:

- As soon as an new application or a server is deployed
- As something unknown on the network changes, breaks, or runs out of resources

In this hour, we'll concentrate on the second type, because the first type is typically pretty easy. If you deploy something new on a known good network and it runs like a pig on roller skates, it's fairly obvious where the trouble lies. What's more, if you get good at troubleshooting the second type of slowness report, you'll be able to specifically troubleshoot the first type as well, rather than just pulling the plug on things.

Limiting Factors

When folks report "network slowness," they're typically reporting "application slowness." Because the application is the fruit of the network tree, let's take a systematic look at what the limiting factors are in any network:

- Amount of bandwidth available
- Routing and switching "latency"
- Application efficiency
- Server factors

The first and most obvious factor in any network is the speed of the shared network that an application lives on. This is referred to as "bandwidth available" and is sort of like the speed limit on a highway.

Bandwidth and Throughput

Raw bandwidth doesn't necessarily mean anything. Just as you don't always drive at the speed limit of the highway, network applications don't always take advantage of the bandwidth available. Your speed on the highway depends on your driving skills, your driving habits (who cares if you drive right at the limit if you stop every five minutes for a bathroom break?), and so on. The speed that your network application actually drives at is referred to as its *throughput*. You can arrive at an application session's throughput by measuring how many bytes are in the packets that compose the network session and dividing this number by the number of seconds the session takes to complete. Here's the formula:

```
Application throughput per second = total application data / elapsed
number of seconds
```

Remember that your total speed on a journey takes into account all roads you must drive on. For example, if you spend half your journey on a highway and the rest on a dirt road with pot holes every few yards, your total driving time might be twice or three times what it might be if you only traveled on a highway. Accordingly, when figuring out what's affecting application throughput, you'll want to consider each "hop" that the application packet needs to traverse.

23

Let's go over commonly available network links and their speed:

- 10 or 100Mbps Ethernet
- 16 or 100 Mbps Token-Ring
- 64 or 128Kbps for consumer-oriented ISDN
- 9.6Kbps (9600bps), 56Kbps, or 1.5Mbps (T1) for traditional leased lines

As you can imagine, your application packet might make half its journey at 100 miles per hour on a Fast Ethernet connection but then would slow down to approximately 1 mile per hour to traverse a T1 leased line. If your packet travels across a 9.6Kbps line, this would be the rough equivalent of traveling at a *hundredth* of a mile per hour. A 56Kbps line does somewhat better, at approximately a *twentieth* of a mile per hour. Nutty!

Latency

Now consider that each "road" used by the application packet also has a tollbooth at each end of it. I'm speaking, of course, of the router or switch that connects the two network segments. This delay is referred to as the *latency* of a device. Latency is usually pretty negligible, but it adds up on every device that a packet must pass through. Some "wire speed" routers and switches don't add appreciably to the delay (sort of like the new electronic toll passes), but others will. You'll have to test to find out.

I was in an awesome class a couple of years ago in which the instructor taught us a quick-and-easy way to measure the latency of any "network toll-booth." Set up two network analyzers on each "side" of a device to capture traffic for station A and station B. Then have station A ping station B.

Record the absolute time the analyzer reports the packet *leaving* the first station (A1) and then record the time of it *arriving* at the second station (B1). Next, record the absolute time that the reply packet comes back from the second station (B2), then the time for it to come back to the first station (A2).

You then perform the following calculation:

    Latency = (A2 - A1) - (B2 - B1)/2

Instant latency analysis. Yahoo!

The idea behind latency analysis is to measure the latency before loading and then to see if it moves *after* throwing lots of traffic at it. Therefore, if I measure 50 to 100 microseconds (.00005 to .0001 seconds) of latency in the evening, but during the day measure 300 microseconds or even 800 microseconds, my device is definitely experiencing an overload, and it should be considered a speed liability.

Here's the bottom line: The route that's used by an application is a *major* consideration when figuring out how fast the application can run.

Application and Protocol Efficiency

Let's consider the example of a driver who stops every few minutes to go to the bathroom. This isn't exactly an efficient way to drive, but some folks do it. Similarly, some applications don't take advantage of certain protocol efficiencies. What protocol efficiencies might these be?

Let's take a look at a concrete example. Novell's "packet burst mode" for IPX/SPX is a way for an application at one end to avoid a "ping pong" effect with the end station. On totally unreliable networks, it's sometimes necessary to get an acknowledgment for each packet transmitted. On a reasonably reliable network, this creates unnecessary traffic. Take a look at Figure 23.1. The workstation on the right gets all the packets it needs in six transmissions; the workstation on the left needs many more to get the same data, because the application on the workstation is insisting on an acknowledgment for each packet. In large quantities, this is extremely inefficient; Novell's burst mode is a way of avoiding this. However, older Novell networks using older clients don't take advantage of this feature.

A way of seriously upgrading the speed of an older Novell network—without a new investment in hardware—is to get the newest Client32 for your DOS or Windows workstations. Make sure that PBURST.NLM is loaded on your 3.x server (no action is necessary on a 4.x server). You'll be amazed at how much faster your network seems to run.

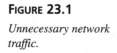

FIGURE 23.1

Unnecessary network traffic.

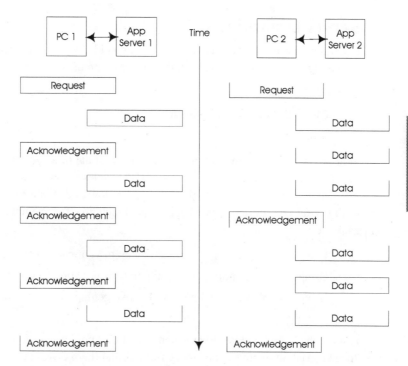

23

TCP/IP also has a "burst mode" called *sliding windows.* Why? Because, when conditions are good, the TCP "window" (the amount of data that may be sent without an acknowledgment) is large, but when conditions get bad, that amount "slides" down to compensate. When conditions are good, it slides back up.

When testing two similar applications' network efficiency, you can simply do the same operation twice, measure how much data was transmitted, and come up with the throughput per second for each. I did this once with two thin-client applications and found that one client was almost four times as efficient as the other. Wow!

Application efficiency typically doesn't change unless the design of the application causes certain events to make the app handle things differently at certain thresholds (more than x indexes? More than x users?), which can affect efficiency. Unfortunately, there's no formula on how to deal with this; you'll have to rely on instinct and then test your theory.

Server Limitations

Every server can run out of resources. Once you identify which server a slow application is running on, you'll want to check the following items:

- CPU utilization
- CPU "waiting for I/O" statistic
- Swapping statistics/RAM available

Sure, every CPU can "run out of gas." But most of the time, you'll see less than 100 percent CPU utilization. Even when a lot of CPU cycles are available, you still can be slow. Why? It all boils down to this: Hard drives are slow as dirt, physical memory is the speed of light. Hard drives don't even begin to approach how fast memory is. Consider these analogies:

- Using cache memory is like reaching up to your cabinet to get a can of beans.
- Using regular memory is like walking to your pantry to get a can of beans.
- Using "swap" (or virtual memory) is like getting in your car and driving to the grocery store for a can of beans.

Is it *that* bad? Pretty close. Even when the CPU is not busy, if your program has to be "paged" back in to physical memory from virtual (hard drive) memory, it takes a long time, and your performance is going to suffer. How much swapping is acceptable? For an answer to that, see the "Baselining" section later in this chapter.

Finally, your application may be disk intensive, regardless of whether there's enough physical memory to go around. Database programs, no matter how well indexed, will suffer performance problems if they're on nonoptimized disks. This *typically* isn't a "new" problem—you'll see this from the first installation of an application. However, if index or database files grow to a certain point, taking up more disk space (and thus taking longer to load), performance may start to degrade. You can see whether your applications are "disk bound" by checking your "waiting for I/O" CPU statistic. If it's a large percentage of the total CPU utilization, you probably have problems.

Measure Twice, Cut Once

The *only* way to know for sure whether you're running out of *anything*—bandwidth, server resources, and so on—is to measure. Everything else is guesswork. What do you measure first? It depends on your theory. Remember, you'll be applying good black box troubleshooting measures when someone tells you that "the network is slow." You'll identify all of the pieces that constitute the whole connection and then rule out one item at a time as the cause of the slowness. If you rule out the local segment for the moment (other people are working fine on this segment) and the route (other people who use that route for different applications are also working fine), you might suspect the server. If the server is working fine for two other applications, but you don't know what's happening on the network segment where the user is complaining, it's time to take measurements on the segment in question.

How do you measure? It depends. For long-term monitoring, distributed network analyzers or management probes are probably best; for short-term problem determination, you can rely on your trusty standalone network analyzer. Intermittent problems are probably better suited to probes, and standalone analyzers for ongoing problems.

Oversubscription

So you hear the cry "the Internet is slow!" In fact, the users say it's slow the great majority of the time. Although the users in question have a T1 connection to their ISP, they say their browsers are going about as fast as they do when they dial up AOL or CompuServe. Yuck!

There were two possibilities: *the users* are the cause of the slowness or the *provider* is the cause of the slowness. You choose to measure network utilization at their DMZ to rule out the provider. You also choose an analyzer that provides general network utilization of the segment, and in particular, the throughput to the ISP router.

Guess what? The *maximum* throughput you see going into the ISP router is anywhere from 64Kbps to 80Kbps—very shy of a T1, and not adequate for the number of users on the network. Because you've made sure, from another station, to attempt to shove more packets through the line (which had no effect), it stands to reason that the router or the provider is at fault. There are no errors on the router; the router's resources are fine. What's more, the router is rated to be able to manage a T1's worth of data at one time. So what's happening?

The answer: These folks are the victims of *oversubscription*, an (unfortunately) common occurrence with ISPs. It happens when an ISP "oversells" its pipeline, kind of like when airlines overbook their flights. You can only get so many folks on, and after that they get bumped and delayed. Looking at Figure 23.2, you can see an example of an ISP that has more "lanes" coming in to its site than it has going out. Naturally, there will be traffic jams.

Figure 23.2

An oversubscribed ISP's users are going to experience "traffic jams."

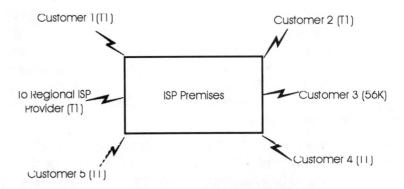

Customer 1 (T1)   Customer 2 (T1)

To Regional ISP Provider (T1)   ISP Premises   Customer 3 (56K)

Customer 5 (T1)   Customer 4 (T1)

Server Out of Gas

Let's say you suspect that the server is not as "zippy" as it ought to be. How do you check? Let's look at an example where a user tells you that her application is running ten times slower than it used to. It's starting to affect her life; she's having to come in at night and complete the run before the new day starts. She's mad as heck and isn't going to take it anymore! She tells you, "This network is getting slower and slower every day."

You know that the application she's talking about is running on a UNIX host. You *know* because you made it a point to say, "Would you show me, please?" Otherwise, a communication jam (between you and her) could send you on the wrong track. As soon as you saw her open a Telnet session to a UNIX host and log on, you *knew*, objectively, that this application lived on a UNIX host.

Check with other users of the UNIX host. Are they having problems? Some of them are disgruntled: "Yes, things are pretty slow." Others are not. You examine *who* is having problems and find that they're mostly people running reports. Because you know that the processing for reports takes place on the UNIX host itself, you naturally suspect the UNIX host as the culprit. If you suspected a network problem at this point, you might time an FTP transfer of a large file to this UNIX host to rule *out* a network problem. You don't, however, suspect a network problem, because all the folks who are reporting problems are largely doing back-end processing on the UNIX host. You decide to monitor the resources of the UNIX host. You perform a vmstat and come up with this:

```
procs   memory         page         faults   cpu
- - - - - - - - - - - - - - - - - - - - - - - - - - -
r   b    avm    fre   re  pi  po   fr   sr    cy   in    sy    cs   us   sy   id   wa
0   0  16894    120   1    0   78  208  312   0    279   1208  94   5    19   54   22
0   0  17091    173   1    8   95  288  872   0    271   2730  180  13   34   33   20
4   1  17112    123   0   48    0  168  635   0    293   3751  386  20   51    0   29
6   1  17050    267   0   48    0  152  652   0    267   4124  359  24   44    0   32
```

Wow! It looks horrible. What in blazes does this cryptic output mean? (Hint: See Hour 8, "Hard Basics: Guide to Being a Hardware Geek," for a verbose description of these column headings.)

For the purposes of *this* discussion, the salient points here are contained in the fre, po, and pi columns. Basically, this output is showing that you have very little memory in the free list and that page-outs (po) and page-ins (pi) are way up.

Remember that paging activity takes a really, really long time in comparison to using physical memory. All this paging activity sure *does* slow things down. To be absolutely sure that this is the problem, you monitor the paging activity during the times the users say the box is slow. There's definitely a correlation. You recommend a memory upgrade, and as soon as the memory is installed, the problem goes away. Excellent!

Certain third-party vendors make graphical long-term server resource reporting tools; if you have long-term problems, it might be worth investing in one of these. The graphical representation of resource use can really be helpful in spotting resource trends that can be dealt with *before* you have problems. (The Microsoft System Monitor is certainly a good start, but even more sophisticated tools are available.)

Baselining

As discussed elsewhere, if you don't know what things look like when times are *good*, you'll have no idea what you're looking for when things go bad. Accordingly, you really want to expend a little effort and create a picture of what your network infrastructure looks like when things are running pretty well.

A couple of words about the length of a baseline: Any good statistical picture must entail a large enough sample to make the data valid. In other words, the American Medical Association doesn't set "normal" lab values from a population sample of alcoholic, anemic computer geeks—they take large samples from healthy people from all walks of life and figure out what the normal range (highs and lows) for cholesterol, iron, white blood cells, and so on should be for most folks. If the doctor finds out that *your* blood has abnormal ranges—and, after all, you've reported to her that you don't feel well—she'll likely investigate what's causing your abnormal ranges.

The same is true of your baseline. You can't expect to take samples during your busiest time of the year and get normal values. Nor can you take a day's worth of data and consider it to be gospel. Instead, you need to take at least a week's worth of data at a time of year when it's business as usual. You can graph this data and keep it for when you have problems. When you do, you take the same measurements and see which statistics "jive" with your baseline numbers and which do *not*. For example, suppose your network utilization on segment 3 never exceeds 15 percent and never has an error rate of more than 2 percent when things are normal. If you find out that its utilization is 65 percent with an error rate of 12 percent, you would probably investigate the segment some more. This is the magic of baselining.

Automatic Baselining

If you have an RMON and SNMP infrastructure, you can use this to baseline your network. Companies such as NetScout and Kaspia can help you out here. Although the initial investment can be steep—you have to make sure that each of your servers, routers, switches, and applications have an SNMP agent, plus you have to expend the effort of configuring the management station—it's only a one time investment, and you'll be provided with baselines for a long time.

If you're not sure whether you need automatic baselining, try manually creating your statistics. It's a lot of work, but it's doable a couple of times a year. Think of it as "closing the store to take inventory"—it's a lot of work, but necessary.

Manual Labor

Here are the two types of performance monitoring you'll have to perform in order to manually baseline your network:

- Server CPU and I/O baselines
- Network utilization baseline

Why no switch or router baselines? Unfortunately, just about every router and switch is different. What's more, the data gathering mechanisms are either proprietary or—you guessed it—SNMP based.

Server Statistics

Let's say you have a UNIX system you'd like to baseline. On Monday, you set up `sar` (System Activity Reporter) to collect performance data each day. Some systems already have data collection enabled by default. To see if you get a report, type

`sar -A ¦ more`

If you don't, data collection probably isn't enabled.

> You can enable `sar` data collection on certain UNIX systems by typing the following command:
>
> **`sarenable`**
>
> If that doesn't work, type this:
>
> **`man sar`**
>
> This should tell you how to enable data collection.

At the end of each day, you take the `sar` output and place it in a text file. You then take the text file and import it into Lotus 1-2-3, Quattro, or whatever spreadsheet you like. You'd do this for a couple of days.

There are two schools of thought on what to do with the individual "day" data. I personally like to graph the entire week sequentially—after all, what happens on Friday doesn't necessarily happen on Tuesday. However, there are those who like to average all the data for the week.

You'll want to produce the following graphs for visual reference:

- A CPU utilization graph broken down into `%User`, `%System`, and `%Waiting for I/O`
- A paging graph
- A memory utilization graph

Because some implementations of `sar` are different, you should see the `sar` man page to see which abbreviation corresponds to which statistic. All the graphs should have "time" as the X axis so that you can see how one graph relates to another. (See the sample graph in Figure 23.3.)

FIGURE 23.3

A sar report converted into a Quattro Pro graph.

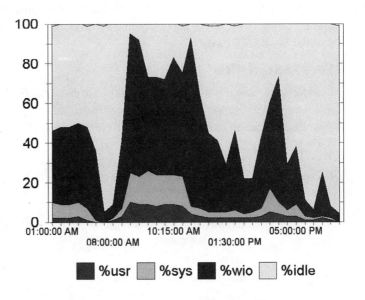

You can see in Figure 23.3 that user activity (%usr), system activity, (%sys), waiting for I/O activity (%wio), and idle time (%idle) all add up to 100 percent. Although you're *not* running out of processors on this graph, you can see that you've got a %wio problem: This is evident when you graph the paging activity; it pretty much follows the curve of the %wio. As with the vmstat example earlier, you probably have a memory and swap problem.

As far as manually gathering statistics from other operating systems is concerned, you need to know the following points:

- NetWare really requires an SNMP management station to deal with its resources; there's no way to extract the server resources manually.

- You've already seen how cool the Windows System Monitor is. You can also use the NT Performance Monitor (PERFMON.EXE) and get it to store reports in comma-separated format, which you can easily import into a spreadsheet.

Commercial packages are also available for tracking the resources of your servers; they're reasonably inexpensive and can save you a lot of work. For example, UNIX users should check out SarCheck by Aurora Software (www.sarcheck.com). A solution like this is a good compromise between performing resource baselining by hand and buying into a full SNMP solution.

Network Statistics

The best manual way to gather long-term network statistics is to use your analyzer. If you have a lot of segments, you should get an analyzer with a probe system such as Observer, LANalyzer Agent, or the Distributed Sniffer. For our purposes, we'll pretend that you only have one segment you're interested in getting statistics on.

Let's say that my shop's only analyzer is the LANalyzer. A LANalyzer allows you to export trend details to a disk file that you can then import into whatever spreadsheet you like. All I do is start it running on Monday, stop it Monday night, and save the trend data to disk (see Figure 23.4). Then I repeat the same steps on Tuesday, Wednesday, Thursday, and Friday.

FIGURE 23.4

LANalyzer can show you details or trends.

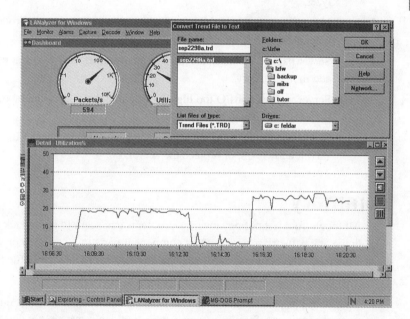

With LANalyzer, I end up with several vital statistics that are sampled every 15 minutes:

- Packets/sec
- Errors/sec
- Percent of network utilization
- Kilobytes/sec

I definitely like to chart the kilobytes per second—this lets me know how quickly my little data highway is actually flowing. I also chart the utilization. Although this pretty much follows the curve of the KB/sec statistic, it can't hurt, and it reminds me how much of my pipe I have left. I don't usually bother with packets per second, but I definitely chart the errors; this should be a long, flat line at the bottom of the graph with very few peaks.

Baseline Bottom Line

After you've done your baseline homework, when a user reports slowness on the network, it's a simple matter to compare values that you're *currently* getting to what they *should be* on your baseline graph. This allows you to know whether these stats are out of line for your network. You can then take appropriate action:

- Network utilization too high?—Seek and destroy the "top talker" using an analyzer.
- Network errors too high?—Seek and destroy the top error producer using an analyzer. Also check the cabling.
- Server paging too high?—Decrease the number of users or apps on the server or add more memory.
- Server waiting for I/O too high?—Upgrade the disk cache or consider a new high-performance disk upgrade.
- Server CPU utilization too high?—Decrease the number of users or apps on the server, add CPUs, or replace the server.

Summary

Although troubleshooting slowness problems can seem to be a black art, when you break down any network session into its component parts in a variation on the divide-and-conquer theme, it quickly becomes apparent which part is the bottleneck on your information highway.

Your family trip can take a lot longer to complete than you expect due to highway traffic or road conditions. Similarly, your application can move slowly due to a variety of reasons—the most obvious being network utilization. Other reasons include server slowdown, router or switch latency, and application or protocol efficiency problems.

Baselining your network is an important step in being able to quickly determine which of these reasons is causing your slowdown; if you don't know how things are when life is great, you have no reference to troubleshoot by. With a baseline, you can compare current stats to "normal" stats—just as a doctor does when diagnosing your blood chemistry—and quickly take action to fix it. You can "manually" take baselines, or you can buy into an SNMP management package that will create the baseline for you. SNMP is certainly the yummier option; however, it's possible to do this on the cheap side—it's just more of a pain in the neck.

Workshop

Q&A

Q Which network analyzers can be used to manually baseline a network segment?

A Just about all the newer ones. The exact technique may vary, but the basic functions for gathering statistics about the segment you're analyzing are the same. Very old DOS-based analyzers might not have the ability to save statistics over a time frame, however. Just ask before you buy.

Q About that latency analysis method: Do the analyzers need to have synchronized clocks?

A No, that's the cool thing about this method. You're taking the total trip time *differences* on both ends. Because the difference between the differences *has* to be the total amount of time the packet spends in the switch or router going *both* ways, you divide that number by 2 to get the latency for a one-way trip.

Quiz

1. You install a new virus protection application on one of your servers. Instantly, you're bombarded with complaints that the network in your building has slowed to a crawl. What should you do next?

    A. Run a network analyzer on your segment

    B. Deny everything

    C. Uninstall the new application

    D. Power down the server

2. Application throughput can be found by dividing the _____ by the _____.

    A. number of workstations, number of routers

    B. total bytes transmitted, time elapsed

    C. total bytes transmitted, workstations involved

    D. number of workstations, time elapsed

3. 10Mbps Ethernet is about _____ times faster than a T1 leased line.

    A. 5

    B. 2

    C. 1

    D. 100

23

4. Major slowdowns can occur when _____ or _____ is not used by a network application.

   A. packet burst, sliding windows

   B. packet windows, sliding burst

   C. windows defenestration, burst appendix

   D. windows burst, sliding packets

5. What's the slowest kind of memory on any server?

   A. Amnesiac memory

   B. Cache memory

   C. Dynamic memory

   D. Virtual memory

6. What constitutes a "disk-bound" application?

   A. When the limiting factor is how fast the disk can go

   B. When the application is strapped to the hard drive

   C. When the disk is going as fast as it can

   D. None of the above

7. When does "oversubscription" occur?

   A. When a provider has more bandwidth coming in than going out

   B. When a provider sells too many tickets

   C. When a network is saturated

   D. When too many Web sites are used by your users

8. True or false? You can easily tell whether current statistics are out of bounds, even without baselining.

Answers to Quiz Questions

1. C
2. B
3. C
4. A
5. D
6. A
7. A
8. False

HOUR 24

Reverse-Engineering Somebody Else's Network

Congratulations. You now know enough to reverse-engineer somebody else's undocumented network. I'm so proud!

You've probably noticed that documentation has been a major theme of this book. And why not? If you've turned ahead to this hour out of desperation, you may well be the victim of somebody else's undocumented network, and you have a good idea of how frustrating it can be. Fret not. This is where we're going to comb the tangles out of that undocumented network and make it into a reliable and manageable beast. It's going to be humming along by the time you get through.

Grab a sharp pencil and take a deep breath, you're about to chart uncharted territory. We'll start off with physical cable tracing and then move on to TCP/IP and IPX/SPX networks. (Why leave out NetBEUI? Remember, NetBEUI is a very simple, nonroutable protocol—it can't be too complex, and a physical cabling diagram is probably enough.) We're going to assume that you've come into possession of a *working* network; it's too tough to reverse-engineer a network that's broken. So, let's hurry and document it before it goes down. The network is up, and today's the day.

Cable Tracing

An unlabeled cable is a troubleshooter's nightmare. After all, it's in the wall, making it hard to know where the heck it's going. Fortunately, most sites only have a certain number of electrical closets, and that narrows the number of locations that you'll need to search.

One tool is an absolute must if you're trying to trace (and label) unlabeled cables. For under $100, you can get an *inductive tone generator* and an *inductive tone tracer*. (Jensen Tools, at www.jensentools.com, is one supplier, but there are others.) The theory behind an inductive tone generator is that it generates such a strong signal on the wire that the tracer can "hear" it—even without touching the wire. Very cool. This allows you to quickly and easily trace a wire from one end to another.

The operation of the generator/tracer pair is pretty simple. Follow these steps:

1. Identify the wall jack or cable end that you want to start with. (I start with "far end" stuff, for reasons you'll see in a minute.)

2. Hook the tone *generator* to the cable (make sure to follow the wiring directions that come with it). Then turn it on.

3. Take the tone *tracer* and do a quick test to make sure everything is working: Follow the wire a couple of feet down, and make sure you can hear a tone— remember that you shouldn't have to touch the cable to hear the tone. Notice how the tone gets stronger as you move toward the cable.

4. Take the tone tracer to a site where most cables seem to "terminate" and wave the tracer near all the cables. If you hear a tone, you're in the right area. Play "hot and cold" (as the tone gets louder, you're closer to the right cable; as it gets softer, you're getting away from the cable).

5. Repeat this at different closets, hubs, and so on until you find the cable.

6. Label it.

You now see why you put the generator at the workstation end. You want to limit the number of places you have to visit with the tracer.

Of course, if you have a very small site with only one or two hubs, you can always have a friend turn a computer off while you're looking at the hub. The hub port light that goes out belongs to the PC that just got turned off. Now you can label the wire appropriately. Still, inductive toners are a lot of fun to use.

TCP/IP Discovery

Your first task in discovering how a TCP/IP network is laid out is to identify the "glue" of the network—the routers! The easiest way to discover the routers on your network is to go to a functional workstation and check the TCP/IP configuration. Go to several in different locations, particularly if you're not sure whether you have multiple segments.

Router Configuration

Can you telnet to the router? Cool. Oh no! It's asking for a password. Hopefully, because you own this router, you have the password. (Check inside the manual's front and back covers; some folks write it in one of those places.) If not, call the manufacturer for technical support. If the manufacturer won't help you, don't despair. Although you *definitely* should have the password in case you need to troubleshoot or reconfigure this router, you still can discover your network without it—it'll just take a little more sleuthing.

Try the following passwords:
- manager
- security
- supervisor
- admin
- administrator
- root
- [ENTER]
- 12345 (and variations on that)
- Your company name (or one word of your company name)

You'd be amazed at how many folks (particularly people who don't document the networks they build) leave the "default" passwords on devices or simply pick "bad" passwords.

Being able to telnet into the router means that you can also create a status report on which interfaces are which network numbers. Write 'em down! Don't know how to show the addresses on the router? Check the manual.

24

Many routers will show you which router commands are available if you type

    ?

or

    help

If you can't find the manual in your shop, check the manufacturer's Web site before buying another copy. Some manufacturers keep the manuals on the Web as a service to their customers.

Another cool and highly informative task you can perform while in the router is to dump the routing table. As nasty as that sounds, it just means that you're going to list all the known routes to that router. All the routes that apply to your organization are going to be in the route table—be sure to write down the list of network numbers (even if the router is not connected to them) with their next hops. The next hop will be a router that knows something more about that network, and it's more than likely only a hop or two away from the network. Repeat this process until you have all the networks written down with a corresponding router identification.

By convention, most routers for a given network segment have low node numbers, starting at 1 and working up to as many routers as there are on that segment.

Once you have an idea of which routers have which IP numbers, you should be able to start drawing a map. Start with the router, draw the network segments off of each, and then play "connect the dots." That is, make correlations between which routers have common network numbers and then connect them (see Figure 24.1).

FIGURE 24.1

Once you've laid out your network pieces like Legos, you can then snap them together using common networks to reveal the entire picture.

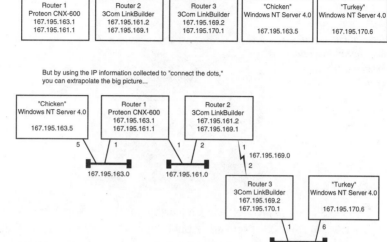

Servers

If you have an idea of what the server names are, you're one step further in the right direction. If not, you'll have to perform name discovery. From an operational workstation, look at the DNS configuration. No DNS configuration? It's possible—some sites don't use DNS, but that's very unlikely if the Internet is in the picture. If you're *sure* that no DNS is available, you have two options for gathering hostnames and IP addresses of servers:

- Check the C:\Windows\HOSTS file on several functional workstations.
- Check the client configuration of several functional workstations.

For the second option, you'll have to be familiar with the client (for example, the Telnet client). Many Telnet clients allow you to put a hostname or IP address in the command line that invokes the program, so check the properties of a working icon to glean hostnames or IP addresses (see Figure 24.2). It's entirely possible that someone has set up an entire office using just IP addresses. I've seen it happen!

24

FIGURE 24.2

The "assessor" icon points to the program NetTerm but supplies the program with the command-line parameter of "assessor."

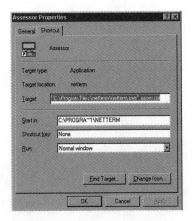

If DNS *is* in the picture, you can usually dump the name table using nslookup, as discussed in Hour 20, "Network Troubleshooters Just Wanna Have Fun." Remember, nslookup doesn't work for Windows 9x; you'll have to check out one of the nslookup equivalents. Some of the "network discovery" tools listed in the next section will also dump any given name table (see Figure 24.3).

FIGURE 24.3

Because nslookup isn't an option for Windows 9x users, you'll have to use a third-party utility. NS-Batch is one way to dump a DNS table.

Once you have either server names or IP addresses for your important servers, connect them to the appropriate segments laid out when you performed router discovery. If the servers are on a segment that you don't know about, perform a "traceroute" to the server, which will show you the segments that it passes through. You can telnet to each hop (because it's definitely a router), gather configuration information along the way, and flesh out your map.

Some people configure their name servers to disallow a name dump from an arbitrary workstation. This is a good security practice but a pain in the neck for network discovery. You'll have to log in to the primary or secondary server and print out the DNS configuration file. On UNIX, you can usually take a look at the /etc/named.boot file:

```
directory /usr/local/named
primary mycompany.com named.company
cache root.cache
forwarders 192.168.1.10
```

This will point you to the data files. (In this case, this is a primary name server; it keeps its database for the zone in the named.company file. Because there's a "directory" keyword in the boot file, you'll specifically find the data file in /usr/local/named/named.company rather than in /etc directory, which is the default.)

24

Automatic for the People

A couple of network discovery tools are available for your use. They are very useful and usually cost less than $100, making them, in my opinion, quite a bargain for what they allow you to accomplish. They work by performing the tasks that you or I would do: running traceroutes, performing name lookups, opening sockets on a destination to see whether they're listening, and so on. However, because a computer has infinite patience doing the most boring and repetitive of tasks, a network discovery tool is *much* more complete than you or I would be!

In particular, these automatic network discovery tools will take a *range* of IP addresses and systematically ping and check many common service ports on each destination. For a large network, this can be tens of thousands of checks (assuming that it checks twenty or so services on each destination, and that there are 254 possible host numbers on a network, and that you have a couple of networks). What's more, if you leave your automatic discovery tool running overnight, you'll have lots of answers in the morning without losing a bit of sleep!

What about proprietary socket numbers for services such as Lotus Notes or GroupWise? Don't worry about them. Once you identify that a server is running at a certain IP address, you can do a more thorough port scan (see Figure 24.4).

FIGURE 24.4

Port scanners such as the Internet Anywhere Toolkit can discover "listening" ports on a server, out of thousands of possibilities.

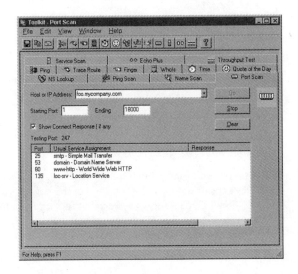

Here's the rule of thumb: Even though it's *possible* to scan every single port in the world using these tools, you're probably best off scanning for a common "server" port, such as telnet (23), SMTP (25), or NetBIOS (139), on all addresses and then performing a more thorough scan on a machine once you find one that offers a common service.

SNMP scanners are also pretty good for network discovery. Although SNMP is a UDP service and therefore can't have a "connection," a program that "understands" SNMP can send SNMP datagrams to a range of TCP/IP addresses and report to you which ones respond. Those that do are likely servers, routers, switches, or "smart" hubs.

You can find these types of tools at the following sites:

- www.tnsoft.com
- www.solarwind.net
- www.tucows.com
- www.shareware.com

For the last two sites, you'll want to look under "Network Tools."

TCP/IP Review

Let's review the salient points of TCP/IP network discovery. You have "known factors" in your "unknown network," such as functioning workstations and/or servers that you can physically get to. You can gather information from these known factors (such as TCP/IP addresses, name server addresses, router addresses, and server addresses) and write down a skeleton of your network that you can then flesh out.

Once you have the addresses of routers on your network, you can telnet to those routers, check out the routing tables, and further discover more network segments. You can use the next hop as a clue to the next router and then repeat this process as often as necessary.

TCP/IP network discovery can be a long and drawn out process, particularly when large numbers of hosts are involved; in this case, automated discovery tools can really help.

IPX/SPX Discovery

Novell servers announce themselves to the network, so it's usually pretty easy to identify them. I tend to concentrate on the NLIST utility from a DOS prompt to show me the name of all NetWare servers (see Figure 24.5). If you're a NetWare 3.x user, you can use the SLIST utility instead to identify which servers you have. The NLIST or SLIST utility will show you the servers' internal IPX addresses—be sure to write them down.

FIGURE 24.5

You can look for servers on a NetWare network by using the nlist *command. To only list bindery-compatible servers, use the* /B *option.*

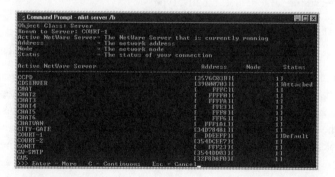

Once you have IPX server names, you can then use the RCONSOLE utility (assuming that the servers are in an unknown location) to connect to the servers. As with TCP/IP routers, you'll need to know the password.

24

If you don't know the RCONSOLE password for your Novell servers, you can still get in if you have the appropriate permission to read the SYS:SYSTEM\ AUTOEXEC.NCF file. Just look for a line that reads something like this:

```
load remote foobar
```

The last word is the remote password (in this case, "foobar.") Secure, huh? It's a reasonable bet that if you find one remote password, it will be valid for each server.

If you can't read the AUTOEXEC.NCF file but you have access to the console of one of your servers, you can type the following:

LOAD EDIT AUTOEXEC.NCF

You'll then be able to read it from there. (While you use the console, you're accessing the files as the supervisor.) You can probably use this password on other servers as well.

Once you get into a remote console, you can type **config** at the console prompt, which will show you the IPX network addresses this server is connected to. Write them down. Remember that each multihomed NetWare server is a router as well.

When you write down each network address and server name, you should have a pretty good idea of what the network looks like. Remember, servers that have a common network number live on the same network: A server "between" two networks acts as glue to tie everything all together. Finally, type

display networks

at the console prompt to make sure you've diagramed a router for each network.

If you have "holes" in the diagram—for example, if you see that you have network numbers that don't have servers attached to them—there might be router "filters" that are keeping you from seeing certain servers or routers. In this case, you might want to check out the track on console prompt command. It will open up the "route tracking" screen. It looks really nuts, but once you get a handle on what you're seeing, it will get easier to use (see Figure 24.6).

FIGURE 24.6

You can track routing requests through the NetWare route tracking screen.

Basically, two types of entries are shown on the route tracking screen: the IN entry and the OUT entry. The IN entry is where other servers and routers tell the server that you're looking at other networks. The OUT entry is where your server tells others about the networks it is connected to. We'll concentrate on the IN entry.

The IN entry contains a bracketed number such as [0000001D:0000C91D5488], for example. That number is the address of the foreign router. You can *try* to use this address in RCONSOLE by hitting the Insert key instead of picking a server name. Then you can enter that address number and attempt to connect. This way, you can connect to a server even if it doesn't appear on the server list.

Of course, you don't have to do *any* of this remote stuff if you know where the servers are. You can simply take a couple of hours to travel around your campus, gather the network information from each console, and stitch it all together into a *bona fide* network map. Of course, because Novell servers also use TCP/IP, the techniques used in the previous section are applicable as well.

Summary

Once you understand the underlying technology of a network, reverse-engineering it isn't hard. However, getting an inductive tone set is a must if you have a lot of unlabeled cables.

From a protocol and network perspective, if servers can talk to each other and to workstations, there's always a "trail" that you can follow. Typically, once you identify the network "glue" that holds the network together, the rest falls into place after a little bit of research. If you have a TCP/IP network, you're in luck, because you can use automated discovery tools to your advantage.

Novell networks are reasonably simple to reverse-engineer; it's just a matter of getting access to the server consoles, either remotely or locally. If you run a mixed IPX/SPX and TCP/IP Novell environment, you'll have to use IPX/SPX *and* TCP/IP discovery techniques.

Workshop

Q&A

Q Some of this network discovery stuff looks like cracker-type espionage. Are you sure I should be doing this?

A If the network that you're performing a discovery on isn't a network that you're responsible for, definitely not. It's considered antisocial and possibly illegal to gather this type of information without authorization. However, if you're the person responsible for this network, you've got to know this information. If someone has not left you a paper trail, you must create one. Just as in the movies, the good guys use some of the same tools as the bad guys—it just depends what your motives and responsibilities are.

Q Any more tips for TCP/IP discovery without automation tools?

A Sure, but isn't it worth $15 to save a couple of hours of your time? I highly recommend the automated discovery tools. I have lost hours of my life manually discovering networks that I could have otherwise spent doing something fun or productive.

One additional thing you can do to dump routing tables if your routers are inaccessible is to load Microsoft's routing to a test NT server, have it participate in the TCP/IP routing protocols running on your network, and then dump the routing table by typing the following command:

```
netstat -rn
```

You can do a similar thing if you have a Linux box; just add the "gated" package to it, have it listen for RIP, and see if you discover anything. This seems like a lot of work compared to downloading and buying a cheap Windows utility, though, doesn't it?

Quiz

1. The "generator" part of an inductive tone generator/tracer pair should be put where?

    A. At the "far end," away from where most cables terminate

    B. At the "concentrator" end, where most cables terminate

    C. In the middle of the cable

    D. None of the above

2. The first thing to find when performing network discovery is the address of a what?

    A. Server

    B. Novell file and print service

    C. Web server

    D. Router

3. True or false? Once you discover all the routers on your network, it's a simple matter to map all the servers to where they belong.

4. True or false? All TCP/IP networks use DNS.

5. You can't find a DNS server for a network that you've been hired to reverse-engineer. A sensible way to find host addresses would be to check the _____ of a functional PC.

    A. network card

    B. router entry

    C. client application configuration

    D. destination hop

6. True or false? All ports should be scanned on every possible IP address on your network.

7. The RCONSOLE password for a Novell server resides where?

    A. SYS:SYSTEM\AUTOEXEC.NCF

    B. SYS:PUBLIC\AUTOEXEC.NCF

    C. SYS:SYSTEM\AUTOEXEC.BAT

    D. SYS:PUBLIC\AUTOEXEC.BAT

24

Answers to Quiz Questions

1. A
2. D
3. True
4. False
5. C
6. False. First you should scan possible IP addresses for a common port and then go back and scan that address for more port possibilities.
7. A

Appendix A

Glossary

1000Base-CX   Extremely fast (1000Mbps) Ethernet, typically strung via copper wire and capable of transmitting a distance of some 75 feet.

1000Base-LX   Extremely fast (1000Mbps) Ethernet, typically strung via fiber-optic cable and capable of transmitting a distance of some 9,000 feet.

1000Base-SX   Extremely fast (1000Mbps) Ethernet, typically strung via fiber-optic cable and capable of transmitting a distance of some 1,500 feet.

1000Base-TX   Extremely fast (1000Mbps) Ethernet, typically strung via copper wire and capable of transmitting a distance of some 330 feet.

100Base-FX   Fast (100Mbps) Ethernet, typically strung via fiber-optic cable and capable of transmitting a distance of some 412 meters.

100BaseT   Fast (100Mbps) Ethernet, supporting various cabling schemes and capable of transmitting a distance of some 205 meters.

10Base2   Coaxial (thinwire) Ethernet capable of transmitting to distances of 600 feet.

10Base5   Coaxial (thickwire) Ethernet that, by default, transports data to distances of 1,500 feet.

10BaseT   Twisted-pair Ethernet capable of transmitting to distances of some 205 meters.

acceptable use policy (AUP)   Originally established by the National Science Foundation, AUP once forbade use of the Internet for commercial purposes. Today, AUP refers to rules a user must adhere to when using an ISP's services.

access control   Any tool or technique that allows you to selectively grant or deny users access to system resources.

access control list (ACL)   A list that stores security information about users and which system resources they're allowed to access.

active hub   An active hub is one that has intelligence built into it (for example, to make it error tolerant). See also *hub*.

adapter   A hardware device used to connect devices to a motherboard. In networking context, an Ethernet adapter/card.

adaptive pulse code modulation   A method of encoding voice into digital format over communication lines.

adaptive routing   Routing designed to adapt to the current network load. Adaptive routing routes data around bottlenecks and congested network areas.

Address Resolution Protocol (ARP)   Maps IP addresses to physical addresses.

administrator   Either a human being charged with controlling a network or the supervisory account in Windows NT. (Whoever has administrator privileges in NT can—but need not necessarily—hold complete control over his or her network, workgroup, or domain.)

ADSL   See *Asymmetric Digital Subscriber Line*.

AIX   A flavor of UNIX from International Business Machines (IBM). AIX runs on RISC workstations and PowerPCs.

American National Standards Institute   See *ANSI*.

analog system   This term is generally used to describe the telephone system, which uses analog technology to convert voice to electronic signals. Many telephones in modern office systems are *digital*, which means that if you plug your modem into the jack, you risk damage to the modem.

Anonymous FTP   FTP service available to the public that allows anonymous logins. Anyone can access anonymous FTP with the username anonymous and his or her email address as a password.

ANSI   The American National Standards Institute. Check out `http://www.ansi/org` for more information on ANSI.

answer-only modem   A modem that answers but cannot dial out. (These are useful for preventing users from initiating calls from your system.)

applet   A small Java program that runs in a Web browser environment. Applets add graphics, animation, and dynamic text to otherwise lifeless Web pages.

application gateway   Firewall device that disallows direct communication between the Internet and an internal, private network. Data flow is controlled by proxies that screen out undesirable information or hosts. See also *proxy server*.

application layer   Layer 7 of the OSI reference model, the highest layer of the model. The application layer defines how applications interact over the network. This is the layer of communications that occurs (and is conspicuous) at the user level. (For example, the File Transfer Protocol interfaces with the user at the application layer, but routing occurs at layer 3, the network layer.)

ARP   See *Address Resolution Protocol*.

ARPAnet   Advanced Research Projects Agency Network. This was the original Internet, which, for many years, was controlled by the Department of Defense.

ASCII   American Standard Code for Information Interchange. ASCII is a common standard by which many operating systems treat simple text.

Asymmetric Digital Subscriber Line (ADSL)   A high-speed, digital telephone technology that's fast when downloading (nearly 6MBps) but much slower uploading (about 65KBps). Unfortunately, ADSL is a new technology that's available only in major metropolitan areas.

asynchronous data transmission   The transmission of data one character at a time.

asynchronous PPP   Run-of-the-mill PPP; the kind generally used by PPP dial-up customers.

asynchronous transfer mode (ATM)   An ATM network is one type of circuit-switched packet network that can transfer information in standard blocks at high speeds. (These are not to be confused with *automatic teller machines*.) ATM packets are called *cells*.

attachment unit interface (AUI)   A 15-pin twisted-pair Ethernet connection or connector.

attribute   The state of a given resource (whether file or directory), as well as whether that resource is readable, hidden, system, or other.

AUI   See *attachment unit interface*.

AUP   See *acceptable use policy*.

authenticate   When you authenticate a particular user or host, you are verifying its identity.

authentication   The process of authenticating either a user or host. Such authentication may be simple and applied at the application level (demanding a password), or it may be complex (as in challenge-response dialogs between machines, which generally rely on algorithms or encryption at a discrete level of the system).

Authentication Server Protocol   A TCP-based authentication service that can verify the identity of a user. (Refer to RFC 931.)

automounting   The practice of automatically mounting network drives at bootup or when requested.

back door   A hidden program, left behind by an intruder (or perhaps a disgruntled employee), that allows him or her future access to a victim host. This term is synonymous with *trap door*.

back up   To preserve a file system or files, usually for disaster recovery. Generally, a backup is done to tape, floppy disk, or other portable media that can be safely stored for later use.

backbone   The fastest and most centralized feed on your network. The heart of your network to which all other systems are connected.

bandwidth   The transmission capacity of your network medium, measured in bits per second.

baseband   Audio and video signals sent over coaxial cable, typically used in cable television transmissions. In particular, the signals are sent without frequency shifting of the wave. (The *Base* in 10BaseT refers to this type of signal.)

bastion host   A server that is hardened against attack and can therefore be used outside the firewall as your "face to the world." These are often sacrificial.

biometric access controls   Systems that authenticate users by physical characteristics, such as faces, fingerprints, retinal patterns, or voices.

bootstrap protocol   A network protocol used for remote booting. (Diskless workstations often use a bootstrap protocol to contact a boot server. In response, the boot server sends boot commands.)

border gateway protocol   A protocol that facilitates communication between routers serving as gateways.

bottleneck   An area of your network that demonstrates sluggish transfer rates, usually due to network congestion or misconfiguration.

bridge   A network hardware device that connects local area networks together.

broadband   A very high-speed data transmission system, capable of supporting large transfers of media such as sound, video, and other data. Unlike baseband, broadband can use several different frequencies.

broadcast/broadcasting   Any network message sent to all network hosts. Also, the practice of sending such a message.

bug   A hole or weakness in a computer program. See also *vulnerability*.

cable modem   A modem that negotiates Internet access over cable television networks. (Cable modems provide blazing speeds.)

call back   Call-back systems ensure that a trusted host initiated the current connection. The host connects, a brief exchange is had, and the connection is cut. Then the server calls back the requesting host.

Carrier Sense Multiple Access with Collision Avoidance (CSMA/CA)   A traffic-management technique used by Ethernet. In CSMA/CA, workstations announce to the network that they're about to transmit data.

Carrier Sense Multiple Access with Collision Detection (CSMA/CD)   A traffic-management technique used by Ethernet. In CSMA/CD, workstations check the wire for traffic before transmitting data.

Cast-128   An encryption algorithm that uses large keys and can be incorporated into cryptographic applications. (You can learn more about Cast-128 by reading RFC 2144.)

CERT   See *Computer Emergency Response Team*.

certificate authority   A trusted third-party clearing house that issues security certificates and ensures their authenticity. Probably the most renowned commercial certificate authority is VeriSign, which issues (among other things) certificates for Microsoft-compatible ActiveX components. A *certificate* is used to verify the identity of a server or a user on the network.

certification Either the end result of a successful security evaluation of a product or system, or an academic honor bestowed on those who successfully complete courses in network engineering and support. Two of the most popular are Novell's CNE (Certified Novell Engineer) and Microsoft's MCSE (Microsoft Certified System Engineer.)

CGI See *common gateway interface.*

Challenge Handshake Authentication Protocol (CHAP) A protocol (often used with PPP) that challenges users to verify their identity. If the challenge is properly met, the user is authenticated. If not, the user is denied access. Refer to RFC 1344 for further information.

channel In networking, a channel is a communications path.

circuit A connection that conducts electrical currents and, by doing so, transmits data. Also refers to a TCP or "circuit-oriented" connection.

client Software designed to interact with a specific server application. For example, WWW browsers such as Netscape Communicator and Internet Explorer are WWW clients. They are specifically designed to interact with Web or HTTP servers.

client/server model A programming model where a single server can distribute data to many clients (the relationship between a Web server and Web clients or browsers is a good example). Many network applications and protocols are based on the client/server model.

CNE Certified Novell Engineer.

COM port A serial communications port, sometimes used to connect modems (and even mice).

common carrier Any government-regulated utility that provides the public with communications (for example, a telephone company).

common gateway interface (CGI) A standard that specifies programming techniques through which you pass data from Web servers to Web clients. (CGI is language neutral. You can write CGI programs in Perl, C, C++, Python, Visual Basic, and many other programming languages.)

compression The technique of reducing data size for the purposes of maximizing resource utilization (for example, bandwidth or disk space). The smaller the data, the less bandwidth or disk space you need for it.

Computer Emergency Response Team (CERT) A security organization that acts to disseminate information about security fixes and assists victims of cracker attacks. Find out more about CERT at http://www.cert.org.

copy access   When a user has copy access, it means that he or she has privileges to copy a particular file.

cracker   Someone who, with malicious intent, unlawfully breaches security of computer systems or software. Some folks say *hacker* when they actually mean *cracker*.

CSMA/CA   See *Carrier Sense Multiple Access with Collision Avoidance*.

CSMA/CD   See *Carrier Sense Multiple Access with Collision Detection*.

DAC   See *discretionary access control*.

Data Encryption Standard (DES)   An encryption standard from IBM, developed in 1974 and published in 1977. DES is the U.S. government standard for encrypting non-classified data.

data link layer   Layer 2 of the OSI reference model. This layer defines the rules for sending and receiving information between network devices.

datagram   A packet. RFC 1594 describes a datagram as "a self-contained, independent entity of data carrying sufficient information to be routed from the source to the destination computer without reliance on earlier exchanges between this source and destination computer and the transporting network."

DECnet   An antiquated proprietary protocol from Digital Equipment Corporation that runs chiefly over proprietary, Ethernet, and X.25 networks.

DES   See *Data Encryption Standard*.

DHCP   Dynamic Host Configuration Protocol. A method for allocating IP addresses to hosts "on-the-fly" rather than assigning them statically. Refer to RFC 1534 and RFC 2132.

digest access authentication   A security extension for HTTP that provides only basic (not encrypted) user authentication. To learn more about digest access authentication, refer to RFC 2069.

digital certificate   Any digital value used in authentication. Digital certificates are typically numeric values derived from cryptographic processes. (There are many values that can used as the basis of a digital certificate, including but not limited to biometric values, such as retinal scans.)

discretionary access control (DAC)   Provides the means for a central authority on a computer system or network to either permit or deny access to all users, and to do so incisively, based on time, date, file, directory, or host.

DoD   Department of Defense.

domain name   A host name or machine name, such as gnss.com. (This is the nonnumeric expression of a host's address. Numeric expressions are always in "dot" format—for example, 207.171.0.111.) See also *zone*.

domain name service (DNS)   A networked system that translates Internet host names (for example, traderights.pacificnet.net) into numeric IP addresses (for example, 207.171.0.111).

DoS   This refers to *denial of service*, a condition that results when a user maliciously renders a server inoperable, thereby denying computer service to legitimate users. For example, a user could fill up disk space or TCP connection tables, making it impossible for other users to work.

EFT   Electronic funds transfer.

encryption   The process of scrambling data so that it's unreadable by unauthorized parties. In most encryption schemes, you must have a password to reassemble the data into readable form. Encryption is primarily used to enhance privacy or to protect classified, secret, or top-secret information. (For example, many military and satellite transmissions are encrypted to prevent spies or hostile nations from analyzing them.)

Ethernet   A local area network (LAN) networking technology that connects computers and transmits data between them. Data is packaged into frames and sent via wires.

exabyte   (Abbreviated EB) 1,152,921,504,606,842,880 bytes.

fiber-optic cable   An extremely fast network cable that transmits data using light rather than electricity. Most commonly used for backbones.

fiber-optic data distribution interface (FDDI)   A fiber-optic cable that transfers data in a ring topology at 100Mbps.

file server   A computer that serves as a centralized source for files.

File Transfer Protocol (FTP)   A protocol used to transfer files from one TCP/IP host to another.

filtering   The process of examining network packets for integrity and security. Filtering is typically an automated process, performed by either routers or software.

firewall   A device that controls access between two networks according to source and destination addresses and ports.

frame   See *packet*.

frame relay Frame relay technology is a public switched network technology. It allows multiple clients to share the same cloud to transmit data from point to point, rather than having a separate point-to-point connection at each site. The providers typically allow clients to transfer information in at variable rates. This is a cost-effective way of transferring data over networks because you typically pay only for the resources you use. Unfortunately, you'll probably be sharing your frame relay connection with someone else. Standard frame relay connections run at 56Kbps, or T1 (1.54Mbps); the actual guaranteed rate is called the *CIR* (or *committed information rate*).

FTP See *File Transfer Protocol*.

full duplex transmission Any transmission in which data is transmitted in both directions simultaneously.

gateway A device on a network where two (or more) network protocols are translated into other protocols. Typical examples of such translation include TCP/IP or IPX/SPX to proprietary (mainframe) protocols, such as the Novell or Microsoft SAA gateway. See also *router*.

gigabyte 1,073,741,824 bytes.

Gopher The Internet Gopher Protocol, a protocol for distributing documents over the Net. Gopher preceded the World Wide Web as an information retrieval tool. (Refer to RFC 1436 for more information on Gopher.)

granularity The degree to which something is subdivided. In security, the extent to which you can incisively apply access controls. For example, setting security for a group is less granular than setting security for a user.

group A value denoting a collection of users. This concept is used in network file permissions. All users belonging to a particular group share similar access privileges.

groupware Application programs that are designed to make full use of a network. They often promote collaborative work.

hacker Someone interested in operating systems, software, security, and the Internet in general. This is the original (and correct) definition from the good old days when hackers were the good guys. Also called a *programmer*.

hardware address The fixed physical address of a network adapter. Hardware addresses are just about always hard-coded into the network adapter.

hole See *vulnerability*.

host   A computer that offers services to users, especially on a TCP/IP network. Also refers to older mainframe computers.

host table   Any record of matching hostnames and network addresses. These tables are used to identify the name and location of each host on your network. Such tables are consulted before data is transmitted. (Think of a host table as a personal phonebook of machine addresses.)

HP/UX   A flavor of UNIX from Hewlett Packard.

hub   A hardware device that allows the sharing of a network segment by repeating signals between ports. (Like the spokes of a wheel, a hub allows many network wires to converge at one point.)

hypertext   A text display format commonly used on Web pages. Hypertext is distinct from regular text because it's interactive. In a hypertext document, when you click or choose any highlighted word, other associated text appears. This allows for powerful cross-referencing and permits users to navigate an entire set of documents easily.

Hypertext Markup Language (HTML)   The formatting commands and rules that define a hypertext document. Web pages are written in the HTML format.

Hypertext Transfer Protocol (HTTP)   The protocol used to traffic hypertext across the Internet. It's also the underlying protocol of the WWW.

IDEA   See *International Data Encryption Algorithm*.

Identification Protocol (IDENT)   A TCP-based protocol for identifying users. IDENT is a more modern, advanced version of the Authentication Protocol. You can find out more about IDENT by obtaining RFC 1413.

IGMP   See *Internet Group Management Protocol*.

Integrated Services Digital Network (ISDN)   Digital telephone service that offers data transfer rates upward of 128Kbps.

Interactive Mail Access Protocol (IMAP3)   A protocol that allows workstations to access Internet electronic mail from centralized servers. (See RFC 1176 for more information about IMAP3.)

International Data Encryption Algorithm (IDEA)   IDEA is a powerful block-cipher encryption algorithm that operates with a 128-bit key. IDEA encrypts data faster than DES and is far more secure.

Internet   In specific, the conglomeration of interconnected computer networks—connected via fiber, leased lines, and dialup—that support TCP/IP. Less generally, any computer network that supports TCP/IP and is interconnected, as in an *internet*. Usually, a local internet is referred to as an *intranet*.

Internet Group Management Protocol (IGMP)   A protocol that controls broadcasts to multiple stations. Part of IP multicasting. See also *multicast packet*.

Internet Protocol (IP)   The network layer of TCP/IP; the method of transporting data across the Internet. (See RFC 791 for more information about IP.)

Internet Protocol security option   IP security option. Used to protect IP datagrams, according to U.S. classifications, whether they're unclassified, classified secret, or top secret. (See RFC 1038 and RFC 1108 for more information.)

Internet Worm   Also called the *Morris Worm*. A program that attacked the Internet in November, 1988. To get a Worm overview, check out RFC 1135.

Internetworking   The practice of using networks that run standard Internet protocols.

InterNIC   The Network Information Center located at www.internic.net.

intranet   A private network that utilizes Internet technologies.

intrusion detection   The practice of using automated systems to detect intrusion attempts. Intrusion detection typically involves intelligent systems or agents.

IP address   A numeric Internet address, such as 207.171.0.111.

IP spoofing   Any procedure where an attacker assumes another host's IP address to gain unauthorized access to the target.

IP   See *Internet Protocol*.

IPX   Internetwork Packet Exchange. A proprietary data transport protocol from Novell, Inc. Loosely resembles Internet Protocol.

IRIX   A flavor of UNIX from Silicon Graphics.

ISDN   See *Integrated Services Digital Network*.

ISO   International Standards Organization.

ISP   Internet service provider.

Java   A network programming language created by Sun Microsystems that marginally resembles C++. Java is object oriented and is often used to generate graphics and multimedia applications (although it's most well-known for its networking power).

JavaScript   A programming language developed by Netscape Communications Corporation. JavaScript runs in and manipulates Web browser environments, particularly Netscape Navigator and Communicator (but also Internet Explorer).

Kerberos   An encryption and authentication system developed at the Massachusetts Institute of Technology. Kerberos is used in network applications and relies on trusted third-party servers for authentication.

Kerberos Network Authentication Service   A third-party, ticket-based authentication scheme that can be easily integrated into network applications. (See RFC 1510 for details.)

LAN   See *local area network.*

Linux   A free UNIX clone that runs on widely disparate architecture, including *x*86 (Intel), Alpha, Sparc, Motorola, and PowerPC processors. Linux is becoming increasingly popular as a Web server platform.

LISTSERV   Listserv Distribute Protocol. A protocol used to deliver mass email. (See RFC 1429 for more information on LISTSERV.)

local area network (LAN)   LANs are small, Ethernet-based networks.

maximum transmission unit (MTU)   A value that denotes the largest packet that can be transmitted. (Many people adjust this value and often get better performance by either increasing or decreasing it.) Some network problems can be tracked down to MTU issues.

megabyte   1,048,576 bytes. (Abbreviated as *MB*.)

modem   A device that converts (modulates) signals that the computer understands into signals that can be accurately be transmitted over phone lines or other media. A modem can also convert the signals back (demodulate) into their original form.

Morris Worm   See *Internet Worm.*

MTU   See *maximum transmission unit.*

multicast packet   A packet that's destined for multiple (but not all) stations, possibly on multiple networks. Stations that want to participate in multicasting must join a *multicast group*.

multihomed host   A host that has more than one network interface. Routers and firewalls typically have more than one network interface.

NAUN   A Token-Ring station's *nearest addressable upstream neighbor*. This is very important to know for troubleshooting purposes.

NE2000   A very popular 10Mbps Ethernet network card, developed by Novell. Many network cards were cloned from this, and it is now a *de facto* standard.

NetBIOS Protocol   A high-speed, lightweight transport protocol commonly used in local area networks, particularly those running LAN Manager, Windows NT, or Windows 95.

`netstat`   UNIX command (also available in Windows) that shows the current TCP/IP connections and their source addresses.

NetWare   A popular network operating system from Novell, Inc.

network analyzer   Hardware or software (or both) that captures and monitors network traffic. It decodes the traffic into a form that can be read by humans.

network interface card (NIC)   An adapter card that lets the computer attach to a network cable.

network layer   Layer 3 of the OSI reference model. This layer provides the routing information for data, opens and closes paths for the data to travel, and ensures that the data reaches it destination.

Network News Transfer Protocol (NNTP)   The protocol that controls the transmission of USENET news messages.

network operating system (NOS)   An operating system for networks, such as NetWare or Windows NT.

NIC   See *network interface card.*

NNTP   See *Network News Transfer Protocol.*

NOS   See *network operating system.*

one-time password   A password generated on-the-fly during a challenge-response exchange. Such passwords are generated using a predefined algorithm but are extremely secure because they're good for the current session only.

OSI reference model   Open Systems Interconnection reference model. A seven-layer model of data communications protocols that make up the architecture of a network.

owner   The person, username, or process with privileges to read, write, or otherwise access a given file, directory, or process. The system administrator assigns ownership. However, ownership may also be assigned automatically by the operating system in certain instances.

packet   Data sent over a network is broken into manageable chunks called *packets* or *frames*. The size is determined by the protocol used.

packet spoofing   The practice of generating packets with forged source addresses for the purposes of cracking. See also *IP spoofing*.

Password Authentication Protocol   A protocol used to authenticate PPP users.

PCM   See *pulse code modulation*.

penetration testing   The process of attacking a host from without to ascertain remote security vulnerabilities. (This process is sometimes called *ice pick testing*.)

peripheral component interface (PCI)   An interface used for expansion slots in PCs and Macintosh computers. PCI slots are where you plug in new adapter cards, including Ethernet adapters, disk controller cards, and video cards (to name a few).

Perl   Practical Extraction and Report Language. A programming language commonly used in network programming, text processing, and CGI programming.

petabyte   1,125,899,906,842,620 bytes (abbreviated as *PB*).

phreaking   The process of unlawfully manipulating the telephone system.

physical layer   Layer 1 of the OSI reference model. This layer deals with hardware connections and transmissions and is the only layer that involves the physical transfer of data from system to system.

Point-to-Point Protocol (PPP)   A communications protocol used between machines that support serial interfaces, such as modems. PPP is commonly used to provide and access dial-up services to Internet service providers.

Point-to-Point Tunneling Protocol (PPTP)   A Microsoft-developed specialized form of PPP. PPTP's unique design makes it possible to encapsulate or "wrap" non-TCP/IP protocols within PPP. Through this method, PPTP allows two or more LANs to connect using the Internet as a conduit.

Post Office Protocol (POP3)   A protocol that allows workstations to download and upload Internet electronic mail from centralized servers. (See RFC 937 for more information.)

PPP Authentication Protocols   A set of protocols that can be used to enhance the security of the Point-to-Point Protocol. (Refer to RFC 1334.)

PPP DES   The PPP DES Encryption Protocol, which applies the data encryption standard protection to point-to-point links. This is one method to harden PPP traffic against sniffing. (To learn more, refer to RFC 1969.)

PPP   See *Point-to-Point Protocol*.

PPTP   See *Point-to-Point Tunneling Protocol*.

presentation layer   Layer 6 of the OSI reference model. This layer manages the protocols of the operating system, formatting data for display, encryption, and translation of characters.

protocol   A standardized set of rules that govern communication or the way that data is transmitted.

protocol analyzer   See *network analyzer*.

protocol stack   A hierarchy of protocols used in data transport, usually arranged in a collection called a *suite* (such as the TCP/IP suite). The actual programs used to implement a protocol stack are colloquially called a "stack" as well (for example, the Microsoft TCP/IP stack.)

proxy server   A server that makes application requests on the behalf of a client and relays results back to the client. Often used for a simple firewall; routing domains are typically different. See also *application gateway*.

pulse code modulation (PCM)   A system of transforming signals from analog to digital. (Many high-speed Internet connections from the telephone company use PCM.)

RARP   See *Reverse Address Resolution Protocol*.

read access   When a user has read access, he or she has privileges to read a particular file.

redundant array of inexpensive disks (RAID)   A large number of hard drives connected together that act as one drive. The data is spread out across several disks, and one drive keeps checking information so that if one drive fails, the data can be rebuilt.

repeater   A device that strengthens a signal so it can travel further distances.

request for comments (RFC)   RFC documents are working notes of the Internet development community. These are often used to propose new standards. A huge depository of RFC documents can be found at http://www.internic.net.

Reverse Address Resolution Protocol (RARP)   A protocol that maps Ethernet addresses to IP addresses.

RIP   See *Routing Information Protocol*.

rlogin   A UNIX program that allows you to connect your terminal to remote hosts. This program is much like Telnet, except it allows you to dispense with entering your password each time you log in. Unfortunately, it authenticates you via an IP address, so it's vulnerable to IP spoofing. See also *IP spoofing*.

router   A device that routes packets in and out of a network. Many routers are sophisticated and can serve as firewalls.

Routing Information Protocol (RIP)   A protocol that allows Internet hosts to exchange routing information. (See RFC 1058 for more information on RIP.)

RSA   A public key encryption algorithm named after its creators (Rivest, Shamir, and Adleman). RSA is probably the most popular of such algorithms and has been incorporated into many commercial applications, including but not limited to Netscape Navigator, Communicator, and even Lotus Notes. Find out more about RSA at `http://www.rsa.com`.

S/Key   One-time password system to secure connections. Because each session uses a different password, sessions that use S/KEY are not vulnerable to packet capture attacks. In other words, even if someone finds out that the password for your current session is "MYSECRET," he or she doesn't know the password for the *next* session, "OUT-TALUCK." (Refer to RFC 1760 for more information.)

Secure Socket Layer (SSL)   A security protocol (created by Netscape Communications Corporation) that allows client/server applications to communicate free of eavesdropping, tampering, and message forgery. SSL is now used for secure electronic commerce. To find out more, go to `http://home.netscape.com/eng/ssl3/draft302.txt`.

secured electronic transaction (SET)   A standard of secure protocols associated with online commerce and credit card transactions. (Visa and MasterCard are the chief players in development of the SET protocol.) Its purpose is ostensibly to make electronic commerce more secure.

security audit   An examination (often by third parties) of a server's security controls and disaster-recovery mechanisms.

Serial Line Internet Protocol (SLIP)   An Internet protocol designed for connections based on serial communications (for example, telephone connections or COM port/RS232 connections).

session layer   Layer 5 of the OSI reference model. This layer handles the coordination of communication between systems, maintains sessions for as long as needed, and handles security, logging, and administrative functions.

SET   See *secured electronic transaction*.

sharing   The process of allowing users on other machines to access files and directories on your own. File sharing is a fairly typical activity within local area networks and can sometimes be a security risk.

shielded twisted pair   A network cabling frequently used in IBM Token-Ring networks. (STP now supports 100Mbps.)

Simple Mail Transfer Protocol (SMTP)   The Internet's most commonly used electronic mail protocol (refer to RFC 821 for more information).

SLIP   See *Serial Line Internet Protocol*.

SMB   Server Message Block. The brains behind Microsoft Networking.

SMTP   See *Simple Mail Transfer Protocol*.

sniffer   Hardware or software that captures datagrams across a network. It can be used legitimately (by an engineer trying to diagnose network problems) or illegitimately (by a cracker looking for unencrypted passwords). Originally a trade name for Network General's Sniffer product, *sniffer* is now used generically to mean *network analyzer*.

SOCKS Protocol   A generic circuit proxy protocol that allows for proxy of TCP-based circuits (Socks version 4) and UDP sessions (Socks version 5). Refer to RFC 1928 for more information.

SONET   Synchronous Optical Network. An extremely high-speed network standard. Compliant networks can transmit data at 2Gbps (gigabits per second) or even faster.

spoofing   Any procedure that involves impersonating another user or host to gain unauthorized access to the target.

SSL   See *Secure Socket Layer*.

stack   See *protocol stack*.

STP   See *shielded twisted pair*.

suite   A term used to describe a collection of similar protocols. This term is used primarily when describing TCP- and IP-based protocols (when talking about the "TCP/IP suite").

TCP/IP   Transmission Control Protocol/Internet Protocol. The protocols used by the Internet.

Telnet authentication option   Protocol options for Telnet that add basic security to Telnet-based connections, based on rules at the source routing level. Refer to RFC 1409 for details.

Telnet   A protocol and an application. Telnet allows you to control your system from remote locations. During a Telnet session, your machine responds much as it would if you were actually working on its console.

TEMPEST   Transient Electromagnetic Pulse Surveillance Technology. TEMPEST is the practice and study of capturing or eavesdropping on electromagnetic signals that emanate from any device (in this case, a computer). TEMPEST shielding is any computer security system designed to defeat such eavesdropping.

terabyte   1,099,511,627,776 bytes (abbreviated as *TB*).

terminator   A small plug that attaches to the end of a segment of coax Ethernet cable. This plug provides a resistor to keep the signal within specifications.

TFTP   See *Trivial File Transfer Protocol.*

Token-Ring   A network that's connected in a ring topology, in which a special "token" is passed from computer to computer. A computer must wait until it receives this token before sending data over the network.

topology   The method or systems by which your network is physically laid out. For example, Ethernet and Token-Ring are both network topologies, as are "star" versus "bus" wiring. The former is a network topology; the latter is a physical topology.

traceroute   A TCP/IP program common to UNIX that records the routers used between your machine and a remote host. Available on Windows as `tracert`.

traffic analysis   The study of patterns in communication rather than the content of the communication. For example, studying when, where, and to whom particular messages are being sent, without actually studying the content of those messages.

transceiver   An essential part of a network interface card (NIC) that connects the network cable to the card. Most 10BaseT cards have them built in; however, in some cases, you might have to get a transceiver for an AUI port to connect to 10BaseT cable.

transport layer   Layer 4 of the OSI reference model. This layer controls the movement of data between systems, defines the protocols for messages, and does error checking.

trap door   See *back door.*

Trivial File Transfer Protocol (TFTP)   An antiquated file transfer protocol now seldom used on the Internet. (TFTP is a lot like FTP without authentication.) Frequently used for "diskless" booting from the network.

Trojan Horse   An application or code that, unbeknownst to the user, performs surreptitious and unauthorized tasks that can compromise system security. (Also referred to as a *Trojan.*)

trusted system   An operating system or other system secure enough for use in environments where classified information is warehoused.

tunneling   The practice of encapsulating one type of traffic within another type of traffic. For example, if you only had a TCP/IP connection between two sites, you might *tunnel* IPX/SPX traffic within the TCP/IP traffic. Nowadays, tunneling often implies employing encryption between two points, thus shielding that data from others who may be surreptitiously sniffing the wire. These types of tunneling procedures encrypt data within packets, making it extremely difficult for outsiders to access such data.

twisted pair   A cable made up of one or more pairs of wires that are twisted to improve their electrical performance.

User Datagram Protocol (UDP)   A connectionless protocol from the TCP/IP family. Connectionless protocols will transmit data between two hosts even though those hosts do not currently have an active session. Such protocols are considered "unreliable" because there's no absolute guarantee that the data will arrive as it as intended.

user   Anyone who uses a computer system or system resources.

user ID   In general, any value by which a user is identified, including his or her username. More specifically, and in relation to UNIX and other multiuser environments, any process ID—usually a numeric value—that identifies the owner of a particular process. See also *owner* and *user.*

UTP   Unshielded twisted pair. See also *10BaseT.*

virtual private network (VPN)   VPN technology allows companies with leased lines to form a closed and secure circuit over the Internet, between themselves. In this way, such companies ensure that data passed between them and their counterparts is secure (and usually encrypted).

virus   A self-replicating or propagating program (sometimes malicious) that attaches itself to other executables, drivers, or document templates, thus "infecting" the target host or file.

vulnerability   This term refers to any weakness in any system (either hardware or software) that allows intruders to gain unauthorized access or deny service.

WAN   A wide area network.

write access   When a user has write access, he or she has privileges to write to a particular file.

yottabyte   Approximately 1,208,925,819,614,630,000,000,000 bytes.

zettabyte   Approximately 1,180,591,620,717,410,000,000 bytes.

zone   One level of the DNS hierarchy. See also *domain name service*.

INDEX

SAMS
Teach Yourself
in 24 Hours

When you only have time for the answers™

Sams Teach Yourself in 24 Hours gets you the results you want—fast! Work through 24 proven 1-hour lessons and learn everything you need to know to get up to speed quickly. It has the answers you need at the price you can afford.

Sams Teach Yourself Windows Networking in 24 Hours

Peter Kuo
ISBN: 0-672-31475-4
$19.99 US/$28.95 CAN

Other Sams Teach Yourself in 24 Hours Titles

Sams Teach Yourself More Windows 98 in 24 Hours
Michael Miller
ISBN: 0-672-31343-X
$19.99 US/$28.95 CAN

Windows NT Workstation
Martin Kenley, et.al.
ISBN: 0-672-31011-2
$19.99 US/$28.95 CAN

Networking
Matt Hayden
ISBN: 0-672-31145-3
$19.99 US/$28.95 CAN

Windows 98
Greg Perry
ISBN: 0-672-31223-9
$19.99 US/$28.95 CAN

Windows 95
Greg Perry
ISBN: 0-672-31482-7
$19.99 US/$28.95 CAN

Upgrading and Repairing PCs
Galen A. Grimes
ISBN: 0-672-31340-5
$19.99 US/$28.95 CAN

PC's
Greg Perry
ISBN: 0-672-31447-9
$19.99 US/$28.95 CAN

Computer Basics
Jill T. Freeze et. al.
ISBN: 0-672-31334-0
$19.99 US/$28.95 CAN

All prices are subject to change.

SAMS

www.samspublishing.com